Mad Men and Medusas

ALSO BY JULIET MITCHELL

PSYCHOANALYSIS AND FEMINISM

MAD MEN AND AND MEDUSAS

RECLAIMING HYSTERIA

JULIET MITCHELL

BASIC
BOOKS

A Member of the
Perseus Books Group

First published in Great Britain by the Penguin Group 2000

Copyright © 2000 by Juliet Mitchell

Published by Basic Books,
A Member of the Perseus Books Group

Set in 11/14 pt Monotype Sabon
Typeset by Rowland Phototypesetting Ltd, Bury St Edmunds, Suffolk
A CIP catalog record for this book is available from the Library of Congress.
ISBN: 0-465-04613-4
00 01 02 03 / 10 9 8 7 6 5 4 3 2 1

For PMR, JRG and EB-E

Contents

Preface

My initial interest in hysteria came from a double perspective – from feminism on the one hand and from psychoanalysis on the other. For both, though separately, hysteria has been crucial.

It is widely argued that hysteria has disappeared from the Western world during the twentieth century. As far as I am concerned, this remarkable claim opens rather than closes the issue. First, I would argue that it has not disappeared – as the frequent use of the word to describe conditions in the community testifies. Rather, it had a brief history as a disease and it is this categorization which has been coming to an end, much as its diagnosis as witchcraft or possession has sometimes terminated in other times and places. Hysteria also migrates. Supremely mimetic, what was once called hysteria manifests itself in forms more attuned to its new social surroundings. What was once a subsidiary characteristic becomes dominant and vice versa.

From my double perspective, two factors stand out as needing examination to account for the disappearance of a historically specific disease diagnosis. The first involves both feminism and psychoanalysis; the second primarily psychoanalysis, and feminism only secondarily in so far as it has made use of psychoanalysis. However, both implicate female–male social relations and our understanding of them – and hence are of concern to the political theory of feminism.

The first factor is the advent of the full recognition of male hysteria. Of all the psychic, mental, emotional or behavioural conditions known to humankind, it is hysteria which has been bound with bands of steel to femininity, and hence very largely to women. Feminism, in seeing hysteria as the protest of the disadvantaged and hence above all of women, has made little of hysterical men except in so far as it can assimilate them to this position, as it has done with working-class men, nineteenth-century east European Jews or male immigrants, or to the position of the traumatized, as has been done with war neurosis from the Great War to the Gulf War. Equating hysteria with disadvantage misses half the problem. This half is the issue of hysterical violence.

Psychoanalysis also made nothing of the male hysteric. It is often remarked that all the great discoveries of psychoanalysis, indeed the theory of psychoanalysis itself, have emanated from work with hysteria. This is certainly true. However, the critical claim that inaugurated psychoanalysis was that men could be hysterical. By espousing and furthering this observation (initiated by Jean Martin Charcot), Freud instituted psychoanalysis as a theory about universal human processes. This would hardly have been possible had hysteria been limited to women. But psychoanalysis, too, slipped from explaining to endorsing its proclivity in women. Two reasons for this can be highlighted.

The first of these reasons arises from a difficulty internal to psychoanalytical theory: that is, the non-elaboration of the hypothesis of a death drive in general, but in particular in relation to hysteria. In the classic account, hysteria is the failure to demolish sexual desires for the mother and then for the father (the Oedipus complex). This, I believe, is only half the picture. Again, as with feminists' accounts of hysteria, what is missing is that there is violence as well as sexuality in the seductions and rages of the hysteric. Reading hysteria through the death drive that Freud hypothesized following the psychoneuroses of the First World War puts the male hysteric back in the picture and fills out that picture to include the 'evil' that is too often omitted.

The second reason, from my double perspective of feminism and psychoanalysis, for why we no longer see the hysteria that stares us in the face is a larger omission. This is the omission of the key role played in the construction of the psyche by lateral relationships. In referring to these as 'sibling' relations I am using the term extensively to include all those who stand in the position of siblings, whether biologically related or not. It is these and their heirs in peers and partners that are missing from our understanding of hysteria. Anthropology has long recognized the significance of these relations (although not in relation to hysteria); psychoanalysis has subsumed them to the vertical child–parent relationship.

Once one brings in 'siblings', hysteria emerges. Likewise, understanding hysteria calls forth siblings. Siblings are everywhere in psychoanalytic accounts – even though they are absent from the theory and the clinical practice. Together with the death drive, they help account for many things we are otherwise puzzled by in social situations if we stay only with the vertical axis of explanation. Any elaboration of the death drive has seen it as either destruction (Melanie Klein) or as the effects of trauma (French psychoanalysis). It is both. It is a drive, or a force, towards inertia or stasis, that can turn outwards in destructiveness towards others. When a sibling is in the offing, the danger is that the hero – 'His Majesty the Baby' – will be annihilated, for this is someone who stands in the same position to parents (and their substitutes) as himself. This possible displacement triggers the wish to kill in the interest of survival. The drive to inertia released by the shock becomes violence. Or it becomes a sexual drive, to get the interests of all and everyone for oneself. There are rules against sibling incest and sibling murder but in smaller ways rules are broken daily – what is the widespread practice of wife-beating but a breaking of that rule that one should not hit someone smaller than oneself?

I am not arguing that the lateral should replace the vertical axis – but that they are brought into conjunction. This conjunction in its turn opens up several perspectives. I have suggested a 'parthenogenetic complex', in which the hysteric perpetuates the idea, voiced initially to himself or among peer groups but in imitation of the mother, that one can make a baby from oneself. This opens out into questions of social practice, *not* single mothers but the fury that can arise against a child when one does not know boundaries or how to symbolize the other as different from oneself. Over and above the many specific issues that can fall within a framework that adds the lateral to the vertical is that this helps us account for hysteria as a universal possibility. The post-modern emphasis on difference has been at the expense of transversality – the variations always present within the universality. Hysteria and lateral relations that take up positions which are simultaneously the same *and* different may make a contribution to resolving this dichotomy, to allowing for a perspective of both/and rather than either/or.

Juliet Mitchell, Ahmedabad, India
December 1999

Acknowledgements

Because, for reasons of confidentiality, I cannot name my patients (1978–1998), I will also not name the many friends, teachers and members of my family who helped me with typing, editing, reading chapters and in less concrete ways through the long gestation of this book. I thank them all for their generosity.

I

Hysteria

1. A BRIEF HISTORY: PAST AND PRESENT

The Taita people live in the Coast province of Kenya. They recognize two categories of illnesses: those of the heart and those of the head. One illness predominant among the Taita is *saka*. Like all illnesses that involve fears, urges or cravings, *saka* belongs to the heart; as the Taita describe it, it is an illness of 'wanting and wanting'. Customarily, the Taita men have herded goats, sheep and a few cattle, and grown and sold cash crops: mainly vegetables, wattle, chilli and coffee. Increasingly, however, they work as domestic or agricultural wage labour away from the tribal reserve. Meanwhile, women have cultivated the basic grain, root crops and greens for eating. Marriage takes place within the tribe and the descent line is patrilineal: women may inherit neither land nor livestock, although as wives or widows they have extensive rights to their use. Likewise, wives and widows are the main purchasers and controllers of consumer goods and define the needs of a household. Their tasks are dependent on the use of money but they themselves can earn only 'pin money' – small amounts for their own domestic use. Taita education seems to emphasize women's dependence and men's enviable privileges. The women have little contact with the world beyond the reservation.

It is almost entirely Taita wives who suffer from *saka* – indeed, as many as 50 per cent of married women may be afflicted at some point in their lives. *Saka* can originate in a mood of restlessness and anxiety or in a self-induced hypnotic state. In its dominant expression *saka* begins with the upper body of the sufferer going into convulsions, her shoulders shaking and her head rolling; then come some or all of the following symptoms: the monotonous repetition of an action or of words that are usually from another (scarcely known) language, closed eyes, expressionless face, loss of consciousness, a trance state, rigidity and teeth-clenching. Sometimes *saka*'s main characteristics occur without any of the preceding convulsions.

Instances which are cited as having triggered *saka* include the sight of a car in an area where such an object is scarcely known; the sudden striking of a match; the intense desire or craving for a particular object, such as sugar, a cigarette, bananas, or an action, such as playing the concertina (a man's instrument). In one woman's case, *saka* was triggered by her wish to hear her son's band play after she had missed it; in another, by her desire to have her husband's blood to suck; in another, by her wanting to drink the water in which her favourite nephew had washed.

Christian elders often consider *saka* the work of the Devil; others think it has been sent by foreigners who, having failed to seduce the Taita women, make them barren instead, by means of *saka*; still others do not regard it as an illness at all, but rather as a deliberate feminine con trick to make husbands procure whatever their wives want.

Treatments range from making sure the woman has what she wants to the prescription of various medicaments and the use of herb-infused smoke; from drinking the water in which a man's lower garments have been washed to becoming a Christian, or performing the *saka* dance. For this dance, the afflicted women line up wearing some or all of the following items, which must be provided by their husbands: a man's felt hat or fez, a hunter's or explorer's red and white bandolier, a man's belt and bells on one ankle. The sufferers wear dresses which may be tied under the shoulder like a woman's or around the waist like a man's. The women carry a man's dancing staff or a young man's walking stick. Gender ambiguity and fluidity is all-pervasive.

The treatments, however, do not seem to produce permanent cures. But such cures as there are, particularly those brought about by the *saka* dance – like the illness to which they respond – involve the negotiation of gender differences. Women crave and get consumer goods that men must pay for (clothes, sugar) or objects or attributes that 'belong' to men (bananas, cigarettes, their clothes, their blood); they want to have and do the things which are prohibited to women but are allowed to men and, at least as a token, the treatments allow this. The gender difference is not absolute, but clearly the illness is experienced by women who can be cured, at least for the time being, if they can temporarily have or do or be the things men have, do and are. Commenting on her observations of the *saka* complex during the 1950s, the anthropologist Grace Harris writes: 'In the *saka* attacks we see what appears at first to be a highly aberrant form of behaviour. The symptoms strike one as being of an hysterical sort, using the term in an everyday rather than a technical psychiatric sense.'[1] The 1950s were a decade in which hysteria was not an acceptable diagnosis or medical concept. Although she backs off from using it and in the title of her essay about the Taita women calls it 'Possession "Hysteria"', with double quotation marks, Harris can find no other appropriate term for the phenomenon which she observed.

Hysteria is a universal phenomenon, a possible response to particular human conditions that can arise at any time or anywhere. Just over ten years ago, in *Religion in Context: Cults and Charisma* (1986), the anthropologist I. M. Lewis wrote that it was incorrect to regard witchcraft, spirit possession, cannibalism and shamanism as discrete phenomena found in different social contexts in different places and times. Instead, he argued, these are just so many aspects of mystical power or charisma; they are the various facets of a single phenomenon. This unity becomes clearer if one asks who are the chief actors in all these apparently different instances. A strict scrutiny of the empirical data produces the answer that in all the apparently discrete cases the actors are the same: occasionally they are disadvantaged men, but predominantly they are women.

Lewis, like Harris, is nervous about using the term hysteria. Yet if we ask the same questions about hysteria, it is no accident that the answers are also the same. They are the same, too, for the many discrete 'illnesses' into which hysteria has been transmuted or, in part, transferred in the twentieth-century Western world. Hysterics may be 'disadvantaged' men, but they are predominantly women. So too are the actors of the many different aspects of Western hysteria such as eating disorders, multiple personality and 'borderline' conditions.

The analogy between mental illness and adherence to 'alternative' religious cults runs *sotte voce* throughout Lewis's book. Lewis's argument is about the interdependence of orthodoxy and mysticism, about, essentially, male and female modes of religious power. The unorthodox mystical cults which he describes are in fact crucial to orthodoxy; they are its essential 'other side'. To take that argument further, in the context of Western medico-psychiatric practices, it is just such an interdependence that we witness between so-called psychic health and hysteria. Hysteria is the alternative or other side of the coin of what is regarded as normal behaviour. Women are thought to be, or assigned to be, its main practitioners.

Hysteria is also the mental condition which provides the relevant point of comparison for both witchcraft and spirit possession, for shamanism and even for cannibalism. However, there is only one reference to hysteria in the index to *Religion in Context*, although there are, in fact, twelve references in the text. Lewis praises Grace Harris's account of *saka* but omits the term 'hysteria', even though Harris had translated *saka* as 'possession "hysteria" '. 'Hysteria' does not therefore appear to be a term that Lewis is prepared to use in this context.

Lewis was criticized for deploying the notion of hysteria in his earlier book, *Ecstatic Religions* (1971), and he clearly wanted to eschew it subsequently. Yet his descriptions clearly point to it. Hysteria and cults cannot be reduced entirely to each other. It is rather that, within the contexts in which they are practised, possession, cannibalism, trance, shamanism are the social expressions and actions which make use of hysteria. The cults which Lewis describes are ritualized forms of hysteria; as they are socially organized, they may well be the obverse of religious orthodoxy, just as hysteria is the flipside of psychic 'normality'. In both transitional societies, such as that of the Taita, where women are in the reservations and men are becoming part of an urban proletariat or unemployed, and the complex societies of the Western world, where by and large religion is no longer a major principle of organization, the human potential for hysterical behaviour and experience may not be made manifest in alternative religions or rituals, apart from in dances or at carnivals; it may instead appear as an illness.

There are, then, forms of behaviour, particular states of being, ranges of symptoms, which seem to have something in common and of which the actors are nearly always women. Those who describe these manifestations try to eschew the term 'hysteria', but are repeatedly drawn back to it.

Except for the rare occasions when it is claimed by artists and

writers, hysteria tends to be an opprobrious term. Is this because, as
the Taita demonstrate, it displays fear and craving – and both are
synonymous with weakness? Such an explanation tallies with the
bobservation that hysteria is expressed by disadvantaged groups such
as women. In which case, we have to add to the weakness that what
is being shown is the power of the weak. Charisma, a demonstrative
egotism, a need to control others, witchcraft, are all expressions of
power. Hence it would be wrong to see hysteria as the protest of the
inferiorized without adding that it is the deployment of weakness as
power. But is even this a sufficient or, in fact, accurate explanation?
Too much today is expounded in terms of power struggles; hysteria
demonstrates how these are only manifest forms. For the powerful
can also be hysterical. There is little to choose in terms of hysteria
between the rhetoric of the prosecutors described in the *Malleus Mal-
eficarum* (1484) and the aberrant behaviour of the witches they were
accusing; and it was the dominant Nazis who drummed up mass hysteria
against the weak, creating panic that the Jews, the Gypsies, the politically or genetically 'undesirable', would displace the Aryans. It is also
important to say that hysteria can be a source of creativity, as it is in
shamanism and charisma, or as it was used by artists such as Flaubert
and the Surrealists to demonstrate its proliferating fantasy aspects
and its flamboyant dislocation of normal thought processes as an
artistically innovative stance. This creative dimension would seem to
be returning in the performative practices prevalent in the West today.

All human emotions, psychic states, and indeed even organic illnesses, take place within specific social contexts. They cannot exist
outside of them. Yet discussions of hysteria are remarkable for a
particular sort of unawareness of this self-evident fact. Clearly, there
are human emotions – love, hate, anxiety, envy, jealousy, pity, fear,
compassion, just to start the list – and there are human behaviours –
making love, fighting, eating, drinking, playing, talking, listening,
seeking revenge – to name the first that come to mind. There are also
both so-called normal and so-called pathological expressions of these
emotions and behaviours which we all come across everywhere. Knowing what they are in the abstract, however, does not help us to
understand them properly, but perceiving them in their different
contexts enables us to build a general picture.

It is not the abstraction but the aggregate of different manifestations that reveals the general condition. For example, finding what different languages have in common enables us to understand something about our universal human ability to speak. Love is defined by the twelfth-century Provençal troubadour as the pursuit of the unattainable ideal; in the black humour of a 1960s joke, the mother of a schizophrenic man is said to have held him as a baby out of an eleventh-floor window in order to declare that this showed how much she *loved* him because she didn't drop him. These two different versions of love serve to prove not that it is not a general human emotion but rather that it is a complex state in which at one time and place idealization may be predominant while in another it will be ambivalence that comes to the fore. Idealization and ambivalence are both inevitable within a state of love. The twelfth-century poet and the twentieth-century mother each allow us to understand different aspects of love, and so enrich our concept of it as a universal phenomenon.

My contention about hysteria follows the same pattern of argument. It has been fashionable in the twentieth-century West to argue that hysteria has disappeared. To my mind, this is nonsensical – it is like saying 'love' or 'hate' have vanished. There can be no question that hysteria exists, whether we call its various manifestations by that name or something else. For hysteria is a potential human experience that we can bring some understanding to by looking at the particular contexts which shape it. I would not expect hysteria to always look the same – any more than I would expect love to do so – but that does not mean that it is not a universal possibility. There are clear links, for instance, between how the Taita understand and deal with *saka* and how the Hippocratic doctors of fifth-century BC Athens conceptualized *usterie* (from which our particular word derives), or how, with the demise of beliefs in witchcraft, Renaissance scholars recreated this Greek illness to produce a humanistic tradition of 'suffocation of the mother'. All yield up similarities and differences within their own contexts which help us to construct a picture of what we now call 'hysteria'. Conversely, there must be specific reasons for the current notion that hysteria (or something that may be recognized as such) has disappeared.

Every context which describes hysteria links it to gender – but not, of course, always in the same way. Historically, the various ways in which gender differences and hysteria are seen to interact should tell us something both about gender as it is defined at any given time and place and about hysteria: for instance, sometimes it is feminine to have the vapours, at others to be a lovely woman caring for the sick, at others to be an emaciated girl. Sometimes 'hysteria' is a medical diagnosis, sometimes just an insult. These diverse expressions could be used for specific historical and cultural analyses. My question, however, is different: Why is hysteria linked to women? Using the psychoanalytic understanding of hysteria as an exemplary case, I challenge the assumption that there is an equivalence between femininity and hysteria, arguing instead that hysteria has been feminized: over and over again, a universal potential condition has been assigned to the feminine; equally, it has disappeared as a condition after the irrefutable observation that men appeared to display its characteristics.

In its turn, my investigation of the gendering of hysteria has led me to question some of the basic psychoanalytic theory that was itself built up from an understanding of hysteria. Thinking about hysteria has led me to a different reading of the Oedipus complex and to the need to insert the experience of siblings and their lateral heirs in peer and affinal relationships into our understanding of the construction of mental life.

Until recently it was argued that hysteria could be found throughout the rest of history and cross-culturally, although it has disappeared today. However, this has been energetically challenged from a postmodern standpoint. Hysteria has been deconstructed and its universality, its unity as a disease entity or illness category, more importantly its very existence at any time or place, has been called in question. The prevalent clinical argument that hysteria has disappeared from hospitals and consulting rooms in the twentieth-century Western world now runs parallel to the intellectual challenge to the existence of hysteria at all. Not only is it said to have 'disappeared', but scholars are finding that it never existed. This scholarly deconstruction is exemplified in a brief, tightly argued essay by the British classicist, Helen King, 'Once Upon a Text' (1993), which challenges the standard work on the subject, *Hysteria: The History of a Disease* (1965), by

Ilza Veith. Under the all-pervading influence of post-modernism, we are made aware daily that traditions are invented. In keeping with this trend, King shows that part of the Renaissance project of finding a tradition for its new humanism in all things Greek was to find its own observed illness in the Hippocratic texts. King argues that the Renaissance invented classical Greek hysteria in order to create its own illness heritage. However, surely, although traditions are indeed created, they are not invented out of thin air: there is always something there that has been selected, embellished, recreated – aspects of the past that have been given meaning in the present. Hysteria seems to be indicated both by the Greek texts and their Renaissance dependants. However unfashionable its 'universalism' and 'essentialism', Veith's history, which regards 'hysteria' as something that really exists, is still very useful because it documents the symptoms over time and place.

For the Hippocratic doctors of the fifth century BC, the dominant symptoms of what we will call 'hysteria' were breathing difficulties and a sense of suffocation. The main sufferers were recently bereaved widows; the explanation offered by most doctors was that the womb, craving the satisfaction of which it had been deprived, was wandering urgently around the body causing pressure on other organs and hence obstructing other processes such as breathing. The cures ranged from remarriage (and so presumed sexual satisfaction) to herbal fumigation through the vagina, to hypnosis. In the third century BC, Galen of Pergamon, who argued that the womb produces a secretion analogous to semen (as has been claimed in both the seventeenth and twentieth centuries), suggested that blocked-up semen or its analogue, in both women and men, could also produce hysteria. There are notions latent here of hysteria as an essential but explosive discharge. The explanations for hysterical behaviour in the ancient world became increasingly sexual until the growth of Christian mysticism and the decline of medicine in the late third century AD.

Christianity, initially and most influentially in the person of Saint Augustine, transformed the hysteric from a sick being (nearly always a woman) with physical and emotional needs which a doctor could help, into a person (again nearly always a woman) who was wilfully possessed and in league with the Devil. Under Christianity symptoms included anaesthesia, mutism, convulsions and imitations of bizarre behaviour (such as swallowing needles and the marks on the body thought to be *stigmata diaboli*). The treatment – or persecution – of the condition was religious or juridical, but not medical. The hysteric most frequently showed herself as a witch or, depending on your viewpoint, the behaviour of witches was characteristically hysterical.

The late Renaissance, referring back to ancient Greece, began the remedicalization of hysteria and the refutation of supernatural religious causes. In 1603, a doctor, Edward Jorden, published a book in England, *Briefe Discourse of a Disease Called the Suffocation of the Mother*, which demonstrated how all the signs that hitherto had been regarded as marks of witchcraft could be found in cases of clinical hysteria. At this time, the treatments matched the renaturalizing of hysteria into a disease that could be cured – so, for instance, energetic exercise such as horse-riding was strongly recommended (again we can see here the theme of physical discharge). As for the ancient Greeks, symptoms that received prominence in the sixteenth and early seventeenth centuries included problems of breathing and choking (the so-called 'suffocation of the mother'), convulsions, fits and compulsive imitations. The vast majority of recorded observations and descriptions of hysteria also noted mimetic imitation, although this feature was not to gain diagnostic significance until the eighteenth and nineteenth centuries. Observing a case of hysterical epilepsy, Giorgio Baglivi (1668–1706), a physician, observed: 'In *Dalmatia*, I saw a young Man seiz'd with violent Convulsions, only for looking upon another Person that lay groveling upon the Ground in a Fit of an Epilepsy.'[2] The relationship between hysteria and epilepsy was to gain ever greater importance until the twentieth century. However, Baglivi's observation also points to the significance of death-like states. One definitional but overlooked feature of hysteria is the particular way in which it relates to death both as concept and as fact.

Of course, with the increasing medicalization of hysteria from the seventeenth century onwards, a larger number of hysterical patients sought help from physicians. However, medical explanations of the symptoms varied. Thomas Sydenham (1624–89), a remarkable physician derided in his time but since acknowledged as a founder of modern clinical medicine and epidemiology, claimed that bursts of anger, fear or pain could be indirect causes of hysteria and that the fundamental problem was an imbalance in the relationship of the mind and the body: the animal spirits which dominated both mind and body had got out of synchronization and caused a disturbance in the body, which was weaker than the mind. The hysterical symptoms he observed included the experience of believing a nail was being driven into the forehead, various pains in the stomach and muscles and spasms of the intestine. Sydenham not only noted the fluidity of the disease but also, importantly, its capacity to assume the form of various physical diseases. In other words, whereas the late medieval and early modern witch would turn into a cat, the hysterical patient from the seventeenth to the twentieth centuries might imitate appendicitis.

Although some doctors still linked hysteria with the womb, as Renaissance and Greek thinkers had done, from the seventeenth century onwards it became predominantly associated with the brain. After the Renaissance, this link marked the most striking change in the way hysteria was explained in the Western world. In turn, this changing explanatory model led the way to a neurological etiology. In fact, looked at through the lens of gender, this shift of explanation introduced a yet more important change of thinking about hysteria: if hysteria was to emanate not from the womb but from the brain, then this also in principle made men and women equally susceptible to it. This could, though, be looked at the other way around: the psychosocial situation of women and men was becoming less distinct and so the apparent femininity of hysteria was thus becoming available to both sexes – hence the need felt by doctors to detach theories of its etiology from the uterus. However, their doing so only created problems.

To sum up: at least in Western societies until the seventeenth century, hysteria was mostly linked to women and its etiology either thought to reside in the womb or in the seductions of the (male) Devil. Although observations of male hysteria were made from time to time throughout history this was rarely problematic. Certainly it was not the impossible contradiction which it was thought to be in the nineteenth century. Prior to this, men could behave like women in certain contexts. Emotional and anatomical bodies only coincide in some, not all, cultures and historical times and even where they do coincide, the coincidence is neither total nor omnipresent: a child of three will complain of a headache in its tummy; or a fed-up Sicilian male will happily complain that his adversary 'makes his womb dry up'; or King Lear, about to go mad, proclaims that he feels 'the mother rise in him'. Some cultures take bodies or body parts literally, seeing them as actors in their own right: a thief steals with his hands, so his hands are cut off.

However, what is interesting here is that once its origin was no longer thought to be biologically gender-specific, once it was a question of the brain and the nervous system, then hysteria's femininity had to be more firmly established; it had to be refeminized. During the eighteenth century refined women having the vapours became synonymous with hysteria. So that although the basic source of the vapours was the brain, it was often argued that these emanated secondarily from the womb. The vapours have been defined as depression, hypochondria or the spleen; in fact they were hysterical and 'feminine'.

By following the history of hysteria in Europe, we can see a shift from defining the female as a biological woman to defining her as characterologically 'feminine'. The natural association that hysteria equals a troubled womb gave way to an ideological explanation of femininity. This opened a door to a prejudice against women which, though far less overtly violent, was no less virulent than that which had accompanied the similar shift from the classical world's natural explanation of hysteria to the transformation of hysteria into witchcraft in the Middle Ages. Even though he acknowledged that he had seen a man with the vapours, the physician Joseph Raulin (1708–84) observed: 'This illness in which the women invent, exaggerate, and repeat all the different absurdities of which a disordered imagination is capable, is sometimes epidemic and contagious.'[3]

By the next century, 'vapours' had become 'nerves'. But at the same time the late eighteenth and early nineteenth centuries saw the reintroduction of a female sexual etiology. Philippe Pinel (1745–1826), rightly famous for unchaining the mental patients in the Parisian asylums of Bicêtre and Salpêtrière, explained mental illness largely in terms of social and psychological stress. Favouring a psychological and humanitarian approach, he recommended and practised friendly close-contact therapy. Pinel designated hysteria 'The Genital Neurosis of Women'. After Pinel, although the bodily symptoms of hysteria continued to be described – anaesthesias (parts of the body which lose sensation), disordered eating, breathing, choking, *globus hystericus*, etc.) – character traits were added which read like a working definition of the 'bad woman': hyper- or hypo-sexuality, flirtatiousness, lying and deceitfulness, manipulativeness, extreme emotionality. By the mid-nineteenth century it was being argued that the charm of femininity was, when found to excess, indeed hysteria.

In the later part of the nineteenth century the French neuropsychiatrist Jean Martin Charcot (1825–93), working too in the Salpêtrière, photographed and classified hysterical patients. Charting the different stages of the hysterical paroxysm, Charcot considered it a neurological disease. He is famous for having demonstrated that it was prevalent in men. Contemporaneously, Hippolyte Bernheim (1837–1919) contended that hysteria was psychological, not neurological. Subsequently, through the different work of Pierre Janet (1859–1947) and Sigmund Freud (1856–1939), the psychological model of hysteria was confirmed and remains dominant to this day. All these late nineteenth-century physicians (in particular Freud) were convinced of the presence of male hysteria.

However, with the supremacy of the psychological model came the belief that, having been 'understood', hysteria had simply disappeared. Veith comments that Freud, by deciphering it, had divested hysteria of the mystical importance that it had had for two and a half millennia. She argues that the hysteric must have come to feel that by being so well understood, there was little to be gained from being hysterical. Veith's is a slightly implausible suggestion. The *Encyclopaedia Britannica* explains hysteria's so-called disappearance differently, although the stress is still on progress: 'The incidence of hysteria appears to have been diminishing over the years in many areas of the world, probably because of cultural factors such as increasing psychological sophistication, diminishing sexual prudery and inhibition, and a less authoritarian family structure.'[4] Surveying her own work Veith comments:

It must be apparent from this brief chronological review of hysteria that the manifestations of this disease tended to change from era to era quite as much

as did the beliefs as to etiology and the methods of treatment. The symptoms
. . . were conditioned by social expectancy, tastes, mores, and religion, and
were further shaped by the state of medicine in general and the knowledge
of the public about medical matters. The more detailed such knowledge
became the greater was the variety of symptoms . . . Furthermore, throughout
history the symptoms were modified by the prevailing concept of the feminine
ideal.[5]

In fact, hysteria's many manifestations have shown some striking
similarities throughout the ages – sensations of suffocation, choking,
breathing and eating difficulties, mimetic imitations, deceitfulness,
shock, fits, death states, wanting (craving, longing) – and treatments
have often veered between assuaging them and punishing them. If the
treatments and conceptualizations vary, mimetic hysteria will look
different at different times because it is imitating different treatments
and different ideas about hysteria. As far as its so-called 'disappearance' is concerned, the question that needs to be asked is: Where did
the hysteria go to?

In the twentieth century, the dominant modes of comprehending
hysteria, from both the analytical and the treatment perspectives, have
been psychiatry and psychoanalysis. Twenty-one years after Veith's
successful and popular study, the history of hysteria was greatly
amplified by the French psychiatrist Étienne Trillat in his *L'Histoire
de l'hystérie* (1986). After starting with the Greeks, Trillat focused on
the period from 1700 until the 1960s, looking at hysteria as it came
to be understood from a predominantly French psychiatric perspective,
in which the aim is to see how the brain's chemistry affects behaviour.

Psychiatry moves forward through ever-increasing classifications;
it refines its knowledge by further demarcations and differential
descriptions. Charcot was the first eminent classifier of hysteria and
Freud, who studied under him for some months, was enthusiastic
about how, by a detailed charting of the symptoms, Charcot had
brought 'law and order' to this unruly condition. But Charcot's work,
though remaining famous, soon had little effect. Both because it
involves the labile desires of the sufferer (as we shall see in chapter
3) and because it can imitate anything or anyone, hysteria ultimately
resists any such constraints or classification. Since it cannot be easily

classified nor any biochemical explanation be found for it, it disappears. The prevalence, then, of psychiatric practices in the modern Western world is also an important factor in hysteria's vanishing. However, as the behavioural sciences have had their impact, the urge to classify and find a biochemistry have waned in recent years.

A recent account of hysteria by a psychiatrist, Philip Slavney's *Perspectives on 'Hysteria'* (1990), reflects this move from psychiatric classification to behavioural modes of understanding. Slavney advocates what he terms a 'dimensional perspective' to the understanding of hysteria; that is, halfway between a disease method, which treats a person as an organism, and a life story method, which considers him or her as an agent or subject. Slavney traces the process since the last century, which has shifted from perceiving the hysteric as someone who is having an emotional response to a major event in their life (for example, to becoming widowed) to the subsequent idea that the nervous system is the weak part of an organic structure – weaker in some than in others – and that this weakness predisposes a person to hysteria. This echoes the change in perception that took place between the sixteenth and seventeenth centuries.

In the latter part of the twentieth century ideas have moved on once more from considering hysteria as a disease to seeing a hysteric as a person with traits rather than symptoms. With this shift the notion of hysteria itself has been replaced by descriptive terms such as 'histrionic'. For instance, the all-important classificatory *American Diagnostic and Statistical Manuals* (DSM) numbers II and III introduce the concept of a 'histrionic personality disorder' to replace 'hysteria'. The substitution reflects the view that hysteria has many associations in its history which are now thought to be irrelevant and hence it should be erased. In fact, in both the literature and the practice, the terms hysterical and histrionic tend to be used somewhat interchangeably. Hysterical character traits change, however, so that, for instance, in *DSM* III, 'immaturity' and 'seductiveness' have been deleted and 'superficiality' added. Slavney lists a constellation of traits – excessive displays of emotion, self-dramatization, emotional lability, ingratiation, need for attention, unlikeability, insincerity and self-deception – which lead then to the simulation of other diseases. A person may *behave* hysterically/histrionically; however, 'hysteria' does not exist as a disease entity. Slavney concludes: 'This could well be the last book with *hysteria* in its title written by a psychiatrist. Although the word is used daily in the practice of medicine, "those who would like to drop it once and for all" seem to have won the battle for control of psychiatric nomenclature, and the next generation of clinicians will no longer find it indispensable when they wish to indicate certain traits and behaviours. *Hysteria*, *hysteric* and *hysterical* are on the verge of becoming anachronisms.'[6] The irony of this triumph of the diagnostic is that the doctors who no longer recognize hysteria's existence continue to refer to it daily. The same could be said of psychoanalysts. Certainly, with few exceptions, until very recently British Object Relations psychoanalytic theory has not considered hysteria officially to exist. Slavney's reorientating of the psychiatric classification of a disease towards the description of individual character traits marks a meeting point where understandings of neurosis turn into descriptions of personalities and life stories. But, given the history of hysteria, one must surely ask: Is it hysteria itself or its classification – psychiatric, medical or psychoanalytic – that has become redundant?

Ironically, the psychiatrist Slavney uses the psychoanalytic material to institute his characterological-behavioural theory. As we shall see, psychoanalytic theory and practice are supposed to resist the story. However, the final section of Slavney's book is entitled 'Hysteria as Story' and considers the first case history of what was to become known as psychoanalysis, that of 'Anna O', pseudonym of Bertha Pappenheim (a patient of Sigmund Freud's senior colleague Joseph Breuer) who became a well-known feminist social worker in Germany in the first part of the twentieth century. Slavney's account exemplifies the shift from the analysis of symptoms to the description of a life history. What is of particular importance in this descriptive mode is that in Slavney's account there are now no 'symptoms'. This characterological approach appears liberal and humane, but it presents serious problems.

Joseph Breuer treated Anna O in 1882 and it is her case history which opens Breuer and Freud's seminal joint work, *Studies on Hysteria* (1895). Anna O fell sick while nursing her dying father. Her symptoms were chronic and incapacitating: an inability to speak her native German or to eat or drink at times, terrifying hallucinations, serious amnesia, an imaginary pregnancy, to name just some of them. Freud's foundation of psychoanalysis, based on an understanding of the dynamics of unconscious processes, largely came out of this work with hysteria.

A symptom such as a facial twitch for which there is no organic reason is explained in psychoanalytic theory as the result of a wish that cannot be realized becoming unconscious but still pressing forward as a physical expression into a person's life. For instance, a young man wishes to have an illicit affair with his friend's mother; the woman's husband intervenes and denounces him for his 'nerve'; the young man experiences the violent rebuke as 'a slap in the face'. The wish and the prohibition against it become unconscious but insist on their presence by becoming an uncontrollable facial twitch. The sufferer has no control over his symptom; he cannot stop it. If, however, its origin is discovered, the symptom becomes redundant. At this point, the young man can take conscious control of the situation and decide either to pursue or to relinquish his wish in full awareness of the prohibition or the realization of the wish. The difficulty in treating a hysterical symptom is that the wish and its prevention can also find an outlet in a different unconscious 'choice' of symptomatic ex-pression. On an idea or wish becoming unconscious, its representation appears utterly changed, as in a dream. Unconscious processes are ordinary thoughts transformed into a different modality. What would be contradictory ideas in conscious life can coexist simultaneously in unconscious processes: there is no 'no'; nothing can be negated; one object/idea can stand in for many others or be displaced along a seemingly (but not actually) endless series of other manifestations. This is called 'primary process thinking' and is utterly distinct from conscious secondary process thought. It is 'primary' because, although conscious thought is 'pushed back' into it, its modality is earlier, 'childish', more 'primitive'. Changing this unconscious thought back into conscious thought is a central task both of psychoanalytic clinical practice and the theory that results from it. The slippage from analysing Anna O's hysterical *symptoms* to describing her *personality*, as Slavney does, is evidenced in his different usage of the term 'unconscious'.

Psychoanalysis had established itself by deciphering and compre-hending the hysterical symptom. With the eradication of the symptom and its replacement by traits there is no process to understand, only something to be described by the observer or enacted by the sufferer. Hysteria ceases to be an object for comprehension; it thus ceases to 'exist' as anything other than a mode of behaviour. Having come to be used to describe the character of an individual, hysteria no longer exists beyond that person's aberrant behaviour. Today, even when unconscious aspects are mentioned, these are not the unconscious processes described by Freud but instead the interactional and interpersonal desires and fantasies which could easily become conscious. Such unconsciousness is not dynamic; it does not work with the primary process logic, which is as different from it as a nightdream is from planning the shopping. Instead it is 'unconscious', as in the words 'unconscious behaviour', which indicate simply something of which we happen at that moment to be unaware; it is not another way of thinking, but merely something we may not be completely conscious of doing – like eating a sandwich.[7] As we will see, this leads to an omission of the crucial conflictual and compulsive, driven element in hysteria.

What we see in this shift from looking at symptoms to considering character traits is simply a further version of a change in the explanatory paradigm. Hysteria is no longer a disease, it is a mode of behaviour and a life story. Freud's famous case of Dora – of which more in chapter 3 – perfectly exemplifies this transition from the patient presenting an illness to a physician to the sufferer telling a story to a therapist.

The disease entity has also vanished into the continued colloquial use of the term 'hysterical'. This shift may have enabled hysteria to disappear into the community, presenting itself as 'hystories',histrionic behaviour, wild rages, compulsive lying, abusive practices and so on. Today, while the family and the work place and new artistic practices have come to house hysteria, its more obviously 'mad' dimensions have become recategorized as new discrete illnesses.

A history of hysteria in modern times demonstrates a certain shift in the social class of the typical hysteric. Although there were plenty of Morgan Le Fays in medieval times, the main population of witches was poor and probably rootless; with the demise of witchcraft and the increased medicalization of hysteria during the sixteenth and seventeenth centuries, there followed a shift in the type of person most likely to be labelled a 'hysteric': hysterics became increasingly middle and upper class, often ladies of leisure (at least in the image that held hegemonic sway over the descriptions). During the nineteenth century the great humanist theorists of hysteria, Sydenham, Pinel and Freud, treated their subject and its practitioners with considerable respect. This respect was not only class-linked. Well before the explanations of madness and mental illness as resulting from demonic possession had declined during the seventeenth and eighteenth centuries, hysteria had come to be regarded as an illness accessible to *medical* help. The psychotic or mad dimensions of witchcraft continued, but without their 'witch' associations. This respect for hysteria – although it was highly uneven – already contributed to allowing that there could be male hysterics. However, once men were regarded as possible hysterics, the positive feminine end could not be theirs – they could not be said to be charming and alluring mothers, as hysterics so often were, and so the description as a whole became once more generally opprobrious. Apart from artists and writers, who operated beyond normal social boundaries anyway, hysteria in males became located at the negative pole – hysterical behaviour was considered more unmanly than it was unwomanly. This pole then got siphoned off into apparently non-hysterical psychotic disorders, such as schizophrenia, or later 'borderline' illnesses.

Ilza Veith's conclusion that throughout history hysteria's symptoms have been modified by the prevailing concept of a feminine ideal is, to all intents and purposes, my starting point. I would argue, however, that its 'disappearance' is in fact one more characteristic of the same phenomenon; one, moreover, that is linked to the advent of male hysteria. My question is: What does hysteria mean clinically? I am particularly interested in psychoanalytic practice where, as in psychiatry, convention sees hysteria as having largely vanished from the Western world. However, I also want to explore more generally what hysteria means for contemporary 'advanced world' cultures, whose historiographers, cultural studies students and performance theorists and artists (as opposed to clinicians) in a post-modern climate are once again finding it so extraordinarily interesting, thus renewing the link between hysteria and creativity. A cross-cultural perspective, in which we can see hysteria appearing in different contexts, acts as confirmation: hysteria's manifestations are clearly visible today, although the reluctance of anthropologists as well as of clinicians to label something hysteria is also still plainly in evidence. These anthropological and historical observations, with their different contexts, add further dimensions to the complex picture of hysteria that emerges today. Above all they help to insist on its continued presence as a particular response to aspects of the human condition.

II. HYSTERIA AND PSYCHOANALYSIS

It was the observation of hysteria which led to the foundation of psychoanalysis. However, hysteria has, to a large extent, now vanished from the psychoanalytic account – and for a number of reasons.

I shall argue that, in particular, the relationship between hysteria and psychoanalysis has been haunted since its inception by a crucial omission: that of sibling relationships. Secondly (and linked to this) is the problem of male hysteria. It is ironic, but necessary, then, to point out that the repressed sibling and the repressed male hysteric came together in the person of Sigmund Freud at the very outset of psychoanalysis. But the repression of male hysteria has had further consequences, which are highly complex. Making a claim for these consequences is certainly controversial. However, I believe that the repression of the male hysteric has partly led to a misdirection of psychoanalytic efforts from looking at the symptoms of hysteria to trying to replace them with an understanding of femininity in general. Feminists and psychoanalysts like myself are both heirs to, and participants in, this turn of events.

Towards the end of her life, Sigmund Freud's psychoanalyst daughter Anna Freud stated that, although psychoanalysis was founded on the observation of hysteria in the last century, late in this century it had still not really understood it.[8] I think this is true. We need to go back to the beginning. For, the shibboleths of psychoanalytical theory – in particular, the notion of the Oedipus complex – while not being incorrect, nevertheless stand in the way of our complete understanding of hysteria. The notion of the Oedipus complex, which takes place when the child is between the ages of three and five, was added to when it was seen how important the earlier, pre-Oedipal relationship of the baby to the mother was. However, both the Oedipus complex and the pre-Oedipal relationship stress vertical, generational relationships between children and parents at the expense of those which I think are at the heart of hysteria, the lateral relationships of siblings, peers and affines (those related by marriage).

The sibling relationship is important because, unlike the parental relationship, it is our first *social* relationship. The mode of psychoanalytic treatment obscures this and the theory ignores it. On the advent of a younger sibling or the awareness of the difference of an older sibling (or sibling substitute), the subject is displaced, deposed and without the place that was hers or his: she/he must change utterly in relation to both the rest of the family and the outside world. If the child is an older girl she is urged to become a 'little mother', a boy to become a 'big brother'. (The asymmetry is noticeable here.) For both, however, murder is in the air. The wish to kill the father (part of the Oedipus complex) who possesses the mother and with her is responsible for the usurper, is secondary to the need to eliminate he/she who has stepped into one's place and has exiled one from oneself. Another baby replaces the baby one was until this moment. Henceforth, a craving for love together with a love/hatred of excessive proximity construct a fragile psyche. If the child is a younger or only child, its mother's inevitable withdrawal evokes fantasies of other babies and often a sense of guilt for their assumed death. But the child is also excited by the discovery of someone like itself, so replicas of the subject are also wanted. Many children create imaginary twins or playmates who wishfully enact their replication. It is the love/hate ambivalence which comes into play in relation to siblings or near-peers that characterizes hysteria. The hysteric never knows whether he loves or hates. It is the catastrophic awareness that one is not unique which triggers the onset of hysteria, in which the displaced child regresses to produce the Oedipal and the pre-Oedipal stages and also the terrors of the traumatic helplessness of the neonatal infant. However, the context from whence the regression takes place is one of sufficient maturity, it is that of a small child whose lateral relationships entail both delights and dangers.

The traumatic helplessness is an experience of possible death. In chapter 5 I contend that we must raise issues of sexuality in conjunction with both reproduction and death in order to understand hysteria more fully. The condition of the human infant is one in which, because it is born prematurely, that is, before it is physically able to tackle the world, it needs a period of prolonged dependence on another human being, offers the ground plan for hysteria.

The 'premature' birth of humans and their early dependence, however, cannot explain why hysteria should be so persistently gendered. Marginal differences in the neonatal conditions of females and males could not possibly account for this overriding factor. Does the social organization of humankind explain the feminization of hysteria? The system of descent passing through the male line (agnatic filiation) that is found in most human societies obviously has a different effect on girls than boys. The gendering of hysteria is testimony to this asymmetry. In chapter 6, I look at how the human condition that leads to possible hysteria is feminized in a particular context of the twentieth-century Western world and its dominant theories.

The years that followed the publication of Breuer's and Freud's *Studies on Hysteria* produced one after another key tenet of the theory and practice that was to become psychoanalysis: symptoms, dreams, slips of the tongue and pen, and so on, were all taken to indicate the representations of some desires which were prohibited, repressed and hence made unconscious. However, such repression was never to be wholly successful: for the tabooed desires (or several conflicting desires) and their unsuccessful prohibition would inevitably return as one symptom or another. The energy of the original desire would fuel this return as a symptom which appeared in a distinct form because it contained simultaneously both the wishes and the prohibition of them. The story that is used as an emblem of these desires is the Oedipus complex – and its prohibition, which was formulated somewhat later, is the castration complex. These two theories derived from the observation and treatment of hysteria and hysterical phobias, but they also fed back into hysteria by way of offering an explanation for it: the hysteric has failed to resolve the Oedipus complex, failed, that is, to internalize a prohibition on parental incest.

In psychoanalytic theory, the Oedipus complex is the 'nuclear complex' which structures the personality and orientates human desire. It is the major axis from which psychopathology, or so-called normality, originates. The Oedipus complex organizes the child's loving and hostile relationship to its parents, which, when transferred on to other people, will be played out throughout its life. The incestuous love for the mother or father (the Oedipus complex) must be utterly demolished. If it is anything less than this, it will 'return' and get in the way of any successful transference of these primary desires on to new people, such as marriage partners. In this argument, the hysteric has not smashed the Oedipus complex, but has only inadequately 'repressed' it so that its desires come back as a symptom or in fantasies and enactments. For, so goes the theory, only through the acceptance of the castration complex can the Oedipus complex be effectively demolished. This is the law against incest, which emanates from the place of the father. The hysteric does not realize that it is just that – an absolute law; instead, he feels something is simply getting in the way of the realization of his wishes. Even if, as we shall see when charting the growth of British psychoanalytic Object Relations theory in chapter 6, subsequent psychoanalytical theories have emphasized a dyadic (two-person) pre-Oedipal relationship of mother and infant instead of the three-person Oedipal situation, or have detracted from the importance of the father's prohibition on the phallic incestuous nature of the Oedipal complex by placing it, not in early childhood but in infancy (around eight months, as does Melanie Klein), nevertheless the Oedipus complex has remained the crucial and central frame of reference.

Although the Oedipus complex, however, was discovered through hysteria, it has blocked our understanding of it. I do not for one moment want to contest the importance of either the Oedipus or the castration complex; what I want to propose is a different ordering which implicates siblings. I propose to invert accepted psychoanalytic ordering, which leads from the Oedipus complex on to the siblings, and suggest instead that it is the initial awareness of the presence of the siblings which produces a catastrophic psychosocial situation of displacement. This triggers in turn a regression to the earlier parental relationships which were without their psychic implications until this moment. Cast back on to babyhood in defence against displacement, the relationship to the parents becomes fully Oedipal. Although on all other occasions Freud emphasizes both regression and 'deferred action' (whereby an event acquires its meaning later), with regard to the Oedipus complex he follows chronology and always puts parents first. Thus he writes:

As a rule a father prefers his daughter and a mother her son; the child reacts to this by wishing, if he is a son, to take his father's place, and, if she is a daughter, her mother's. The feelings which are aroused in these relations between parents and children and *the resulting ones* between brothers and sisters are not only of a positive or affectionate kind but also of a negative or hostile one.[9] [My italics]

and

When other children appear on the scene the *Oedipus complex is enlarged into a family complex*. This, with fresh support from the egoistic sense of injury, gives grounds for receiving the new brothers or sisters with repugnance and for unhesitatingly getting rid of them by a wish.[10] [My italics]

This chronological approach is contrary to psychoanalytic method, which constructs the past from the viewpoint of the present. In Freud's account, love and hate derive from the parental relationship and are subsequently transferred to siblings. I read these events the other way around: faced with a sibling, the child regresses to its wish for infantile unity with the mother; it is then that it finds the father in the way. Of course, there are plenty of feelings between infants and parents before this moment, but it is the experience of complete displacement by a sibling or equivalent that causes the regression which turns these emotions into the psychic organization of the nuclear or Oedipus complex which in its turn must be demolished. Feelings for siblings and peers cast their shadow over relations with parents. The birth of a new sibling is of course the most visible shock, but the presence of older ones takes on the meaning of displacement of the subject, as we shall see in the case of 'Dora' in chapter 3.

Sibling relationships are the great omission in psychoanalytic observation and theory – its practice, as set out by Freud and all subsequent psychoanalytic theorists, militates against seeing their importance. Psychoanalysis's ignoring of sibling relationships has turned hysteria into a no-go area, as hysteria cannot, I believe, be understood without an understanding of lateral relationships. Once resurrected, siblings come out of their hiding places and are everywhere noticeable. In *The Interpretation of Dreams* (1900), for instance, while discussing the fact that he has never known a woman (we should note it is a woman) who did not dream of murdering her siblings, Freud comments:

Children are completely egoistic; they feel their needs intensely and strive ruthlessly to satisfy them – especially as against the rivals, other children, and first and foremost as against their brothers and sisters . . . before the end of the period which we count as childhood, altruistic impulses and morality will awaken in the little egoist . . . If this morality fails to develop, we like to talk of 'degeneracy', though what in fact faces us is an inhibition in development. After the primary character has already been overlaid by later development, it can still be laid bare again, at all events in part, in cases of hysterical illness. There is a really striking resemblance between what is known as the hysterical character and that of a naughty child.[11]

Yet, though once we think of siblings, they seem to be everywhere, they never get taken up into the theory. Eighteen years after this comment from *The Interpretation of Dreams*, while analysing the case of a Russian aristocrat obsessional neurotic who, on account of a recurrent nightmare, became known as the 'Wolf Man', Freud found exactly this pattern of an underlying hysteria. We shall see in chapter 2 how crucial was the Wolf Man's relationship to his older sister and how this set up a regression in him, not, in his case, back to form the Oedipus complex, but to fantasize about something yet more primitive, the so-called 'primal scene' of the intercourse between his parents. The primal scene is a perfect image for an originary absence of the subject at the very place where he comes into being – we are not present at our own conception. It is, however, the catastrophe of sibling displacement which occasions a retrospective imaginary perception of this 'unimaginable' event. Hysteria protests this displacement, this absence of the subject.

Psychoanalytic anthropology has mostly had the Oedipus complex in mind when applying psychoanalytic theories to ethnographic observations. I earlier selected Lewis's account because many of the rituals, practices and illnesses he observed bear a resemblance to hysteria. In polygynous societies, such as those of northern Somalia, the wife who fears replacement develops *sar* – hysterical behaviour which must be assuaged by gifts from the husband. The jealousy is lateral and is a response to displacement. Seen through the lateral relations of siblings, the account could benefit from psychoanalytic input in a way which is inhibited by the need to prioritize the Oedipal schema. For anthropological accounts of hysteria-like conditions actually describe lateral relationships to affines: husbands, wives and peer cohorts.

Or again, let us look at 'wanting', the characteristic which defines the Taita illness of *saka*. Nineteenth-century literature uses the word 'longing', a term taken up by the early Freud; it expresses itself like some desiring will-o'-the-wisp endlessly wanting what it cannot have. Flaubert's *Madame Bovary* shows an example of a typical state in which a person is only interested in people who are not interested in them. There was also the disease which the nineteenth century referred to as 'nostalgia', which is absorbed into the psychoanalytic observation that 'hysterics suffer from reminiscences' – a child would be so nostalgic for its wet nurse that it could never settle down with its mother. 'Wanting' is central to a Freudian theory of hysteria. The age-old observation that the hysteric mimes or imitates is replaced in psychoanalytic theory by a specific understanding of mimesis in the context of 'wanting': one wants what the other person wants and mimes that person's desires.

It is easy to pose an Oedipus constraint on this wanting; indeed that is quite accurate. However, it also needs to be read through the advent of the sibling. Before it was redesignated as anorexia nervosa, anorexia was called 'anorexia hysterica' – eating disorders are widely observed as a prevalent feature of hysteria. 'Normal' food fads occur at exactly the stage of displacement by a sibling: the toddler, for instance, may try to get back to being the baby at the breast, or alternatively may never touch milk again. The anorexic teenager may be regressing to infantile faddishness and ambivalence to the breast. This is not the mother's breast *per se*, but the breast the new baby has usurped. The younger child on whom the realization dawns that he is not the older sibling will also both fear the advent of another and want to regress to infancy, that is, a time when, as he thought, he got all the attention. An actual sibling is the concrete embodiment of a general condition in which no human being is unique – he can always be replaced or repeated by another.

Within the psychoanalytic theory of the Oedipus complex, hysteria is part of the wearisome condition of humanity, because humankind, as Fulk Greville expressed it in the sixteenth century, is 'born under one law but to another bound'. With the castration complex, the human propensity to wish and want comes into conflict with the human laws that proscribe the realization of these wishes. The prohibition comes with the sexualization of wishes. Just as childhood dreams show the satisfaction of a range of wishes, so in the regressions of hysteria there are more wishes and wants than just those of parental incest, which is really the ultimate – but not exclusive – expression of what cannot be had or done. If we see the onset of hysteria as the catastrophic moment of the subject's displacement – which archetypically occurs when subjects become aware that they can be replicated by a sibling, either in mind or actuality – then this also coincides with a time when all 'wanting' is not only intensified but also sexualized. Sibling or peer group sexual play around the ages of three to five years is so common as to be regarded as developmentally normal.

Once siblings are read into the account, a number of puzzles clear up: reading the earliest case histories of hysteria is otherwise to be amazed that the emphasis that emanated from them was only on sexuality – not, as is so clearly the case, on sexuality in conjunction with trauma and death. When a death wish against siblings, not only against the father of the castration complex, is recognized, then the now-you-see-him, now-you-don't of male hysteria becomes clearer; wayward mythologies such as Freud's own *Totem and Taboo* (1913), which fantasizes the ganging-up of brothers but which otherwise fails to connect with his clinical material, fall into place. The very notion of a disappearance of hysteria can in part be blamed on the emphasis on Oedipus. Reading in the sibling does not produce a miracle explanation that solves the problem of hysteria once and for all. Rather, it offers a sense of relief: that something still major and crucial in theory and observation, the Oedipus complex, has been acting as an unnecessary obstacle, a block of stone which, for all its importance, nevertheless obscured the view.

*

In chapter 6 I argue that some theories, in particular those of Object Relations, together with the emphasis on femininity in the interwar period, take us further away from understanding or even recognizing hysteria. Because these are developmental theories they tend to miss the crucial importance for hysteria of regression: confronted with a sibling, the infant *regresses* to wanting to be the unique baby it previously was. This small child is older, though, and rivalrous and competitive, and there has probably been sibling or peer sexual play, so regression to a fantasized merger with the mother comes under the sign of sexuality. It also bears death in train, for as well as murderous rivalry the child who was king is suddenly no one, annihilated, in danger of psychic death.

Freud's case of *Dora* (1905) (see chapter 3) is a *locus classicus* for our thinking about hysteria. It was written before any hypothesis of a death drive (in *Beyond the Pleasure Principle* (1920)). Hysteria, I argue, needs to be understood also in relation to the death drive. The absence of this perspective in the theory of hysteria is related to the suppression of male hysteria. And this suppression, in its turn, takes us back to the way in which the dominance of the Oedipus complex obscures our view. Whatever our particular family constellation or kinship network, or the reproductive technology involved in our conception, we are all conceived of two parents: society elaborates this biological fact, which gives plausibility to the timelessness and placelessness of the Oedipus complex – it is everybody's human lot. And hysteria in its generality finds a plausible explanation as a malnegotiation of the universal Oedipus complex. The wanting that the Taita note in *saka*, or that is present within the cults and practices observed by Lewis, or the Greek account of the wandering, hungry womb, was also considered central by Freud. He argued that the 'wanting' that the hysteric exemplifies takes place within the specific context of the dependent infant's wanting of the parents; that is to say, its fantasies about those who care for and protect it. When these wantings have a 'phallic' dimension, they become prohibited (the taboo on parental incest) and subsequently the fantasies of necessity become unconscious. If the Oedipus complex could not be found in the deciphering of the symptoms, then to the psychoanalyst the illness was not hysteria.

From a psychoanalytical point of view, when men had to leave the battlefields of the First World War because they had all the symptoms that in women would have been classified as hysteria, it was this incessant Oedipal longing which was regarded as the deciding factor as to whether or not they were in fact suffering from hysteria. The men's symptoms included non-organic limps, paraplegias, paralyses, headaches, amnesia, nightmares, insomnia, contractures and, above all among the British, mutism. What could these men have been 'wanting' when they were traumatized on the battlefields of France? One answer tended to dominate all others: conditions of bonding in the army allowed for the return of repressed homosexual desire. The boy's passive Oedipal love for his father was being brought into play. But even at the time the explanation seemed somewhat strained; it concentrated on one aspect of the condition at the expense of something far more straightforward: the trauma of war violence. Indeed, in time, a diagnosis of 'traumatic neuroses' won the day and hysteria 'disappeared'. The connection between hysteria and trauma is crucial, though. I take this up in detail in chapter 9, but it is a theme that runs throughout this book.

The First World War, then, reintroduced the probability of fear and trauma in the etiology of hysteria. The anthropologist-psychiatrist W. H. R. Rivers (1864–1922), recently brought to popular attention through Pat Barker's novel *The Ghost Road* and the film of *Regeneration*, initially trained as a doctor and psychiatrist. He was well informed about psychoanalysis and instrumental in its dissemination earlier this century. During the war he ran Craiglockhart hospital in Edinburgh for officers repatriated from the front for non-organic illnesses (later officially referred to as 'shellshock'). Shellshock was supposed to be traumatic because the new technology meant the shock was so quick that it could not be mentally processed. Rivers considered the then neologism an unfortunate misnomer for the illnesses he was treating as it ignored the significance of the sufferer's *preceding* terror of death in the etiology of his illness – the fear that came before the shock.

Rivers must have been correct in his assessment of shellshock as an inadequate explanation of the illness he was treating at Craiglockhart: soldiers in the American Civil War, before the advent of the fast-blasting shell, had responded in similar fashion – they too must have feared death *before* the blow. However, in addition to the preceding terror are the *post hoc* fears. The physical and chemical components of modern warfare have subsequent effects – which are almost certainly both organic and imaginary; most people exposed to such warfare from Hiroshima onwards must live with the permanent fear of unknown effects, even if they suppress this fear in the interest of daily life. However, in all warfare, fear would seem to be present both before, during and after the fighting – fear of annihilation or of possession by an unknown deadly disease or vengeful enemy is omnipresent.

The sufferer of the illness in the situation of war has not only been a victim of aggression but has also been an aggressor. In many cultures, including late twentieth-century Western culture, the taking of life, however completely rationalized as justified killing, is taboo at some level (or some aspects of it are considered seriously to offend). By considering the victim of the illness only as a victim of war, we are missing the point. What the soldier, sailor or airman may also be suffering from is the knowledge that he has broken a taboo and that in doing so he has released his wish to do so – his wish, his 'wanting' to murder, to kill his sibling substitutes. Terror produces madness: an ill veteran of the Vietnam War described how in the general carnage he had let a young boy live only to find, to his fury, that a fellow American had shot the child in the head. Listening to this personal account by chance on the radio, I was momentarily confounded to learn that he had wanted the child to live, not from compassion but because he wanted to see him tortured.

In addition to shock and fear of death, the person who becomes hysterical following a war is also unconsciously dreading vengeance or possession by the person he has killed or threatened. This killed person who returns as a revenant is a notion that is very close to the psychoanalytic concept of a 'return of the repressed'. In chapter 2 we will meet the revenant for Freud – his dead baby brother, who set a pattern of enmities/friendships in his relation with younger men, but who, more importantly, appears as a 'symptom' within psychoanalytic theory and practice. The dread of the revenant can be enacted in hysterical possession or conquered in poetry. It is to this phenomenon of the return of the dead friend who is the enemy – one's 'brother officer' – that Wilfred Owen referred in 'Strange Meeting' (1918).

Wilfred Owen was himself for a time a patient of Rivers at Craiglockhart before he went back to the front to be killed at the crossing of the Sambre canal in 1918. In 'Strange Meeting' he writes about his imagined encounter with a German soldier he had shot. The German is Owen's own mirror double (his sibling peer) and talks to him of the 'pity of war'. Owen puts into the German's mouth the terms he had used previously when writing from his own perspective. His slain foreign double now mimes the earlier Owen:

> 'I am the enemy you killed, my friend.
> I knew you in this dark; for so you frowned
> Yesterday through me as you jabbed and killed.
> I parried; but my hands were loath and cold.
> Let us sleep now . . .'

Concern about the return of the dead and of the broken taboo on murder is widespread; the wish to break the taboo rather than the breaching of the taboo itself must take some responsibility for the notion of the revenant. Enacting through ritual ensures against haunting. In Birifu, northern Ghana, the offence against the earth is a predominant concern: anyone who has shed any human blood on the earth, for whatever reason, must go through 'rituals of inversion' and carry out a number of revolting acts otherwise avoided, such as eating off 'dirty' steps or consuming a medicine supposed to be concocted of human flesh. In Birifu, it is said that in taking into oneself what one has done to another, one 'takes out the dream' – the dead will not return. In carrying through rituals of inversion, the people of Birifu acknowledge that there was a revolting element in the original killing (it had offended the earth). Disgust and shame are characteristic of hysteria, as they are of the child of around three years of age to whose reactions the hysteric regresses. Failure to carry through this ritual carries with it the risk of possession. In hysteria we see the haunting that arises when enactment is neither turned into poetry nor ritualized (as, through the appearance of the Ghost, a murder by a brother haunts the play of *Hamlet*).

Hysteria is preempted by the ritual. The shared ground of hysteria means that we can see a number of parallels between the social tasks of ritual and individual psychic responses elucidated by psychoanalysis. The notions of 'reaction formations' or of 'undoing' what one has done are strikingly parallel to these rituals. In the first the individual reverses an experience so that, for instance, he acts disgust when he feels pleasure he should not have had; in the second, he compulsively goes back on some experience that was likewise illicit. Psychoanalytic conceptualization absorbed many of the processes it observed in the hysteric and that are found enacted in other cultures. However, 'possession' was weakened to '*besetzung*', as in 'to take possession of a building', and poorly translated into English as 'cathexis'. It seems to me, though, that we have assigned 'possession' to elsewhere (for example, to the Taita) but that it is everywhere among us, just reinterpreted in terms such as 'projective identification' (the process through which one individual puts unwanted feelings into another and then identifies with that person). Projection is a powerful process. It is seen very clearly in instances of jealousy. The jealous person finds the feelings intolerable, so he both gives the feelings to another person and then may make the predicament real – as I will show Iago does to Othello, in chapter 8. A 'disturbed' child may be 'possessed' by the hysteria of a parent. The paeditrician and psychoanalyst Donald Winnicott once described the crazy behaviour of a young boy. He suddenly realized that the child was trying to tell him what no one except the child knew – that his mother had mad episodes.[12] Because of its apparent disappearance from the Western world, I have selected to examine possession, in chapter 7.

The experience of a haunting that would arise in Birifu if the ritual of inversion were not carried through might not be so very different for the actor from the 'haunting' proclaimed by sufferers of Gulf War Syndrome and the like. One can be 'haunted' by the sense that one is harbouring some inexplicable disease or that one's offspring will be the bearer of some deformity. Indeed, the group aspect of a phenomenon such as Gulf War Syndrome may be a substitute for the failure of society to provide a ritual. However, the hysterical dimension of responses to war experiences does not exclude the possibility that there are also organic illnesses or genetic consequences to contemporary warfare. There is no reason why people cannot suffer simultaneously from something that is organic as well as from an ineffable fear of it and at the same time also be haunted for having broken a taboo which, moreover, may be one which they unconsciously wished to break and whose flouting may consequently also be illicitly exciting.

We will see later the tragic case of Allon White, a young lecturer with leukaemia, who was haunted by his dead sister and terrified of both death and his sibling wish to have got rid of his sister. We contain multitudes of possibilities which are only mutually exclusive to the enquiry that is trying to organize them. Even the discarded notion that the shock from shells happens so quickly that it triggers hysteria had plausibility because one of the characteristics of hysteria is that the hysteric does not have access to the process of mourning, which takes time – both actual and psychical. Mourning requires the acknowledgement that the dead person is gone for ever and cannot return. When this psychological state is achieved, then there can be an internal image or memory of the dead person, instead of a kind of incubus within. The hysteric still has the incubus or revenant.

If the breaking of the taboo and, with it, the release of the unconscious wish to kill is an underlying factor of war hysteria, then the deeper relationship of the symptoms of First World War soldiers and those of middle-class women in the consulting rooms of nineteenth-century Europe becomes more explicable. Illicit wishes for murder were returning from repression for the men in the same way as were illicit wishes for incest. This equation of the breaking of the taboo against murder and the breaking of the taboo against incest is contained in the original story of Oedipus, who not only marries his mother but also murders his father. However, for both to come together, as they appear to do in hysteria (that is, the near-identity of murder and the urgent sexual wanting), the ground plan of sibling hate/love needs to be read into the account. The child wants to be in the place of the sibling, to murder the usurper of its place, but it also loves it as itself and as it is/was loved itself and also as it wants to be loved itself.

In *Hystories* (1997), a recent study of hysteria, Elaine Showalter suggests that the underlying factor in hysteria is a response to a situation experienced as untenable. This fits in with explanations of helplessness: the terrified soldier, the Victorian woman idol, the inarticulate working-classes are all powerless. Citing Weir Mitchell's unpublished case of 'uncomplicated hysteria in a male', treated in 1876, Showalter notes (as Weir Mitchell did not) that his patient, Robert Conolly, who suffered from the clock-like movements of so-called 'pendulum spasms', was a watchmaker. She goes on to ask: 'Could it have been that Conolly's distaste for his finicky and monotonous labor was so great, his inability to articulate it so deep, that his body simply created compelling symptoms/symbols of his dilemma? Nineteenth-century male breadwinners could not admit that they hated their work and found debilitating symptoms useful . . . Conolly developed a body language that expressed his preference not to fulfil his role.'[13] It is this impossible position, Showalter suggests, which unites women and powerless men in their hysterias. While I think such inarticulate powerlessness is an important constituent of hysteria, as is clearly shown by the Taitas' *saka* illness, in itself it is an inadequate explanation. Certainly, helplessness in the present reactivates the dependent conditions of humankind. However, powerlessness, helplessness, hatred of one's work, do not reveal conflict – it is the oddity of behaviour that indicates there is a meaning behind it that has been transformed into a hysterical symptom. If Conolly's were hysterical *symptoms*, as I believe they were, they must also have contained unconscious conflicting wishes.

Furthermore, Conolly's pendulum spasms were driven, compulsive behaviour so that, even were he to wish to do so, he could not stop. As we shall see in chapter 5, it was partly in order to account for this compulsive reiterativity that the hypothesis of a death drive was formulated. Most Independent Object Relations psychoanalysts reject the notion of a death drive – instead, we need further to refine our understanding of it. Death and trauma are crucial to the onset and manifestations of hysteria. Today, a fascination with trauma has ousted hysteria in such programmes as the movement to recover memories of childhood abuse. In fact, memory (or its absence in hysterical amnesia), trauma and death all come together in hysteria. This is a conjuncture I consider throughout this book. The hysteric cannot acknowledge that death is absolute – this refusal to accept the meaninglessness of death is manifest in the suicide of the poet Anne Sexton (a diagnosed hysteric), as it is indeed in the story of Don Juan. A hysterical identification with the violence of the thing that is experienced as traumatic is also a part of the rage that is the other side of the charm of the hysteric. In a postnatal depression a mother may have felt herself to have 'died' in giving birth. This will bring up childhood experiences of annihilation. Her experience of psychic death will be violent; she screams murderously at her baby but is charming to her husband, just as when she was a little girl she courted her father when she felt the violence of her mother's rejection when her mother seemed to love her brother better. Aspects of trauma, memory and the question of a hysterical response to being 'unrecognized' are focused on in chapter 9.

A trauma blasts body and mind. Before and beneath the flamboyant pantomime of the hysteric's seductive behaviour is the experience of a body that is not there. This has rightly been explained by the French psychoanalyst Monique David-Menard as a body which cannot be symbolized. I explore what this means and why it should be so when I consider the absent body of the hysteric in chapter 7. However, psychoanalysis is famous for its status as an anti-Cartesian theory: that is, one in which there is no separation of mind and body. But the theory has been unable to contain its own insight: the notion of repressing Oedipal desire embraces the notion of repressing the representation of the idea of the desire; this representation becomes unconscious, and the effects (feelings and emotions) are discharged through the body. However, the hysteric does not represent. He is blasted by trauma, actual or imagined, and, on recovering, he both evacuates and dramatizes, presenting rather than representing: the fantasies of his mind are the actions of his body, so his hurt feelings are presented as a physical wound. One of my patients saw his leg weep – this was a painful pun on the idea that a physical sore 'weeps' and that, being a man, he must not weep in his distress. Nevertheless, something has happened to these presentations – for they are not simply enactments, since the unconscious has been at work in the transformations of the symptom.

The importance of retaining an awareness of the peculiarity of the hysterical symptom and its indication of unconscious processes at work is made evident if it is compared with a psychosomatic illness. Between the world wars the notion of the psychosomatic illness became fashionable and, to a great degree, replaced diagnoses of hysteria. There is, of course, always an interaction between a mental state and a physical condition; a state of mind affects the body and the state of the body affects the mind – but in different ways. A psychosomatic condition can be summed up in the aphorism, 'You don't need to be depressed to get a cold, but it helps.' One may know one is depressed and be unable to prevent the cold developing – which would involve conscious or preconscious processes. However, it is the transformational aspect, the distortions, displacement or condensations which make the symptoms so bizarre – as in the weeping leg – that it is obvious that something conflictual and unconscious is at stake. If one suffered from a perpetual cold because one's lover had rebuked one for being emotionally cold when one was in fact being warm to another man, then the symptom – the cold – would be hysterical. Without this concept of unconscious processes, such questions as what is happening in the hysterical body cannot really be approached. It is simply not the case that all hysterics are inarticulate. Indeed, the very prevalence of 'hystories' as a late twentieth-century mode of expressing hysteria argues strongly against this.

Current explanations that the body 'speaks' because the social position of the sufferer is weak and cannot be articulated in language seem like contemporary versions of earlier accounts of hysteria. It seems like prejudice – oppressed people are uneducated and use their bodies instead of language. In such accounts the notion of social denigration replaces the seventeenth- and nineteenth-century ideas that some people suffer from organic inferiority or degeneracy of the personality.

However, to argue for a moment against myself, if there can be 'hystories', where is the transformational, conflictual dimension necessary for this to be a mode of hysterical communication? Our everyday, so-called 'secondary process' language is sequential and thus cannot express two conflicting ideas at the same time; the nearest we can get to this is the oxymoron – for instance, 'sweet sorrow'. A story looks like an ordinary sequential use of language. Is this so? 'Hystories' are known in psychoanalysis as 'bovarism', or the propensity to believe one's fantasies as though they were reality. Flaubert studied his own as well as other cases of institutionalized hysteria as models for his portrait of Emma Bovary. 'Bovarism' comes close to pseudologia – a self-referential language system in which the subject tries to enhance his own importance and interest to other people through fantastic self-important fantasies or lying. Lying has long been noted as a mode of hysterical expression. Is there something in the 'lie' that could be described as a conflict, something therefore transformational about the mode of the lie which, in turn, underlies the propensity to recount 'hystories'? 'Honest Iago', whom I discuss in chapter 8, exemplifies this possibility (his appellation is an oxymoronic indication of contradiction). The lie can be seen as an unconscious wish which would otherwise be prohibited; it thus contains both the wish and the prevention of its realization. With Iago I shall look at whether the lie is a transformation in a way comparable to the body symptom of conversion hysteria.

Hysteria has long been divided into conversion hysteria and anxiety hysteria. In conversion hysteria, the idea is converted into a bodily expression; in anxiety hysteria the anxiety is so extreme that the subject takes avoidance action. So, for instance, flying represents such an illicit desire and such a prohibition on it that a phobia results and there is a complete inhibition – an absolute fear of flying. Initially Freud thought that anxiety resulted from the repression of sexual wishes – the later notion of a primal anxiety suggests that as well as this the infant has an anxious reaction to life and the possibility of helplessness and death.

Psychoanalysts were involved, usually as army psychiatrists, in both world wars. As Freud was at pains to point out, there were no actual psychoanalytic treatments of war neurosis (the conditions did not allow them), only the application of certain ideas. However, both wars had a major impact on psychoanalytic theories. From the viewpoint of the study of hysteria, the most influential concept introduced after the First World War was the importance accorded to primal anxiety. Important too was the hypothesis of a death drive. Finally, crucial too was the formulation of a different metapsychology – that is, of the id, superego and ego being superimposed on the unconscious, preconscious and conscious. In this theory, the ego can be partly conscious and partly unconscious (which it is in hysteria). The superego, which acts as a moral judge over oneself, is established by internalizing the rule of law embodied in the father – those very prohibitions against one's pleasures that the notion of a castration complex addresses; the superego is an internal authority where the father is an external one. It is weaker in women than men and virtually absent in the hysteric. However, with this latter observation, we can see once again that we are faced with the onset of the collapse of hysteria into femininity (see chapter 6).

As the traumata of the First World War provoked a retheorizing of psychoanalysis, so new theories followed on from this – most particularly ego psychology (and the subsequent hostility to it of Jacques Lacan) and Object Relations Theory, which became particularly strong in Britain. For Freud and for Freudians, the idea that a death drive is in conflict with a life drive (a drive which subsumes sexuality) was still contextualized within the fantasies of the Oedipus complex, and, increasingly, the pre-Oedipus complex. I suggest that this confinement to oedipality means certain dimensions of the hysterical response to the world wars were missed and indeed continue to be missed in subsequent violent situations.

The Second World War, like the first one, occasioned hysteria-type reactions. Attitudes to these varied from the idea that they were impossible, since hysteria had disappeared from the Western world, to violent fury with men who produced hysterical symptoms or behaviour because they had failed both the armed forces and the Western notion of manhood. By the end of the 1940s, as in the interwar period, the notion that hysteria had disappeared was prevalent once more, for current theories simply could not contain the idea of the male hysteric.

Within psychoanalytic theory it had become doctrine that if there was no evidence of an unresolved Oedipus complex, then the illness could not be a proper hysteria. However, as the observation of male hysterics in the last years of the nineteenth century had already disappeared into the notion of the Oedipus complex, there was some tautology in the situation. The notion of trauma was reintroduced. Charcot had observed that the male hysterics he treated had suffered from trauma and once more, the psychological casualties of the First World War were assigned 'traumatic neurosis'. For all the psycho-neuroses – anxiety, hysteria, obsessionality – the Oedipus complex was crucial. After a pre-psychoanalytic phase which argued that the prevalence of hysteria in women was the result of the previous traumatic sexual abuse of the girl child, the female hysteric also became understood within the framework of the Oedipus complex.

The Oedipus complex, however, was a concept engendered at the turn of the century, at the height of a veritable obsession with parental incest. Incest or 'incasta', 'unchastity', has always been a moveable feast – although mother–child sexual unions seem to have been very widely tabooed. Twentieth-century psychoanalysis has added the importance of the mother to the late nineteenth-century supreme father.

As we will see through the psychoanalytic story of Don Juan in chapter 8, perhaps the greatest effect of an acknowledgement of male hysteria was that it was exactly this that became normalized. Today's hysteric is an everyday Don Juan (male or female) – creative but seducing, lying, someone for whom death has no meaning, transmitting jealousy and causing chaos wherever they go. But as an artist he has also found his creative programme in some of the performative preoccupations of post-modernism which consciously put into effect much of what hysteria is unconscious of. In a performance or in performative language, speech enacts, puts on stage, what it wants to say; words *do* things. The French philosopher Jean-François Lyotard, a quondam spokesman of 1960s revolutionary optimism, declared 'the stakes of post-modernism as a whole [are] not to exhibit truth within the closure of representation but to set up *perspectives* within a return of the *will*'.[14] This is a good manifesto for hysteria. However, it presents a problem for psychoanalysis, which works within the framework that there is truth within the closure of representation and urges that one cannot have all one wants and wills. The hysteric, both in body symptom and in the lie, is enacting what he wants or wishes were the case.

The categories within which hysteria is confined have changed. The secularization of the Western world, for instance, has led to the demise of spirit possession and witchcraft in an uneven way since the eighteenth and nineteenth centuries, and so to that particular explanation of hysteria becoming defunct. However, this does not mean that hysteria itself has disappeared – instead, it has become interpreted in an alternating medical or characterological way. With the rise of neurology, what had become a female characterological condition became once more medicalized, but this time as a malady of the mind. Hysteria became the object of the rising science of psychiatry. Then, when what Ian Hacking described in his book *Rewriting The Soul* (1995) as the 'sciences of memory' replaced the soul as the seat of the human psyche around the 1860s, the scene became set for a different understanding – that offered by psychoanalysis. This contained its own demedicalization and set the seal on this epoch of treating hysteria as a disease. However, hysteria lived on.

Psychiatric accounts of hysteria led during the first part of the twentieth century to its reclassification into discrete parts, such as eating disorders or multiple personality. The psychiatric aim is to find entities which are amenable to drug treatment. This left 'histrionic' behaviours and relationships to the behaviour therapists or to families and workplaces. Psychoanalytic theories worked within the confines of the Oedipus complex, adding the pre-Oedipal mother and child. They replicated this in the treatment situation, interpreting maternal and paternal transferences, only to find that hysteria was no longer 'there'.

The prevalence of the male hysteric ensured he became normalized as the post-modern individual – a latterday Don Juan, uninterested in fathering, just out to perform.[15] There has always been a creative potential in hysteria; the emptying-out of the subject allows for creativity as well as for traumatic response. The issue then becomes how conscious or unconscious, how driven to create is the hysteric (as was Dostoevsky, whose hysterical epileptic fits took place as a prelude to a burst of writing) or, on the contrary, compelled to repetition until death (as with Don Juan).

Hysteria has only disappeared from sight in the clinic – in the real world, it is everywhere around us. In a climate in which one does not speak clinically of hysteria, I once apprehensively suggested to a patient that the several hospitalizations he had experienced might have been for hysteria. Having initially dismissed the idea, he went on to admit that no organic causes had been found for his symptoms, and that the late twentieth-century diagnosis he had eventually received for his apparently severe cardiac problems was 'Devil's grip'.

Hysteria, although of course under different names and with diverse explanations, is to be found across all cultures and has been observed by anthropologists as well as by psychoanalysts. At the turn of the century, when both psychoanalysis and anthropology were establishing their disciplines, incest obsessed both scientists and practical do-gooders, who feared its prevalence with the spread of urbanization. At this time, anthropologists, like psychoanalysts, emphasized *descent* and *filiation* – the relations between parents and children. However, where the practice of the various dominant psychotherapies replicates up to the present time the parent–child situation in the therapist–patient dyad, the observation of other cultures does not perpetuate this focus. In cross-cultural studies after the Second World War, the importance of *affinity* – including marriage partners as well as lateral peer and sibling relations – began to rival 'descent' theory. Unfortunately, this has not benefited an understanding of hysteria, for as this concept came in, hysteria disappeared from circulation. Affinity and laterality, I believe, need to be used to restructure psychoanalysis as theory and practice and hysteria needs to be reconsidered in both anthropology and psychoanalysis, if we are ever to see where it has hidden itself.

Lateral relations start in childhood with siblings and peers. Brothers and sisters and, following on from this, collateral partners, wives and husbands, are positioned differently from parents – this lateral 'positioning' is a crucial factor in the gendering of hysteria. The existence of mass hysteria, which is essentially a peer group phenomenon, or the prevalence of hysterical behaviours such as imitated anorexia in girls' boarding schools, indicate that the limited vertical parent–child axis of explanation is both inappropriate and inadequate.

Noting sibling relationships is crucial. Freud, himself a sufferer from hysteria at the time of the founding of psychoanalysis, was haunted by his rivalry with his first playmate, his nephew John, one and a half years his senior, but also far more particularly by the death of his younger brother Julius; the hysteria of Dora, the young woman famously analysed by Freud, came on in childhood when she had to renounce her fused identification with her older brother. In chapter 3 I look at the classic case of Dora, this time with a focus on her relationship with her brother, who effectively never features in all the many readings of the case that have been offered since Freud first presented it in 1905. I also examine Freud's own hysteria in order to show what was present at, and what absent from, the creation of the dominant psychoanalytical understanding of hysteria at the time of its inception.

I suggest a picture of hysteria which looks like this: a catastrophe in the present is experienced as traumatic. This may be something beyond normal human endurance – the blasting to pieces of your mate beside you in the trenches – or the sufferer may have used some

minor incident to create an experience of trauma, such as the striking
of a match or the sight of a car in the case of the Taita women. As
with physical pain thresholds, the tolerance levels vary from individual
to individual – one person's distress is another person's trauma.
Trauma, actual or induced, or transmuted from a catastrophe,
breaches defences. In coping with the present experience, the person
regresses to a catastrophic state, an infantile or childhood situation.
I suggest this state is one in which the person has felt in danger of
their own non-existence – somebody else seems to be the same as
them. If someone is the same as oneself, then the sensation can be,
'Who am I? I thought I was the baby – but here is another baby: I
thought I was my parents' favourite child, but here is another one.'
In protesting against this by trying to become again the only baby or
favourite offspring, the hysteric regresses so far that the differentiation
between mind and body is no longer clear, just as (we assume) it is
not in infancy. By which time he is utterly dependent and helpless. The
dread of the death-like experience of trauma, which is the equivalent of
an absence of subject or ego, is warded off by a mimetic identification
with another person. This may well be with the mother for whom he
wants to be the only baby – this possibility has contributed to our
not seeing the sibling as the cause. At the same time there is a frenetic
mobility (or a frozen reaction against it) which prevents the unbearable
thought, a thought that would 'kill' him. One of my patients used to
shake her head wildly, in a way that reminded me of an infant's
'headbashing' against its cot, whenever we got near something she
did not want to think about. In turn, this mobility is exciting, in the
same way as for a child who is being jiggled on a knee or playing
horsey-horsey, and hence, in a generalized way, it can be felt as
sexually stimulating; the desire or 'wanting' – even craving – for its
repetition is felt as an urgent need to fill the hole that has been opened
up by what is experienced as, or what actually is, trauma. Frenetic
talking, compulsive lying, can be the verbal equivalent of excited and
grandiose movement. The vortex this mobility creates draws in those
around the hysteric, whose own potential hysterical vortex (which
we all have) responds. To a degree, everyone is vulnerable. Though
the idiom is somewhat dated, T. S. Eliot, in 'Sweeney Agonistes'
(1932), which could be read as an autobiographical account of some

hysterical (and hysterically creative) aspects of his own work, inserted a prose poem:

'Hysteria'
As she laughed I was aware of becoming involved in her laughter and being part of it . . . I was drawn in by short gasps, inhaled at each momentary recovery, lost finally in the dark caverns of her throat, bruised by the ripple of unseen muscles . . . I decided that if the shaking of her breasts could be stopped, some of the fragments of the afternoon might be collected, and I concentrated my attention with careful subtlety to this end.[16]

Hysteria is as broad and expansive as human culture. It cannot be neatly packaged in narrative, either historical or medical. All aspects of the condition radiate out to touch yet others. In the same way, this book should be viewed as a verbal picture rather than a narrative. Its structure is like a dandelion flower, a compositae in which each floret is an independent unit but each is needed to make a connected whole. The chapters I have written here are a few florets, but there are others waiting to be written. However, even these few, like the dandelion, spread rapidly, sometimes into unexpected areas.

Hysteria, as a response to certain aspects of what it means to be human, is everywhere. Its name and the understanding of it changes – both geographically and historically. Some aspect of this 'human condition' insists that hysteria over and over again is reassigned to women or to 'femininity'. The acknowledgement of male hysteria has entailed the banishing of hysteria. Twentieth-century understandings of hysteria – in particular the psychoanalytic – excluded it at the very moment they contemplated it, because they completely 'foreclosed' on relations with siblings in favour only of parents. This is the besetting problem of Freud's otherwise world-historic understanding of hysteria.

2

Sigmund Freud: A Fragment of a Case of Hysteria in a Male

'Things are fermenting in me; I have finished nothing; am very satisfied with the psychology, tormented by grave doubts about my theory of the neuroses, too lazy to think, and have not succeeded here in diminishing the agitation in my head and feelings . . . After having become very cheerful here, I am now enjoying a period of bad humour. The chief patient I am preoccupied with is myself. *My little hysteria, though greatly accentuated by my work, has resolved itself a bit further.* The rest is still at a standstill. That is what my mood primarily depends on. The analysis is more difficult than any other. It is, in fact, what paralyzes my psychic strength for describing and communicating what I have won so far . . .'[My italics]   Sigmund Freud, 14 August 1897

'I am apparently much more normal than I was four or five years ago.'   Sigmund Freud, 2 March 1899

In 1895 Joseph Breuer and Sigmund Freud published *Studies on Hysteria*. The two key tenets of psychoanalysis – the importance of infantile sexual fantasies and the different mode of thought of the unconscious mind – had not yet been formulated. However, with hindsight, we can see that crucial aspects of these concepts emerge implicitly from the *Studies*. Above all, this is the material on which psychoanalysis is founded as a theory and as a practice. It was hysteria – both his own and that of his patients – rather than any other mental condition that opened up for Freud the role of unconscious processes and of sexuality in the psychic life of humankind. Many of the future concepts of psychoanalysis may be seen in embryo in *Studies on*

Hysteria, but there is one that is not: the Oedipus myth, later to become known as the Oedipus complex, which Freud only seems to have started considering important in the autumn of 1897, some three years after writing *Studies on Hysteria*.

Freud presented four full case histories in *Studies on Hysteria* and Breuer one, that of 'Anna O'.

Of Freud's four, Frau Emmy von N suffered from convulsive tics, clacking of the tongue, stammering, anorexia, neck cramps and zoophobias – all of which had come on after the premature death of her husband (she was rumoured to have poisoned him). His second case, Fraulein Elizabeth, was treated for her inability to stand up and her shifting but incapacitating pains in the legs, which prevented her from walking even when she could stand. These had started when her sister had died of a heart attack – Fraulein Elizabeth had long desired her sister's husband and the painful leg came on when she was out walking with him (although she also recalled that her father, who had also died of a heart attack, had been in the habit of resting his legs on her leg in exactly the place where the paralysis occurred).

Number three, Fraulein Katharina, suffered from breathlessness and feelings of suffocation. The breathlessness had started when she had witnessed her father and her sister making love. This was two years after she had woken to find her father lying on top of her. Both with Katharina and a certain Rosalia H (a singer with a constricted throat who is mentioned but not given a full case history), Freud initially disguised the father as an uncle and, with Katharina, her sister as a cousin. His fourth case, Miss Lucy, was an English governess in love with her employer, who suffered olfactory hallucinations and a split consciousness.

What we see, then, in Freud's case histories in the *Studies* is a merging of vertical and lateral relationships. Fathers, husbands, brothers-in-law and siblings all play important parts. Even Katharina's hysteria is not solely the product of a relationship with her father, for she is clearly perturbed by and probably extremely jealous at seeing him with her sister – it is this that triggers the hysterical suffocation. In all these cases Freud does *not* see the Oedipus complex which subsequent psychoanalysts such as Didier Anzieu believes is staring him in the face and which Ilsa Grubrich-Simitis perceives as the proleptic omission from this first embryonic statement of psychoanalytic ideas. When he finds it, he finds it in himself some time in the late 1890s, during the self-analysis he conducted while in an intensive relationship with his close friend and fellow doctor Wilhelm Fliess, two years his junior, and with his long-term patient Herr E.

It is not, I believe, chance that the notion of an Oedipus complex emerges from an analysis of *male* hysteria – above all Freud's own and Herr E's (as well as that of some other, less well documented male patients). Freud's analysis of his women patients led him first to the notion that hysteria was caused by an actual seduction by the father, as in the case of Katharina. For a time Freud thought that this was also the case for himself, his younger brother Alexander and E. He realized that this was not so, and that adults were expressing infantile wishes: boys for their mothers and girls for their fathers. But in analysing himself, Freud missed the context of these certainly crucial Oedipal relationships: E and Fliess were, for better and worse, his 'brothers'. Without an awareness of the effect sibling rivalry has on the subject, making him (in this case Freud himself) regress to a frantic attempt to become once more all and everything to the mother, male hysteria, even as it was being 'discovered', was set to disappear.

Freud had enthusiastically espoused the proposition of male hysteria following his study visit in 1885 to the Salpêtrière hospital in Paris where Jean Martin Charcot had been demonstrating the hysterical behaviour of both male and female patients. Then he discovered it in himself. But at the same time, by not seeing something hysterical in his transference to Fliess and by substituting first his Oedipal love for his mother and then his resolution of the threat of castration from his father, he repressed it. Through the main part of his overwhelming friendship with Fliess there was also a certain irritability and sexual compulsiveness with his wife, Martha. His deep, displaced affection for his sister-in-law, Minna; his Don Juan dreams; his repeated rejection of those of his followers whom first he most adored and then could not tolerate when they wished to be like brothers to him instead of sons; his terror of plagiarizing the work of others; ultimately his hysterophobia – all took up the slack of hysteria in the man. The fact that Freud's father died during this period was almost certainly crucial. In time Freud was able to overcome any hysterical identification with his father and instead mourn him. Through this process he overcame his own hysteria (he became, in his own words, 'far more normal').

The discovery of the Oedipus complex and subsequently the castration complex – largely through another male hysteric, Little Hans, a phobic five-year-old – established the parents as all-important. Freud did seem to cure his own *petite hystérie* through resolving something in relation to his father (his mother remained problematic up to and including the day of her death – he was unable to attend her funeral). The hysteric protesting against displacement or annihilation 'tries on' the ultimate annihilation of death and comes back from it, as in a child's game. Freud had a number of points when he identified with his dying father, but after his father's death in 1896 he seems to have been able to accept death's finality and mourn his father. Once mourned, the lost person can become an object with whom the mourner can identify and become like. The hysteric, in his identification, as it were *becomes* the other; the person who has mourned identifies with an internal image of the other and can become both like them and different from them. After his father's death was mourned, Freud became a father: both like but not identical to his dead father.

Freud's own hysteria seems to have been cured by his mourning of his father. This means that hysteria can be overcome by a successful negotiation of the Oedipus complex. What it ignores is why the Oedipus complex is experienced as so intense and so difficult in the first place; it ignores the fact that mother and father are so important and so problematic because others besides oneself have claims on them. These others – in Freud's case, Wilhelm Fliess as an emotional reincarnation of his dead brother – are the fall-out when something enables the hysteric to resolve his hysteria through the resolution of the Oedipus complex. Just to persist with Freud as an exemplary instance of a widespread problem, although he recovered, he was never able to tolerate lateral relationships with men as peers. In this case, peers are brothers. The other fall-out from a self-cure through the father is analogous at an intellectual level to Fliess at an actual level: it was male hysteria which got dropped from the agenda.

Hysteria in general became the victim of this demise of the male hysteric. The hysteric becomes hysterical because there seems to be something intolerable around that threatens his unique existence, something that prevents him from being who he is. He mistakes this preventing him from being who he is as preventing him from getting what he wants. He wants his mother, or lots of new clothes, or too much of something to eat. This wanting to *have* the mother or father and their substitutes always dominates in pictures of hysteria; it obscures the desperate need to *be* someone. The person who threatens one's being, the sibling, is an object of intense ambivalence: love and hatred. (All developmental psychology studies testify to this sibling ambivalence.) In the presocial relationship to the mother, there has certainly been the ambivalence to which Melanie Klein in particular gives great significance; it is in relation to having: one loves the mother for giving the breast and hates her for removing it. I suggest that when the sibling presence provokes the ambivalence as a response to being or not being (the prompt for Hamlet the hysteric's 'to be or not to be'), the person regresses to the ambivalence connected with the mother of having and not having – exemplified, for instance, in hysterical bulimia.

When Freud overcame his hysteria, because he did so through a relationship to the father and not through a resolution of sibling problems, the ambivalence connected with 'being' remained. This ambivalence, which prevented him from having male peers, was also in evidence in subsequent psychoanalytic attitudes to hysteria.

What Freud bequeathed to psychoanalysis was mostly the negative side of the ambivalence that hysteria has towards itself. And not for the first time in hysteria's history. Freud's relationship to this founding illness of psychoanalysis was always a troubled one; he could not quite leave it alone and oscillated between the ecstasy of thinking he had understood it to a phobic avoidance of it as something elusive, ungraspable, contaminating and dishonest.

In his ground-breaking *The Interpretation of Dreams* (1901), Freud is famous for using his own as well as his patients' dreams to decipher the process of dreaming. However, a similar use of his own hysteria, as well as that of his patients, is not perceived as important. In fact, it was his work on his own hysteria which led to Freud's wider understanding of psychic life. In psychoanalysis, at every level, the personal, the subjective and the objective observation are intertwined.

Working on oneself was later institutionalized as the rule that the trainee analyst must undergo a full analysis herself. I have no intention of attempting a psychobiography of Freud. However, there are a number of reasons why Freud's hysteria should not be neglected.

An essential element of psychoanalysis involves a particular on-going dialogue about one's own and another person's subjectivity. Yet Freud said that there could be no such thing as self-analysis, since, if one could analyse oneself successfully there would be no neurosis. One would understand one's own unconscious mind which – no longer being unconscious – would then have no power to dominate, direct or drive one. Therefore Freud notoriously used his friend Wilhelm Fliess, the Berlin ear, nose and throat specialist, as his interlocutor, so that his 'self-analysis' was not a monologue but was conducted through another person. Psychoanalytic understanding has always been reached by grasping something via a relationship with another person. For it works on the principle that something that, in a sense, one has 'lost' or not found about oneself is discovered in that relationship with the other person (alternatively, there can be something about oneself that has resided from the very beginning in the other, some very early inter-connectedness). Although they have been ignored, early sibling relationships again offer a good model for this same/different self-and-other situation. That Freud should have chosen Fliess as his 'other' is interesting, for, of course, he also became an object of Freud's hysteria.

Sigmund Freud and Wilhelm Fliess met in Vienna in 1887 – Fliess was visiting from Berlin and they were introduced by Josef Breuer. The intense friendship between the two men that ensued has been subjected to various interpretations. I believe that it had a great deal to do with a largely creative hysteria. What I will note here is that both were interested in sexuality – Fliess from a biological point of view (what would now be considered an endocrinological perspective) and Freud initially from the neurological and then increasingly from the psychological viewpoint. They each had an enormous admiration and the deepest affection for the other. However, they treated the topic of sexuality like a shared secret, with all the excitement that implies. Fliess was ambitious for fame, hoping to chart the sexual periodicity of human beings and thereby show how this determined the gender and the birth dates of babies, and, even more ambitiously, the dates of illnesses and of death. Fliess's ideas were not all so bizarre: his linking of possible contraception to times within the menstrual cycle was inspired. Freud's ambition was more focused on trying to understand what had hitherto not been understood.

Fliess was a German, married to a wealthy Viennese while Freud was a relatively poor Austro-Hungarian. However, they were both Jewish and they moved in the same social circles; they were also both 'men of science' with young families. In addition to frequent visits between the two families, Freud and Fliess met on their own for what they called 'congresses', when they talked and talked about their ideas. Even before the catastrophic end of their compulsive friendship, one can see that Freud's idealization of Fliess was slightly tinged with the envy and jealousy of rivalry. But the positive gain to Freud's creativity through his identification with Fliess's wilder flights of fantasy seems to have outweighed any more negative aspects of their relationship. Freud's letters to Fliess are excited, honest, witty, funny, humane and self-aware – a testament to the enormous importance of their friendship. Also, Fliess's 'mad' creative influence did not finish with the end of their relationship; afterwards, Freud's own flights of fancy continued, although more guardedly.

To ignore the part played by the hysterical element in Freud's 'self-analysis' is to repress the relevance of the male hysteric – as Freud himself, his followers, his critics and even modern-day commentators, both psychoanalytic and feminist, have done and continue to do. The repression of male hysteria haunts the theory and practice of psychoanalysis; psychoanalysis must also, I believe, share responsibility for both the so-called 'disappearance' of hysteria in the twentieth century and for our very partial understanding of it. Freud's 'little hysteria' constitutes an important starting point from which we can re-examine hysteria from the perspective of its repression: hysteria in men.

One specific way to think about the place of hysteria in the foundation of psychoanalysis and, reciprocally, how psychoanalysis handled hysteria, is to think about the relationships which are reflected within Freud's thinking in the 1880s and 1890s. That is to say, the reproduction of his interaction with his patients, his colleagues, his family, his friends: his personal history. There is no question here of a wild analysis that simply labels Freud a male hysteric. I am concerned not with Freud the individual, but with the operation of hysteria itself. At no point does my analysis exceed Freud's own comment: 'The chief patient I am preoccupied with is myself. My little hysteria, though greatly accentuated by my work, has resolved itself a bit further.'[1]

Nor am I concerned with an academic survey of Freud's work on hysteria. Rather, my task is to observe hysteria as it moves between people or as people become hysterical, either as a brief episode or as a more pervasive way of life. Hysteria can be dominant for life, a brief response to an episode, or a series of feelings that can always return on another occasion. It has been said of Montaigne that he seems to write entirely about himself, but then one realizes that he is everyone. Though Freud is writing in a different idiom and with a different purpose, the same could be said of him. My purpose here, though, is to show through the specificity of Freud the universal possibility of hysteria. Because of the part played in psychoanalysis by the analysis of the analyst, the specific context for its insights is thus the testing of hysteria on the pulse of the doctor.

But the doctor, in this instance, is male; Freud 'cured' himself through his self-analysis in which he used Fliess as a transference-object. However, unfortunately, the cure eliminated male hysteria at the same time. Looking back to his pre-psychoanalytic days in his 'Autobiographical Study' Freud recalled his reception in Vienna when in 1886 he returned from studying in Paris with Charcot:

[A]n old surgeon . . . broke out with the exclamation: 'But, my dear sir, how can you talk such nonsense? *Hysteron (sic)* means the uterus. So how can a man be hysterical?' I objected in vain that what I wanted was not to have my diagnosis approved, but to have the case put at my disposal. At length, outside the hospital, I came upon a case of classical hysterical hemi-anaesthesia in a man, and demonstrated it before the 'Gesellschaft der Aerzte'. This time I was applauded, but no further interest was taken in me.[2]

Freud had staked a great deal on the significance of the presence of hysteria in men, as established by Charcot. This retrospective account of his reception presents a situation in which his heroic stance was ignored or denied by the Viennese medical community. It is true that Freud's notion received considerable opposition in Austria – he claimed that the most favourable response from his colleagues was: 'Well, maybe in Paris but not in Vienna,' and that mostly they denied his views outright.

The Viennese medical community's resistance to the idea of male hysteria may have been caused by a particular aspect of anti-Semitism. An immigrant community from the country to the town is often thought to manifest hysterical behaviours (its members do not know 'who they are'). There was a steady flow of Jews (such as Freud himself) into Vienna from eastern Europe. There may have been a prevalence of hysteria among them, but, equally, to be associated with immigrant Jews may have been something the resident Viennese wanted to avoid. Hence, they labelled Jews hysterical.

However, Freud's reaction to this initial rebuttal of his work in Vienna was more interesting and more important than it appears at first sight. On the surface it looks as though he fought through thick and thin on scientific grounds to defend his observation of the male hysteria he had witnessed. He claims later that his mentor, the famous brain analyst Theodor Meynart – who had been adamant in his opposition to the possibility of male hysteria – apparently confessed on his deathbed that his own resistance to the notion had been the result of the appalling recognition that he himself was a male hysteric. But in fact, if we compare Freud's sponsorship of male hysteria with his later unwavering determination to combat all opposition to his emphasis on the determining role for psychic life of infantile sexuality (or other tenets of psychoanalysis which are less pertinent here), a stark contrast emerges. In his espousal of male hysteria there seems to have been a considerable element of posturing and plenty of the typical hysterical positioning of himself as a victim – or 'martyr', as Freud called it, with his constant unhysterical self-insight. The result is that whilst never reneging on his observation, Freud let the subject of male hysteria fade from the limelight. Freud published three pre-psychoanalytic papers and lectures on the topic between 1882 and 1885, and then *Studies on Hysteria* in 1895, in which no man features. Only much later, in 1923 and 1926, did he analyse two historical male figures who come within the category. First was a seventeenth-century victim of demonic possession, the painter Christof Heizzman, who presented with a melancholia but whose hysterical possession Freud saw as the medieval equivalent of contemporary hysterical illnesses. Second was the writer Fyodor Dostoevsky, a hysterico-epileptic whom Freud fitted into the Oedipal/castration complex pattern.

Studies on Hysteria is a crucial text both in the development of psychoanalysis and in any understanding of hysteria. My focus here on Freud's self-analysis and the hysterical dimension of his psychopathology, rather than on the women patients of the *Studies*, has to do with the place and history of male hysteria and its disappearance into the notion of the Oedipus myth. When, later, the position of Oedipus (the desire for incest with the mother) was seen to be resolved if the father's prior claims to her were acknowledged (that is, the law of castration was submitted to), then hysteria became a failure to accept this prohibition. The task for men was clear: accept the law of the father and you will not be a hysteric. This is what Freud did. He resolved his male hysteria first by becoming Oedipus in his wishes and then by overcoming these fantasies in the interests of his fatherhood – intellectual and familial. He recollected a scene in which he had desired his mother when he was a small boy and was terrified that she had been taken away from him as a punishment. Because of the generational complexity of his family, Freud first thought his adult half-brother, not his father, was responsible for his mother's absence (she was giving birth to a sibling). The confusion about who was the actual father may have contributed to his strengthening insistence on the father in the theory.

Not only did Freud's emphasis on Oedipus eliminate the male hysteric and realign hysteria with femininity, it also allowed for the repression of a key relationship: that between siblings. Freud was offended by Fliess's lack of enthusiasm for his discovery of the significance of Oedipus. Did Fliess unconsciously realize that there was something in his own relationship with Freud – a hysterical brotherhood – that was missing from the Oedipal interpretation of Freud's condition?

When Freud, however, lost interest in male hysteria as a *cause célèbre*, it disappeared in a special way. Consciously in his letters the topic opened the way first for reflections on his brother as a hysteric and then on himself; unconsciously, he absorbed it back into himself, either as resolved and sublimated erotomanic tendencies or, having been repressed, it came back itself like a symptom which, because it was not fully understood, would not quite go away. Because male hysteria was thus repressed, it has continued to haunt psychoanalysis, structuring both the thought and the therapy by its omission. For the moment it is important to note that though it is often stressed that Freud repeatedly abandoned his close male friends, this is not usually linked with either his own recovery from hysteria or with his dropping of male hysteria as a topic for consideration. Such a link, however, seems crucial.

Freud's diagnosis of his own condition during the 1890s shifted. At first he believed he was suffering mainly from neurasthenia, one of the three 'actual neuroses', the other two being anxiety neurosis and hypochondria. 'Actual neuroses' – a term little used today – were thought to be caused by current sexual difficulties such as enforced abstinence, lack of satisfaction resulting from methods of contraception (or the lack thereof), impotence in the man causing frustration in the woman or inhibition in the woman causing frustration in the man. Freud displayed symptoms of all three of the actual neuroses: neuralgias, depressions, tremors, railway phobia, fatigue, intestinal problems, nasal difficulties, nervous irritation and, above all, respiratory and cardiac disturbances.

What is interesting here is not to speculate on which or what factors could have led to Freud's actual neurosis – how can we know? – but to note an early slippage on the part of clinicians generally between the diagnosis of actual neuroses and that of hysteria, so long as the hysteria was manifest in women. It was common for clinicians in the nineteenth century to note that neurasthenic women had a 'hysterical admixture' in their condition – Freud himself concurred with this on a number of occasions. Now obsolete, neurasthenia was at the time given as a diagnosis for fatigue or exhaustion of the nerves. However, hysteria was regarded not as an actual neurosis but as one of the 'defence neuroses' – that is, there was some hereditary factor attached and its cause was not a current *actual* problem. Increasingly, however, Freud himself questioned the notion of a hereditary factor and replaced it with the notion of some disturbing event in early childhood, even in infancy. This event, which had taken place in the *past*, distinguished hysteria from an actual neurosis, where the disturbing situation was a *present* one. In time, Freud became convinced that the causative occasion in the past was a sexual event, a passive sexual experience later specified as an assault or seduction by the father or nursemaid on the son or daughter. Charcot, who had 'discovered' male hysteria had noted the prevalence of traumatic accidents as precipitators; his male subjects had usually suffered work- or violence-related accidents. The trauma factor was taken up by Freud and a familiar switch occurred: women in particular were considered to have suffered from *sexual* trauma in the past.

That neurasthenia in women was mixed with hysteria blurred the distinction between the 'actual' and the 'defence' neuroses. In Freud's own work, an absolute separation between the two became less and less tenable; in hysteria it seemed that a present event triggered memories of a past one whose meaning only became clear in the present. Thus, a child who was sexually abused did not understand this event in a sexual context until another event gave it meaning later. However, it was common for these earlier distinctions to be resolved by their being gendered: men were neurasthenic while women were hysterical. Nevertheless, when in mid 1897 Freud started work on his own self-analysis, he diagnosed himself as suffering not from neurasthenia, as before, but from a '*petite hystérie*' – the same condition as that with which his famous hysterical patient Dora was afflicted. In this important period of self-analysis, then, Freud thought of himself as hysterical, and there seems no reason why we should not take his word for it and thereby learn from it. His self-analysis involved male hysteria, not neurasthenia or an 'actual neurosis'.

During the 1880s and 1890s Freud's physical symptoms and psychic difficulties were manifold. They circled around displaced expressions of a dread of death (he called it his 'death delirium') which itself was evident in his compulsive wish to determine his own death day. It was throughout this period that Freud underwent the most intense phase of his friendship with Wilhelm Fliess: 'no one can replace for me the relationship with a friend which a special – possibly feminine – side demands'.[3] Placing a crazy faith in the mathematical calculations that emerged from Fliess's interesting if bizarre and aberrant theories of periodicity in human life, Freud originally decided he would die in

1896 at the age of forty and then, when that point passed, at the age of fifty-one or fifty-two. This prediction has been variously understood, but to me it seems that by thus choosing and selecting his death day Freud was trying to 'control' the ultimate uncontrollability of death – a task hysterics always set themselves in various ways. That death has dominion over mankind is unacceptable: this is an important factor both in the fascination with and actuality of suicide in instances of severe hysteria.

However, Freud and Fliess tried to control death not through suicide but by making predictions based on mathematical calculations of dates. All aspects of Freud's ensuing illness testify to the necessary failure of this heroic effort – for the dread of death is enacted in the body. Freud's ill body bears witness that the panic is greater than the solution he found: 'As for me, I note migraine, nasal secretion, and attacks of fears of dying . . . although [a friend] Tilgner's cardiac death is most likely more responsible for this than the date.'[4] Interestingly, though, in this comment, Freud is sowing, unawares, one of the seeds of his subsequent estrangement from Fliess: his heart condition is due not to the calendar as Fliess would have him believe, but to a hysterical identification with a friend who had just died. Such an identification with a dead person, through fits or paralysis, is common throughout the long history of hysteria.

Although Freud had moments of mimetic identification with his dying father, these would have appeared to be within the range of the normal; Freud's reaction to his father's death has no signs of full-blown hysteria; quite the contrary. His hysterical identification with death is noted by him just prior to his father's death when he thinks his illnesses are all hysterical symptoms which show he has 'become' his recently dead friend Tilgner. Each of his symptoms – such as palpitations, cardiac pains, etc. – is a sign that he has identified with a dead person. When again he dreams a great deal about death in 1898 (two years after his father's death) it is at a time when Fliess has been at death's door. The death of someone one's own age, or, like a sibling, within a year or two of one's age, is more likely to trigger a hysterical identification than that of an older person. The example of outbreaks of hysteria in English girls' schools in the mid 1960s at the time of a polio epidemic to which teenagers were particularly vulnerable is a clear example of this phenomenon (see chapter 10).

In the preface to the second edition of *The Interpretation of Dreams*, Freud writes, 'For this book has a further . . . significance . . . which I only grasped after I had completed it. It was, I found, a portion of my own self analysis, my reaction to my father's death – that is to say, to the most important event, the most poignant loss, of a man's life.'[5] Freud's father, Jacob, died on 23 October 1896. Some days later, Freud wrote to Fliess a moving account of a dream and of his feelings: 'the old man's death has affected me deeply'.[6] Three weeks later he noted: 'What I am lacking completely are high spirits and pleasure in living; instead I am busily noting the occasions when I have to occupy myself with the state of affairs after my death.'[7] Before one can accept one's own mortality, one needs to have internalized in mid-life the idea of a dead parent. The difficulty of doing this marks the mid-life crisis. The work of mourning means the dead person is psychically understood to be lost and gone forever, but instead of his presence a representation of him or her can be established and permanently called on and used as a memory. This internalization of a lost person through a representation of them in mourning is the very opposite of the hysterical identification which denies the loss.

Yet before the process of internalizing an image and remembrance of a mourned person can take place, there is this mode of identification which is part of everybody's hysterical experience – through mimetic identification we become in our symptom the dead other person. Simone de Beauvoir tells how she felt sudden compassion as she watches her dying mother try to speak. As she recounts this to Sartre, Sartre notes that de Beauvoir's mouth is enacting exactly the mouth of the mother she is describing. Freud was to expand on the hysterical identification with death in his study of Dostoevsky of 1926, but already in 1897 Freud was noting the commonly observed identification of the hysteric with the dead person. He wrote to Fliess of a patient: 'The most recent result is the unravelling of hysterical cataleptic fits: imitation of death with rigor mortis, that is identification with someone who is dead. If she has seen the dead person, then glazed eyes and open mouth; if not, then she just lies there quietly and peacefully.'[8]

Freud was later to write that hysterics love where they hate. Simone de Beauvoir felt great hostility towards her mother, but as her mother lay dying in great pain a sudden love overcame de Beauvoir. There is always ambivalence in human relationships. However, ambivalence also plays a part in hysterical reactions. Ambivalence is a theme that crops up time and again in Freud's letters to Fliess. Rather than think through the ambivalence with which an important death confronts us, the hysteric 'becomes' them, experiencing what he imagines they experience.

There are two extreme ends of this process of mimetic identification. On the one hand is the sort of pathology of which multiple personality syndrome is the clearest expression. At the other extreme is the creative experience which Keats called 'negative capability', that is, the poet's capacity to experience the world so intensely that he 'becomes' in his imagination, say, the bird which he is watching. In the case of multiple personality syndrome, each of the sufferer's feelings is represented in isolation from the other as a discrete character whom the patient mimes and uses to contain feelings he cannot accept. Swinging between these two extremes of severe pathology and creativity, is hysterical identification – the process of experiential identification in which one imagines oneself into and as another person, in a process which is partly conscious and partly unconscious. This is sometimes mistaken for empathy, but it is not empathy, for in empathy one knows that the person in whose feelings one is participating is other than oneself.

Freud was later dismissive of the common observation that hysterics identify with other people to an unusual degree, asserting instead that this property of hysteria was superficial: hysterics do not simply identify with the other person; instead, they identify with what the other person desires (or, more accurately, what they imagine the other person desires). In fact, I think in hysteria both types of identification, that is, with the other person and with their desires, take place, although it is easy to neglect the element of desire. Why then would Freud have identified with the death of his friend, Tilgner, or that of his father? Behind the romantic wish to 'cease upon the midnight with no pain' there lay for Freud both ambivalence towards the dying person and the triumphal excitement that it was not him who had died; and it was only he, the mimer, who could 'magically' come back from the dead. Freud's reaction to his father's death was 'normal', but before an important person is fully mourned it is usual for some hysterical identification to take place: one is like the dead person before one fully realizes one is not. This often becomes prolonged in instances of war violence.

As many scholars have pointed out, Freud's reaction to his father's impending death doubtless involved his ambivalence towards his father as an object of his feelings – wanting to replace him, but not wanting to because of his love for him. It would also have involved an identification with what Freud imagined it would be like to face death. In a letter to Fliess, Freud thinks of himself as an old man: 'I would like so much to hold out until that famous age limit of approximately fifty-one, but I had one day that made me feel it was unlikely.'[9] It is not unlikely that Freud's father would both have 'liked to hold out' and not face death but also at the same time have welcomed death as a release from the illnesses of old age. We can see Freud's confusion between himself and his dying father in this much-interpreted dream which took place after his father's death and yet in which Jacob Freud is still alive. In it Freud confuses the date of his father's first wife's death in 1851 with his own birthdate of 1856; it has therefore become known as the '1851–1856' dream. There are many possible interpretations (and many have been offered) of the dream; here I will just point to the coincidence of 1851 and the age of fifty-one when Freud expected to die. Freud seems to have confused his father's second and third marriages; in fact he has also put the date of his father's second marriage in 1852 as 1851. Though (as a result of one of Fliess's calculations) Freud believed he would die at age fifty-one. With the confusion and amnesia (both of which are his father's old age symptoms) of ages in his dream, Freud marries his mother and gives birth to himself at a date which coincides with his own projected death. Freud first believes in his death at fifty-one/ two after nine (the number is mentioned) pregnant months of cardiac symptoms. Like any anxious child he once feared that his mother (and thus himself) might die like the first wife.

The projected age of Freud's death at fifty-one- or -two arose from Fliess's notion of a male menstrual cycle of twenty-three days, as opposed to the female cycle of twenty-eight days. Fliess also pioneered the notion of human bisexuality, of a male cycle and a female cycle, which were both part of each individual; the cycles add up to 51 (23

+ 28). But why should Freud and Fliess have got involved in these bizarre calculations? When it was Fliess, the younger 'brother' who almost died, as it was his infant brother Julius who had died, Freud's fears for his friend were quite openly mixed with triumph that it was Fliess not Freud who faced death. This has often been commented on. A transference is a present-day 'new edition' of a crucial infantile relationship. But which relationship was Freud dominantly transferring? This is not commented on. Surely it was a sibling relationship – someone with whom Freud felt both identical and different?

Freud had a 'transference' relation with Fliess. Amazed at having found someone 'who is an even greater fantasist than I am',[10] Freud thought 'through' Fliess, so that when the friendship ended it was because something disturbing, 'mad' or hysterical about the friendship could no longer be sustained. Even while both men were in the grip of friendship, Freud could write: 'I no longer understand the state of mind in which I hatched the psychology; cannot conceive how I could have inflicted it on you. I believe you are still too polite; to me it appears to have been a kind of madness.'[11] Freud engaged Fliess in this hysterical condition by making him the person without whom he could barely survive. In his letters he wrote: 'It is obviously no special favour of fate that I have approximately five hours a year to exchange ideas with you, when I can barely do without the other – and you are the only other, the *alter*'[12] and, referring to Fliess, 'another one is an urgent necessity for me';[13] 'Without such an audience [as Fliess] I really cannot work.'[14] Freud almost felt he did not exist without Fliess.

Without the other through whom he can live, the hysteric can only enact his hysteria for the other to see, offering himself as a spectacle, discharging his emotions into dramatic actions of wild illnesses, the famous 'attention-seeking of hysteria', the acts towards which Freud's mentor Charcot was a somewhat voyeuristic witness in his studies at Salpêtrière hospital. Hysteria involves a relationship – one cannot be a hysteric on one's own. It always engages the other, inducing a reciprocity or a refusal. If the other refuses to participate in the free flow of mutual identification (the *folie à deux*), then the hysteric demands to be a spectacle – only something one can look at or observe. At Salpêtrière Charcot stared at and demonstrated his patients for others' gazes in staged 'theatrical' performances, or he reproduced the images of his patients in a panoply of photographs. The symptom of a hysterical attack, Freud noted, is an action. In these instances the audience is the crucial 'other', but if the other participates, as Fliess and Freud did in their creative *folie à deux*, then the other is sufficient audience.

With Fliess, Freud was able to share his hysteria, exchanging with him illnesses and creativities. But by 1898, Freud is protesting too much about the value of their mutual identification:

I am so immensely glad that you are giving me the gift of the Other, a critic and reader – and one of your quality at that. I cannot write entirely without an audience, but do not at all mind writing only for you.[15]

Until there is a jocular disidentification:

My head and your head are evidently, even though unsteady, two very different heads, because mine, in spite of all its lability, did not prevent me from having a good period. But I can do something that you cannot do – replace headaches or cardiac pains with ridiculous back pains.[16]

The nature of the hysterical identification is one of unhappy confusion or happy fusion between self and other: but when two people are fused or confused, then whose feelings, whose body, whose ideas are these? We can see this question underlying the topic over which Freud and Fliess quarrelled – the issue was 'bisexuality' (hysterics are considered highly bisexual). The problem between them was even more relevant – it was plagiarism. 'Bisexuality' indicates a two-fold object choice: that everyone can love a woman and/or a man. Colloquially, the word is used to indicate something about the person as a subject; psychoanalytically it refers not to any predisposition in the person but to the fact that everyone starts with bisexual object choices; one of these desires 'should' be repressed. Freud acknowledged, somewhat too insistently, that the notion of 'bisexuality' originated with Fliess. Fliess felt used and his originality betrayed by Freud's deployment of it – it became a key tenet of psychoanalytic theory.[17] Thereafter the source of any idea was a problem which continued to haunt Freud. Plagiarism is a kind of hysterical enactment: one has taken over the other who, in a sense, thus becomes non-existent or dead. When a sibling dies one becomes once more the beloved child but psychically speaking one has usurped the dead rival's place.

In all his subsequent professional relationships, Freud was most anxious – excessively anxious, even – to attribute credit to whomsoever he thought it was due. Thus, he embarrassed his first collaborator, Josef Breuer, by at times nearly insisting that Breuer (whose patient Anna O worked out the 'talking cure') was really the originator of psychoanalysis. Plagiarism, whether conscious or unconscious, concerns the absence of boundaries; it is not the same as stealing because one appropriates what is the other's as though it were one's own. Probably one can only stop it once one regards it as stealing, in other words once one knows one is taking something from someone else who is different from oneself. Freud's dreams of the period show him at work with the problem. In one of these dreams, the 'Three Fates', one of the Fates is rubbing her hands together to make dumplings or 'knodel'. (Professor Knodel was a well-known plagiarist of the period.) Freud recalls his mother showing him how the epidermis, if rubbed in this way, produces the dirt or dust to which we come on death. In the dream Freud is a thief who steals overcoats from lecture halls: he wants to wear another man's mantle. We can see Freud shifting from being a plagiarist (Professor Knodel) to being a thief. In another dream he wants to step into someone else's shoes. He also earlier identifies with his old nurse, Monique Zajic; he has a dream in which he steals a purse just as Zajic had in fact stolen his own pocket money. Plagiarism and the identifications triggered by death are clearly linked. Freud is the same as Zajic, being the same is plagiarism, but when he steals he is becoming conscious of the fact that he wants what the other has; it is not that he unconsciously *is* the other. The 'Three Fates' later play a central role in Freud's analysis of King Lear of 1912 – a short essay about a play which is very concerned with death and with a madness that starts as hysteria.

Freud's case of a hysterical patient, 19-year-old Dora (examined more fully in chapter 3), has become a *texte célèbre* both of the women's movement and of psychoanalysis. After he had written the essay in January 1901 Freud himself was pleased: 'It is the subtlest thing I have written so far.'[18] It was due to be published in the autumn of 1901 but Freud withdrew it and, in March 1902, wrote to Fliess:

'When I came back from [my visit to] Rome, my enjoyment of life and work was somewhat heightened and that of martyrdom somewhat diminished. I found my practice had almost melted away; I withdrew my last work from publication because just a little earlier I had lost my last audience in you.'[19] Understandably, the editor of Freud's letters, Jeffrey Masson, comments that 'with the loss of Fliess's friendship and interest in his work, Freud felt that there was no one who would care about what he was writing'.[20] Understandably, because this is precisely what Freud himself says. But Freud's mood is one of cheerful triumph, not of hurt pride. Abandoning any hope of immediate recognition, he had instead applied for and received an excellent university post in Vienna – he could visit Rome, look after his patients and support his extended family. Some six months later there was still no pique or reproach to Fliess. In other words, the mood belies the interpretation. In fact, even before the delay with the publication of 'Dora', Freud had already behaved strangely. 'Dora' had been accepted for publication by Theodor Zieman in the *Monatschrift für Psychiatrie und Neurologie* when Freud changed his mind and sent it instead to Brodman at the *Journal of Psychology and Neurology*. Brodman rejected it on the grounds that it breached confidentiality. Did Brodman make a decision over the one issue – that of confidentiality – which is always problematic in psychotherapy? At the time Freud left it at that – again, from his mood, it seems he was relieved. Reading back through Freud's subsequent distaste for hysteria, was he not, among other reasons, also relieved to have transferred an interest in the daytime confusions and fusions of hysteria to an interest in night-time dreams, and to have freed himself from overinvolvement with Fliess?

The (pathological) problem and (creative) strength of the friendship with Fliess did not revolve, as has been claimed repeatedly, just around the *degree* of transference in it – but the *kind* of transference it embodied. The kind of transference here was a hysterical transference in which the subject does not know what belongs to whom or who is who. Freud took refuge from his hysteria in his paternity – becoming the father of his children and soon the father of a movement. Delaying 'Dora' only points to Freud's incipient distaste with hysteria (although there may have been other more important reasons). It was, of course, not only distaste that Freud felt but also fascination – from a psycho-analytical point of view these are two sides of the same coin. Freud put aside both these aspects – and did so with relief. What Freud had postponed indefinitely were not his hurt feelings nor his inadequate theory or therapy, but working out fully the meaning of his own male hysteria. He was delighted, relieved to have cast it off. But where did he cast it, and at what cost?

It was not then because he had lost his audience with Fliess but because he could no longer think through the 'other' (nor did he want to) that Freud withdrew 'Dora' from publication and accepted its rejection with relief. Issues of confidentiality are almost impossible to resolve when there has been an underlying confusion between people. As we shall see in the next chapter, in the case history, Freud, who had been too confused with Fliess, makes sure he is absolutely demar-cated from Dora. With Dora, Freud may have missed perceiving his countertransference responses (that is to say, his own feelings) and the full import of his patient's bisexuality, because to have noted either or both would have entailed resuscitating the problems of his friendship with Fliess.

Following on René Girard's thesis that human sociality is based on primal mimesis, that is that the infant becomes human through his photofit identification with a parent, Ourghourlian, in his 1991 study of hysteria *The Puppet of Desire*, described the hysteric's particular identification and mimesis of the other person as a malign 'appropri-ation'. Indeed it can come to feel like that. Freud's hysterical interaction with Fliess was 'benign', in so far as it remained largely creative for both men. In more malign instances the hysteric wants (and often manages) to get 'under the skin' of the other. One of my patients was so compelled to get under another person's skin that he had to avoid it at all costs – he was phobic about any substance that, quite inappropriately, he thought could get under the skin. It is important to remember that hysterics, like small children, take metaphorical phrases literally. Most important, I think, is that the process of identification becomes so absolute because it involves the potential hysteria of both parties. The hysteric is never alone. The libidinal investment present in group pseudologia and lying facilitates the hysterical process of identification. The result can be mass hysteria, outbreaks of group phenomena such as anorexia hysterica in girls' schools, political rallies, or a *folie à deux*.

Apart from himself, and the women he and Breuer wrote about in *Studies on Hysteria*, Freud worked during the initial period of psychoanalysis with a number of patients whose neurotic difficulties were partially or predominantly hysterical. The one whose case history has been most fully extracted from the letters to Fliess and from *The Interpretation of Dreams* is 'E'. Following an essay by Eva Rosenblum, both Didier Anzieu and Douglas Davis, who have reconstructed the case history, note the blurring of therapist and patient roles of Freud and 'E': the two men are not fully distinguishable as together they produce the universal Oedipus complex. The relationship also shows male hysteria in action.

'E' was a patient whom Freud treated for five years around the turn of the century. He was a diagnosed case of hysteria – an 'illness' that had developed in his youth. Freud learnt as much about himself as he did about his patient during 'E''s treatment – and a great deal for psychoanalysis. 'E' and Freud also had a number of symptoms in common and shared certain aspects of their reconstructed infantile histories. 'E''s fits of profuse sweating, tendency to uncontrollable blushing and dread of going to the theatre were traced back to his fantasy that he would 'deflower' every woman he set eyes on. Freud, too, had a crucial 'deflowering' incident in his history. 'E' had failed botany at the university and Freud commented, 'now he carries on with it as a deflorator'. Freud remembered how he too was a deflorator. When he was a small child, he had snatched and destroyed his niece Pauline's yellow flowers.[21] This incident became a crucial part of the ground plan of Freud's own later fantasies of defloration. According to the theory that developed from his and similar cases, the conflict for 'E' was between his compulsive wish to seduce and his phobic restriction on going out (agoraphobia), so that he could not do so. A paradigmatic illustration of such a conflict is where an hysterical woman tears off her dress with one hand and clasps it tightly to her with the other, thus both expressing her sexual desire and simultaneously refusing it. In fantasizing seduction scenes, in imagining trips to the theatre and suffering from the agoraphobia that prevented him going out, 'E' was enacting this conflict simultaneously in his mind and through his bodily actions. As a result, 'E' was a Don Juan in his fantasies and abstinent in his practice (indeed, rather like Mozart's Don Giovanni, whose endless affairs are listed in the abstract by his servant Leporello but are never depicted as consummated.

During the five years of 'E''s treatment Freud too would seem to have been experiencing heightened sexual conflict. Freud's own 'Dream of Irma's injection' in *The Interpretation of Dreams* is the model (or 'specimen dream') demonstrating a psychoanalytic method of interpreting dreams. It involves his wife's pregnancy with the baby (who happens to be Anna Freud) which they are determined to make their last. Freud is elsewhere concerned with the inadequacies and miseries of poor contraception (which he had good reason to think Fliess's theories would go some way towards solving). The dream indicates that abstinence is the only solution for an already large family – Anna was the Freuds' sixth child in twelve years. Since its first publication in 1901 this dream has been subject to extensive additions as commentators have been challenged by Freud's open admission that he did not wish to pursue as far as he might some of the associations he had to his dream. Freud did in fact confess to a younger adherent and colleague, Karl Abraham, that he did not want to pursue in a published text his association to the sexual fantasies referred to in the dream – that it was he who possessed all the women in it. Was Freud, like 'E', a Don Juan in fantasy, in compensation for his self-imposed abstinence? It is certainly possible. In a letter to Fliess he notes that collectors are enacting Don Juan fantasies – his own subsequent collection of antique figurines ('stone' statues) was superb. To Fliess, he claims he sees himself as a 'conquistador' and uses the opening line of Leporello's 'catalogue aria' from *Don Giovanni*, a 'List of all the Beauties . . .', to announce his first published works, thereby making the writing of many books an obvious sublimation of having many women.

'E' and Freud both had a phobia of rail travel and it was 'E''s association to his phobia that unleashed Freud's interest in his own symptom: '["E"] demonstrated the reality of my theory in my own case, providing me in a surprising reversal with the solution, which I had overlooked, to my former railroad phobia.'[22] The phobia, Freud said, was due to infantile gluttony – and though we learn no more about this, it would link with what Freud was to call the hysterical *greed* for love. In hysteria, which in my account wants the mother that the sibling has taken, sexuality is predominantly oral and 'hungry'; hence the prevalent symptom of eating disorders. Freud would seem to have felt that if he did not get to the station early (the table first) he would miss the train (meal). With the many sisters that followed the birth of his brother, he may well have been right. (Hence, too, in my account, the link with cannibalism: in wanting to become once more the only baby the rivalrous sibling both wants and does not want to eat the mother's breast.) Both Freud and 'E' 'recollected' being seduced by nursemaids in their infancy. 'If the scenes . . . come [to light] and I succeed in resolving my own hysteria, then I shall be grateful to the memory of the old woman who provided me at such an early age with the means for living',[23] he told Fliess. For both Freud and 'E' this seduction turned out to be not a reality but a fantasy. Together Freud and 'E' provided crucial material first for the notion that hysteria was caused by sexual abuse in infancy (when they believed their own and Freud's other patients' fantasies) and then for the theory that it was caused by the inability to overcome infantile fantasies of incestuous relationships with father or mother – the Oedipus complex.

For Freud, his 'brothers' 'E' and Fliess came increasingly to occupy structurally similar places in their relation to him. With Fliess, Freud seemed to merge in a shared fascination with illness and death, and with 'E' in shared sexual fantasies. Both men acted as objects of transference. This, however, is both to read the later theory of transference back into the emergent notion of it and to use the concept of transference and countertransference in a very generalized way. What or which crucial relationships were being 'transferred' both ways? In fact, the concept first of transference and then of countertransference grew out of the creative but highly disturbing material of hysterical identification – they were salvaged from the facts of hysterical confusion of identities. These concepts are the crucial means by which one after another psychoanalyst has saved her or himself from the mutual seduction set up by the human proclivity to hysteria which would be bound to be repeated in the treatment relationship. With his women patients in *Studies on Hysteria* it would seem that Freud was clear about his difference from them. This difference, at the same time, prevented him using an ability to identify with the other in order to understand what was going on. With 'E', a male patient with obvious hysterical features, Freud was overjoyed that he could understand his patient through the fact that they shared many of the same fantasies and problems. (Initially, he thought that, quite coincidentally, they shared similar *actual* histories of having been seduced as infants.) Subsequently, from this tangle of hysterical identification, Freud (visibly through the case of Dora) extracted the patient's involvement with the analyst – the patient's *transference* of intense infantile feelings. It was left to later psychoanalysts to draw the full benefit of the observation that the analyst's transferred feelings on to the patient (her *counter*transference) may be no less intense than the patient's own feelings. But, even before this was documented, the centrepoint of the analytic training was designed to enable the psychoanalyst to understand herself as *a patient* – to see what her dominant transferences may be. The necessary technique of understanding the 'transference' (and subsequently the analyst's countertransference) acted along with the deployment of the Oedipus complex to remove the hysteria inherent in the mode of treatment – instead of being enacted as hysteria it became part of the theory and practice.

Freud and Breuer would seem to have covered up many of the difficulties and failures that arose in the treatment of 'Anna O'. The problems centre on a too-great and too-confused involvement of doctor and patient. Yet were they to have stayed too distant, psychoanalysis would never have been born. Anna O, the 'first' patient of psychoanalysis, became entangled with Joseph Breuer, Freud's senior in medical practice and co-author of *Studies on Hysteria*. Freud subsequently claimed that Breuer abandoned Anna O when she admitted to fantasies that she was pregnant with his child. If so, this may well have been the last straw – but something in their relationship had already set the therapy in that direction before it proved too much for Breuer who fled his patient. Before finally leaving Anna, Breuer renewed his endangered marriage with the conception of his youngest daughter; Anna O then imitated this pregnancy. Breuer and his wife called their daughter Dora.

There were preconditions which helped Bertha Pappenheim ('Anna

O') and Joseph Breuer find the shared psychic ground on which they met. When she became ill with hysteria, Bertha was nursing her dying father; Breuer was old enough to be her father. Bertha identified with her father to such a degree that looking in the mirror she saw his dying face and a death mask instead of her own head. Thus, for Bertha, who already confused herself with her father in her fantasies, it was a short step to confuse herself with her doctor. On Breuer's side, his mother, who had died when her son Josef was only three years old, had been called Bertha. Bertha Pappenheim was therefore of an age, twenty-one, when she could have been both the young mother from Breuer's past and, in the present, the mature Breuer's daughter. As they came from the same social background, it is as though doctor and patient could have encountered each other in some human void or vortex of confused identities opened up by death and by the coincidences of names, ages and wants and desires. Their egos, overwhelmed by a scarcely conscious dread of crucial deaths, exercised poor control over their relationship, so that when Bertha thought she had conceived her doctor's baby, Breuer could well have felt as confused and 'mad' as his patient – in which case he was right to leave the treatment. Neither could possibly have been aware of the pitfalls of this relationship. Love and hate are emotions that easily ignore the boundaries between people; madness too knows no boundaries. Although the heterosexuality of the sexual attraction between Breuer and Bertha may have been more explicit, the attraction was not really so very different from that between Freud and Fliess – which Freud also had to abandon. With the case of Anna O (whom Freud described in a 'First Lecture on Psychoanalysis in 1910') the doctor–patient relationship seems so obviously to involve father–daughter sexual fantasies that it is easy to overlook additional relationships. For instance, Anna's mother could have constituted what André Green has called 'a dead mother', in his paper 'The Dead Mother' in his collection of essays On Private Madness (1986). According to Green, a 'dead mother' is not actually but only psychically 'dead' – she is a depressed or bereaved mother who has lost another child. However, Anna had an actually dead sibling and Breuer her doctor as a 3-year-old had a mother who had died. Both the infant Anna and the infant Breuer would have experienced 'dead mothers' – Breuer's in actuality and Anna's emotionally dead because of her earlier bereavement. This shared history would have contributed to their confused identities.

What, however, is this shared, potentially creative madness where people meet in the absent egos of hysteria? There are many things to be said about hysterical identification; here I shall only select some features that can be used to illustrate hysteria throughout this period of Freud's life and work and its place in the advent of psychoanalysis. Paradigmatically, the model for this identification is that of the mother and preverbal infant. The infant strives to find out what the mother wants, and reciprocally the mother understands the infant through her identification with its signs and sounds. This period of mutual identification has been described by D. W. Winnicott as, from the mother's perspective, a time of 'necessary madness', when a social relationship extends the biological connection.[24] I watched a mother and small baby on the bus the other day: they bit each other, hugged, fought and giggled crazily – a number of us joined in their laughter. The mother had lost her own ego boundaries in becoming for a time her 'unbounded' pre-egoic baby. A later hysterical regression to this stage echoes this fusion/confusion which can resemble temporary madness.

Freud labelled his relationship with Fliess 'feminine'. Freud and Fliess seemed to embrace a biological identity reminiscent of the imagined bodily unity of mother and baby. In so far as from the baby's perspective he was merged with the mother, it was 'feminine', but pathologically lovers may try to recreate this: 'Your sleepiness now explains to me my own simultaneous state. Our protoplasm has worked its way through the same critical period. How nice it would be if this close harmony between us were a total one; I would always know how you are and would never expect letters without disappointment.'[25] 'As a consequence of the secret biological sympathy of which you have often spoken, both of us felt the surgeon's knife in our bodies at about the same time, and on precisely the same days moaned and groaned because of the pain.'[26] The baby does not have words to describe its feelings – the mother understands them, through feeling them in herself for a short period of time.

Throughout the 1890s, in his urgent effort to understand hysteria, Freud became involved in a creative but hysterical relationship with

Fliess, in which he was thinking through Fliess. Then, as with the pathology of overinvolved lovers or mothers and babies who stay identified for too long, their friendship had to come to a sudden, catastrophic halt. Freud, however, still expected Fliess to share in his experiences: 'I still do not know what has been happening in me. Something from the deepest depths of my own neurosis set itself against any advance in the understanding of the neuroses, and you have somehow been involved in it . . . I have no guarantees of this, just feelings of a highly obscure nature. Has nothing of the kind happened to you?'[27] 'Things are fermenting in me . . . tormented by grave doubts about my theory of neuroses.'[28] Yet to be wrong felt to Freud more like a victory than a defeat – he had moved on from his overidentification with Fliess.

The theory that Freud was abandoning was his notion that hysteria was caused by the patient having been actually seduced in infancy or early childhood. In the first theory, the infant would only become hysterical later as the sexual meaning of this incest or abuse was deferred till puberty when it was then dominantly believed that the individual became sexual for the first time. Throughout his self-analysis, which separated him from Fliess, and his analysis of patients such as 'E', Freud searched for this original scene of what today would be called 'abuse'. As late as Christmas 1899 he thought he had found it for 'E' and thus could foresee the end of his lengthy treatment:

You are familiar with . . . my dream which obstinately promises the end of 'E''s treatment . . . and you can well imagine how important this one persistent patient has become to me. It now appears that the dream will be fulfilled . . . Buried deep beneath all his fantasies, we found a scene [of seduction] from his primal period (before twenty-two months) which meets all the requirements and in which all the remaining puzzles converge. It is everything at the same time – sexual, innocent, natural, and the rest. I scarcely dare believe it yet. It is as if Schliemann [the famous German archaeologist] had once more excavated Troy, which had hitherto been deemed a fable . . . [29]

What came to replace this notion of an original scene of seduction for Freud was the idea that the seduction was not a reality but a fantasy. Even if the abuse is a reality, as it sometimes is, it is the fantasy of it that is invoked in hysteria and indeed more generally in human psychic life. Infantile desire for first the mother, then the father, is universal – actual abuse is particular. Human beings outlaw relationships which are regarded as incestuous because they desire them. If they did not desire them, there would be no need to prohibit them. This, and the allied notions of repression and the unconscious mind, constitute the idea of a universal Oedipus complex; these are the foundational concepts of psychoanalysis. Yet the notion of an Oedipus complex which was developed from insights into hysteria tolled the demise of hysteria as a subject of analysis.

But something from these days of early insight by Freud into his own and his patients' hysteria persisted against the grain of subsequent theories. In 1918, working with an aristocratic Russian, the 'Wolf Man', Freud commented that he had found a layer of hysteria beneath his patient's dominant obsessionality, and beneath this hysteria – a real scene: in this case one in which, at eighteen months, the Wolf Man had witnessed his parents engaged in intercourse from behind. The Wolf Man subsequently hoped to bear a baby in his bowel. His intestinal problems, which expressed this fantasy, were one of his hysterical symptoms. Freud's comment on the Wolf Man is not expanded into further thoughts on male hysteria – though we could usefully develop them that way. However, just as important is his assertion from observing the Wolf Man that, beneath all other neurotic disturbances in man or woman, there is a layer of hysteria.

The 'minimal' actual occurrence remains important in psychoanalytic theory. Freud suggested that the mother's bodily care for the infant constituted for the infant the sensation of a real seduction. In the interwar years in Budapest, Sándor Ferenczi took the intrusion of the parent's sexual feelings into the affectional demands of the infant as a starting point for a revised mode of therapy. Today, Jean-Paul Laplanche in France has developed a theory around the notion that the infant tries to translate the messages (the 'enigmatic signifiers') of the parent's desire. All these theories are concerned with the question of infantile sexual desire – showing that it is not just something innate, but rather something induced by the circumstances of prolonged and intensive nurturance of the human child. I believe this is correct, but if we add in the sibling or peer group sexuality in which the small child is involved, we will see that it is a regression on the part of this child, with its normally awakened sexuality, back into the potential sexuality of the parent–infant relationship that is at stake. The child regresses to an infantile position but with the later perspective of its sexual self – a sexuality that has probably been explored in games of 'doctors' or such like with siblings or peers. This is hidden by the exclusive focus on the Oedipus complex.

There was a homology between the new theory of fantasies – the 'founding' theory of psychoanalysis which remains dominant to this day – and the end of the friendship with Fliess. As Freud was to describe many years later, in *The Ego and the Id* (1923), the process of thinking means that motor discharge can be postponed; one can think instead of doing. In his relationship to Fliess, as in his relationship to his hysterical patients, in particular to 'E', although Freud was thinking and urgently trying to understand, he was also enacting in his behaviour exactly what he was trying to grasp intellectually. If thought can delay motility, so motility, and more generally 'enactment', can distract from – or even utterly inhibit – thought. This observation was to become recognized in the therapeutic situation as the danger of 'acting out': instead of thinking about the problem in the session, the patient (or analyst) enacts it in the world outside. It can happen to both patient and therapist – for instance, the hysterical American poet Anne Sexton, instead of thinking about her compulsion to seduce, had an affair with one of her therapists – her therapist was not thinking either.

The hysteric definitionally acts or performs: when Anna O talked instead of enacting the scenes of her fantasies – she *told* Breuer what her symptoms were performing – she invented 'the talking cure'. However, acting out has remained a problem for the therapy that was devised to cure it. Psychoanalysis aims to bring enactment into language; thought is a precondition of language but the hysteric is acting, enacting and performing or even evacuating thought through explosive language (as in 'road rage') in order to prevent thought. Freud's enactments of his *petite hystérie* with Fliess and 'E' provided him with all the material with which to understand hysteria. For instance, to take the already mentioned railway phobia, Freud enacted a compulsion to get to a railway station incredibly early at considerable inconvenience to himself until he realized that, as with 'E''s problems with railways, for himself, too, it stood for having to get to the table and the food first, before his siblings got there. Behind this is the suggestion of 'E' and Freud both needing to get all the women as well as all the food: the Don Juanism. The very process of having to think about his enactment in his self-analysis 'cured' Freud's hysteria. Or, to put it another way, while he was still enacting his hysteria as friend and therapist, he could not fully *think* about it. Furthermore, when he *acted*, his theory reflected the action: he found in himself and his patients *actual* – enacted – scenes of seduction. When he felt triumphant that his theory of *actual* seduction was wrong, Freud's *actual* relationship with Fliess was fatally endangered; unconscious enactment no longer stood in the way of thinking. But likewise thinking was also at the base of the new theory. In Freud's emerging theory of the existence of infantile sexuality, the child only *thinks* he or she has been seduced by the father. What is needed to rescue the theory of hysteria from this impasse is the application of the idea of 'deferred action'; that is, what an infant hears or sees before it can understand it, is given a bizarre meaning by the child when it is older. One can witness children playing out this problem: I know I was not the only child, learning to read through posters on the bus, who wondered what Bill Stickers had done to merit his prosecution ('Bill Stickers Will Be Prosecuted'). The Wolf Man does not understand as an infant what he overhears his mother tell her doctor about her bowel symptoms; later he gives it a literal meaning. His mother has said she cannot live like this; the Wolf Man later adopts her complaints – having intestinal problems that he thinks might kill him – which, in turn, would also have been associated, through the child's notion of anal birth, with possible death in childbirth.

The hysteric is convinced that he has actually been seduced in order not to have to think about sexuality. The idea that he has been actually seduced enables him to go on experiencing sexuality as though 'in actuality'. This experiential thinking is what we can understand as 'fantasy'. In deploying fantasy, the fantasist is not concerned with trying to discover whether something is true or untrue, but rather he is enjoying his own version of events, even if it is a frightening version. In fantasy we are endeavouring to reproduce, to replicate in the mind's eye and the feelings of the body, what we want to happen in practice.

It is this characteristic that led Freud to see that dreams and neurotic symptoms have the common aim of 'wish-fulfilment' – of getting what we want. When we wake up we know a dream is not true, but while we are dreaming it, we experience it as reality, however far-fetched or impossible it may seem in our waking state. The dream and the neurotic symptom realize our wants as though in actuality: I want not to see something happening, so I become hysterically blind in order to fulfil this wish. In *Othello*, the pseudologist Iago starts off knowing he is making things up but comes to believe the world of lies which he has created – as, of course, do others. Experiential fantasy or lying acts as a defence against intellectual thought or truth-seeking thought no less than does enactment or 'acting out' as it came to be called.

Developmentally, the baby hallucinates the breast in its absence, the toddler is the train engine he pretends to be, the young child tells stories, but the adult is supposed to distinguish between fantasy and reality. The level of distinction between fantasy and reality varies between different societies or social groups, but the hysterical element in everyone rejects this distinction – for in hysterical behaviour fantasies are lived as though they were reality. The apparent disappearance of hysteria from Western society is bound up with the advent of the psychoanalysis which it inaugurated. The period of Freud's manifest hysteria was over by around 1900. 'Thinking', and speaking the very theory and practice of psychoanalysis, had replaced it.

There is, of course, a crucial distinction between fact and fiction and between actual abuse/seduction and fantasy, between truth and lying. But the important distinction here is in their subjective dimension. Put into words or deeds, the hysteric's fantasies may be kept within the bounds of performance or stories, but because of an unconscious driven element they can also spill over into perversion and lies. It was to suggest a kind of verbal perversion that the French psychoanalyst Christian David deployed the term 'bovarism'. These tales are usually of sexual derring-do with violence intermingled. The quality of conviction is powerful. One patient in my early days as an analyst was carrying me along with an epic (but untrue) account of the adventures he had had as he had come that day to the clinic where I worked, when I nearly burst out with a laugh of deep shock. In his story, he had arrived at his destination and found me dead; the description was extremely vivid and disturbingly 'convincing'. My patient had no inkling his story would have any effect on me; I was part of him, admiring with him his prowess.

The *petite hystérie* of Freud demonstrates the presence of hysteria in a man. It tells us that hysteria involves a desperate and exciting degree of mental and bodily identification whereby one thinks and feels through another person who, though all-important, is not experienced as a separate being; not, in other words, as another person in an 'object relationship'. It shows how feelings do not become thoughts that might be represented but are instead expressed in the body.

The notion of the Oedipus complex, in which, as an essential process of becoming human, 'everyman' desires his mother yet must demolish that desire, sets out man's task. A boy may want his mother but he cannot have her in actuality nor even in fantasy.[30] The so-called 'negative' or feminine Oedipus complex, in which a man wants to be his mother and desires his father is recognized but never gets as much attention in the theory. Because it is not accorded proper attention in the practice and theory it has become 'unconscious', but it has surfaced again as a homophobia which is prevalent in many psychoanalytical institutes. The attention now drawn to this homophobia means that we miss the crucial importance of hysterophobia in the theory as a whole.

The poorly explored male negative Oedipus complex indicates how the notion of the overriding importance given by psychoanalysis to the Oedipus complex (negative or positive) has blocked our understanding of hysteria. Because the Oedipus complex was discovered through *male* hysteria it bore the marks of the resistance to the possibility of hysteria in men. The negative male Oedipus complex – that is the man's passivity in relation to the father – had to carry the weight of explaining both male hysteria and homosexuality. Too often the two have become conflated. Hysteria, to the contrary, is essentially bisexual. The often enormous importance placed on the 'love object' by the hysteric (man, woman or child) conceals the fact that it is wanted not as an object in itself but for purposes of identification or as a source from which the hysteric may receive love or acclaim for him or herself.

While psychosexuality has been the focus of most psychoanalytical work on hysteria, the importance of death has been much overlooked. But reading the construction of Freud's hysteria from his dreams and letters one wonders how death escaped attention, as one is similarly bemused after reading *Studies on Hysteria* where fantasies of death are all-pervasive in the symptoms and identifications. Death, in hysteria, is a presence in the body.

On a number of occasions Freud referred to the significance, for his psychic life and his male relationships, of his younger brother's death. It is the failure to work this into the psychoanalytic theory that surely explains the omission from the early theory of the significance of death – above all for the hysteric's symptoms and enactments. To miss out on the importance of the sibling is to miss out on the place of death. Even without a sibling death, the wish to kill siblings or the sense of being annihilated as a unique subject by their presence is a crucial aspect of the human condition. We can see how Freud's family situation may have had something he wished to avoid when developing the theory of the Oedipus complex.

The dates are somewhat uncertain, but Freud's brother Julius would seem to have been born when Freud was around one and a half and to have died at six months, shortly before Freud's second birthday. About the time of Julius's death, Monique Zajic, the woman whom Freud calls his nurse, was accused of stealing and was sent to prison. During this period Freud played and fought with the children of his half-brother Philipp – John, eighteen months his senior, and Pauline, the same age as himself – like brother and sister. Zajic had looked after all the young children while their mothers worked.

Freud's father was forty, his mother twenty and his half-brothers by his father's first marriage twenty-five and twenty-two. When, in his self-analysis and in the period of his active hysteria, Freud was reconstructing these first years of his life spent in Freiberg, he and his wife Martha were expecting Anna. After Julius's death, Freud's sister Anna was the last child to be born in Freiberg before Freud's parents moved first to Leipzig, then to Vienna. Freud never liked her; she married his wife's brother.

To read the account of the Freud circle of interfamily connections is to get a vivid picture of a kinship system that was near endogamous.

But what is also striking is both the degree and kind of intermarriage that took place – which often reveals the sibling relationships on which the marriage would have been psychically based. Freud's (and all subsequent psychoanalytic) emphasis on the intergenerational Oedipus complex indicates a massive repression of the significance of all the love and hate of sibling relationships and their heirs in marital affinity and friendships.

There are, however, a number of instances which point both to the importance of siblings and to the repression of this importance. For example, the time when Freud was reconstructing these events and connections between his present and his past, was also the time of his discovering the significance of the Oedipus story. In his first writings (in the letters to Fliess) which give an inkling of the importance Freud was to place on this scenario for human existence, Hamlet vies with Oedipus as representatives of the myth of infantile desire for the mother. However, Freud, for a number of reasons, explicitly labelled Hamlet a hysteric and settled on Oedipus instead as the universal norm. In other words, his choice in itself banishes the male hysteric in favour of Oedipus.

Hamlet's 'sexual alienation in his conversation with Ophelia [is] typically hysterical', wrote Freud. So too is the displacement (which is the same as Don Juan's) in which he murders Ophelia's father instead of his own. Hamlet suffers unconscious guilt because he wanted to do what his uncle did – murder his father. This is comparable to Dostoevsky's history: Dostoevsky's hysterical epilepsy was an identification with his father who had been murdered – by someone else. 'And does [Hamlet] not in the end, in the same marvellous way as my hysterical patients, bring down punishment on himself by suffering the same fate as his father of being poisoned by the same rival?' Hamlet the hysteric never knows what he really wants. Oedipus, though, unlike Hamlet, actually achieves the desired union with his mother, actually kills his own father, and is punished for it, but he is not haunted by the endless 'wanting' that Hamlet suffers. Freud, who knew Shakespeare's plays backwards, makes an interesting slip:

How does Hamlet the hysteric justify his words, 'Thus conscience does make cowards of us all'? How does he explain his irresolution in avenging his father by the murder of his uncle – the same man who sends his courtiers to their death without a scruple and who is positively precipitate in murdering Laertes?[31]

In fact, Hamlet does not murder Laertes – Ophelia's brother – with whom he fights a duel; he murders Polonius, Ophelia's father. This slip indicates Freud's own repression of sibling murderousness. The conclusion of his thoughts on Hamlet indicates how near to the surface of his mind sibling rivalry was: Hamlet's father (also called Hamlet) is murdered by his rivalrous brother, who wants his wife as well as his throne; that is, there exists a lateral rivalrous wanting of the same woman and a murderousness between brothers.

Given the fact that his half-brothers were his mother's age, Freud may have been particularly prone to paternal–fraternal confusion, so that in his work he was relieved to settle on the proper father as being at the heart of the Oedipus complex. Freud had a recurring memory of himself as a child in Freiberg, crying desperately because his mother had disappeared. His half-brother, Philipp, teasingly opened a cupboard to show him that his mother was not there. Philipp had been instrumental in having Monique Zajic imprisoned for theft. In a letter to Fliess, Freud recollects his childhood panic when Philipp puns about 'boxing up'. This word play indicated to Freud both his mother's pregnancy and Zajic's incarceration. The association Freud made suggests that as a child he may have been uncertain whether his father or his half-brother was responsible for 'boxing-up' his mother and hence for her pregnancy. But if we acknowledge the importance of siblings, then the transference of a wish to get rid of the sibling into wanting to dispose of the father makes the coincidence of the two figures a more generalized phenomenon. Of another male hysteric described to Fliess, Freud writes:

A 25-year-old fellow who can scarcely walk because of stiffness in the legs, cramps, tremors and so on. A safeguard against any misdiagnosis is provided by his accompanying anxiety, which makes him cling to his mother's apron strings like the baby he once was. The death of the brother and the death of the father in a psychosis precipitated the onset of his symptoms.[32]

The death of baby brother Julius in the context of the rivalry with John, his half-brother's son who seemed like an older sibling to him, was crucial for Freud: 'I greeted my one-year-younger brother (who died after a few months) with adverse wishes and genuine childhood jealousy; . . . that his death left the germ of [self-] reproaches in me . . . [My] nephew and this younger brother have determined, then, what is neurotic, but also what is intense, in all my friendships.'[33] Fliess was born the same year as Julius. As he is fixing on the Oedipus story, Freud associates to dreams that display his own triumphant survival in relation to the possible death of Fliess (Fliess had been very ill) and two other rival brother figures – Victor Tilgner and Ernest Fleischl von Marxow – who died prematurely. Fratricide illustrates how hysterics love where they hate and hate where they love: 'My emotional life,' wrote Freud, 'has always insisted that I should have an intimate friend and a hated enemy. I have always been able to provide myself afresh with both, and it has not infrequently happened that the ideal situation of childhood has been so completely reproduced that friend and enemy have come together in a single individual.'[34]

In producing his masterpiece *The Interpretation of Dreams* (1901), Freud explicitly chooses not to identify with Hamlet the hysteric but with his creator, Shakespeare, who at the time of writing the play was mourning the recent death of his father. Freud's personal hysteria is resolved but at the cost of displacing male hysteria (which is enacted in transferences with 'brothers' like Fliess and 'E') on to an unresolved Oedipus complex in relation to a father. In its turn this theoretical gesture makes for the 'disappearance' (or, I would argue, 'normalization') of hysteria. When it reappears, hysteria is returned to women.

There are numerous discussions and theories about the earliest mother–infant bond: Are the two fused so that the infant must separate, or are they already separated by birth so that the infant seeks fusion? This repeated question seems to me somewhat misplaced. The small child has a unique relationship with its mother or carer. When a sibling arrives (or some equivalent is imagined) its world disintegrates: the infant has been replaced by another, so who has it become, where does it stand? In this emergency of its sudden non-existence or meaninglessness, it regresses to being the baby at the breast or in the womb: this is the enactment and the fantasy of fusion in which it is both baby and mother for the degree of fusion makes them one and the same. Fusion, or the fantasy of it, follows some degree of later separation. For a long time, Freud was convinced that it was he who stole the florins for which his nurse was imprisoned, only to discover in midlife that Zajic had indeed stolen them herself from him. Freud had confused himself with Zajic (who in this context was his mother substitute) in the act of theft, in wanting what she wanted – he had achieved the fusion the child demands. In his dreams at the time of his hysteria Freud merged with menstruating mother figures, but he also dreamt that he was carried by them like a small child. Separated as a child from the mother the hysteric regresses to the imagined fusion of infancy. This merged or fused identification with the mother figure is the so-called 'femininity' of hysteria in both boys and girls – the result of the catastrophic displacement brought about by the sibling that comes to occupy the space where one's existence was hitherto recognized.

The Oedipus complex and later the notion of a castration complex allowed the exclusion of sibling rivalry as a determinant of psychic and subsequent social life siblings precipitate the Oedipus complex. There are many occasions, catastrophes and traumata that depose or displace the individual throughout life but to some extent they will be re-editions of this first social situation in which another, who is too similar to oneself, usurps the throne of infancy. One can either choose to adjust to this displacement or one can protest hysterically against it.

Brothers and sisters get scant attention in Freud's work or in subsequent psychoanalytic theory and practice. This is connected with the 'disappearance' of hysteria. At the time of the dominance of hysteria in the foundation of psychoanalysis the problems and permutations of psychosexuality received all the emphasis as the explanatory factor – death did not feature. Violence and hostility were noted but not given a place in the theory model until the castration complex was first observed in the phobias of 'Little Hans', a child whose father described them to Freud in 1909. It was formulated as a theoretical concept some seven years later. Wanting to murder thus only found its place in the theory with the castration complex and its successive hypothesis of a death drive which Freud (controversially) proposed in *Beyond the Pleasure Principle* (1920). It is usually wrongly considered that by that time Freud was no longer interested in hysteria.

Subsequent accounts of Freud's portraits of hysteria rely on the early work, with its emphasis on sexuality and the absence of a notion of 'wanting' death. If, however, we reread these early works through the later formulations, the scant references to relationships of brothers and sisters, in which sexuality and murderousness are prominent, are brief but they are shouting to be recognized: 'In none of my women patients . . . have I failed to come upon this dream of the death of a brother or sister, which tallies with an increase in hostility';[35] and, 'hostile feelings towards brothers and sisters must be far more frequent in childhood than the unseeing eye of the adult observer can perceive'.[36] Indeed, in *The Interpretation of Dreams* Freud comments that he had not thought to observe sibling rivalry among his own children – this was during the period of his self-analysis with its resultant emphasis on Oedipus. Freud's was the unseeing eye. He resolved to remedy the situation with observations of a nephew. But some years later, it was Little Hans who repeatedly asked his mother to drown his baby sister in the bath. Hans (described more fully later) was unable to leave the house because he feared seeing horses. His sister had just been born. Hans's Oedipal fantasies show clearly the significance of this sibling birth. Hans, a case of hysterical anxiety, is also the link between castration, death and Freud's later attempts to understand hysteria. Freud adds footnotes to the case in 1923 and uses it for his worries about hysteria in *Inhibitions, Symptoms and Anxieties* (1926). Hans, like Freud himself, was a male hysteric whose hostility to his sibling could not be fitted into an Oedipal schema. The importance of siblings (their death or fantasies of their murder) and their place within the construction of hysteria have all been underestimated in psychoanalysis's attempts to base all interpretations on the intergenerational model of parents and children, first of parental seduction and then of Oedipal fantasies of incest.

3

Dora: A Fragment of a Case of Hysteria in a Female

With the second wave feminist movement, 'Dora' became a household name. Her hysteria made her a protofeminist heroine. Some argued that her illness was an unsatisfactory alternative to political protest, others that hysteria was the only means available to her of contesting the oppression of patriarchy. In Freud's account, Dora sees herself (and most feminists agree) as the victim of men's 'exchange of women', in which her father is prepared to trade her in the interests of retaining his own extramarital affair. Certainly Dora is stuck and her hysterical symptoms reflect what she experiences as the impossibility of her position. The case history also gives us a neat psychoanalytic account of hysteria as the failure to negotiate and resolve the Oedipus complex: Dora wants to love a woman (originally her mother) as a man would love, and receive a man's love (originally her father's) as a woman would expect.

Following the discovery by her parents of a suicide note, an 18-year-old, Ida Bauer (disguised in the case history as 'Dora'), is brought for treatment to Freud by her father. Her father, a wealthy Jewish businessman, had consulted Freud earlier for his own complaints at the suggestion of a friend, Herr K. Herr K is the husband of Herr Bauer's mistress. Dora is the younger by eighteen months of the Bauers' two children. According to Dora, Herr K has made sexual advances towards her and there is an implication that he would want to marry her in the advent of his own possible divorce. Dora suffers from a *petite hystérie*. Her mild hysteria consists of a range of troublesome physical symptoms for which no organic cause can be found. The symptoms are often connected with breathing and speaking – loss of voice, breathlessness, asthma – or with disturbances of internal organs such as bowels and appendix. Bringing the two areas together are similar unhealthy discharges of the throat and vagina. She drags one foot and is always fatigued and irritable. Dora exemplifies the hysterical propensity for easy and absolute mimetic identification with the characteristics or actions – real or imagined – of another person.

Prompted by Freud's interpretations of her words and actions, Dora tells Freud of the sexual entanglements of the two families, of which she sees herself as the victim. Dora thinks her father would allow her involvement with Herr K in exchange for silence and acceptance of his own affair with Frau K. At each juncture, Freud does not disagree with Dora's account, but instead asks her what she gains from her involvement in the story.

The case history consists of a clinical presentation of the family history, followed by an account of Dora's hysterical identifications and an analysis of two dreams, which show how dreams can be understood to reveal the satisfaction of otherwise illicit wishes. These wishes are not exclusively, but tend to be predominantly, sexual – although in this context sexuality must be taken to include a far wider range of wants than just genital urges. In his approach to the case, Freud is out to demonstrate a theory of the importance of wish-fulfilment and of the Oedipus complex, rather than one of hysteria.

Dreams are not in themselves either hysterical or 'normal'; they are simply a different mode of thinking from conscious thought. However, Dora's dreams, in showing her various desires and identifications, do indicate the irreconcilable positions she wants to take up but which she cannot take up in waking life. Her hysteria lies in the fact that her ego cannot unify these irreconcilable positions and at the same time she will not renounce them.

In the first dream – a version of a recurrent dream – a house is on fire. Dora's father is rescuing his daughter and her brother. Her mother wants to stop the escape in order to retrieve her jewelcase. Her father refuses. They get out and Dora wakes up. In the second dream, Dora is in a strange town. She finds a letter from her mother inviting her home now that her father has apparently died. She has a long and bewildering journey through a wood to the station. When she associates to this, it turns out to be a journey a suitor of hers undertook.

Then Dora arrives home to find her mother and the others at the cemetery.

Dreams can largely be translated into everyday thoughts through the associations the dreamer makes when she or he has been able to suspend inhibitions and censorships. Freud asks for Dora's associations and together they build up a verbal picture of aspects of her psychological and emotional life as well as a recollection of incidents that seem really to have taken place.

Dora left the treatment prematurely and when she returned to try and continue it, Freud refused, as he did not believe she was motivated to recover. The case has been both widely admired for its virtuoso demonstration of a theory and widely criticized for the 'patriarchal' stance Freud himself seems to have adopted towards Dora.

Freud called his essay a 'Fragment of an Analysis'. The focus is on the dreams; my concern, however, is with the hysterical manifestations and the social relationships. We have seen how Freud has been quite clearly identified with hysteria. In particular he seems often to have been fused and confused with his patient 'E' and his friend Fliess. There is no such confusion or identification with Dora; there is no shared hysteria here. The account of Dora shows the distance Freud had taken from any identification with his patients. For, his father now dead and mourned, he could set up this image within and 'become' a father, not only to his children, but to his patients, as well as to the young analysts he was starting to gather around him. Whereas previously therapist and patient had been in a lateral relationship such as that exemplified by Freud and 'E' in the 1890s, now, with the parental transference in place, they were in a hierarchical relationship of father and child.

Dora, a hysteric, got the worst not only of Freud's paternal posturing but also of his own need for it. For, when Dora came to see him, Freud needed desperately to get away from his own propensity to hysteria. The last thing he wanted was to try and understand his hysterical patient by identifying with her in too unmediated a manner, as he had done with 'E'. The result is the dismissive distance Freud established between himself and Dora which has annoyed feminists but attracted some psychoanalysts, relieved that they too are not hysterics and that hysteria can be left mainly to women patients.

There are a number of problems with the feminist position, even though it is not, in a sense, an incorrect reading. It makes Dora a double hysteric. Like any hysteric, Ida Bauer (the Dora of the text) presented herself to Freud as the victim of other people's failures and machinations. A reading of the case history that merely notes the mistakes and failures of Freud's patriarchal analysis simply reinforces Ida Bauer's position – it makes Dora Freud's victim, just as she is a victim of the 'exchange of women' in history and in her own family. Such an argument also misses a particular aspect of Freud's stance which is crucial for the nature of the treatment and the future of hysteria: Freud protests too much. As we will see in a number of different contexts, Freud betrays his doubts by his dogmatism.

At times, when he is writing about Dora, Freud's sense of psychological paternity seems more like a patriarchal pose, thereby revealing both its precariousness and its proximity to a hysterical condition in which it would be only an *imitation* of fatherhood. Where the position seems most strenuously asserted, there it is most fragile; where the arguments are most dogmatic, therein lie the points of doubt. As once he sought an actual event of infantile sexual seduction as the instigator of a later hysteria, now Freud looks for an unresolved incestuous Oedipal love as the *causus belli* of hysterical protest. It is not that this is necessarily an incorrect explanation; it is that Freud's own insistence on it marks his uncertainty, an uncertainty to which Dora would doubtless have become attuned. So too it is the *uncertainty*, not (as is argued) the *certainty*, of Freud's patriarchal attitude that would have communicated itself through his overstrong protestations.

Freud's father died in 1896. Four years later, a reluctant Ida Bauer was brought by her father for treatment of a number of hysterical problems – the most troubling of which was a persistent voicelessness (*aphonia*). Through his self-analysis which was terminated in the publication of *The Interpretation of Dreams* in 1901, Freud had largely worked through his hysterical identification with death through his diseases and come instead to mourn the loss of his father. He could now no longer conflate himself in a hysterical manner with an actual person, but instead had to identify with an imago, an inner image of fatherhood based on the dead father who was known to have been both good and bad. However, such processes are rarely, if ever, absolute.

For her part, Ida Bauer did not want to consult Freud but, once there, she would have wanted to find out what Freud wanted and then to have identified with whatever it was. What Freud wanted was too insistent and hence too uncertain for her to identify with. He wanted her to confirm his theories, forgetting that in his own observation, hysterics identify with what another wants – but not if that wanting is too strident because it is too much in doubt.

The case history was designed as a confirmation of *The Interpretation of Dreams* and largely consists of the analysis of two dreams. Dreams are only a process of 'dreamwork' which brings the day's preconscious thoughts into alliance with unconscious (probably infantile) wishes so that they can be fulfilled in the dream and thus allow the dreamer to sleep satisfied. Although Freud's own analysis of Dora focuses on her dreams, in order to examine the nature of hysteria as Freud found it we need to look instead at her hysterical symptoms and decipher the points of identification she had with another's wants. This has been done before with regard to other actors in Dora's social milieu, but much less in relation to Freud himself, her somewhat insecure, overemphatic, male therapist. There has also been virtually no account taken of the part played in Dora's life by her successful older brother, Otto Bauer, future leader of the Austro-Hungarian Marxist Party.

Dora's is not a flamboyant hysteria but one whose almost manageable symptoms are modelled on the behaviour or condition of close relatives and friends. All these friends and relatives are endlessly ill, not just mentally with threatened suicide or *taedium vitae*, but physically – whether for organic or strategic reasons. It is, without doubt, the sick body that holds centre stage in this portrait of Dora's life. Of the men in Dora's circle, Herr K would seem to have been unusually free from ill health. Dora is interested in sickness, however, so this healthiness already makes him problematic as a point of identification for her. The healthy Herr K does not seem to get what he wants, however – he gets neither his wife nor Dora. Dora's father's illnesses, on the other hand, seem to have completely dictated the places and procedures of family life. The Bauers move between town and country on the pretext of his health, but in fact to suit his affair with Frau K. Throughout the case history, Herr Bauer is described as having numerous serious physical conditions, among them syphilis, gonorrhoea, tuberculosis, a debilitating cough and breathlessness. These would appear to have been either genuinely organic or deliberately manipulative. The latter were not hysterical because the manipulation was not at all unconscious but, on the contrary, quite consciously intentional. His lying about his affair was likewise deliberate, not habitual or compulsive as it would have been if it had been hysterical. Some of Herr Bauer's organic illnesses, such as a diffuse vascular condition and a detached retina leading to permanently impaired sight, would seem to have been the result of an earlier bout of syphilis.

Outside the main actors in the case history, we are told that Herr Bauer's brother, Dora's uncle, had been 'hypochondriacal' – presumably not organically ill – and a boy cousin, who had been a bedwetter in childhood, was currently dangerously ill with appendicitis. Dora's elder brother Otto had had all the usual infectious illnesses of childhood, but had had them mildly. He too had been enuretic in childhood, wetting himself in the day time as well as at night. Otherwise, Otto and Herr K are healthy – and, therefore, from a hysterical perspective, not very useful as models.

Of the women, Frau Bauer suffers from gonorrhoea caught from her husband, abdominal pains and a discharge necessitating a spa cure. Frau K becomes ill (we are not told with what) whenever her husband comes home. A girl cousin suffers from gastric pains when she becomes jealous of her sister's impending marriage. An aunt with an unhappy marriage dies with uncured marasmus, an unexplained wasting of the body. All the women's illnesses are, therefore, linked to their relationships with men.

We could say, then, that the currency of sexuality in Dora's family is not so much that of the sexual or reproductive body as that of the sick body. However, it is Dora's father, Herr Bauer, who is the sickest of the lot, and he is sick because of sex. For Dora and her family sexuality and sickness are linked: 'Her father, then, had fallen ill through leading a loose life . . .'[1] But although Herr Bauer gets sympathy for his ill health, his daughter is also angered by his making use of it to get whatever he wants. It heightens her ambivalence towards him: she is both compassionate and hostile. She is also envious. If Herr Bauer gets his way through sickness, why shouldn't Dora? The price, however, is sickness.

Dora suffers from gastric pains, *dyspnoea*, a cough, asthma, *aphonia*, catarrh both from the throat and the vagina, breathlessness, hoarseness and irritation of the throat, loss of appetite, vomiting, irregular periods, continual constipation, appendicitis or perityphilitis; she drags her right foot and at one point has a fever, probably as a result of influenza; during one reported illness she apparently has convulsions and delirium. After her treatment with Freud is over, Dora suffers from six weeks of *aphonia* and returns to Freud with a right-sided facial neuralgia, seeking to renew her therapy. But Dora's illnesses are mimetic copies: she had modelled herself on the hysterical aunt with the wasting disease. When she complains of piercing gastric pains, Freud asks her 'Who are you copying now?' Imitating we know not who, a specific constellation of her symptoms also indicates that through them she has gone through an imaginary childbirth. Her answer to Freud's questions about bedwetting suggest that she may have been confused with her brother, for she too had been enuretic in childhood.

Freud posits sexual fantasies as lying at the root of hysteria and that hysterics mimic other people's desires. I suggest that the late nineteenth-century hysteric specifically mimicked not just sexuality but, overwhelmingly, the sexuality of the endlessly sick body. Of hysterical symptoms it is said that the mind makes a mysterious leap into the body. The body through which Dora expressed her mental dilemmas was a body that was modelled on the sick bodies that characterized her social milieu. In other words, it imitated disease and so hysteria was understood as a disease. The thrust of Freud's final understanding of Dora's hysteria is that in her symptoms she has predominantly (by no means exclusively) identified with a man and loved as a man – in the second dream, her own suitor. Mainly, according to Freud's analysis, she has become her father in order to be successful in her love of the women her father loves. We should not, however, underestimate the fact that it is through his sick body that Herr Bauer is able to get what he wants. Does Dora, the hysteric, identify with a man to get a woman or does she identify with the most effectively sick body, which in this case is a man's, in order to get whatever she wants? The two possibilities, of course, overlap and coincide but they are not identical.

Sick bodies are treated by medical doctors. It is as such that Freud first becomes acquainted with the Bauers. At his friend Herr K's suggestion, Herr Bauer consults Freud about some consequences of his syphilis. Nearly everybody mentioned sees doctors. Dora has made a profession of making sure they cannot help her. Nevertheless, she keeps consulting them. Why? At one point in the case history, Freud comments:

The motives for being ill often begin to be active even in childhood. *A little girl in her greed for love does not enjoy having to share the affection of her parents with her brothers and sisters; and she notices that the whole of their affection is lavished on her once more whenever she arouses their anxiety by falling ill. She has now discovered a means of enticing out her parents' love,* and will make use of that means as soon as she has the necessary psychical material at her disposal for producing an illness. When such a child has grown up to be a woman she may find all the demands she used to make in her childhood countered owing to her marriage with an inconsiderate husband . . . In that case ill-health will be her one weapon for maintaining her position. It will procure her the care she longs for; it will force her husband to make pecuniary sacrifices for her and to show her consideration, as he would never have done while she was well; and it will compel him to treat her with solicitude if she recovers, for otherwise a relapse will threaten. Her state of ill-health will have every appearance of being objective and involuntary – the very doctor who treats her will bear witness to the fact; and for that reason she will not need to feel any conscious self-reproaches at making such successful use of a means which she had found effective in her years of childhood.[2] [My italics]

Sick bodies need doctors. In disentangling himself from such patients as 'E', in noting the surplus of erotic satisfaction in the hypnotic and suggestive cures he had tried to practise, Freud had come to devise the notion of 'transferences'. These are described in the Dora case: 'What are transferences? They are new editions or facsimiles of the impulses and phantasies which are aroused and made conscious during the progress of the analysis; but they have this peculiarity, which is characteristic for their species, that they replace some earlier person by *the person of the physician* [my italics].'[3]

Over the years of psychoanalytic work, emphasis on the importance of the transference has increased, but as regards the different figures deployed in the transference, it has actually declined. It has focused on the parents – first the father, then the mother. As well as siblings, we have overlooked the importance of the ultimate transference figure. This, at the time of Dora, was the physician – a medical man who was interested in the whole person but whose professional speciality was the sick body. Whatever his particular personality, this medical doctor occupied a charismatic position – one could want to get well for the sake of his blue eyes, or rather, because he wanted to achieve a cure; or one could want to delay the cure to prolong the relationship – a wish that may well have been mutual. The person of the doctor was not the cure or its absence but, like an actual change in circumstances to which Freud refers in the Dora case, he could be the means to it: 'The postponement of recovery or improvement is really only caused by the physician's own person.'[4] Prior to the rise of psychoanalysis, treatments in vogue for hysterical patients had been hypnosis and allied cures that used 'suggestion' – suggesting, for instance, that the patient is not suffering or would feel better. The suggestive element that remained from these therapies, in which Freud was involved, is retained in the figure of the therapist. The psychoanalytical therapist does not suggest but the patient can believe that she does.

Ideally by being ungratified, by not getting what he wants from his doctor, the patient's yearning can be resolved by the end of the treatment. Although clearly often it is not – for, as the French psychoanalyst François Roustang says, psychoanalysis may never let go. But that is not my concern here. What is of importance is that the manifestations and symptoms in hysteria will assume a form that suits the therapist.

In going to Freud, Dora would seem to have come to see yet another doctor at her father's insistence, and she brings with her a plethora of physical ailments. But doctors' tasks change. At the time of 'vapours' in the late eighteenth century or of 'nerves' in the mid nineteenth century, the doctor might have been aware of blood circulation or of neurology. The doctor was a major figure throughout the nineteenth century, but during the second Industrial Revolution his importance intensified, particularly in respect to women. Womanhood itself, in its sexual difference from manhood – menstrual periods, pregnancy and childbirth – became a medical problem. With compulsory elementary schooling and increasing labour law restrictions, children were fast becoming an economic drain rather than an economic asset. There was a significant decline in fertility and the emphasis in reproduction shifted to fewer, healthier, 'medicalized' babies who could be well brought up and 'morally' educated by the mother. It was in this context that there was the rise of so-called 'moral motherhood' (with single women as school teachers) and commensurately an increase in the medicalization of childbirth and of women's reproductive capacities.

According to general feminist analyses and to the sociologist W. Seccombe's account of this particular period, *Weathering the Storm* (1993), the doctor's influence changed pregnancy, which had previously been regarded as a natural event, into a medical problem. The male doctor reached pre-eminence, not only in relation to women and their reproductive capacity, but also for children, who, being fewer in number, must be assured fit. As the literary critic Mary Poovey has shown, birth spasms and hysteria were frequently compared; only women had both. If we think of reproduction as the result of a relationship between two people, then, on the one hand, it is this mutual relationship that hysteria particularly resists. On the other hand, because of the strong medical interest and the definition of women as those who get attention as mothers, it is this reproductive capacity that it is most likely to mime. Pseudocyesis, or pregnancy fantasies, in women and men have always been fundamental to hysteria in any place or time. Here I am looking at the bonus of their medicalization. The medicalization of pregnancy in the mid nineteenth century made its imitation all the more attractive to the potential hysteric. It also increased the likelihood that hysteria would be gendered 'female'.

Freud was neither a gynaecologist nor an obstetrician, although he compares and contrasts himself with the former and, like his senior colleague Joseph Breuer, had previously been a family doctor. As Breuer's patient Anna O had had a phantom pregnancy, so Dora fantasizes about childbirth and stands transfixed for two hours gazing at Raphael's Sistine Madonna. As we will see more fully later, pregnancy and childbirth are central hysterical fantasies. If the sexual and reproductive body is a sick body, then the sick body of the hysteric may take reproductive forms miming pregnancy and childbirth to please the doctor who is known to be interested in these conditions.

A hysterical symptom uses a physical predisposition as an oyster uses a grain of sand to make a pearl. There is 'somatic compliance' wherever the psyche adopts the willing body for its expression; so Dora may have had a physical weakness of the chest which she made full use of by adopting a hysterical cough when, for instance, she was imagining oral sexual intercourse and was both attracted and repelled by it. It is this use of the body that, for Freud, differentiates hysteria from other psychoneuroses, as psychological illnesses were coming to be called. However, perhaps as Dora's symptoms were physical they expressed a shared interest with Freud the physician.

As a professional, who does Freud think he is? There is considerable slippage. In writing about Dora he refers to himself predominantly as a physician. But in his task of presenting and reconstructing the case history he compares himself to an archaeologist. He also calls himself a psychoanalyst: the techniques that so far can be fully specified as analytical are those of understanding the transference and of dream interpretation. Most particularly, Freud defends himself from accusations of prurience by referring to himself as a therapist who talks to a young girl about sexual matters, quoting a hypothetical patient who is relieved to find: ' "Why, after all, your treatment is far more respectable than Mr X's conversation!" '[5]

From Dora's point of view, however, she has come to see a physician about her sick body, like any good nineteenth-century middle-class woman hysteric. But during the two-month treatment she learns that what Freud wants to hear about are her Oedipal fantasies. Dora is understandably confused.

Freud himself is clearly not too sure, either. As with his patriarchal attitude, he has a tendency to protest too much about being a scientist. For instance, he is keen to show himself as a man of science and not as a writer of stories: 'I must now turn to consider a further complication to which I should certainly give no space if I were a man of letters engaged upon the creation of a mental state like this for a short story, instead of being a medical man engaged upon its dissection.'[6] Freud the physician is *en route* to being the therapist who has 'eyes to see and ears to hear' a patient who, even if her lips are silent, 'chatters with [her] finger tips'. Freud states that his task in the treatment of Dora is to *translate* pathogenic into normal material. That is an analytic, or even a linguistic, task, not a medical task. But over and above this Freud believes it is the unspoken that must be said.

And Dora complies. When she first came to see him, Freud would probably have taken her *history*, explaining that this was a new 'talking cure' – hence why Dora and Freud would have found her most troublesome symptom to be her *aphonia* – speechlessness. By the time she leaves, in what Freud interprets as an act of revenge in which she is giving him notice like a servant, she has learnt that a physical excitation is converted into a psychical symptom. The original slap in the face with which she had greeted Herr K's sexual proposal returns to her as a facial neuralgia. She brings further *aphonia* and this neuralgia back to Freud in the hope of renewing her treatment: it is as though her symptoms were saying 'Now I have got what you want.' She may even have developed these symptoms in order to identify with what she thinks Freud wants. But Dora is also fence-sitting in the history of hysteria – looking back to the bodily symptom of the disease and forward into the speech of the talking cure.

There are also Freud's 'wants' to take into account. In these, Freud is no less confused than Dora. Freud had wanted to stay an acceptable 'man of science'. For the sake of his friendship with Fliess, which at the time of Dora's treatment was both reaching new heights of emotional intensity and already on the edge of collapse, he had wanted to find an organic basis for the notion of bisexuality, a notion which is crucial to the understanding of hysteria. Freud had adopted the ideas of both organic causation and bisexuality from Fliess; but Fliess had accused him of plagiarism and of giving the ideas away. Freud's insistence on Dora's love for Herr K (and behind this her father) and his equally strong insistence that he had failed in his treatment of her because he had missed the import of her love for Frau K (her bisexuality) is testimony to Freud's own confusion with Fleiss's wants. Fraught with ambivalence as his feelings for Fleiss were, these wants could only be partially and imperfectly sustained. The 'Dora case' is testimony both to Freud's ambivalence in his wants and to Dora's conflictual hysterical response in trying to keep pace with them while at the same time resisting them. The hysterical symptom mimes what is wanted; because of ambivalence and conflict (Freud did not at any point whole-heartedly believe Fleiss's organic biology) what is wanted is difficult to decipher. As a consequence, the hysterical symptom is doubly hard to grasp; it contains its own conflict and the conflict in the person with whom there is an identification. In addition there is the resistance – the dilemma of not wanting to do what is wanted.

Dora's apparently dominant identification at the time of the treatment is with her father; like her father, she tries to use a sick body to get what she wants. On the surface, it would seem that the endlessly mimetic hysteric tries to achieve what he wants by imitating whoever seems best at it. But beneath this – and far more persistent – is the fact that he mimes whoever he is most jealous of. At the time of the treatment, Herr Bauer fits the bill on both counts. During the course of the treatment, the nature of the transference means that Dora transfers her wishes from her father on to the perceived desires of her physician, whose perceptiveness she also probably envies.

But Dora is placed on the cusp of change – the physician to whom she takes her sick body is turning into a therapist who is interested in reconstructing the incomplete story she has to tell. Dora, however, upstages her therapist by telling stories better than he can. At least, that is the skill that she takes away from the treatment. At the time, Frau and Herr K are sitting shiva for the death of their young daughter whom apparently Dora used to love and look after. It was through her care of his children that Dora had attracted Herr K. At the end of her treatment with Freud, or perhaps *as* an end to her treatment, Dora goes to offer her condolences to the bereaved Ks, with whom she has lost touch. Instead of condolences, Dora recounts to the grieving parents the full history of the two families' actual or intended infidelities. Confronted with Dora's story, both the Ks acknowledge their guilt and Dora leaves. The child's death does not signify; the story is all.

Today's Doras still have their body's desires, their 'greed for love', as Freud put it, in their coughs or wasting bodies but telling the story is where most of the passion has gone. For the professionals to whom hysterics and their families now turn are more likely to be 'listening' therapists than 'curing' physicians. And so, hysterics have gone from using the sick body to deploying the sexual story as the main manifestation of their condition. A passion of wanting inhabits both these forms, however. As Descartes realized, passion can cross boundaries; passion can go wherever it wants. It can also go wherever the shaman, through his or her use of that passion, directs it. With the talking cure and the story, sexuality moved from the body into language. It is not, as Fredrick Crews argues in his essay 'The Unknown Freud', the notion of paternal seduction or parental abuse that links psychoanalysis and recovered memory therapists, it is the story.

However, it is essential to note that, despite its origins as a 'talking cure', psychoanalysis, properly speaking, does not deploy the story. In this it is different from many of the therapies that may in part derive from it. Already at the time of Dora, Freud was rightly worried by the seductions of the story, by language as sexuality. The psychoanalytic method is one of free association. The psychoanalyst asks the patient to say without censorship whatever comes into his head. It is surprisingly difficult and hysterical patients are particularly adept at being able to avoid this prime requirement of the treatment. If one freely associates rather than making an effort to tell a coherent, logical story, then all kinds of surprising juxtapositions occur. One may also make slips of the tongue or say something which clearly has a meaning other than the one that was intended. We would need to use the German text to properly appreciate this in Dora's case. However, when Dora recalls in an association to her first dream that her father has said he will not let his children 'go to their destruction' and also tells Freud that her brother got all their childhood illnesses first and then gave them to her, both she and Freud can recognize in the lingo and innuendos of their day that she is talking about masturbation – a subject she wishes to avoid.

However, as 'the talking cure' grew in popularity, so did the hysterical ability to imitate it. Lying has always been noted as a characteristic of hysteria; in fact, there is an easy slippage between telling a story and telling stories where the fantasy cannot be distinguished from the truth. It is a remarkable fact that somebody who has truly mastered the art of lying does not make the lapses that the ordinary person is prone to. He cannot free-associate, he carries on with his story, covering any gaps with a further 'memory'. The unconscious processes do not break through the immaculate structure of the hysterical lie or the pseudologia. The lying of the hysteric was, according to the Hungarian analyst Ferenczi, the explanation for Freud's hysterophobia. Ferenczi thought that Freud never forgave his first hysterical patients who told him their fathers had seduced them when they were children.

The Dora case is read by psychoanalysts and feminists alike as an exemplary instance of patriarchy in its heyday. It is commonplace to note the patriarchal suppression of Dora's mother to a marginalized position of housewife's neurosis, of making life difficult and of being ill-educated and lacking culture; she appears not to count in either the life history or the text. But social relations abhor a vacuum. If Freud is neither quite sure of himself as the powerful physician nor as an authoritative father figure, something else must occupy that space. Contrary to first impressions, it is Dora's mother and her substitutes who occupy the space left empty by the doubting father-physician. In dismissing the mother through his patriarchal prejudice, Freud may have been echoing Dora's father (who, after all, is having a somewhat florid affair with another woman) and also Dora (who is very angry with her mother at one level, and dependent on her at another). However, the text does not bear this dismissal out. In other words, our task is not to reclaim Dora's mother from neglect (as, in particular, Object Relations therapists and feminists have done) but to fully appreciate her presence in the text. At times, the importance of her mother to Dora is made explicit. So Freud tells Dora: The dream shows 'that we were here dealing with material which had been very intensely repressed'[7] – '[T]he mystery,' says Freud to Dora, 'turns upon your mother.'[8] As the listener to Dora's tales, Freud is not her father but her mother in the transference. Dora not only tells things to Freud the therapist, she talks to her mother.

Frau Bauer is actively trying to bring Dora up to be a moral mother like herself – engaged in the hard work of looking after the home and family, in particular in trying (in vain), by endless cleaning, to keep it free from disease. Dora resists her mother's efforts on this front – she is, after all, very interested in disease. However, on the level of the symptoms and unconscious processes, Dora clearly identifies with her mother. Her hysterical identification with her mother's gonorrhoea, for instance, manifested itself as a vaginal discharge. As Freud put it, Dora 'identified herself with her mother by means of slight symptoms and peculiarities of manner, which gave her an opportunity for some really remarkable achievements in the direction of intolerable behaviour . . . The persistence with which she held to this identification with her mother almost forced me to ask whether she too was suffering from a venereal disease.'[9] In common with many physicians of the time, Freud thought children of syphilitic fathers had a predilection to hysteria, since syphilis could lead to eventual madness. Dora, too, would have been aware of this. To become a woman like her mother, at the end of the nineteenth century, was to become potentially mad; her feared syphilitic heritage from her father was the danger of insanity. What is Dora's hysteria anyway but a madness and a fear of madness, an identification with the madness one fears? (In the twentieth century, a fear of madness has been considered one feature of a 'borderline condition'.)

I suggest then, as many a psychoanalytic and feminist critic has demonstrated before, that Freud the therapist seems to have colluded with his patient's and her father's dismissal of the mother. As Freud sees it, the 'father was the dominating figure in this circle'.[10] However, I do not consider that the text of Dora's case history similarly colludes. In other words, I am arguing that the mother was firmly in place as a dominant figure at the beginning of psychoanalysis – in *Studies on Hysteria* we have Breuer's famous reiteration of 'reaching down to the mothers' as a synonym of unconscious processes. The mother is there at the beginning of psychoanalysis because she was there in the patient's material and there as an important figure in social reality. What we have in the text of Dora is a portrait of a powerful woman, the wife and mother of a prosperous, socially successful Jewish family, dominating her family and household and trying, against the odds, to keep it clean and proper. Nevertheless, because of her venereal disease and her husband's adultery, she provides a complex and problematic sexual model for her adolescent daughter. Furthermore, even in its details, I believe that this is a highly realistic portrait of the situation and role of the mother in those social circles at that time.

When Dora came to Freud, then, at the turn of the century, we can see that mothers were powerful and important figures behind the strictures of patriarchy, and that sexuality among the bourgeoisie was rampant and profoundly subject to sickness. It was around this conjuncture that Freud the doctor started to shift his ground to become Freud the psychoanalyst. And hysteria was at the centre, indeed was really the cause, of this shift.

The male physician diverted the patient's bodily need for the other person on to himself in the transference but in the process he ran the risk of becoming the mother to whom one brings one's stories. The movement from male physicians and sick bodies to stories for mothers can all too easily get caught up in the ambivalent idealization of motherhood in the Western world. This idealization goes from the rise of moral motherhood after the second Industrial Revolution to the construction of psychological motherhood particularly after the Second World War: the mother's responsibility for the moral and educational propriety of her children transforms in the twentieth century into the so-called 'good-enough mothering' which becomes her children's passport to psychic health. This applies to the actual mother and, in the transference, to the therapist as mother. Dora's case shows the importance of the father disappearing into the importance of the mother and, commensurably, of the physician becoming the therapist.

The presence and complexity of psychosexuality in the etiology of hysteria is also demonstrated by the case of Dora. In psychoanalytic observation and theory the psychopathologies are only exaggerations of what is referred to as 'normality', a condition Freud labelled 'an ideal fiction'. It is not only that we can all be hysterical, it is also that the structures of our experience are the same whether they are 'normal' or hysterical, and only the exaggerations of the latter will throw the former's moderation into relief. We all both more or less succeed and somewhat fail to resolve an Oedipus complex: Dora in her hysteria makes more of a meal of this process than most people. Conventional thought makes us want to rigidify Dora into a fixed position of hysteria, but the point is that it is exactly her hysteria which exaggerates the lability and mobility of desires and the objects of them. We find it hard to follow unconscious thought processes which do not abide by the notion of either/or but instead always indicate both/and. Freud is both the father in the transference *and* the mother; Dora may want to attract Herr K *and* adore Frau K (or her father *and* her mother); she may want to please a physician with her sick body *and* be getting the idea that the emerging therapist is interested in listening to her so she will return to ask Freud's help with symptoms both of facial · neuralgia *and* speechlessness, and so on.

Freud the psychoanalyst recognized this simultaneity of desires but his text and his conscious argument find it difficult to do so. So, for instance, he will comment that Dora tells her mother things so that her mother will pass them on to her father; but, of course, it is *both*. Dora wants both to tell her mother *and* for her mother to tell her father (otherwise she could have chosen other ways). The conscious argument occludes the mother but writing also sometimes reveals a thought that has not yet come to consciousness: Dora's mother is written into text.

Endorsing the importance of Dora's gynaeocophilia, that is to say, her love for a woman, Frau K, who in psychoanalytic theory is the 'heir' to the mother, Lacan has emphasized that Dora becomes uninterested in Herr K only when she learns he doesn't want his wife, whom Dora adores. Herr K has told her, 'I get nothing from my wife', a phrase which repeats what her father told Freud about his own marital relations and which he may well have told his daughter (Dora recounts how as a child she was her father's confidante). The shift from looking at the father figure to centring on the mother figure was to be crucial in the future understanding of the psychoneurosis of hysteria. Its buried presence in the Dora case, however, was to be the focus of criticism – from both Freud himself and his psychoanalytic critics. However, this criticism misses the lability of hysterical desire. Dora tries to attract Herr K by becoming a little mother to his children, only to discover that nobody in her social world seems to want mothers as objects of their love. But there is no resting point for her desire. She becomes like her father in order to 'have' Frau K, just as she would once have wanted to be in his position to the mother she had imagined as her love object. Yet there is more, and other, to Dora's, or any girl's, wish to be male than that contained within the notorious theory of penis envy to which it gave rise.

By definition, an emotion is mobile. Too much emphasis has been put, first in the theory of hysteria and then in the theory of femininity (see chapter 6), on the girl and/or the hysteric moving from a primary love for the mother to a secondary love for the father and back again to reinforce the first as the 'truest' (Frau K over Herr Bauer or Herr K). It is the lability itself that counts, rather than the object: Dora is desperate for attention from whomsoever she can get it. When she realizes this attention is not genuine (i.e. is motivated by love for another, not herself) as in the case of a governess (who flattered her as a means of access to her father) and then Frau K (who loves her because she really loves her father just as Dora loves the K children because she really wants Herr K's attention), she is, in both her own and in Freud's account, beside herself with fury. When is one 'beside oneself' except when one has been displaced, one's place occupied by another?

While Dora's mother has been ignored by Dora, Herr Bauer, Freud and critics alike, there is one even more strikingly buried player in Dora's life history: her brother Otto, older by eighteen months. Otto is mentioned, but only in passing, and his significance as a main actor in Dora's condition totally overlooked: 'During the girl's earlier years, her only brother . . . had been the model which her ambitions had striven to follow,' says Freud. 'Her brother was as a rule the first to start the illness and used to have it very slightly, and she would then follow suit with a severe form of it.'[11] May she not likewise have learnt that, although she caught all her childhood illnesses from her brother and managed to have them extremely severely, this did not make her the most wanted child?

I referred earlier to Freud's comment on how sickness was a means whereby a child wrested the parent's attention from another sibling: 'A little girl in her greed for love does not enjoy having to share the affection of her parents with her brothers and sisters; and she notices that the whole of their affection is lavished on her once more whenever she arouses their anxiety by falling ill.'[12] Dora's brother Otto appears in the associations to the first dream: Dora's father is saving his two children from a fire but his wife wants to stop to rescue her jewelcase. Dora's association is to a recent argument between her parents about her mother wanting to lock at night the door to the dining-room which was the only way out of her brother's room. The association leads Dora to recollections, first that her brother wet himself at night and during the day and then, after some resistance, that she, Dora, had also done this until just before her first nervous asthma attack at the age of eight. Dora also has a memory of a scene from her infancy when she merged with her older brother, holding on to his ear while she sexually gratified herself. Following the usual Oedipal emphasis, Lacan sees this as the emblematic scene which sets the way for her later identification with her father, her merging with a boy later becomes her tendency to identify with a man. A lengthy footnote, the only extended discussion of Dora's brother, however, can lead the argument in a totally different direction:

Dora's brother must have been concerned in some way with her having acquired the habit of masturbation; for in this connection she told me, with all the emphasis which betrays the presence of a 'screen memory', that her brother used regularly to pass on all his infectious illnesses to her, and that while he used to have them lightly she used, on the contrary, to have them severely . . . In the dream her brother as well as she was saved from 'destruction'; . . . he, too, had been subject to bed-wetting, but had got over the habit before his sister . . . Her declaration that she had been able to keep abreast with her brother up to the time of her first illness, but that after that she had fallen behind him in her studies, was in a certain sense also a 'screen memory'. It was as though she had been a boy up till that moment, and had then become girlish for the first time. She had in truth been a wild creature; but after the 'asthma' she became quiet and well-behaved. That illness formed the boundary between two phases of her sexual life, of which the first was masculine in character, and the second feminine.[13]

Although it is attached to a real occurrence, a 'screen memory' is not a replica of actual events but a resumé of what has been significant in the form of an icon that stands in for the overall experience. In this case Dora sees herself as her brother's equal (or as being the *same* as her brother) until her asthma attack. We need to look at this 'sameness' of Dora and her brother. When Freud first asks Dora about bedwetting, she recalls that her brother's problems went on to his sixth or seventh year; she then acknowledges that she too bedwet, but not for so long – not, she says, until her 'seventh or eighth year'. This slip suggests a number of possibilities. It may indicate the confusion between herself and her brother in Dora's mind, as she would have been six when he was seven and seven when he was eight. But it is notable that Dora's enuresis lasts until just before the onset of her nervous asthma at the age of eight – it may therefore be that, as with the infectious illnesses, Dora has this problem more severely than her brother. Certainly a doctor was brought in to treat her problem whereas there is no mention of this with her brother. At the time bedwetting was thought to indicate masturbation or sexual abuse. Shortly before treating Dora, Freud had written to Fliess of a male patient: '. . . a child who regularly wets his bed until his seventh year, must have experienced sexual excitation in his earlier childhood. Spontaneous or by seduction?'[14] Freud linked this childhood bedwetting and Dora's current vaginal discharge with her ultimate secret of the masturbation she practised in childhood and perhaps was continuing in the present. At the time of the treatment, masturbation was a dominant topic in general medical and paediatric circles. When, however, Freud surveyed his case history and added his footnotes in 1923, more than twenty years after the initial writing of 'Dora', he criticized his earlier overriding emphasis on the etiological significance of masturbation. By the 1920s masturbation was no longer thought to cause madness.

If we put the few references to Otto together, an interesting picture emerges of Dora's hysteria. Illness was, is, a standard means of getting more attention when one is jealous of one's siblings. However, this general observation needs to be placed in the specific situation of Dora, which in turn may lead us back to a general observation. Dora merges with her brother while she sucks her thumb and pulls his ear, an image that both Freud and Lacan see as her key masturbatory position. As well as leading to a later masculine identification, Dora is simply pleasing herself in an infantile trance state. Otto becomes the model for her ambitions. Until she was eight she would have rivalled, envied, emulated and tried to surpass the brother with whom she was closely identified. As well as indicating masturbatory habits, micturation often stands for ambition; bedwetting is in general a sexual symptom; certainly wetness (in particular diseased fluids or untimely oozings) is the currency of sexuality within this case history. Whether or not there was sexual play between brother and sister beyond the infantile masturbation, there clearly was an identification from Dora to her brother which suddenly received a catastrophic setback when she was about eight. This catastrophe was, I suggest, triggered by the doctor who was called in to deal with her enuresis. At this point, unconscious hysterical symptoms replaced the fraternal identification. Dora was a bright, precocious child, so much so that her father made her his confidante early on. Of such children, Freud writes that Oedipal love is 'more intense from the very first in the case of those children . . . who develop prematurely and have a craving for love'.[15] Otto sided with his mother in family disputes; in modelling her ambitions on her brother, Dora would very likely have been disappointed in the lesser attention she would have got from her mother and instead fixated early on her father by way of compensation. The Oedipal story is the result of Dora's failure to be like, as good as, or just *be* her brother. It is the sibling situation that thrusts Dora back on to loving her mother and her father.

This, then, is Dora's story: as an infant she merged with her older brother, as small children do with older ones; as a young child she wanted to be like him in every way. The scanty evidence and the circumstantial likelihood indicate that her mother gave more attention to Otto than to Dora, who did her best to remedy this situation by always having the normal childhood illnesses, which she caught from him, more severely in order to get more attention. At eight, something to do with her continuing enuresis and the consultation with a doctor was catastrophic. The doctor emphasized that Dora's enuresis was due to nervous weakness and then, when asthma took over, that her chest was weak, too. Outbidding her brother in illness had led to Dora being the weaker vessel and Otto the stronger. With this understanding Dora became demure and feminine, turned for love to her father and grew apart from her brother. Freud suggests that Dora was relieved the doctor did not discover her secret masturbation. I suggest she was also intensely disappointed; the doctor did not acknowledge that Dora could get sexual pleasure just as easily as could her brother. Boys may masturbate but girls have weak bladders hidden inside their bodies. Dora was thus granted neither a masculine status nor a very positive feminine one.

After the doctor's visit, Dora could not be a boy, yet to be a girl was to be weak and ill. The history shows her trying to find her place in the family. Herr Bauer had encouraged his daughter's love by confiding in her and then betrayed this intimacy by demonstrating its insignificance in comparison with his 'secret' sexual love for Frau K. Her father's relegation of Dora to childhood by this preference, after his elevation of her to femininity, foreshadowed the similar acts of the governess and Frau K, who first confided their amatory secrets to her and then made her realize she was only a conduit to her father. She thought she was wanted as a woman, only to be told she was a child. When sharing confidences turned out not to be a guarantee of femininity, Dora tried the other possibility: becoming a little mother to attract some attention to herself as a potential woman – but Herr K, though attracted by this pose, wanted her not as a mother for his children but as a sexual object. This was exactly the position Dora had had to abandon when her father had his affair with Frau K and stopped confiding his secrets to her.

While as a teenager Otto Bauer insisted that it was important not to be overinvolved with the troubles of their parents, his sister became obsessed with them; he got out while she got deeper and deeper in. But there was, in fact, no place for her there in the family where she was neither boy, girl nor woman, yet neither was there any position she could assume outside the network of kith and kin, as we can imagine Otto as a young man at the turn of the century was able to find.

The social relationship, then, that had triggered Dora's Oedipal desires and the failure of their resolution was a sibling one. She had wanted to be positioned as a child in the family like her brother, only to discover that she was not like him in gender and that (probably) he, first-born and male, had their mother's love. So, having turned to her father in her new demureness and weakness, she was first rewarded and then rejected. We learn that Dora's friendship with her brother was over but it had provided a basis for future jealousy, love and hate. All these found expression in hysterical wanting – her desperate 'greed for love' and her deeply depressed sense that she was lacking. Both Dora's femininity and her hysteria would seem to have been dependent on her not having a defined position within the family. They both emerged in her eighth year with the collapse of her active masturbation and her assumption both of 'femininity' and of hysterical asthma.

In another case of childhood hysteria (a phenomenon that was widely discussed in the last decades of the nineteenth century) Krafft-Ebing, in 1877, described an 8-year-old girl who had masturbated from the age of four and who engaged in intercourse with boys who were ten to twelve years old; the girl had even contemplated murdering her parents so she could enjoy herself with boys.[16] Though abuse was much discussed in medical circles at the time, precocious sexuality was considered a sign of emotional instability where today we would certainly hypothesize an earlier sexually abusive relationship. The point here is that childhood hysteria was already recognized and commented upon at the time of the treatment of Dora. However, although Freud clearly states the onset of Dora's hysteria in childhood, he makes little of it. Neither his commentators nor critics seem to notice it either. What is therefore missed is that Dora's hysteria *precedes* her being an object of exchange between men who each are old enough to be her father. Although subsequently there are a number of indications of Dora making a father identification, the hysteria emanates in childhood from the moment of the breakdown of her identification with *her brother*.

Looking back on her childhood, Dora is confused about ages – which, as already discussed, points to a fusion between herself and Otto. If Dora became a demure little girl and a hysteric in her eighth year, Otto, then nine or ten, would have been about to go to the Gymnasium for boys – leaving Dora, who was very bright, only the somewhat limited classes for young ladies as her educational future. Freud argued that Dora was relieved that the doctor did not discover her masturbation when he investigated her bedwetting – although this may also mean she despised doctors as stupid. In fact, by failing to acknowledge that Dora could masturbate and that she could therefore have pleasure just like her brother, the doctor, with his diagnosis of 'nervous weakness' of the bladder (and then the chest), dashed her hopes and turned her into 'a little girl' – with all the disadvantages this implies.

'I know nothing about myself,' was her reply, 'but my brother used to wet his bed up till his sixth or seventh year; and it used sometimes to happen to him in the daytime too.'

I was on the point of remarking to her how much easier it is to remember things of that kind about one's brother than about oneself, when she continued the train of recollections which had been revived: 'Yes, I used to do it too, for some time, but not until my seventh or eighth year. It must have been serious, because I remember now that the doctor was called in. It lasted till a short time before my nervous asthma.'

'And what did the doctor say to it?'

'He explained it as a nervous weakness; it would soon pass off, he thought; and he prescribed a tonic.'[17]

From masturbatory bedwetting to femininity via the doctor's tonic; a femininity in which Dora tries first to be a passive sexual object and then an active mother: neither work for her. She wants to be her brother, and in her brother's position. Her hysteria takes over this longing. But Dora's slippage from six or seven to eight years is ignored by Freud. Such slips of the tongue should be the very matter of psychoanalysis. This could well indicate that Freud unconsciously wanted to avoid the significance of Dora's relation to Otto, which would have placed in jeopardy his emerging emphasis on the Oedipus complex, which was to become and to remain the shibboleth of psychoanalysis.

Confirming this Oedipal and pre-Oedipal emphasis, Lacan gave a brilliant, and now well-known description, of the foundation of the ego in what he described as the 'mirror phase'. The baby who puts the spoon in its ear experiences its body as uncoordinated. If it looks in a mirror it sees itself as unified. The chaotic, atotic movements of the infant become cohered in a unified *gestalt*.[18] This is an inverted image (a mirror image) which illusionally coheres what would otherwise be experienced as fragmented. The British analyst and paediatrician, Donald Winnicott adopted and changed this notion, seeing in the mother's regard, the mirror which reflects the infant's self.[19] Though different, both accounts have validity. But they both miss the peer and sibling as mirror. An infant, even of a few months, becomes joyfully engaged with the kinesics and movements, facial games and grimaces of another child in a way that is quite different from its relationship with either a mirror or a mirroring by the mother. The playful movements, facial expressions, gambolling of this older child surely also act as appropriate containers for the still uncoordinated movements of the infant?

Dora had no younger sibling, no one arrived to depose her from her sense of where she stood, i.e. her position as baby. But looking in the mirror of her brother she would have seen her unitary self. In Otto, Dora had a focus for her identification with another child. Here was a sibling whom she could be the same as, but over whom she could also excel through illness to get attention from parents and physicians, if the going got tough and he was preferred. But when she tried for Otto's sexual position through their shared masturbation (their bedwetting), her masturbation was not noticed; instead, she was said to have a weak bladder and her place was to stay weak and ill. To suggest that some actual sexual relationship took place between Otto and Ida (Dora) is not far-fetched. The recurrent dream of the fire and the associations to wetting oneself are highly indicative of sibling incest. When Dora assumed the place of her own suitor in the second dream, in her journey through the woods to the station, could this not suggest that a sibling sexual relationship has further assisted her confusion with a lateral male – not a vertical, intergenerational one like her father or Herr K?

Having an older brother, Dora is exiled from her boy-like self just as effectively as she would have been had she had a younger sibling. She tries for an Oedipal relationship instead. But her mother is already captivated by her first child, Dora's brother; Dora tries (and for a time succeeds) in winning her father instead. This pursuit of the father, however, is still a part of her craving for a mother. But so long as an analysis only charts the trajectory of the intergenerational wanting, the reason why hysteria falls to women will be missed along with the various secondary places accorded to sisters in any kinship system. Hysteria itself will also be missed or said to 'disappear'. The hysteric feels catastrophically displaced, non-existent, because another stands in his place. The desperate, exuberant protests, the labile identifications and demonstrative sexualizing of every contact are a way of asserting an existence that has gone missing. Dora is trying to find a place for herself.

When Dora came to Freud for treatment, to Breuer's disparagement, he had been treating 'E' for five years. In the very middle of the Dora case we find this statement:

When, in a hysterical woman or girl, the sexual libido which is directed towards men has been energetically suppressed, it will regularly be found that the libido which is directed towards women has become vicariously reinforced and even to some extent conscious. *I shall not in this place go any further into this important subject, which is especially indispensable to an understanding of hysteria in men.* [My italics][20]

What is Freud referring to here? Is this a suppressed Don Juan turning to men? If so, this indicates not homosexuality but the bisexuality of hysteria. What is important here is how, once again, when the question of sexuality arises in conjunction with male hysteria, it is rapidly put aside. But the same is true for the relationship between death and female hysteria.

Object Relations psychoanalysis and much feminist analysis has rallied to the impossible predicament of Dora used as an object of exchange at the expense of realizing that there is something deadly at the centre. The case history itself does not seem to notice it. Dora comes to treatment because of a threatened suicide; she tells the story (that has been made more complete by the brief therapy) to the bereaved Ks and no mention is made of any concern for the dead child she is supposed once to have loved. Herr K is transfixed by her as she walks past ignoring him, and he is knocked over by a carriage (in a footnote to this incident Freud comments on the possibility of suicide by proxy). The male hysteric and his sexuality, the female and her courting of death and destruction, need to be brought together.

4

Where Has All the Hysteria Gone?

'Within a few years the concept of hysteria will belong to history
... There is no such disease and there never has been.'

A. Steyerthal, 'Was ist Hysterie?' (1908)

'This could well be the last book with "hysteria" in the title
written by a psychiatrist.'

Philip Slavney, *Perspectives on 'Hysteria'* (1990)

Throughout most of the twentieth century it has been supposed in
clinical and scientific circles that hysteria has disappeared. According
to this pervasive view, hysteria had a late Victorian heyday, a heroic
fin de siècle moment and, after more than 4,000 years of recorded
history, it simply vanished. But *what* exactly disappeared? And what
do we mean by 'disappeared'? Hysteria has had both a medical and
a colloquial usage. However, it is only as a medical diagnosis or
pathological entity that it has apparently disappeared. As a descriptive
term for a mode of behaviour, it has been used from at least the
eighteenth century BC, when the first known inscription concerning
an equivalent condition was made on Egyptian papyrus. Hysteria's
appearance and disappearance must, then, have as much to do with
the rise and change of medical practice in the twentieth century as
with the absence or presence of hysteria itself.

What, then, of hysteria's reappearance at the end of the twentieth
century? The hundredth anniversary in 1995 of the publication of
Breuer's and Freud's *Studies on Hysteria* became an occasion for the
psychoanalytic and, to some degree, psychiatric worlds to reconsider

'hysteria'. But these centenary analyses did little more to sustain serious interest than the sporadic conferences held on the subject that have taken place throughout the century. However, they are at least acknowledgements from the clinical edge of a veritable fascination with hysteria that has been emerging within the Humanities and Women's Studies departments of universities, particularly in North America, as the century changes. Repressed in the medical or clinical context for much of the twentieth century, hysteria has returned with a vengeance in the academies. When Ilza Veith wrote *Hysteria: The History of a Disease* in 1965, except from France, there were very few articles and even fewer books on the subject – and these were mostly out of print. However, by 1993, the Modern Language Association of North America was listing sixty-seven theses submitted for that year with 'hysteria' in their title. The American historian Mark Micale noted some 400 studies made in the decade from the mid 1980s to the mid 1990s.[1] Nevertheless, hysteria had still not reappeared as a clinical diagnosis.

Many explanations of hysteria's disappearance from the Western world, and several concerning its reappearance, have been forthcoming from a number of quarters. After noting some of those connected with its disappearance that seem pertinent, I shall look at the question within a psychoanalytic framework. I shall argue that the disappearance of hysteria as a diagnosis is connected with the advent of male hysteria as a discovery (or, more accurately, rediscovery) in the last decades of the nineteenth century and again during the First World War. Hysteria 'disappeared' into its psychoanalytic 'cure' and re-emerged as the trauma theories (Recovered Memory syndrome and False Memory syndrome) of contemporary therapies. This 'cure' involves the centrality in both the theory and the practice of the Oedipus complex. More importantly, clinical hysteria has disappeared into various modes of behaviour in the community – which is why the colloquial use of the term is as prevalent as ever.

In Micale's 1995 account, during hysteria's latter years the concept had become so overextended as a diagnostic term that it seemed as though everything and anything, from an eating disturbance to a major breakdown, could be labelled 'hysterical'. Before hysteria was broken down into its alleged constituent parts, it had been an all-inclusive term; so it slowly ceased to have any diagnostic value until it was deconstructed and its parts reclassified. However, this all-inclusive nature of hysteria is not new. If one is to chart the rise and fall of the popularity of hysteria as a diagnostic category, it seems important to specify its distinctive features at a particular historical time.

The diagnosis of hysteria had declined to near vanishing point by the First World War. During this period there were major nosographical and nosological changes, so that what had previously gone under the name of hysteria became classified as something else. Effectively, a large, general category was broken up into numerous smaller units. Where Charcot, in Freud's terms, had brought 'law and order' to an amorphous complaint by arranging and classifying its myriad symptoms, turn-of-the-century doctors proceeded to break apart its elephantine structure. New neurological and biochemical tests enabled the separation of first epilepsy, then syphilis, from their contamination by hysterical disorders that could look the same. The discovery of X-rays and the increasing sophistication of physiological and organic testing furthered the process of the appropriation of the mental by the physical.

From the field of psychiatry at the turn of this century a new understanding of psychosis also snatched territory from hysteria. Within the context of diagnosis, the final deathblow was probably delivered by the interwar concept of psychosomatics which formulated a causal relationship between mind and body, where previously the process of the formation of conversion symptoms in hysteria (in which an idea in the mind is expressed in the body) had been regarded as largely mysterious. Micale notes:

A more or less unbroken textual record of hysteria runs from the Ancient Greeks to Freud. Yet in recent generations, a drastic diminution in the rate of occurrence of hysterical neuroses has taken place. Furthermore, those cases that have appeared tend clinically to be much simpler and less flamboyant than their counterparts in centuries past. This development has now been registered in the official rosters of mental diseases, which have deleted the hysteria diagnosis. After twenty centuries of medical history, this extraordinary disease is for all intents and purposes disappearing from sight today. Nobody knows why.[2]

Micale's partial explanation that the whole has been decomposed into the many parts seems borne out by the medical facts. Some of the most widely known syndromes of today, such as anorexia nervosa and multiple personality disorder were once subgroups of hysteria. Its post-First World War large-scale dismantling, nevertheless, left something of hysteria intact. Micale's argument calls hysteria's disappearance an 'illusion' or a 'pseudo-disappearance'. Reading Micale's account it is as though, if we search through the cupboard of now carefully separated items, we will find one, a bag of left-over bits, marked 'hysteria'. There is some contradiction here: Did this 'extraordinary' disease, as Micale puts it, vanish or did it get deconstructed and largely relabelled?

There have been other versions of the story of hysteria's disappearance, usually more romantic than Micale's. Etienne Trillat discusses the mystery of its vanishing in his major history of hysteria in France, published in 1986, which concludes: *L'hystérie est morte, c'est entendu. Elle a emporté avec elle ses énigmes dans sa tombe'* (Hysteria is dead, that's for sure, and has taken its mysteries with it to the grave).'[3] Two decades before this Ilza Veith argued that the end of hysteria's mystery was the end of hysteria. By way of explanation, Veith suggests that Freud's work on hysteria in the 1890s demystified it; and that, without its mystery, there was no profit or so-called 'secondary gain' to be had for the patient from producing it. Such an argument takes the manipulative behaviour of the hysteric (which certainly exists, but as one among a number of characteristics) as the condition's defining feature. This is untenable in itself and the argument is historically highly dubious, for, whatever their diverse explanations – whether of genetic degeneracy, wandering wombs, nervous predisposition, being in league with the Devil or sexual abuse – most epochs have 'understood' hysteria in their own ways. However, such comprehension has singularly failed to deter its practitioners. The 'mystery' approach – when it was jokingly renamed 'mysteria' – took a particular Western nineteenth-century view, which linked hysteria to a specific version of femininity as itself a 'mystery'. For Veith's thesis to have validity, the understanding of hysteria reached by Freud would need to have been absolute and definitive. Neither hysteria as a mental illness nor psychoanalysis, with its aspirations to scientific status, could pretend to such a complete explanation: as an object and as a method of research, both illness and any understanding of it resist closure. However, Veith's argument does raise the issue of the relationship between a changing medical practice and its illnesses.

The nineteenth-century Western medicalization of hysteria did lead in various ways to its eventual decomposition and to new specific categories. The increased psychologization of hysteria, for instance, led away from notions either of hereditary or organic degeneracy. In itself this may have contributed to hysteria's apparent demise. Looking at chlorosis (the green sickness) and the other somatic complaints in nineteenth-century Britain, the historian of science Karl Figlio noted how, once these physical illnesses came to be seen as psychological, they also tended to vanish. It may well be, however, that the psychological aspect of comprehension, not comprehension in itself, is the vanishing point. Freud observed how a diagnosis of hysteria in a sanatorium was the end not the beginning of the matter: there was no further interest to be taken in the patient. Even today, we still use psychological diagnoses as though they were tantamount to saying there is nothing there. The step from dismissal to disappearance may not be so very large. A conflictual tension would then exist: as psychiatry increasingly medicalizes itself, some of its illnesses become valid and treatable while others disappear into the colloquialism which dictates that, if it is all in the mind, it does not exist. In English, at least, the hysteric may parody this process: turning a medical *complaint* into a personal *complaint*. Unlike most other 'mental illnesses', no one has yet proposed that one can treat hysteria with a drug, which may therefore account for making it a particularly suitable candidate for 'disappearance' from psychiatry and for its prevalence in the colloquial.

Rather remarkably, there has been no explicit protest about the oddity of the sudden disappearance of hysteria. However, as though there were nevertheless somewhere an almost unconscious awareness of the peculiarity of the situation, the most recent scholarship has started to argue for the non-existence of hysteria in other historical periods as well. Into this category we can place Helen King's claim that the notion that Hippocrates was the father of the Western medical diagnosis of hysteria can now be forever discredited. The idea of hysteria in ancient Greece was, King argues, a Renaissance invention, something read back from a period with a diagnosis of hysteria on to a condition which, misleadingly, appeared similar. In King's argument, what the Greeks described bears no resemblance to Renaissance or nineteenth-century accounts of hysteria. The Greeks explained many conditions as emanating from the malfunctioning of women's reproductive organs; to King, descriptions of comparable symptoms such as fits, choking, breathing difficulties and a late translation of a Greek adjective for things uterine as 'hysteria', does not make for the same illness. And just as King questions the presence of hysteria in Greece, so other scholars such as Merskey and Potter have also shown how what a previous generation believed was 'hysteria' in the descriptions of the Ebers and Kahun gynaecological papyri of Ancient Egypt, was not 'really' any such thing. With these scholars' work, the twentieth-century 'disappearance' of hysteria takes on a new dimension: Has hysteria ever existed at all as an entity that can be defined? The question from the historians must be asked of its clinicians.

It is common to hear both psychiatrists and psychoanalysts dispute hysteria's existence in such a way that is unclear whether they are describing a twentieth-century phenomenon or endorsing the perspective of the historians, with whose arguments they are unlikely to be familiar, who claim it never existed. However, the picture is not completely uniform. During the 1930s the psychoanalysts Sandór Ferenczi, in Budapest, and Ronald Fairbairn, in Edinburgh, were both interested; more recently, British psychoanalyst Eric Brenman prefaced his contribution to a panel on hysteria in the early 1980s with the observation that when he had discussed the subject with colleagues none could define it and none actually used the category. However, everyone recognized hysteria and found the recognition useful whenever they encountered its presence in a patient.

From a medical psychiatric perspective, Philip Slavney writes:

... *although the word ['hysteria'] is used daily in the practice of medicine* [my italics], 'those who would like to drop it once and for all' seem to have won the battle for control of psychiatric nomenclature, and the next generation of clinicians will no longer find it indispensable when they wish to indicate certain traits and behaviours. *Hysteria, hysteric* and *hysterical* are on the verge of becoming anachronisms.[4]

So absolute has been hysteria's clinical 'disappearance' that the *USA Diagnostic and Statistical Manuals* (DSM) II and III from the 1950s onwards do not list it; instead, it has been replaced by the concept of the 'histrionic personality disorder'. The argument for the shift is manifold: that hysteria presents itself with such variation as to be a meaningless concept; that especially in its most dramatic form, so-called 'conversion hysteria', it has vanished; that its variegated history is confusing – as Slavney says, it has 'so many irrelevant historical connotations'; that the word 'hysteria' is opprobrious. Commenting on the confusion of the concept, Slavney tries to pin down the butterfly by dividing hysteria into three types: a disease of the body that can afflict the mind; an affliction of the mind expressed through the body; and behaviour that produces the appearance of a disease. He examines the history of its treatment as a disease, as a dimension of the personality, as goal-directed behaviours, as life stories. But this division of the way hysteria is regarded, whilst interesting, is established by Slavney only in order to toll its death knell.

The paradox of the presence or absence of hysteria within psychiatry is, then, yet starker than the general observation. The 1980 *Diagnostic and Statistical Manual* continues its earlier elimination of hysteria, but 'histrionic personality disorder' seems a thin disguise, especially as it is usually referred to as HPD, in which the 'H' is understood indifferently as either hysterical or histrionic. A sufferer must show significant distress or maladaptive social or occupational behaviour. According to the definitions of the *DSMs*, the histrionic patient is always performing, choosing a number of different parts selected to suit the environment. HPD is characterized by excessive emotionality and attention-seeking. Placating and demanding behaviour follow each other in quick succession; found almost always in women, it is nevertheless a masquerade of femininity. The problem arises when we realize that a prospective patient must display four of the eight criteria for diagnoses that define this behaviour; but, as there are eight criteria, it is possible that any two patients can have no overlap of their defining features. In fact, the eight categories are really no more than specifications of general qualities. The psychiatric diagnosis is only an updated version of what one Victorian churchman described as 'the charm of the feminine in excess is the frenzy of the hysteric'.

Or it could be read as a version of King's account of 'diseases of women' in Hippocratic medicine. Thus, when hysteria disappears as an illness, its left-over attributes are ascribed to 'women's behaviour' or to the characteristics of femininity.

Although Micale has observed that the 'fall' side of the rise and fall of diseases in general is rarely investigated, the extreme lack of intellectual curiosity about hysteria's sudden demise seems remarkable. If hysteria does not exist, what were our nineteenth-century medical predecessors describing? What were women suffering from? A defining feature of hysteria is that it is mimetic: it may be that its very 'disappearance', its reappearance in the academies of today and its stop–go characteristic in earlier epochs, are themselves imitations of a condition. This I believe to be as much the case with the general historical situation as it is of the individual and personal one. Hysteria may have been divided into other illnesses or apparently have lost its appeal on being comprehended, but, endlessly imitative, it has also vanished and reappeared with fashion in an unconscious game of hide and seek.

What then is this disappearance? It is certainly not one thing; for no single explanation will suffice. Although I believe beyond a shadow of a doubt that hysteria 'exists', indeed that human beings could not exist without its potentiality, its so-called 'disappearance' is an important feature of its contemporary existence. For that reason, I shall note pertinent explanations of its disappearance and conclude with a more general speculation. A fragmentation of the syndrome has occurred, so that hysterical manifestations have each become separate psychological or medical entities. But, if hysteria's 'disappearance' is also an illustration of its mimetic ability, then it may have moved from being a disease to becoming a characterological trait. If hysteria has been 'solved', 'cured' and dispensed with as a medical or psychiatric category, then renamed as 'histrionic personality', the hysteric may imitate the cure which no longer treats him as an ill, but rather as a disturbed, person. While the nineteenth-century Alice James, sister of novelist Henry and philosopher William James, took to her bed with paralysis, twentieth-century poet Anne Sexton dressed and performed flamboyantly, twisting and contorting her body, because, in her own words, 'she didn't know she had one' (see chapter 7). That it is no longer diagnosed as a *disease* does not necessitate that there is no longer hysteria. I believe hysteria is still prevalent, even as a serious pathology – as indeed Anne Sexton's proved to be, resulting in her child abuse and suicide. It can also masquerade as normative behaviour – as, for instance, in the case of compulsive Don Juans or 'honest' Iagos (see chapter 8). As a characterological trait it is easily absorbed into the general culture – particularly where performance is valorized.

The psychoanalytic division of hysteria into two types has prevailed in many medical, psychiatric and psychoanalytic circles in this century. The division is into 'anxiety' and 'conversion' hysteria. No one denies that anxiety may, at least in a colloquial way, make people behave hysterically. In a clinical context anxiety hysteria is most commonly manifest in phobias. Phobias are very widespread in the community, but they are also true clinical symptoms because they reveal the element of conflict between a wish and its prevention which, for psychoanalysis at least, defines a symptom. 'Conversion' hysteria was first named and explained by Freud. When it is argued that hysteria has vanished, it is usually 'conversion' hysteria that is being referred to. According to Freudian theory, an idea that cannot be expressed is 'converted' into a bodily symptom – one of the meanings behind a patient's frequent choking fits was that he had decided that it was better to swallow 'a can of worms' than to open it, but it had 'stuck in his craw'. What is relevant to hysteria's so-called disappearance is that twentieth-century forms of treatment do not favour manifestations in bodily enactments. The practice of administering psychotropic drugs, electric shock treatment or brain surgery, or the restriction of the patient to the limited time and place of a consulting room where only talk is allowed, inhibit the flamboyant forms of mental illness that once flourished either in lunatic asylums or in family homes.

The phenomenon of 'conversion hysteria' has largely been replaced by the notion of 'psychosomatic illness' – in these organic conditions there is quite evidently no organic cause, but there is no conflictual element as in a hysterical conversion symptom or a phobia. The concept of the 'psychosomatic' is always presented as a step forwards, but actually it resolves the mind–body interaction by reducing it. By assuming that the mind and the body relate to separate areas but are in a mutually influential relationship to each other, it restores the very Cartesian dualism that 'conversion hysteria', and earlier psychoanalysts' preoccupation with the understanding of it, first called in question. Without doubt there are psychosomatic conditions, but psychosomatic and conversion are not substitutable terms. The conversion symptom expresses an idea through the body, an idea which has been repressed but which has returned as a bodily expression. In the psychosomatic illness there are clear disturbances of physiological function. Someone may be reluctant to leave home because he does not yet feel independent. Were the results to be an unusual vulnerability to skin rashes so that he stays in the family home, then he would be succumbing to a psychosomatic condition. If the wish not to leave home were because of a conflict between his wish to rely on his father and his wish to kill him, it might be that he did not want to 'stand on his own two feet', which this symptom would facilitate. Were one of his legs to become paralysed he would have produced a hysterical conversion symptom.

The classic psychoanalytical treatment asks the patient to suspend deliberate, conscious thought, that is, to 'free associate'. It is a difficult task. There may be no thoughts. But more usual is that many different thoughts crowd in simultaneously and, from habit, the patient tries to select or create a dominant thought. But this non-selection and non-hierarchization is one manifest expression of what is called 'the primary process'. It is also an essential mode of hysteria. The psychoanalytic method of treatment releases what we could call a hysterical characteristic of thought and then tries to put everything into organized words. It subjects simultaneity to the structures and hierarchies of language: in other words, if it is successful, the psychoanalytic practice utilizes and then eliminates one of the manifestations of hysteria.

Contemporary concern with eliminating hysteria, either as a clinical entity, or as a useful heuristic concept, is also part and parcel of the fashion for attacking all claims of anything to universality. Along with such an assault on universalism goes a critique of the transhistorical. Hysteria, with its 4,000 years of recorded history and its worldwide crosscultural presence, is clearly an appropriate representative of those two *bêtes noires* of contemporary, particularly post-modern, thought: universalism and essentialism. Obviously, everything is unique and therefore nothing can be absolutely universal. There are, however, some general conditions within which people exist which will not be identical but will have sufficient shared features to elicit responses, which are both general and specific. Hysteria, I believe, is one such response. The current shift in perspective may suggest that what is at issue is not so much a challenge to the existence of hysteria as a challenge to universalism as such. If this is the case, then once more the problem is not with hysteria but with the thought systems that are operating to define or eliminate it.

Hysteria may well not be a disease, or rather it may be a 'disease' only in cultures which confine certain behaviours to the 'disease' category. It makes more sense, therefore, to limit the disease category to a historically specific time and place than to relinquish what is observed, both as subjective experience and as objective phenomenon. Different epochs and different cultures have had, and still have, their own explanations for hysteria: the most prevalent late twentieth-century Western view is that it does not really exist. However, hysteria escapes our range of definitions, in particular definitions which try, as psychiatry does, to produce *diseases* of the mind.

Ancient Greek Hippocratic medicine did not distinguish in the same way as its twentieth-century equivalent does between the physical and imaginary movement of the uterus (*pnix hystericus*); according to Hippocrates, the various movements of the womb, whatever their origins, could lead to suffocation, vomiting, speechlessness, coma. The English Renaissance (via Italy) adopted and adapted 'suffocation of the mother' as a synonym for hysteria. But this lack of distinction between the physical and the imaginary does not mean that the condition described was not therefore what we would understand as hysteria; all it indicates is that this particular distinction between organic and non-organic was alien to Greek modes of thought. Indeed, it has been argued that the Greeks were systematically trying to root hysterical symptoms in biological causes. In the movement of passion through the mind and the body, Greek thought resonates more with that aspect of hysteria than does our own. By contrast with classical Greek thought, a common understanding in the twentieth-century Western world is of a particular set of physiological symptoms for which no organic basis can be found. But again, this definition is dependent on our medical culture that 'murders to dissect', a culture built on differentiation as a basis for classification. Once again, it is not that hysteria is necessarily organic or non-organic, but that our definition always demands a distinction between the two. This creates problems, for such distinctions may not have mattered to the ancient Greeks or the twentieth-century Taita.

If a high degree of mimetic behaviour is possible for hysteria as it manifests itself in the individual, surely it is possible for it to act similarly within a society? Also, given that hysteria can act positively in an active identification with another disease or a condition, so that it looks, for instance, like epilepsy, it would be likely that it can also act negatively – it can become an 'invisible illness'. The issue then becomes not so much that later medical or religious ideologies have ascribed a condition to a society that itself did not recognize it, as King suggests happened to ancient Greece via the Renaissance, but rather why some societies recognize and name certain states and behaviours as hysterical (or with a word such as *saka*, which can translate as hysteria) and others do not do so.

The feminism of the 1970s was very largely responsible for the reappearance of hysteria in the academies. The women's liberation movement of the late 1960s had protested against the prevalent stigmatization of women as hysterical by accepting and then overturning its implications: the hysteric in her many guises – as a witch or as Dora – was a protofeminist heroine protesting against patriarchal oppression. In particular, she was refusing a situation where women are created definitionally as objects of exchange between men; being so-called 'sexual objects', in the idiom of the 1960s and 1970s. The 1980s both endorsed and questioned this interpretation of hysteria as a radical protest. Now the late second wave or 'third wave' of feminism sees that initial reascription as futile: hysteria has not shed its denigrating connotations and many feminists argue women should relinquish Dora – a lifelong hysteric – in favour of Ibsen's Nora (*The Doll's House*) as a model, a woman who renounces her hysterical dependence on father, then husband, to seek her full humanity through an alternative, female morality.

The 1990s have witnessed an increase in new disease entities of unknown origin. A question mark hangs over such conditions as muscular entropy or chronic fatigue syndrome – are they organic, caused either by physiological stress or viral infection, or are they psychological? The bridge category of 'psychosomatic' will not work for these diseases, as no particular psychological feature can be found and the 'diseases' are produced *en masse* by everyone, but neither as a contagious group phenomenon nor as an individual response. A psychosomatic illness belongs to a specific individual's conditions and life history, whereas these diseases are generic: many people, whatever their individual circumstances, can have them. These disease entities are mass events. After considerable research, Elaine Showalter, literary critic and historian of hysteria, has emphatically labelled them 'hysterical'. Considering them from a psychoanalytical perspective, one cannot be certain: there is no evidence available on these illnesses of the infantile conflict or of the overdetermined expression that characterizes hysteria. Although they lack the sexual factor, in some ways these illnesses are analogous to neurasthenia or the 'actual' neuroses of the last century. And equally, as with those earlier conditions, there is speculation about their organic, hereditary and environmental origins. Today's conditions are often ascribed to the stresses of the new technologies, as the earlier ones were made the responsibility of urban industrialization. They are mass experiences in an era of mass communication.

The 1990s, like the final decades of the previous century, have seen either an enormous increase in the amount, or in the recording of the amount (or most likely both), of sexual and physical abuse of children and of recollections by adults of abuse in their childhood. The notion of false reminiscences highlights the problem of the relationship between fantasy and reality. If these illnesses that trace their origin to abuse are not organic, if this abuse is more fantasy than actuality (relying thereby on past conflictual wishes), and if the telling of the story reveals an oscillation between amnesia and compulsive supervalency of thought about it, then there is a strong possibility that we have hysteria.

Most of the arguments for the disappearance of hysteria from the clinics of the Western world in the twentieth century seem to deploy some characteristic intrinsic to the nature of hysteria which is no longer visible, rather than account for its vanishing through some factor specific to the historical epoch. They do not, therefore, amount to explanations. Arguments that the psychology of the 'illness' of hysteria, its amorphousness, the opprobrious nature of the term, its effervescence in mimesis, are responsible for its demise, do not really add up. All these features, or equivalents, are found in other eras and places – they are a part of the hysterical condition and its treatments. The partial exception to this is Micale's account of the redefining of the hysteria concept at the turn of the century and the subsequent naming of its separate parts. But even with Micale's account of the deconstruction of hysteria we can find analogies: in the seventeenth century, certain features of what in other times were labelled hysteria fell under the designations 'melancholia' and 'hypochondria'.

There are, however, aspects of the 'disappearance' of hysteria in the twentieth century that I wish to emphasize which do not seem intrinsic to hysteria but rather relate to specific historical conditions – although again these are not unique. By this I do not mean to endorse a popular explanation that sexual liberation has done away with the need for hysterical symptoms because there are now no repressed desires that have to 'return' from unconsciousness as symptoms. Such an explanation makes little sense in terms either of the date of its demise in the first years of this century, or of the relationship between sexuality and psychoneurosis – however, it does lead to the possibility that the balance between perversion (enacted hysteria) and hysteria (fantasized perversion) may have swung in favour of perversion. I do believe, in addition to other explanations, that hysteria in the West specifically 'disappeared' into its psychoanalytic treatment. After the discoveries of psychoanalysis, language and the story (narrativity) instead of the body have been deployed by the hysteric as a major means of enacting a mental conflict. In such a situation, hysteria is not cured by psychoanalysis (although it can be), but rather it becomes camouflaged within linguistic mimesis and the Oedipal or pre-Oedipal constellation of the treatment that psychoanalysis imposes upon it. These are not, of course, exclusive explanations – they merely indicate how hysteria may appear to have disappeared when all it has in fact done is change colour.

The factors of the psychoanalytic cure and gender-specificity are related. Girls both have a predisposition to early language acquisition and a very different relationship from boys to the Oedipus complex. The shift during the century from psychoanalysis as an aspirant medical science to a therapeutic discourse has been paralleled by the shift from the predominance of the male analyst to the female therapist. It may be, as the historian of psychoanalysis John Forrester suggests, that a talking cure attracts women who are socially prescribed to be gossips;[5] what, however, interests me is that early language use, where sounds are being imitated, is more mimetic, as is second language learning, where imitation also plays a key role – it is this mimetic use of words that the hysteric, who is always engaged in regression, deploys. In organic conditions such as strokes, the patient loses speech in the order in which language was most recently acquired; in hysteria, he loses his first language and retains his second. Anne O spoke English not German, the Taita women sometimes use foreign words and are speechless in their own tongue. Hysterical language concerns archetypically a regression to the girl's identification with her mother, in which there is often a free play between sense and un-sense – a baby copies its mother but the mother also imitates her baby in early speech development. Language is not only symbolic and representational, it is also an imitative physical process of mouthing sounds. Just as, at the end of the nineteenth century, there was an exchange of melodrama between the theatre and the hysterical patient, in which each borrowed from the other, so today the hysteric is well able to imitate the process of putting what masquerades as a repressed idea into conscious words – a technique psychoanalysis originally learnt from the hysteric. Dora commenced her hysteria and femininity with her 'weak' body. More ill than her brother, and as a girl definitely assumed to be the weaker vessel, she went to her doctors with myriad sicknesses. After going to see Freud, however, she ended up telling her story.

The breaking up of hysteria into its constituent features confirms its gendering: multiple personality, borderline conditions, dissociative states, tales of infantile or childhood abuse, eating disorders (particularly anorexia and bulimia), witchcraft – all have a 70–95 per cent female population. When we ask, as with the non-orthodox religious practices described by I. M. Lewis, who are the actors of these illnesses, the answer is clear: women. There is, however, one 'illness' related to hysteria which did not at the outset have a distinctly female population:

schizophrenia. After the apparent 'disappearance' of hysteria earlier this century, schizophrenia, a 'new' illness, became the most prevalent of psychological illnesses; indeed it took over in popularity from hysteria for at least two-thirds of the twentieth century. In this connection I wish to emphasize what Micale omits to look at in detail: that it was the mad and psychotic dimensions of hysteria that became siphoned off into schizophrenia, which is not gender-specific.

In 1911 Eugen Bleuler in Zurich relabelled *dementia praecox* with Emil Kraepelin's 1893 term 'schizophrenia' – one of the psychoses. The label stuck. According to the Belgian historian of hysterical psychosis Katrien Libbrecht, schizophrenia absorbed patients who before would have been diagnosed as hysterical. This is contentious – many clinicians argue the other way around: that the earlier nineteenth-century hysterics were so mad that they should have been labelled psychotic. Schizophrenia has been an important category of mental illness throughout the twentieth century. However, today the diagnosis of 'borderline' is more likely than schizophrenia to have absorbed what was once hysteria. As Libbrecht notes: 'The hysterics of the past have become the borderlines of the present.'[6] The term 'borderline' indicates that the psychological malady sits on the border between neurosis and psychosis. Again, the idea that the diagnosis of 'borderline' has absorbed hysteria is contentious, but we should note that men are allowed to be schizophrenic or borderline – and male hysteria has to go somewhere. However, after a gender-neutral start, now more women than men are considered borderline. The familiar pattern reasserts itself: first schizophrenia, then borderline conditions start as gender-neutral and then become female-dominated. This certainly supports Libbrecht's contention that both incorporate hysteria.

What was happening in that initial take-over bid of hysteria by schizophrenia? Before he went to Berlin to practise as a psychoanalyst, Karl Abraham worked for three years with Bleuler and Jung at the Burghölzli clinic in Zurich. Afterwards he wrote to Freud comparing hysteria and *dementia praecox*, as he still called it. He and Freud discussed the differences. Abraham had proposed that, where the hysteric loves other people, the patient suffering from *dementia praecox* has withdrawn his libido on to himself, thus becoming predominantly narcissistic and apparently asexual but in reality autoerotic. In reply Freud comments that the hysteric clothes his early narcissistic autoeroticism in imagined love scenes of erotic meetings and seductions and is fascinated by them, whereas 'patients who turn towards dementia and lose their resemblance to hysterics produce their (sexually infantile) phantasies without resistance, as if these had now lost their value, rather as a man who has abandoned his hope of marriage throws away the souvenirs, ribbons, locks of hair etc., which have now become worthless'.[7] Freud also commented that Jung had been right to suggest that one could cure hysteria by producing the splitting processes requisite for a mild *dementia praecox*, what would today be called a 'schizoid' condition. This was, I think, correct.

The Zurich group, most notably Jung, did not consider that there was any possibility of a sexual etiology for schizophrenia – and an asexual account has almost invariably dominated the diagnosis. Indeed, Jung in particular was opposed to the notion of a sexual etiology for any of the neuroses. Freud's and Abraham's analysis of an etiology for schizophrenia involving autoeroticism had no staying power; the idea that it was asexual won the day. Without a disturbance of sexuality in the history, there could be no affiliation of the illness to either men or women. Indeed, at the beginning of the century, males had outnumbered female schizophrenics, although this was the other way around by the 1960s. I would contend that the Abraham/ Freud suggestion, that schizophrenia involves withdrawal from the erotic world into autoeroticism while hysteria apparently displays object love, is crucially important. However, I shall argue in the next chapter that the object love of hysteria is the demand to receive love (a greed for love) which in fact feeds autoeroticism.

In Libbrecht's terms, after the First World War schizophrenia 'overran the world'; she argues that its success as a diagnosis was due to the fact that it resisted the problem of sexuality: 'Bleuler's capacious schizophrenia group which avoids . . . differential diagnosis with the hysterical psychoses and rejects the role of sexuality, gains the suit.'[8] This, I think, is true. However, I believe we can be more specific. What was, and is always, the psychotic dimension of hysteria disappeared into schizophrenia during this century. In part the psychotic dimensions of hysteria had been excluded from psychoanalytic

treatment and it became the 'untreatable schizophrenia'; in part schizophrenia became a hiding place for hysteria.

Moving to Object Relation psychoanalysts (Kteinian and Independent), Libbrecht rereads the triumphant analyses of psychosis by these
clinicians after the Second World War as failures to discover the
hidden hysteria:

Rosenfeld's publication [of] the analysis of Mildred [see chapter 6], first
presented in 1947 at the British Psychoanalytical Society, is historically of [the]
greatest importance. It notably regards the first publication of a successful
therapy with an adult psychotic woman within the Kleinian tradition, i.e. the
first *psychosis under transference*. A rereading of the Mildred case, however,
shows that there is no question of schizophrenia here, but on the contrary of
a severe hysteria, which some would probably label as hysterical psychosis.[9]

Where once the female hysteric had provided the model patient for
psychiatrists and psychoanalysts, by the middle of the twentieth century it was the 'neutered' schizophrenic who had replaced her. Sometimes schizophrenia as a diagnosis was the construction of a new
disease entity (it did not exist as a category of illness before the end
of the nineteenth century), which, like anorexia, had once merely been
a dimension of hysteria – in other words, it could be seen as a result of
greater diagnostic sophistication. Sometimes the diagnosis of schizophrenia arose as a result of hysterical mimesis by the patient, which
was not always so absolute as to become the thing itself (as Mildred
had achieved for her analysis). For example, in 1956, Dr Martin
Orne, a psychiatrist and psychoanalyst working in Boston, made an
important rediagnosis. Orne rescued the woman who was to become
the bestselling American poet Anne Sexton from a schizophrenic ward.
He recognized that Sexton's hysteria had enabled her to more-than-act,
to mime so completely that she almost became a schizophrenic – with
all the appropriate symptoms and behaviours and apparent thought
disorders which had become definitions of schizophrenia.

Originally, when Anne sought help following the birth of her second child,
she had been diagnosed as having post-partum depression. When I first saw
her in therapy in the hospital in August 1956, a year after the birth of her
daughter, her thoughts and behaviours were not really consistent with the

presumptive diagnosis. As I began to get to know Anne, I realized that she was showing ideation that one might expect in a patient with a thought disorder. Fortunately she happened to mention that she was spending time with two patients who suffered from a schizophrenic disorder, and thus I became aware of her tendency to take on symptoms that were like those of people with whom she was currently interacting. Indeed, because of this tendency, I was even more careful not to have Anne stay in a hospital setting any longer than was absolutely necessary, lest she adopt new symptoms from other patients.[10]

This was a perfect illustration of how the hysteric could perform and mime the currently fashionable illness. If the doctors in hospitals wanted schizophrenia, then that is what hysterics would become. Thus, hysteria 'disappeared', or camouflaged itself, in other more contemporary illnesses, as it had once done in, say, epilepsy.

Although an interest in hysteria was already in decline in the first decade of the century (giving way to *dementia praecox*/schizophrenia), paradoxically it was, I would argue, the extensive hysterias of the First World War that capped its 'final' disappearance. The officers and men who were invalided from the front on both sides displayed hysterical symptoms. However, a hysteria diagnosis was quickly disputed. Although it had been with male hysteria that Charcot had made his name, Freud had, rightly or wrongly, attributed his own unpopularity in Viennese medical circles in the 1880s to his espousal of the diagnosis. It has been widely suggested that the massification of male hysteria during the First World War was simply unpalatable to the medical community – or, more generally, to standard images of 'maleness'. If the soldiers with non-organic paralyses, amnesia, catatonia, mutism and all the other 'hysterical' traits could not be labelled 'hysterics', and men should not be hysterics, then the simplest solution to this dilemma would seem to have been to allow the decline of the category itself.

By 1914 infections and contagious diseases were no longer so major a wartime problem as they had been in all previous wars. Psychological distress slipped into the breach. During and after the First World War (and in every war in which the West has engaged since) the argument has raged as to whether these psychological symptoms are the result of battle trauma or whether they are hysterical. If they are to be thought of as hysterical, I would argue, along with all psychoanalysts, that there needs to be some place for sexuality and unconscious processes in the etiology. At first medically qualified psychoanalysts (for example, Abraham and Ferenczi) sent to treat soldiers at the front, recorded hysteria and found Oedipal conflicts therein. Psycho-analytically informed opinion more generally, responding to these mass breakdowns of the First World War, initially argued that under the threat of death there was a return either of repressed homosexual longing for the father of the 'negative' Oedipus complex or alterna-tively of Oedipal wishes for the motherland as a substitute for the mother. Both postulates confined the diagnosis to the Oedipus com-plex, 'positive' with the mother, 'negative' with the father. Either explanation could have involved hysteria as it was understood within psychoanalysis at the time.

Psychiatrists such as W. H. R. Rivers, who had enthusiastically read Freud on the unconscious, had little truck with the official classification of shellshock ('the unfortunate and misleading term "shell shock" which the public have now come to use for the nervous disturbance of warfare',[11] as Rivers put it). But for Rivers, the trauma produced psychological effect. For Charcot, much earlier, it had also been crucial. Trauma could unhinge the male. It mattered to Charcot that male hysterics were 'macho' masculine working men, not effete or feminine; Freud, a Galician Jew, was less squeamish, although he called one of his hysterical male patients a 'Hercules of a man'. The need for men not to be feminine spelt the demise of the hysteria diagnosis. The men who were suffering from war or traumatic neur-osis, like their predecessors the male hysterics of the Salpêtrière, were finally assessed as having no sexual dimension to their symptoms. So, ultimately, although much of the psychoanalytic understanding of the problem was retained and, in particular, the impact of unconscious processes was emphasized, sexuality as a determining force was not. The Oedipal explanation had put too little weight on the traumatic shock. The explanation in terms of trauma reversed the situation: too little weight was put on sexuality. Charcot had been pre-Freudian; after 1918 psychoanalysis, in respect of the importance of sexuality, became pre-Freudian, too. Furthermore, if there was no sexuality there could be no hysteria. Traumatic neurosis or schizophrenia took over. The notion of a death drive arose from observations of both trauma and hysteria in the First World War.

However, there is, of course, sexuality in the response to war trauma. If we understand war victims as suffering from traumatic stress alone, how do we account for the rampant sexuality of war? The violent random encounters, the seemingly inevitable rapes and gang rapes that accompany killing? Sexual violence seems to 'automatically' accompany war violence.

In fact, how has it been possible to ignore the intimate relationship of rampant sexuality and war violence? The question is very large. Here I can only make some suggestions that link it with my theme of hysteria and psychoanalytic theory. Within psychoanalysis, sexuality has been regarded as Oedipal. The practice of psychoanalysis, and its influence beyond its own confines, has therefore led to the disappearance of hysteria in another way: by Oedipalizing all relationships, men could avoid being seen as hysterics – they were either homosexual, in a negative Oedipus complex, or 'normal', that is heterosexual, in a positive Oedipus complex – and hysterical women merely appeared ultrafeminine.

Oedipal relations involve identifications with reproductive parents. War sexuality (rape) is the ultimate detachment of sexuality from reproduction and the attachment of death to sexuality. What does this mean? It is hysterical sexuality. In an identification with the mother, a girl looks like a mother; in a hysterical identification, as Anne Sexton put it, 'A woman is her mother/That's the main thing.' There are hysterical daughters who become hysterical mothers. The baby, then, has no independent significance because the hysterical mother has never reconciled herself to the fact that, as a little girl, she could not have babies. She has not mourned this fact and hence, as nothing is lost, nothing can be represented or symbolized. The baby has no meaning in this imitation of motherhood, manifest, for instance, in repeated childbirths, the compulsive need for more and more babies which Penelope Mortimer captured so well in her novel *The Pumpkin Eater* (1962). However, the hysterical woman at least looks like a mother. But such an imitation of motherhood is untenable by a man unless socially condoned, as in the practice of ritual imitation childbirth, the *couvade*.

The hysteria, then, that is, despite our blindness, so noticeable in war surely involves brothers – enemies or compatriots (see chapter 1). This is missed because, in the theory and clinical practice of psychoanalysis, parents are all. The hatred has been taken up in the killings of wars; the desire and the prohibitions on these murders are evident in the hysterical dimensions of traumatic stress reactions, in the non-organic illnesses and hysterical stories. The proximity of love and the violent hate and the conflict involved in these responses are excluded from the drug treatments of psychiatry and the consulting rooms of psychoanalysis with its stress on Oedipal relations. The hysteric in an Oedipal identification is only imitating.

When the boy child realizes his place with his parents is occupied by another he will revert to infantile strategies to win back his mother, or, if that fails, his father's love in order to resecure that love for himself alone. He may hate his mother for the love she has given to his rival sibling; he may hate his father for his role in the production of a rival. But a true male hysteric is not involved in reproductive sexuality – his love for others is a masquerade concealing the fact that it is really a love for himself alone. As with the 'pumpkin-eating' woman, his own subsequent parenting, at best highly ambivalent, is a kind of accident. How many men whose wartime rapes produce babies ever actually father the babies? In a weakened version we can see this unwillingness to father (or ignorance of the significance of reproduction) at work in the 'absent' fathers of today's struggle with changing family forms.

In the Western world today there is also a more attenuated patrilineal identification than in most of our history: the boy displaced by a sibling has a less marked-out alternative position than before. He is not quite so clearly superior to a sister as in the past, but nor, if he is a younger son, does he have possibilities of prodigality or going into the Church. The violence of the rivalry will be taken up by other lateral relationships – in war with other men, in peacetime with cohabiting partners. If the partner is a woman, a baby who displaces the father will reinvoke all the sibling hatred. It is nearly always argued that when violence erupts from men to women (as it does universally), it is the mother, who represents the all-powerful being that makes men feel helpless, who is under attack. This is probably so, but it is the mother who has given birth to the sibling. In this sense mother murder is secondary; the primary hatred is against the one person who stands in one's place and thereby renders one helpless to the point of 'non-existence', the 'sibling'.

Within the clinical setting of a psychoanalytic consulting room, the transference that emerges with hysteria is sibling rivalry. Sibling rivalry does not exclude Oedipal and pre-Oedipal loves and hates – rather, it has been conventional psychoanalysis which has excluded the lateral possibilities. In an article 'Hate in the Counter-transference', D. W. Winnicott describes the hating feelings of a therapist towards his patients. It is an important and necessary corrective to the emphasis usually placed on the patient's envy and hatred of the analyst-as-mother, but the framework remains the same – it is understood as that of an intergenerational feeling. Elsewhere Winnicott has stated (against Kleinian theories of the infant's innate envy) that he knows from his intensive and extensive work as a paediatrician as well as an analyst that the mother's hatred *precedes* the baby's. This may well be so – but where does the mother's hatred come from? The mother may sense that she is displaced by the baby. If she was previously so displaced in her own childhood, it would have been by a sibling who occupied the same space. There is a moment described in Winnicott's article when, despite all his acceptance of his own hating, he cannot tolerate something. A psychopathic boy who has been staying in his home has driven Winnicott beyond endurance. Winnicott finally places the child outside the door where he can be as awful as he wants, but not in the *same place* as Winnicott. The too-close lateral relationship triggers hate.

If we return to formative childhood situations such as displacement, which both mother and father feel on the birth of their baby, this would originate in their own displacement by a sibling in their own childhoods. This would explain why there is a relationship between hysteria and perversion: perversion is the enactment, hysteria is the fantasy: the exhibitionist wants to show off but is prevented from doing so and thus his action is a public secret. The hysterical symptom, such as the adult Anne Sexton's dressing as a little girl, reveals the fantasy of showing off and simultaneously not being allowed to. Both perversion and hysteria contain the lightning-switch proximity of love and hate: the transformation of violence into sexuality and back again. As I have suggested, there is perverse violence as well as perverse sexuality: it is the breaking of the taboo on murdering one's brother Abel or the weaker taboo on murdering one's sister. (Murdering one's sister is the weaker taboo because it consciously has to do with cultural prescriptions – in some circumstances it can even be 'right' to murder a sister who has shamed the family; however, it is probably also weaker because the cross-gender displacement by an 'inferior' girl excites a weaker wish to murder – less wish, less prohibition.) If hysteria has disappeared from the consulting rooms, it would seem to be in part at least because, with the sibling transference untheorized and unpractised, it has gone into the perverse sexual violence of war and of the family home.

Daily one hears the epithet 'hysterical' applied to individual or group behaviours and actions. Suddenly I have a sense of the completely absurd; I have read so many books, heard so many categorical statements asserting that 'hysteria has disappeared'. How can it *not* exist, when we keep talking about it? I have wondered and worried for so long – what was I seeing in my clinical practice, among neighbours and friends and not-such-friends, in myself, in my colleagues, on the news? Some completely schizoid argument has subdued us all: How can hysteria have disappeared when one talks about it, thinks about it, sees it all the time?

We are in a state of change today such as in Western history accompanied the decline of witchcraft and the rise of the medicalization of hysteria. Anthropologists remark on the sudden disappearance of witchcraft when a new order takes over. Now it is hysteria's turn to vanish. One can only be speculative about the causes of present changes. The coming closer together of men and women economically, politically, even socially with the decline in the importance of reproduction, means that hysteria is no longer contained in the polarization of male inquisitor, female witch; male doctor, female hysterical patient; rational husband, hysterical wife. At the end of the twentieth century in the Western world, both genders can be hysterical in ways that are more immediately similar. Although war hysteria is still the province of men, in 'peaceful' relationships women can be violent if they feel displaced and engage in a sexuality which is, either actually or in terms of the resultant child's meaning, non-reproductive.

The Surrealists made their minority manifesto from the tenets of hysterical flamboyance, passion and demonstration. Today the social situation which favours a conscious, public enactment in place of private driven symptoms is best summed up in the philosophy of post-modernity which eschews metanarratives, truth, representation in favour of fragmentation, the proliferation of desires, the ascendancy of the will and the act and language that gets one what one wants. This is the valorization of performance and performativity. In continuing to work on the Oedipus and castration complex against his own hysteria, Freud was also fighting a modernist battle against the disintegration he was to live through before his death in exile in 1940. Hysteria has not disappeared, and never can – it is important to recognize it before it is normalized not as a momentary reaction, but as the way in which we predominantly live.

5

Sexuality, Death and Reproduction

Hysteria has not, then, disappeared from the twentieth-century Western world; it is rather that this world manifests a hidden hysteria and is not recognizing this. It is not just psychoanalysts who have chosen any name rather than 'hysteria' for a syndrome they observe, it is the professional world in general that has done so. For hysteria to be acknowledged, it has to be assigned to the 'other' – any person or group who is not oneself. When that relegation is not assured, then there is something intolerable in hysteria when it is brought too close to home. Social science techniques of participant observation, psychoanalysis's constant examination of analyst-as-patient and, above all, the re-emergence of male hysteria have moved hysteria recently from its relegation to the domain of 'the other' into the heart of society's 'self'. As it has moved from a place outside the centre into the centre, it must be denied all existence. This is an immensely important change of scene. So, what is it that is so intolerable about hysteria?

Freud argued that there was a biological bedrock beneath the construction of the psyche; he located in that bedrock a fundamental repudiation of femininity by both genders. He did not elaborate what it was that no one wanted in femininity beyond indicating that for a man it was intolerable to have a passive relation to another man, although a passive relation to a woman, as to a mother, was acceptable. But a hatred of a specific aspect of passivity is a weak explanation, even with regard to femininity. When we consider that femininity has replaced hysteria as the explanation for certain sorts of behaviour it becomes completely inadequate. The repudiation of femininity is indicatively similar to the contemporary rejection of hysteria. The hysteric too may well be protesting against passivity if for this we read 'helplessness' in the face of a feared annihilation. We certainly do not want to get involved in this experience of helplessness, but is that sufficient reason for a fundamental repudiation of hysteria as a condition or for the assignment of hysteria always to the 'other'?

Among the identifiable characteristics of the hysteric is the charm of the small child. However, there is also something deadly there. It is when the charm reveals this deadliness that we shrink away – admirers of Dora do not notice her indifference to the Ks' child's death. Often more starkly than this, in conjunction with playfulness and a sense of comedy, something evil is released which involves violence and cruelty. To this we need to add the driven, addictive force which accompanies hysteria and so draws others in or infects others – such as in witch hunts or extremist political rallies. The hysteric's audience is compelled to respond or join in. All this is missed if we deconstruct the overall category of 'hysteria' into separate parts. This is why the very deconstruction of hysteria by the twentieth-century 'advanced' world may in fact therefore be a technique for its avoidance. For instance, the multiple personality has an evil alter. Clinicians diagnosing it reflect this split and dismiss one character. In hysteria the good and evil, love and hate, are in a flip-flop relation to each other.

However, three areas need to be addressed to try and understand what it might be that repels thought about hysteria. These three areas are death, sexuality and reproduction. Again, because my material for these reflections comes largely from a clinical psychoanalytical practice, I am proposing to think about a possible explanation within a psychoanalytic framework, whilst making combinations and alterations that are somewhat unorthodox. Freud proposed the notion that we come into the world with a death drive and a life drive which includes a sexual drive; these operate as opposing forces. However, what we see in hysteria's rampant, seductive, destructive, sexuality is a combining of the two in the sexualizing of death wishes, of violence.

It is not just that in hysteria sex and death have come together as a fused drive; it is rather that something violent has been sexualized. If a therapist seduces a patient, or a patient a therapist, it is not in the best interests of either; if a father makes love to a daughter or even if the daughter is a pubescent Lolita, there is little kindness there. The sexuality is unlikely to be about a relationship, it is more likely to be about a desperate need for something that is forever missing. Anne Sexton described her ability to seduce as follows:

It's not that I want to go to bed with him; I want to be sure he loves me. This [wanting] is like pills or drugs but much more complex.[1]

Sexton discussed this fatal attraction with her therapist. She recognized an underlying pattern: lovers were stand-ins for some unavailable person:

. . . it's not that I'm beautiful; it's just that I can make some men fall in love with me. The aura of this thing is more strong than alcohol. Not just sleeping with them: it's a ritual. If I want to push it I just say 'I need you' . . . I'm going to die of this, it's a disease; it will destroy the kids, and my husband. Ever since [my father], ever since my mother died, I want to have the feeling someone's in love with me . . . A fine narcotic, having people in love with me.[2]

We need to put this description of the underlying experience of seducing in the context of a double absence. Sexton relates her need to death: every lover fills the void left by a dead or unavailable person and every lover in his turn becomes an absent person. As her biographer Diane Wood Middlebrook has noted, Sexton not only has the profoundest of identifications with the dead but her poems describe how she makes the dead live again in projections on to the living – for instance, she sees one lover as her dead grandfather. This insistent habit makes both the dead and the living infinitely losable but never really lost, never completely dead. So, for instance, the dead grandfather, mother or father cannot be properly mourned, as they are always turning up as new lovers. In his turn the new lover is always someone who is not there.

This process of displacing the dead can be echoed in the transference in a psychoanalytic treatment – the therapist is not a re-edition of a loved or hated person but rather a replacement for someone who is felt never to have been there. However, by refusing to actually stand in as a replacement lover, the analyst's non-presence in his own right in the treatment can hopefully enable the patient to allow the dead to die. If the therapist in reality becomes the lover (who is anyway only a stand-in for a missing person), then the process is unending – the patient can only accumulate more lovers who are really 'missing persons' and revenants until, Don Juan-like, a patient such as Anne Sexton joins them in a death without meaning. Sexton's suicide, like her 'playing dead', like her lovers who stood in for dead people, would seem to have been a death in which there was no recognition of finality nor sense of other people. Here, then, we have sexuality as death, or perhaps better put as 'missing persons', both as lovers and as herself. Anne Sexton identified with one of the missing people (grandfather, father, mother, her Nanna). Sexton illustrates a common pattern of taking as apparent objects of her love only lovers who enacted these missing persons – people who leave are attractive, those who stay have no psychological value. Compulsive seduction is a meeting place of ghosts. Both the lover and the love object are substitutes for people who have never been felt to be there.

There is, however, a further factor which makes death the context for sexuality; that is, the subject's own sense of rivalry. In Anne Sexton's case, which is only an example, this is described as her rampant competitiveness, first with her sisters, then with peers (in the broadest sense, from fellow writers to sexual partners). As part of the struggle for recognition of oneself there can be a violent urge not only to do better but to have more than others, in particular more than one's peers. If we trace this back to childhood, we can see that the displaced child, who experiences the displacement as a trauma, wants to have what the baby has (for instance, the mother's milk) as well as to *be* the baby. According to Somali tradition, a wife is possessed by the envious *sar* spirits when her husband replaces her with another wife. Her envy thus encompasses both envy of the new wife's belongings and a sexual jealousy of this wife's position with her husband.

The hysteric, in experiencing displacement as trauma, then repetitively re-enacts this trauma. The re-enactment can be through compulsive sexuality, for trauma and sexuality are analogous experiences. The effraction of the subject's protective skin, which is an essential part of trauma (the breaking of the actual skin in the case of physical trauma, of an imaginary boundary in the case of psychic trauma), is comparable to the sense of a breaking open of the mind/body in sex.

This opening of the body is more commonly associated with female sexuality, where normative heterosexuality is penetrative. However, both genders are of course vulnerable to sexual entry, just as both genders can seduce and 'take the other in'. This general human vulnerability to penetration is probably related, once more, to human-kind's premature birth, in which the neonate has not sufficient active powers to grab the nipple but must have it put in its mouth. Human beings are unusual in that any and everyone can be penetrated – this vulnerability makes penetration always a threatening possibility. Although there can be intense erotic grooming, affectionate feeling and sensual bonding among same-gender higher mammals, there is little evidence of same-gender sexual penetration or incorporation.

Human orality and penetration may be closely linked with sexuality modelled on feeding, because only the human does not have oestrus but instead year-round sexuality. Animals of course have year-round feeding, but they have seasonal sexuality which does not map on to feeding patterns. Human year-round sexuality repeats year-round feeding. From the evidence of seduction and rape (as in wars) in the sex/death of hysteria, we may speculate that sexuality is established in humans in addition to the biological animal drive, at the moment of neonatal trauma. The neonate is in danger of death if the carer/provider should fail; however, at the very same moment it must submit to the penetration of caring (feeding, cleaning) and incorporation of holding (as an extension of the womb). Caring for the infant's body and the traumatic absence of caring coincide as an experience. If no one answers the cry of the baby, its body may be felt to fragment, but if the carer does clean and tend the child then there is also intrusion into the body. Likewise, the baby's experiences of being held protectively and of being overwhelmed are closely related, life being ensured by being held and death being threatened by suffocation and incorporation, coincide. We see the tension of experiences which are simultaneously life-giving and death-threatening in later agoraphobia and claustro-phobia. Because of our utter dependency on the carer in infancy, and our year-round sex drive, which is physically modelled on this, the baby can feel life-threatening risk and simultaneously have a focus of sexual excitement in the experience of penetration and incorporation.

Freud's hypothesis of a death drive arose from general psychoanalytic observations of patients' compulsion to repeat traumatic experiences. Why might one have repetitive dreams of terrifying war experiences? The earlier experience of the absence of the essential caretaker seems to underlie this phenomenon. Freud hypothesized a death drive as innate and in perpetual struggle with an equally innate life drive linked to a sexual drive. The hypothesis I am suggesting, however, combines the sexual drive with the death drive as well as with the life drive, as maybe innate, but all activated by the initiating trauma of the conditions of life. Against the death drive and sexual drive I would set the life drive. This life drive is activated by the presence of caretakers, as opposed to their absence. This suggestion is not some quibble about theory, it addresses the whole issue of how to think about the phenomena seen in analytical sessions by all psychoanalysts, whatever their orientation.

Because of my focus on hysteria, the same observation of compulsive repetition that made Freud posit a death drive makes me want to include the activation of potential sexuality in a generalized traumatic moment. In certain contexts, we could say, killing is raping and raping is killing. This sexuality will only be activated in later experiences of trauma, such as war, or in a displacement which for some people will be experienced as traumatic. It is by noting the combination of killing and rape in war, among other instances, and the resultant hysteria in men that I have come to this suggestion of death and sex drives as being constituted in the same moment. I see the sexual drive as a mobile drive, that is, activated along with a death drive at the moment of trauma, but which is also present in the life drive, where it plays its crucial role in forming unions. The caring presence of the caretaker can ensure that sexuality is attached to a relationship of presence rather than bound to the compulsion of absence, as it so clearly was with Sexton. Outside the traumatic repetition, then, sexuality will be part of the life drive which will include with it, but should never be reduced to, a drive to reproduction. But because it is also bound to the death drive, it too will be repetitive, indeed often compulsively so. The life drive is activated by the caretaker providing the infant with a sufficiency of what is needed in terms of care and protection to ensure life.

All human sexuality can take place with a wide range of objects:

the subject's own body, the body of someone in another or the same category as oneself, with animals, mechanical objects, with different parts of the body. This was systematized by the long lists of sexual perversions compiled by psychopathologists such as Krafft-Ebing and Havelock Ellis at the end of the nineteenth century. Some degree of 'perversion' is present in all so-called 'normal' sexuality. It is likewise present in the symptoms of neuroses and psychoses. In so far as human sexuality seeks satisfaction rather than an object (except in the theories of 'attachment' or for Object Relations (see chapter 6)), it is in a sense necessarily perverse. This drive to satisfaction can find an object, in which case sexuality will be part of a life drive; or it can fail to become attached to a satisfying object and thus seek satisfaction in an objectless universe in which case it will be bound to the death drive. Although, as mentioned earlier, cases of rape may be repetitions of violence against the mother who gave birth to a sibling who displaced one, there is, I believe, beneath this an even more profound objectlessness – there is no one there and the actual person or the imagined person that the actual person represents, only fills this void. As Sexton said, her lovers represented people who were not there.

If we assume that sexuality is a biophysical drive, it is nevertheless one that is necessarily expressed and formed in a social human context. A baby's sexuality would seem to be really the surplus of pleasure and satisfaction it gets when it is being fed and cared for. But this is precisely *not* the sexuality we witness in hysteria. Hysterical sexuality seems both compulsive and not necessarily pleasurable, as though it is a need (as Sexton saw) rather than a desire that is being met. Hysterical sexuality is always bound up with both autoeroticism, seduction and rape. As with rape, it *seems* that seduction involves another person while autoeroticism only makes use of the subject's own body and fantasies. Yet we need to ask: In what sense *does* seduction involve another person? Is it perhaps a means of drawing all towards the self rather than a way of attaching oneself to the other? We could say that the other person is used for the purposes of autoeroticism.

The first extensive accounts of male hysteria by Charcot in the latter part of the nineteenth century all cited traumatic shock as the instigator. When Freud heard his patients, female and male, describe their having been seduced by their fathers in childhood, this seemed to constitute a passive experience of shock. Still today, when patients tell their therapist of such seductions, the therapist's first reaction is not to wonder whether or not the story is true or false, but rather to register that the account is an account of a state of shock. The communication of this shock makes it easy for the therapist to become 'shocked' herself and to think that actual incest or abusive violence has taken place. The traumatic shock experienced by the patient becomes the moral shock of the therapist. This is one of the reasons why it should never be the task of the therapist to investigate what actually happened – that task must fall to others. But the shock itself is crucially important.

The recipient of a shock is, by definition, passive. The shock also implodes the body/mind. When, in the process of recovery, a fantasy is constructed, this fantasy bears the marks of both the shock and the implosion. Violence, trauma, shock, break-in – they all penetrate. When a soldier witnesses his neighbour in the trenches being blown up or shot or knifed, the shock he experiences is a penetration of a body boundary analogous with the body-blasting of his fellow combatant. An industrial accident, surgery, sexual abuse, beating – all have a shared lowest common denominator of breaching body surfaces. The mind will experience the breaching in the same way.

I do not believe all impingement or penetration must necessarily become sexualized. We will see in chapter 9 how, instead, the human capacity for memory can occupy the breaches caused by a trauma, but in hysteria this breaching *is* sexualized. In fact, it would seem to be that the sexualization of the trauma replaces memory. The hysteric does not remember. An actual trauma also wipes out memory. The hysteric unconsciously models himself on this process and becomes amnesiac in order to create a traumatic shock. The Taita woman used the shock of seeing a car in an unusual place as a trauma. We can plausibly imagine that she would then have not known where she was and have needed to be helped or enticed with presents in order to resume normal life. One can have a hysterical reaction to an actual shock or one can create a shock in order to produce a hysterical reaction. We are all familiar from our friends or ourselves that when we want attention we break, say, our favourite object. The entrenched hysteric repeats and creates shocks for himself; these shocks entail the blasting of memory. The broken object, rather than the feeling that caused the breakage, becomes the focus of attention – the feeling can then be forgotten. With memory blasted, the shock can be sexualized. The shock itself becomes an end in itself. The memory entailed a peopled world – the shock creates an empty world. Winnicott describes a psychically ill baby who cannot retain the object he throws away but instead frenetically throws it over and over again.[3] This movement, like hysterical sexual movement, is the body surviving the shock, the physical experience of shock has in itself to sustain sufficient survival.

If we imagine a suckling infant from whom the breast or bottle is suddenly, violently, removed, the surplus of pleasure it was experiencing in feeding will turn to shocked distress. However, the baby shows no signs of 'remembering' the feed; instead, the shock that replaces its pleasure will have a frantic quality to it – it is as though the shock has transformed the pleasure into a frenetic protosexuality. If the breast/bottle had been withdrawn in a non-traumatic manner, the pleasure could have been used as an early step on the road to memory. The infant would have made pleasurable sucking movements which would have indicated a hallucination of the object that was providing the pleasure – and hallucination is a step towards remembering the object. With a shocking disruption this possibility is eroded.

Winnicott compares a well baby with an ill baby. He records how the 'well' baby will take a spatula off the doctor's table and suck it, making it its own, then throw it down and get pleasure from retrieving it. However, as we have seen above, an already disturbed baby will not mouth the spatula but will only throw it down with increasing, compulsive frequency, getting more and more frenetically excited as it does so. The toddler who is 'well' will get pleasure from throwing away an object, such as a spoon, that symbolizes its mother – thereby mastering her absences – and satisfaction from retrieving it, from getting her back in play. An unwell child will throw away the object until it is tired out and not get satisfaction on retrieval. Like this disturbed baby or like the baby from whom the breast is traumatically, suddenly withdrawn, the soldier in the trenches may have been experiencing something warm and reassuring from the proximity of his comrade when a violent death suddenly, traumatically removed this contact. The shock converts the previous pleasure of contact to a desperate, painful excitement, a kind of survival–sexuality kit which could well lead to rape or compulsive, violent sexual encounters. The frenetic repetition is the mark of the death of the 'other' and of his own survival – it is sexuality in the interest of the surviving self.

Hysterical sexuality regresses to and repeats the excited compulsive mastery of the trauma of absence and the break in the self. That is, there is excitement but no satisfaction. Active seductions like those set up by a Don Juan depend on the 'throwing away' of the object. To all appearances seduction is the opposite of this: it seems that the successful seducer gets more and more 'objects', as Don Juan gets more and more women. But hysterics would indicate that there is little satisfaction in attaining the object, only considerable, desperate excitement in the game of casting away – like the baby who can only throw away the spatula, Don Juan gets his 'kicks' from breaking troth. A seduction demands an audience, actual or 'in mind'; someone has to 'see' the conquest. A Don Juan knows his wife or a previous Donna Elvira is 'watching' his seduction of the next pretty maid in the row. The baby frenetically throwing away the spatula, although it seems entirely self-absorbed, will tire of the enterprise if no one is watching and will turn to another desperate activity such as head-bashing. On the other hand, the child that can get satisfaction from having or retrieving the object does not need always to have an audience for its game.

There is unmastered pain at the centre of seduction. We can witness the pain in the symptoms of hysteria and in hysterogenic zones which mock erotogenic parts of the body. Erotogenic zones are areas of the body where sensual satisfaction can take place – some, such as in kissing the mouth, through its function in pleasurable eating, will have a predisposition to being eroticized. Erotogenic zones are ones where contact has been made. It seems to me that, contrary to an erotogenic zone, a hysterogenic zone, which is a painful zone, occurs where something has *not* happened, where one cannot have what one wants and the feelings are thus painful. First Charcot, then more extensively Freud, demonstrated that these painful points were in fact libidinized – they were associated with illicit sexual pleasures. For instance, in *Studies on Hysteria*, Frau Cacilie's leg hurt at the point where her father had rested his leg while she dressed its deteriorating condition (thereby inducing sexual fantasies in her). According to Freud, the pain of the hysterogenic zone acts to conceal the underlying sexuality. I would put it the other way around: first we have pain, then the sexualization of pain; or sometimes they are almost instantaneous, so that in the very moment the hysteric is in danger of experiencing pain, he sexualizes it in order to feel excitement rather than pain. Frau Cacilie was suffering from the pain of jealousy, she hoped to steal her sister's or her mother's husband. Instead of an erotic point where Frau Cacilie would have felt she had got what she wanted, the point is where a feeling hurts – she has not got what she wants. The symptom and the predisposition to becoming the place of a symptom which is the hysterogenic zone, indicate not just a repressed sexual desire but, like the baby with the spatula, that excitement stands for pain.

It is at the point where seduction needs an audience that the link to hysterical autoeroticism takes place. Although seduction can appear to be the most intimate and focused two-person relationship which takes place to the exclusion of all others, I would argue to the contrary: that for the seduced no less than for the seducer there is always another person around in the fantasy. Seduction has the structure of many jokes, in which there are always three people: the one who makes the joke, the one towards whom hostile or sexual aggression is directed, and the one in whom the aim of producing pleasure is fulfilled. If we take a married Don Juan as an example: Don Juan is the joker, the hostile and sexual aggression is directed at the wife, the pleasure in fantasy will be fulfilled in the women to be seduced.

The hysteric notoriously recounts how he has been seduced – as did Dora. At the same time the hysteric who is telling the story of his seduction is seducing the listener. But seduction elicits not only the seductability but also the seductiveness of the other. There is probably always some element of seduction in any non-violent sexual encounter. In hysteria, however, it is the seduction, not the consummation, that counts. It is not, as Freud and more particularly Lacan have argued, that there is something about sexuality which in itself is necessarily unsatisfiable; it is that its seductive element cannot be satisfied by consummation – it can only be repeated. This repetition marks the pain of the subject's displacement and beneath that the acute awareness of something that is missing (which is the quality that is at the heart of seduction).

The seducer is always seductive, drawing the other in by his charms. At one level this is an acknowledgement of the need for another, a recognition of the human lack of self-sufficiency. At another level, when excessive, it is a drawing in of the other to fill the seducer's sense of utter emptiness. It is this need to be filled that links seduction, when it shifts from the normal to the excessive, to the trauma which breaches the person, emptying out his memory and his experience. Remembering always that hysteria involves regression, what is being played out in this, its prevalent mode of a positive relationship – excessive seduction?

A catastrophe makes the hysteric feel threatened as a subject. As a result he hates all who would seem to tread on his existence. Prototypically such a catastrophe is the arrival or pre-existence of a sibling who appears to replace him. Hate is a reaction of the need for survival – the urge to humiliate the other when one is in danger of being annihilated oneself. Hate is very strong in perversion and also in hysteria – in both, hatred appears as sexuality. In conjugal relations it is often easy to experience the partner as standing in one's place, to hate him or her, but then to clothe this hatred in a sexual relationship. There is hatred, too, in excessive seduction.

It is commonly argued that hate and love are easily and quickly reversed into each other; but love is really missing in the frequent oscillations of hysteria. Freud claimed the hysteric loves where he hates; I would argue instead that he sexualizes where he hates. It is true that love and hate do not belong to the same area of experience but sexuality can belong to either love or hate. Love can turn to hate when the subject's existence is threatened, but hate cannot turn to love. Hate is an emotional response to the need to survive in hostile conditions. It is because the need to survive comes first and foremost in any traumatic situation that hate has been described as 'older than love'. Hate can be attached to any object in the interest of destroying it.

Love, whether for another person, an object, or for oneself, in the form of self-respect, is a positive emotion that comes about when there is no threat to our survival. Because of previous long experiences in which it has felt secure, there is every possibility that a child will love its new sibling before it arrives. This love becomes hate, however, if the threat to the ego seems too strong. In terms of relationships, love comes before hate but in terms of a primacy of emotions hate is older than love. One hates when one's survival is threatened: born helpless as we are, anything that echoes that predicament evokes hate; anything that saves us from it evokes love. The hate can end when the threat to survival is removed. Love can come in its place – but this is a new experience, it is not hate turning into love. However, when one's love for another is suddenly exposed to the possibility that that person may annihilate one, then the love itself can turn to hate.

This is clearer if we deploy a popular distinction between love and being *in* love. 'In love', a state not considered within psychoanalytic theory, is a better term for the sexuality that is experienced as a state of being which is intoxicated over and above a bodily desire. 'In-loveness' can turn to hate and hate can become 'in-loveness'. Through the character of Dmitry Karamazov in *The Brothers Kara-mazov* (1880), a novel which in addition to all else offers many masterly portrayals and accounts of hysteria, Dostoevsky describes this in-love/hate oscillation:

'[T]o fall in love is not the same as to love. One may fall in love and still hate.' 'You must believe me when I tell you that never before had I looked at a woman with hatred . . . with the kind of hatred from which there's only a single hairsbreadth of distance to love, the most reckless love.'[4]

It is not then correct that hysterics love where they hate. It is rather that hysterics sexualize hatred. To look at this process more closely, we need to involve the concept of the death drive so seriously missing from studies of hysteria. The death drive is a 'drive' precisely because it drives the organism towards a state of inanimacy, or inertia, to stasis or even literally death. The hypothesis of the death drive – and it is no more than a hypothesis – arose from observations which came to prominence in the First World War. It is usually argued that the death drive can only be seen when it is fused with sexual drive, for example when a person gets satisfaction from destroying and hurting either another person (sadism) or himself (masochism). What Freud called 'a pure culture' of the death drive may be visible in melancholia, when the person has been completely identified with a dead or lost person from the past, so much so that this person lives on in the melancholic. In fact, hysteria suggests another focus.

All drives seem to be repetitious, to go over the same ground again and again. In so far as it relates to a trauma, the death drive compulsively repeats the apparent 'annihilation' of the subject: this can be witnessed in the repetition of a traumatic nightmare. As, clearly, a repetition of such experiences is profoundly unpleasurable, the death drive goes beyond the principle that the organism always seeks pleasure. The risk-taking, the compulsive seductions, the driven lying, the need to repeat the performance in hysteria would seem to bear witness to a need to repeat the trauma as a means of survival, but also as a drive towards death. It is as though, at the moment of threatened annihilation, the hysteric has identified with the death embodied in that moment. In his own mind the hysteric has 'murdered' the sibling who is so like him but then he realizes that he is the same as the murdered one. As Freud wrote of the hystero-epileptic fits that took Dostoevsky into apparent death:

We know the meaning and intention of such deathlike [epileptic] attacks. They signify an identification with a dead person, either with someone who is really dead or with someone who is still alive and whom the subject wishes dead.[5]

The hysterical identification with death differs from the melancholic because it is sexualized – the symptom, here the frenetic excitement of the fit, displays the sexualization. There is, however, a further manifestation of the death drive which, although it is discernible in any psychic illness, seems particularly characteristic of hysteria: the so-called negative therapeutic reaction. One of the reasons why hysteria may be thought to have disappeared this century in the West, is its resistance to cure – the doctor's need to succeed would prefer to banish the illness than to seem to fail. Freud was chagrined by the length of treatment that 'E' required; he would not consider accepting Dora when she asked to come back in treatment because he knew she did not want to recover. All the patients I have dealt with who have had predominantly hysterical problems have not only surprised both themselves and me by the length of their treatment but only came into psychoanalysis after they had tried several other therapeutic or analytic cures.

The predominant feature of a strong wish not to get better would seem to arise from an unconscious sense of guilt. However, the hysterical person has a desperate need never to feel guilty. This non-guilt reaches the point where he is not responsible for anything: if he puts a hot saucepan on a wooden table and burns it, the fault lies either with the table or its owner. If occasionally responsibility or even guilt is acknowledged, then, listening to the confession, I as a psychoanalyst am surprised, even impressed, until I realize that it means nothing. This can lead to serious difficulties in cases of abusive behaviour: the counsellor or therapist may believe the confession of guilt but the confession was only what the abuser in his hysteria realized was wanted by the counsellor or therapist. I once confronted a patient with a report that had been given to me of their abusive behaviour to an infant. I was deeply impressed by the concern evinced – the patient could remember nothing of the occasion but was fully prepared to accept it had happened and that it was serious. It was some time before I realized this was only a perfect imitation of a concerned position – the incident had no meaning for the abuser at all.

Loving the sibling before it is born and often afterwards, too, the child hates it only when it is experienced as threatening his unique subjecthood. In the Bible we are enjoined to love our brothers as we love ourselves. Psychoanalytic theory neglects this command. If the subject, however, thinks he must obey it, then the guilt for the murderous fantasies becomes deeply unconscious. If the hate continues and the fantasies are not repressed then perverse behaviour results in which the subject is both physically violent and sexually seductive. A subject suffering from an unconscious sense of guilt does not feel guilty; instead he feels ill. It is, then, necessary to stay ill so as not ever to feel guilty. Hence the cure does not work; there is a 'negative therapeutic reaction'.

It is usually thought that the death drive, when seen in conjunction with the sexual drive, operates outwardly as sadism or destructiveness and inwardly as masochism. Thinking about hysteria leads us to a somewhat different formulation. When under threat the hysteric turns to hate. This hate is then sexualized. Anne Sexton, for instance, sexually abused not her younger daughter, whom she loved, but her elder daughter, whom she tended to hate. At the same time the hysterical subject asserts his survival and existence through a sexuality of his own. As with sexualized hatred or sadism, this is essentially narcissistic and uses the other person for autoerotic purposes. It is always about the subject's self even though the fantasies and actions may seem to be about others. The compulsive seduction is to make someone else (a third party) jealous; the sexuality is a marker only of the subject's survival. In so-called 'arctic hysteria', prevalent among the Inuit of Greenland, neglected women gather together to entice the men through seductive games after a long, hard winter in which both social and individual survival seemed sometimes in question. Hysterical sexual success can be compared to a meal for a starving person – if it satisfies, the hysteria is over, if it is insufficient, the 'wanting and wanting' continues and the search for something else to satisfy it must be repeated over and over again.

We have, then, on the one hand, a self-assertive, autoerotic sexuality which marks the hysteric's survival and coats his hatred of the rival; on the other hand are his loving relationships which are not hysterical. Hate belongs to ego survival and the death drive, love to the life drive. But how does the question of reproduction fit into this picture?

To look at this, I am going to examine cases of pregnancy fantasy in both a boy child and an adult male hysteric. It has been widely observed that the hysterical male avoids fatherhood, either actual or psychical. What has been less widely noticed is the degree to which he can often imagine he is pregnant and capable of giving birth. Boys' and girls' fantasies about having children are commonplace – but they have not been integrated into an account of later psychic development. The hysteric – male or female – has the child's relationship to reproduction. A wish to avoid the question of male hysteria may have been responsible for the lack of significance given to these all-pervasive procreative fantasies of children.

The point to which the adolescent or adult hysteric regresses in relation to reproduction is to this general childhood concern with being able to have babies. 'Little Hans', the first child to be described from the viewpoint of psychoanalysis, offers an exemplary case. In 1909, Freud wrote up the case history of 'Hans', a small boy whose father sought advice by telling Freud of his son's hysterical phobia which displayed clear Oedipal problems. In the process of the telling of the story, a further theory emerged: that of the castration complex. Little Hans would not go out of the house for fear of seeing a horse. It was not just any horse that Hans feared – it was a horse which he saw fall and possibly die. This was his phobia. Horses turned out to be frightening representations of Hans's father. The argument goes that Hans's sexual desires for his mother have suffered the blow of his realizing that his powerful father has got there before him – Hans wishes him dead, but then fears that his father will either kill him or castrate him for his presumption in desiring his mother. In *Totem and Taboo* (1912) Freud elaborates this idea through a reconstruction of mankind's history taken from his anthropological reading and from the material indicated in his own and his patients' fantasies. The totemic father of this reconstructed prehistory monopolizes all the women of the tribe until his sons murder him. This reconstruction sets up a hypothesis of the dead father, like the murdered Laius, as the centre of this possible original society. The wish for the father's death, which is mythologized in *Totem and Taboo*, at an individual level was perceived in Hans's phobia – for Hans, the dead horse represents his wishes for his father's death, which then become the terror of punishment in kind; in other words, the boy fears his own death or castration, that is, the blinding of Oedipus.

Little Hans is one of the early exponents of a new category of illness: anxiety hysteria. He is also a little boy. His phobia is triggered by his mother giving birth to his sister (his first and only sibling). Freud does not make much of this sister, but perhaps the crucial factor that she has displaced the little boy is evident in Freud's choice of pseudonym for her: 'Hans' (who in an earlier unpublished version of the case had been called Herbert) has a sister whom Freud calls 'Hanna' – like two peas in a pod.

Hans is very keen indeed to be able to give birth to babies. He makes and plays with his 'children' and reassures his father that they will both be able to produce them in the future. His father asks Hans, 'Who did you think you have got the children from?' to which Hans answers, 'Why, *from me*.' When told that boys cannot have babies, Hans asserts that he is in fact a mummy. It turns out that the horse

Hans fears is not only his virile father but also his mother in child-birth. Hans wants and fears giving birth. The horse that he witnessed fall down in the street into a prostrate position, Hans associates with childbirth as well as with death. Hans's imaginary children are mainly based on his real live playmates but one in particular, a little girl, is pure invention, and the name he gives her is associated with a particular kind of sausage he likes. From this sausage baby it is a short step for Hans to explain that he imagines giving birth as a pleasurable event, like defecation. The hysterical little boy has, then, produced the baby both by and from himself. For both schizophrenics and hysterics, birth and reproduction are considered parthenogenetic: babies are the result of autoerotic, in particular anal erotic, fantasies.

The case of an adult tram worker, treated in 1921 by the Hungarian psychoanalyst Michael Eisler,[6] places at the forefront the hysterical male wish to become pregnant and give birth. As Lacan has gone to some lengths to demonstrate,[7] the tram worker's is not a psychotic delusion.

Problems begin for the tram man when he falls from his tram and has a recurring acute pain below his left rib. There is no discernible organic reason for this pain and after a period he recovers – only to fall ill again with compulsive acute attacks of pain in the left loin so excruciating that he is unable to sit or lie down except with a bolster. The fits (like Dostoevsky's hystero-epilepsy) are announced by periods of extreme irritability, particularly towards his wife.

Through dreams and associations it transpires that, following the initial fall, the patient was thoroughly investigated with X-rays and various probes. This experience was both frightening and exciting for him, as it echoed a childhood experience of his in which he witnessed a neighbour whose pregnancy terminated in the dead foetus being broken up and removed by surgical implements. The tram worker's symptoms are enacting a dramatic childbirth. Eisler links this to homosexuality – his patient's wish for penetration by a father – and to anal autoeroticism. Lacan emphasizes that the patient is asking the Oedipal question: Am I a man or am I a woman? However, it seems to me that both explanations are viable, although they omit certain crucial features. They pay no attention to the parthenogenetic charac-ter of the hysterical childbirth fantasy. Nor do they make anything of the sibling problem that arrests the tram worker at this stage of development or to which he regresses after the accident.

The tram worker is certainly preoccupied with fertility, yet has been unable to father a child himself. (His wife already has a daughter by a previous relationship.) The tram man longs for a child but only wants a son who will be like himself. He plays with the wish to be able to bear babies inside him. Like 'E' and Freud and many hysterics, the tram worker has a fascination with plants which, after all, vegetatively reproduce. (Children see plants grow probably more than they witness animals copulate.) There is also an interest in eggs and hens which seems to have been a common hysterical theme before battery chickens. This is well illustrated by a boy described by the renowned psychoanalyst Hélène Deutsch who wants to produce an egg from his anus as it seems hens are able to do.[8]

If the tram man is asking through his hysterical symptoms whether he is a man or a woman, he is certainly not asking about the need for both sexes to be involved in reproduction. His models are either a mother and baby with no father around, the egg of a hen with no rooster, or the seeds of a plant. Dora looks at the Sistine Madonna (presumably imagining an immaculate conception), Little Hans gets his babies from himself, the tram man imagines a son as a clone – all three want to reproduce themselves without involving another person.

The tram worker is the eldest of many siblings, to whom he relates only with difficulty. He is scathing about the eldest of his sisters, whose birth he remembers his parents excitedly anticipating. The birth of his youngest sister is actually the event which has precipitated his hysterical symptoms. He seems preoccupied by sisters and anxious that women in general (who clearly represent his sisters) should be 'kept in their place' – a place he regards as utterly inferior. His brothers, we are told, are of little interest to him, except for a now-dead one about whom he has a mildly uncomfortable conscience because the boy had drowned when the tram man had lent him money to go swimming. While driving his trams, the tram man ran down a pedestrian and killed him by cutting him in two. He also hurt a small boy who had survived. As with Little Hans's falling horse, falling down in the street (his own accident and the earlier accidents he caused) suggest both childbirth and death. The dead pedestrian and the aborted baby about whom he fantasizes both recall the tram man's wishes for his siblings to die. In his pregnancy fantasies the tram worker gives birth to a *dead* foetus, as perhaps Dora, in her Madonna fantasies, was conceiving one who would ultimately be crucified. There is the violence of death in these autoerotic fictions of conception and parturition, as there is in sexuality itself.

These death wishes, however, are not absolute. What they show is a child's knowledge (or ignorance) of death, in which it is not ultimate. The tram man dreams of rows of small coffins filled with dead children, but twice, when he looks again, to his amazement the children are dancing (when they see him looking they become dead again). The wish-fulfilling element in this corresponds to the childhood stage at which we still believe death to be reversible.

Eisler focuses on the anal autoerotic, passive homosexual aspects of his male hysteric, suggesting that his patient has no strong heterosexual feelings for his wife; Lacan stresses the Oedipal positioning of the subject as undecided about being masculine or feminine. Lacan emphasizes that the tram man does not recover from his hysteria because he is simultaneously excited and fearful of the instruments which are used to investigate his pains – these are the link with the instruments that he witnessed being used on the neighbour whose dead foetus was broken up and extracted. Both the issues of sexual difference and Oedipality are present but so too is the red thread of sibling rivalry, which is not integrated into either account.

The tram man's delusional jealousy of his wife is noted by both psychoanalysts with a nod towards his eldest sister, but then its origins are traced to his Oedipal feelings for his parents. Yet surely it is sibling rivalry that underlies this jealousy:

It has already been stated that his wish for male offspring was determined by narcissism. Other relics of unduly potent infantile narcissism came forward as certain paranoid phantasies, which however only gave evanescent indications, and proved very variable. *Of these I have already mentioned jealousy. It had reference, however, not only to his wife's former love affair, but developed into delusion-like phantasies of her possible infidelity, for which he wished to atone by murder of the late lover.*[9] [My italics]

The tram man tells Eisler he is angry with his wife because of her deception over her former lover and daughter – he claims he did not know about them when he married her. In fact, it seems more than likely that he did not *want* to know he knew, and that his choice of wife was based on the excitement of his jealous–murderous fantasies. In marrying a wife with this history, the tram man would unconsciously have been attempting to survive his unbearable feelings which had originated with sibling hatred. He would have been both assuaging his guilt and at the same time enjoying the fantasy of 'righteous' murder of a rival. Yet again we see that to omit the crucial role of sibling rivalry in hysterical symptoms and behaviour is to miss what takes place subsequently between lateral relations such as those with partners and peers.

The tram man finds it impossible to accept that women have a particular part to play in reproduction. Thus, in fantasy, he is able to become pregnant while in reality he is unable to father. I would contend, in contradiction to theorists such as Lacan, that the case of male hysteria in relation to reproduction is no different from that of female hysteria. The classical psychoanalytical account of sexual differences revolves around the resolution of the Oedipus complex. This is the 'ideal' non-hysterical resolution in which the boy gives up his wishes for his mother and acknowledges that his father's place will one day be his with another woman if he relinquishes a claim to it in the present. By contrast, a girl more or less gives up her wishes for her mother and instead hopes in the future to be in her place, an object of desire for the man (the father substitute). In doing this, she must give up absolutely the claim to the man's position. Hysteria becomes simply the failure to resolve satisfactorily the Oedipus complex. Because of the relegation of hysteria to non-existence, the other half of the infantile story is missed. This half of the story is that all children want to have babies and both genders have to give this up in the present of their childhood. If they give it up, girls and boys do so differently. Girls know that if they do give up the idea of having babies now, they will be able to have them, and so be in the place of the mother, in the future. Boys must give up such thoughts absolutely. Hysterical men and women do not give up the wish to reproduce from themselves – both sexes maintain this in an identical fashion.

The point at which the hysteric exists is the one where the child's belief that it can have a baby from just its own body is maintained. A woman hysteric, no less than a man, refuses ever to give up the notion that *as a child* one can be pregnant and give birth. In regressing to this childhood, in fantasy the hysteric gives birth to himself as a product of his autoeroticism. This child to which the hysteric regresses will not relinquish the notion that children can produce babies.

How in the so-called 'normal course of events' do children come to give up the omnipotent fantasy that they can give birth? From where does the prohibition on producing babies from one's own child body emanate? It is too easy to point merely to the reality, the reality that small children may put pillows up their jerseys, that hysterical tram men may only feel comfortable with their tummies resting on bolsters, that hysterics may have bellies inflated by phantom pregnancies, but that, even with today's reproductive technologies, still only male insemination and female pregnancy will result in a baby. Where is the cultural law that imposes the need to give up the fantasy of childhood parthenogenesis? Is this a law uttered by the mother to a boy that not now or ever will he be a mother; but equally strongly, to a girl, that psychologically and symbolically she can only be a mother in the future if she accepts herself as not being a mother now in childhood? The man who can psychologically father and the woman who can psychologically mother have accepted that neither as children nor as adults can they produce babies from only their own bodies. The hysterical father or mother, on the other hand, who may have many actual children, has never given up the possibility of having children in childhood. In this case the new baby is not symbolized – the hysterical parent does not know the baby is a separate unique individual produced from two people. The baby in this case is a presentation of the fantasy baby of childhood. It is important not to confuse this state of affairs with the social phenomenon of 'single motherhood' – a single mother may well accept that there is a father to her child and, to the contrary, many a married man or woman may hysterically, in their fantasies, not know this to be the case.

The autoerotic quality of hysterical production (and it really is not a reproduction but a *production*, carrying all the implications of that word) is easy to miss because the hysteric can create around himself many fantasies apparently concerning other people. However, the prototypical knight on a white charger who is the imaginary impregnator is there solely to give attention to the hysterical subject who is asserting her own omnipotence through producing babies essentially on her own; he is there neither as a subject in his own right nor as someone who can be an object of *her* desires. Not being there in his own right, or as an object of desire, he cannot be a father. Similarly, the Don Juan male lines up many a woman, but none can be a mother to his child. He does not desire them; they are additions to his list.

Hysterical sexuality and the hysterical production of babies (both of which may be elements within any apparently 'normal' sexuality or reproduction) are imbued with a deadliness which arises from the hatred, jealousy and murderousness of being displaced. This is not to say there is no love in the hysterical person, only that such love is not the hysterical part. The love would seem to come from the relationship, the attachment to others, whereas the hysteria comes from the absence of, or break with, such relationships.

Hysteria also has almost always been thought of as intimately bound up with the mother. With the move towards seeing the mother as crucial in the transference in the Object Relations theories that developed after the First World War, the analyst tells the patient that he the patient cannot be like her the analyst. The analyst thus acts as the prohibiting agent, the lawgiver who must prohibit the patient from imagining he can have babies, within the treatment. This prohibition may resolve the hysteria by insisting on the patient giving up omnipotent parthenogenetic fantasies. However, because it is unformulated in the theory, the practice, which may be pointlessly punitive, may drive the hysteria to flourish elsewhere.

In psychoanalytical theory, the 'object' is a term which refers to a person. 'Object relations' are those relationships which an individual maintains with people in his environment towards whom his feelings and emotions are directed. There is nothing whatsoever derogatory about the term – quite the contrary. Because the hysteric's fantasies and behaviour are replete with such human objects, the underlying fact that these objects are wanted only as an audience, or as a confirmation that the hysterical person is loved, is easily missed. The hysteric wants to *be* loved, not to love. The child who wants to produce babies omnipotently does not want any relationship to another human object with which to do so – nor does the adult hysteric who has regressed to this position. The sexuality involved is thus necessarily masturbatory, but again, with an emphasis on the object relations of the Oedipal phase, this feature is also easily missed.

The case of Little Hans marks for Freud a transition in his theories (emergent in 'Dora') from attributing the etiological importance of masturbation for a subject's mental life to a widespread desire for other people. Hans has been told to stop masturbating, but this has merely a deferred meaning for him, a command that becomes worth obeying only when he believes there is a danger of losing his penis if he continues to want his mother. The focus of the theory therefore started to shift from noting the significance of the prohibition on masturbation to stressing the castration complex; from noting the hysteric in relation to himself to noting him in relation to 'others'. The problem was now conceived in terms of the object relationship. This demotion of masturbation from a position of etiological significance meant that the understanding of hysteria also suffered a setback.

Masturbation, autoeroticism and narcissism are core states of hysteria. Displaced in the world, unrecognized, the hysteric becomes both 'empty of herself' and overfull of an overassertive ego. This hysterical ego or 'I' is the sexual, narcissistic 'I', and the body is the self-sufficient body of autoeroticism. The hysteric's object love is only there to gain the love *from* objects – there is no love *of* objects. Self-pleasuring fantasies of self-sufficiency are crucial. There is a much discussed, widespread masturbation fantasy known as 'a child is being beaten'. In it, there are three levels. In the first stage, the child (usually a girl) is excited by imagining another child (usually a sibling) being beaten (usually by the father). The second stage cannot be retrieved from the unconscious and is therefore necessarily a hypothesis: what is proposed as the content of this fantasy which cannot be accessed is that the child being beaten is the masturbatory child's own self. This fantasy rests on a third stage, which is physical – it is the rhythmic sensation of the clitoris, that is, its beating with excitement.

This common fantasy highlights the features of hysteria to which I have drawn attention here. In it the first wish is to see the sibling hurt and demoted. But this sibling is, I believe, often confused with a fantasy baby the hysteric has produced. The father who is beating the child in Freud's initial account is often replaced by an imagined husband or lover who is father of the beaten child/baby. The second stage can only be deduced because the subject of the fantasy herself feels that she has been so displaced by the sibling that she does not exist; the 'not there' of the subject is represented by this stage of the fantasy not being there – only deducible.

In Object Relations psychoanalysis, the therapist is often taken to stand for the mother. Despite this, it misses the mother's role as symbolically prohibiting masturbatory parthenogenetic fantasies. The clinical practice repeats the situation of childhood; the therapist represents the mother who, not of course in so many words but nevertheless in effect, prohibits the child from being like her: able as yet to have babies. The prohibiting father of the castration complex is matched by the prohibiting mother of this 'parthenogenetic complex'. To distinguish between hysterical, parthenogenetic reproduction and masturbatory sexuality on the one hand, and two-person sexuality and reproduction on the other, the theory needs to question the nature of its own 'object relatedness'. Too often the actual presence of two people as in a heterosexual marriage or as in the patient–therapist relationship obscures the dynamic that there is psychically only one person there, desperately seeking to be seen. The prohibition on what I am calling the parthenogenetic complex means that in an ideal case a child will give up this wish, and *because he has given it up*, be able to symbolize it in the future. If the parthenogenetic baby has been relinquished, the actual baby in the future will be able to be realized as a separate entity because it has been symbolized, not seen as a replica of the self.[10] Hysteria shows us how sexuality moves across the death and life drives. Hysterical sexuality only mimes reproduction – it is the sexuality of the child who imagines he can have a baby. War sexuality demonstrates hysterical sexuality shed of its mockery of hysterical reproduction. It is not Oedipal sexuality but a sexuality that murders the possibility of meaningful reproduction. A woman can, so to speak, get away with the imitation of motherhood; it is more difficult for a man – war violence displays the 'a-procreativity' of hysteria.

6

From Hysteria to Motherhood

I. THE MALE HYSTERIC AND THE RISE OF
OBJECT RELATIONS THEORY

After the First World War the theoretical resolution of the question
of what is hysteria bifurcated along gender lines, although this went
unrecognized at the time. Male hysterical responses to war led to a
new consideration of the place of trauma in the construction of psychic
life, to notions of the death drive, and to a reconceptualization of
terror and shock (which gradually lapsed into the wider and more
unclear category of anxiety). Anxiety vied with sexuality for supreme
place in psychoanalytic theory – and won. Along with hysteria, sexuality increasingly vanished from the account. Except, that is, in one
area: femininity. The theorization of sexuality was almost exclusively
limited to female sexuality throughout most of the rest of the century.
To put it schematically and in a somewhat reductive way, an interest
in male hysteria developed as a very wide-ranging concern with the
conditions of human birth and the psychic results of the very earliest
relationship with the mother, a very early Oedipal or pre-Oedipal
relationship, whereas interest in female hysteria slipped into a preoccupation with female sexuality and the construction of femininity. In
turn this too became predominantly understood in the early relation
to the mother.

That the obvious factor of trauma, terror and violence as conditions
that produce a hysterical response in combatants should lead to
theories of birth and earliest infancy is interesting. Again, hysteria
provides us with at least part of the explanation. Where hysteria in
women shades easily into femininity, hysteria in men appears as the
very opposite of masculinity. 'One sometimes slaps a baby to bring
it to,'[1] noted General Patton of a hysterical soldier he had abused.
The 'unmanly' behaviour of the male hysteric in war is answered by

the widespread response that he is 'infantile'. The 'infant' is the preverbal baby, unable to explain himself, reacting in his body. First the 'infantile', that is the neonatal and pre-Oedipal period of life, was investigated in psychoanalytic theory after the First World War (and given a further strong impetus after the Second World War) and then the 'feminine' was brought in. Except for ego psychologists and lacanians, for whom the position of the father remains supreme, the relationship with the mother has been the dominant area for theorization right up to the present day.

Although there is no record of any denigratory attitude on the part of psychoanalysts towards the male hysteric, the focal concern of psychoanalytical theory has made it unwittingly complicit in the equating of male hysteria with the infantile. Then male hysteria in turn becomes feminine, as the formation of femininity is likewise seen to take place in the earliest infantile period.

The baby aspect of the male hysteric is, as it were, taken seriously and that baby accorded the respect that otherwise always eludes the hysteric. After the Second World War, the baby was deemed so crucial that its first few months seemed to explain its entire future development. For instance, if the mother was not 'good enough', the baby could develop a 'false self'; or the baby was so envious of the mother's breast that this influenced all future relations with women. Once the 'infantile' male hysteric had led to the infantile *per se*, the male hysteric disappeared, leaving just the infant in his place. Battle combatants with non-organic illnesses were labelled as having 'traumatic' or 'war' neuroses rather than hysteria. The fears of the baby, some 'primal dread', were released in these subsequent traumatic neuroses. Male hysteria was banished with the very infantile scene which hysteria itself had opened up. No one after the late nineteenth-century resolution of the controversies about male hysteria any longer denied that, if there was hysteria anywhere, then men must be able to be hysterics. It therefore followed that, as these soldiers could not be labelled 'hysterics', logically hysteria did not exist either. Female hysteria followed male hysteria into oblivion, and what had been labelled 'hysteria' became, for better or worse, femininity.

The combatants' traumatic neurosis naturally revolved around violence, anxiety and dread. It did not involve sexuality. The demise of the notion of male hysteria saw likewise the demise of sexuality from dominant psychoanalytic theories and practices. Given that the adult problem was always seen to originate in an infantile situation, it was logical that the combatants' traumatic neurosis had to find its origins in the fears and violence of the baby. And so, when the theory focused on the fearful and violent pre-Oedipal baby, sexuality was largely missing from the picture. However, this was not entirely and absolutely the case. After all, the observation and concept of infantile psychosexual fantasies was (together with the concept of the unconscious) the first major theoretical plank of psychoanalysis. Despite this, its diminution was a very clear trend. Briefly, the study of infancy focused on the violence and anxieties of the baby and its need for the mother's care. Although analysts like Ferenczi in the 1930s and Jean-Paul Laplanche today, brought sexuality into the picture, it was and is as the mother's or parent's sexuality intruding into the baby rather than vice versa. The sexuality of the male hysteric went elsewhere: it was enacted outside the hospital or consulting room as compulsive brief encounters, short remedies for desperate wanting or as violent rape.

Even beyond the stage of a traumatic response to war violence, hysterical sexualization by men has continued to be missed because, like the theories and ideologies of hysteria in general, its practitioners have projected the problems on to women: Don Juan makes women jealous so he himself will not feel the green-eyed monster, the sibling rivalry, that underlies his hysterical reaction.

So if that is what happened to male hysteria, where did female hysteria go? Quite simply it became femininity. It was generally considered that at one end of the spectrum hysteria became a parody of ultrafemininity; at the other end was motherhood. As Michel Foucault put it, woman was hystericized all the way 'from the nervous woman to the mother'. However, Foucault's observation totally misses the point: motherhood can be hysterical. Hysteria was made woman, not vice versa.

The map of the theories that resulted is complex. Although they have come to overlap, I shall first look separately at the area that male hysteria gave rise to – the mother-and-infant relationship; and then at the femininity, female sexuality and motherhood into which female hysteria has been absorbed. The dominant psychoanalytical theory which addresses the first area – mother-and-infant – grew out of analytical theories based on the experiences of soldiers in the First World War and the Second World War. This is 'Object Relations' theory.

There are various theories that stress the interactions of object relationships in the construction of the human psyche. They have in common the proposition that the organism can never be seen in isolation but always in relationship with its environment. The 'object' is another human being, who is himself, of course, also a subject – so 'object' implies nothing derogatory, as it often does in colloquial usage. The emphasis of object relationships is on the 'relationship' to the other or from the other. I shall look at two major, influential theories: Kleinian and 'Independent'. Kleinian theory addresses, predominantly, the relation of the baby *to* the mother; that associated with the so-called British School of Independents addresses the relationship *from* the mother. From the perspective of all Object Relations theories, Freud's model is viewed as 'intrapsychic', a so-called 'one-person' psychology, whereas what is needed, it is argued, is a 'two-person' psychology.

In the first formulations by Freud of a sexual drive, the drive has a source in the body: the aim is satisfaction and its task is to seek out an object through which it can achieve that satisfaction. In this sense, the object can be anything or anyone: a man, a woman, a fetish, an animal, a hallucination, the subject's own body as the object of masturbation, and so on. It is simply the object through which satisfaction may or may not be realized. For Freud, when the object is found, firstly it is not welded to the drive that finds it, and secondly the psychic finding of the object is really a refinding of a prepsychic object. So, for instance, when the child takes the mother as its Oedipal object it is finding in the mother the breast that had originally nurtured it. The breast is not an object, except retrospectively, because at the time the neonatal infant did not distinguish between itself as subject and the other as object – from a psychic point of view the baby was in a state that was 'preobjectal' and 'presubjectal'. The growth of Object Relations theory in the 1930s changes this.

With Object Relations theory the baby is born with one object already in place that satisfies or frustrates it, the mother, and other objects are but substitutes for her. Before examining this further we should note how already this theory changes the terrain for hysteria. In Freud's model we can see the experience of hysteria informing the theory: the hysteric wants and wants and will try to get satisfaction wherever he can, but, because his sexual drive is unresolved, he will never finally achieve it. For Freud, both the endless driven search for satisfaction without any fixed object (even if carrying your Taita husband's bandolier will suffice for the moment) and its possible failure are intrinsic to the theory. In Object Relations theory, either the baby or the mother is responsible for managing the degree of satisfaction or frustration. In the theory, it is not that the hysteric is driven to find and cannot find satisfaction, it is that his condition, should it exist at all, encapsulates the failure either of the mother or of the baby to provide or accept this satisfaction and frustration appropriately. Again, this demonstrates how these new object-relational theories of mother-and-infant effectively excluded hysteria as an object of study. If, however, hysteria has vanished in these theories, the profound and novel work of Object Relations theorists should not be negated; the marks of that vanishing can still be traced and something can be reclaimed. Indeed, if we factor in hysteria into the work we can account for some of the omissions and difficulties present in the theories as they are currently deployed. I shall select aspects of the theories to demonstrate these problems and then indicate what it is that prevents hysteria from being read back into the Object Relations account. Hysteria exists; if it is missed in the theory, it will be missed within the treatment, even if aspects of it will be 'cured' under another name.

The general argument of both Kleinian and 'Independent' Object Relations theory can be summed up by adjusting an aphorism of Winnicott. Winnicott claimed that there is no such thing as a baby without a mother. We need to add: nor is there a mother without a baby.

During the 1930s, Sandor Ferenczi, a Hungarian analyst who, together with Freud, had been interested in hysteria, telepathy and the occult, was developing theories and practices that revolved around the needs of the infant from the first months of life. Melanie Klein, briefly, and Michael Balint, fully, were analysed by Ferenczi and trained by him in Budapest. Klein moved to Berlin, where she became a patient of Karl Abraham until his premature death in 1926. (Abraham stressed the importance of the mother and of the maternal transference.) In 1926, at the invitation of Ernest Jones, Klein visited the British Institute of Psychoanalysis in London to lecture – and stayed. Balint, meanwhile, continued in Budapest until he came to Britain as a Jewish refugee just before the start of the Second World War. By this time Balint's and Klein's emergent Object Relations theories had developed in very different ways.

Within Klein's work there are a number of concepts which are useful for understanding the hysteria they exclude. I shall select her particular understanding of the so-called 'primal scene', the specifically Kleinian notion of the schizoid-paranoid position, the 'depressive' position and the primary and all-important place she assigned to envy. Everything described by Kleinians relates not to the real situation but to the unconscious fantasy of the situation (although, of course, the real situation affects the fantasy).

Klein and Kleinians argue that from the beginning there is some primitive phantasy of an object towards which the life and death drives are directed. The phantasy, always spelt with a 'ph', is unconscious. The baby at first does not feel driven towards the parents as whole objects but to parts of them: there is a primitive phantasy of a phantasmagoric breast and a phantasmagoric penis, though these are confused with each other in the first unconscious imaginings of the 'primal scene' of the parent's intercourse. Klein agreed with Freud that there is a primordial conflict of life and death drives; but unlike Freud's notion of a death drive, Klein's must have intrinsic to it an object. It is the death drive that changes in Kleinian theory: it is at root a primal envy which manifests itself as a destructive force which attacks all it envies. Klein's is not, then, a drive to stasis, fragmentation or the inorganic, that is objectless, state, as in Freud's notion; on the contrary, it is a drive directed *at* the object. Late in her life Klein formulated the expression of the death drive as a 'primary envy' which also has its object the mother – who possesses all that the infant wants but also has the power to bestow or withhold.

In the earliest months of life, according to Klein, the baby experiences what the object has to offer as all good or all bad, the schizoid-paranoid position. The breast, which Klein calls a part object (as it is only a *part* of the mother yet it is *all* to the baby), is 'good' if it is present and satisfying and 'bad' if it is absent and frustrating. But the infant also projects the love and the hate of its life and death drives on to it, so the object is split: idealized on the one hand and feared as a persecutor on the other. From the outset, there is ambivalence – but at this point it is split simply into 'good' and 'bad'. If overwhelmed by the anxiety which is occasioned by this persecutory part object, the infant will either try to deny its existence or to control it omnipotently. If these phantasies and mechanisms are retained until later life, they will be psychotic; in normal development, although always latent, they dominate only the first four months of life, shading thereafter into the next 'position' to be assumed in relation to the object.

The next object relationship for Kleinians is the so-called 'depressive' position. In this element of the theory, somewhere around the middle of its first year of life the infant, again always in phantasy, begins to perceive that the person who gives and the person who refuses, the person whom it both loves and hates, are one and the same – prototypically, its mother. In having this relationship to a whole person, who can be both 'good' and 'bad', the infant learns that ambivalence towards the same object can be tolerated. The infant no longer projects, but instead feels concern for the damage it phantasizes it has done to the mother, or that it still might do through its sadism. Where the schizoid-paranoid anxiety comes out of the infant's fears of being violently attacked, the concerns that result from depressive anxiety are for the consequences of the damage the infant feels it has done and might do – and which would entail losing the mother. This depressive position, which is an early Oedipal position in Klein's theory, is resolved through feeling concern for the object, through wishing to repair the putative damage; if this is achieved, then the infant can move on to other object relationships.

In Kleinian theory, the object is a given and the focus is on how the infant in phantasy enacts the relationship to the first objects. In the transference situation, the analyst stands in the position of the object, the patient in the position of the infant-in-the-process-of-becoming-a-subject. The infant projects, identifies, splits, envies, feels sadism, love, gratitude, concern towards its object; although the theory subscribes to the notion that what the infant does to the object is matched by what happens to itself, this latter intrasubjective pole is far less well described. Thus, when the infant in the paranoid-schizoid position splits its object, there is a split in itself – but of this we learn little, because the entire focus is on what the infant does to the object. This, in a sense, excludes hysteria simply by virtue of its perspective: the hysteric is concerned with what is done to him, not what he does to the object who cannot really be said to exist outside his egoistic framework.

Kleinian theory places strong emphasis on the innate life and death drives. In particular, Klein's late work stresses the dynamics of envy, which it sees as a direct expression of the death drive in relation to an object: the infant envies all the mother possesses – of all of which she can also deprive the infant. In my account, the hysteric is jealous of a position and only then envies what the occupant of the position may have.

The Independent Object Relations school, of which Balint was an early proponent, reverses the emphasis: this school claims that it is what the object provides or does not provide for the infant that leads to pathology or psychic health. For most Independents there is a primary love coming from the infant, but no death drive innate within the infant; there is aggression that can go well or ill according to the appropriateness of the care the infant receives. Although Balint had developed his theories independently of Klein, in Britain there was considered just one 'Object Relations' approach right up to the 1950s. The differences that only eventually led to the development of an 'Independent' school of thought can be traced to the Second World War. In 'controversial discussions' during the war, the British Object Relations theorists, headed by Klein, had already distinguished themselves from the Freudians, headed by Anna Freud (who, as a last-minute refugee from Vienna, had settled with her father in London). But the war and post-war work of Bowlby and Winnicott, with their emphasis on the mother, foreshadowed a further split among Object Relations theorists. There is no one single school of thought among Independents. Whereas, although Kleinians may vary, augment or disagree with each other's theories, yet they refer back to and use the vocabulary of Klein (the possible exception being Wilfred Bion), there is no comparable figurehead among the Independents. One Independent, however, D. W. Winnicott, can be used here as, although hysteria is not a condition which he describes, many of his insights and theories are useful for illuminating hysteria as I see it.

Because he was a paediatrician as well as a psychoanalyst, Winnicott was very attentive to the patient's body. What, for example, is the child feeling when it throws an object, stutters, squirms, and so on? For Winnicott there is in every human being a potential 'self' which can come to feel true, authentic and real, or it can, through too much compliance and fear, develop as a 'false' self. For Winnicott neonatal helplessness and utter dependency are crucial; they form the particular all-important basis from which the human being grows. The infant seeks not simply gratification or satisfaction but physical and emotional contact. Before any 'drive' can be used there must be a 'self'.

The entire dependence of the infant makes both men and women always fear the woman/mother on whom that dependence rests. The baby will start life feeling chaotic but, if the mother recognizes the baby sufficiently in and for itself, it can begin to feel real; if she does not, it will either continue to feel chaotic or become compliant to the version of itself which the mother wrongly sees – it will become a 'false self'. The false self is constructed both so the world can be managed and so some residual true self may be protected. Created as a result of misrecognition, the false self builds itself up on a series of erroneous identifications, copies of other people. It is here, in the false self, that we must look for the missing hysteria.

When the object fails by inadequacy, or intrusion, or through misrecognition, according to Winnicott, there will develop some degree of falseness. Again, as with Kleinians, the analyst stands pre-dominantly in the position of the object (mainly the mother); however, Winnicott's emphasis is not on what the infant-patient does to him but on what the infant-patient makes of what the analyst gives or fails to give. The psychotic or person with a false self comes to therapy in search of recognition; for Winnicott he must regress and start again. This perspective is helpful for hysteria, which likewise focuses on what is done to the person who becomes hysterical. Hysteria is a reaction to something that happens – this is Winnicott's perspective.

Both dominant schools of Object Relations theory – Kleinian and Independent – offer a good phenomenology and some useful concepts on to which we can reread aspects of hysteria. However, there are a number of problems.

Both are developmental models: the neonatal infant grows upwards and onwards to health or pathology. If something goes wrong, he must go back a few paces and start again. Against this perspective, even childhood hysteria is essentially regressive: struck by some experience that either is or can be converted to a trauma, the hysteric (individual or group) reverts to a childhood or infantile mode of behaviour. Development can show us the position arrived at and the stage, position or relationship reverted to – but the regression brings with it all the moss that has been gathered and what is reverted to is never the same as what was there 'in the first place'. Balint and Winnicott, and Independents generally, argue that regression is crucial in the therapeutic situation: one can go back and renegotiate the object relationship with the therapist. But I would argue that hysteria is itself a regression. Furthermore, a developmental model *per se* has a tendency to suggest that the path to psychic health is the proper path and all other courses are deviations from it. If, instead of development, we look from the perspective of regression, then, from necessity, the deviation or the pathological is presented as the model. The focus is on what has gone wrong, instead of what should go right. If one looks at pathologies, then, as Freud said, one can understand something of so-called psychic health, but it will only always be as an 'ideal fiction'. Quite contrary to this, a developmental model which is oriented to health sidelines the neuroses (obsessionality as well as hysteria) and tends to a moralizing certainty about health or normality.

Freud argued that psychoanalysis can only treat the neuroses because in the neuroses there are object relationships. In the neuroses, feelings for the other person in the patient's history can be transferred to the analyst and, within this process, understood. Therefore, to a Freudian, though psychoanalysis has things to say about psychoses, due to the absence of a transference relationship it cannot fully treat psychotics. Psychotics have repudiated relationships. Object Relations theorists, however, claim to treat psychosis. The first treatment of psychosis was recorded as a breakthrough. However, by definition,

Object Relations practitioners must be able to deal with psychoses because there are in this theory from the outset always object relationships. If there are always object relations, there will also always be transference – psychotic as well as neurotic. The treatment of psychoses, then, is not a new departure of the practice, but an automatic consequence of the then new theory.

Founding psychoanalysis in hysteria, Freud underplayed, or at times missed, a crucial dimension of it – one that sealed its 'disappearance' on the rise of Object Relations theory. For hysteria poses a special problem to the Object Relations approach: the object relationships of hysteria (its so-called alloeroticism, or apparent erotic attachments to other people) are not true object relationships. 'Objects' abound but the hysteric has identified with or imitated the object to such a degree that the object relationship is necessarily a masquerade, 'phoney' or false. The hysteric has a hunger for love which must come *from* the other, not a love (or hate or envy) *of* the other – except where the other affects the hysteric by either getting in his way or failing to offer him something. The 'object' for the hysteric is not another subject. This was missed from the outset. In his theory, rather than in his observation, Freud took the hysteric's imagined lovers as people he really loves, whereas they are only people whom he wants to make sure love him. With Object Relations the assumption that there are always people whom one loves, hates, envies, and so on, is completely endorsed. This is at the cost of the narcissism and autoeroticism that can – and in hysteria do – underlie what looks like an interest in the other person.

Obviously, no one is born on a desert island. The question is: What is meant by an object relationship? There is some confusion of terminology: narcissism, schizophrenia and paranoia all deploy fantasy objects in any theory. However, in Freudian/Lacanian theory, these narcissistic and psychotic states repudiate any awareness that the object is a subject in its own right. Object Relations theorists, to the contrary, chart how the object is treated or used and take all uses, even repudiation or denial, as relationships to the object. We can see how this plays out in practice. For instance, when Breuer and Freud described Anna O in 1895, and again in 1910, she was diagnosed as a hysteric and thus as 'neurotic'. The assumption was that she *had* relations with other people which were transferable. Some later Object Relations theorists, noting the severity of her condition, have contended, however, that her illness was a psychosis; the fact that she had relations to other people was not a problem, as all of us, 'healthy', neurotic or psychotic, have these relations – we just make different uses of them. However, as hysteria is commonly regarded as a neurosis, then what Anna O suffered from was not hysteria but some psychotic condition. The theories place the 'illness' according to their pre-existent models.

I propose to look briefly at a case of schizophrenia in Kleinian treatment from the 1940s which the Belgian historian Katrien Libbrecht has relabelled hysteria (see chapter 4). Because of the problem of transference, at the time the controversy between Freudians and Kleinians was whether or not one could treat psychoses in analysis. If all relationships are object relationships, then, by definition, they are analysable. As a successful analysis of schizophrenia, the case in point was hailed as a breakthrough – it is an impressive treatment by any standards, in which the analyst learns from his patient by seeing which of her feelings she has projected into and on to him. Libbrecht contends that there is hysterical psychosis here and that many analysts have missed the hysteria.

The case I shall consider is Herbert Rosenfeld's treatment of Mildred, a schizophrenic woman of twenty-nine who showed marked splitting and depersonalization. At the time he started seeing Mildred, in 1944, Rosenfeld himself was in a training analysis with Melanie Klein, and the paper he later produced, 'Analysis of a Schizophrenic State with Depersonalization' (1947), was rigorously Kleinian. When he came to reconsider the case forty years later, Rosenfeld's language was less strictly Kleinian: he then described his patient as someone who had lost all feelings and believed she had lost herself; she had split off parts of herself and projected them into her analyst – she wanted to get inside her analyst and lose herself there but this made her terrified that her analyst would intrude into her. I propose not to reanalyse or even reclassify Mildred, but simply to look at the case through the perspective of hysteria as I am attempting to delineate it. As with Eister's tram man and Freud's Dora, I have gleaned information from the case that is not prominent in the presentation.

Like Dora, Mildred presents with numerous physical complaints, such as a more or less permanent 'flu', which in the idiom of the day were called 'functional' (that is, they can affect the functions, but they have no known organic cause). Like Dora, and many psychologically invalided combatants, Mildred is regularly speechless. The transference relationship is called 'psychotic' because Mildred brings her schizoid splitting habits to bear on the treatment – often not managing to get to the sessions, or turning up very late because she has not interpreted the events of getting up, having breakfast, washing, catching the bus and coming to see Rosenfeld as linked procedures – she has separated, or 'split', them. The relationship with Rosenfeld is also 'psychotic' because in it Rosenfeld becomes a persecutory Devil father. This is the schizoid-paranoid position of Kleinian thought.

So, what would the case look like if we were to use the category of hysteria and the understanding of it that I am trying to advance here? Mildred's younger brother Jack, of whom she has been intensely jealous, has been killed in the war. Following this, she cannot recover from a series of illnesses; she is driven by illnesses. She has had what she calls 'influenze' for four or five months. She feels 'dead' and depersonalized – not knowing who she is, feeling dead to herself.

If we are to think of this as hysteria, then, as with Anna O, this depersonalization of Mildred can also be interpreted as a defence against any sexual feelings emerging within her therapy sessions. Hysterics who sexualize everything often present as the very opposite – precisely because the sexuality is an overwhelming expression of wanting, it must be hidden and enacted elsewhere. Such is the case with Mildred. She will have none of the transference of sexuality – of her positive libidinal feelings towards members of her family – to her therapist that he tries for. Instead, Mildred acts her sexuality outside the treatment in what sounds like a fairly florid manner. She has a massively seductive encounter with a man called Denis, who has a comparable life history to her own. Denis tries uncontrollably to seduce Mildred while his wife is away giving birth to their child. As a result, Denis has a breakdown. Mildred also has intense friendships with women, whom she apparently loves but of whom she is extremely jealous. When, in therapy, Mildred does start to have sexual feelings for her analyst, these, we learn, are 'displaced, *as always*, on to a young relative whom she scarcely knew [my italics]'.[2] She cannot abide her analyst's interpretations because they get inside her – thus he becomes a persecutor. But nor can she stand her adored mother's slightest criticism or interference either. She tells her analyst that she shouts at her mother that she didn't ask to be born; in other words, indicating that she didn't want to leave the womb, and that her life is her mother's responsibility. She wants so much, yet she cannot bear any frustration, screaming at anyone whom she feels thwarts her in the slightest. Mildred wants to get inside her mother and both enacts this by staying warm, half asleep in bed for days on end, and also repudiates any such wish. Because she denies all her sexual and erotic feelings, they are experienced by her as what others are doing to her – she wants to get inside her mother and then her analyst, but she experiences this as a horror of her analyst getting inside her. The desires come back, turned into their negatives, from outside as illness and persecution. And what is this persecution? In the Middle Ages 'witches' were supposed to be penetrated by the Devil; Rosenfeld is just such a penetrating 'Devil Daddy' for Mildred, whose 'influenze' may have been a pun on ghostly influences.

In other words, we can rewrite this case as the story of a young woman who wants and wants what she cannot have and cannot be. What Mildred cannot be is the brother, who was everybody's favourite but who was killed. Her brother's death precipitates the insistent illnesses which bring her into treatment. In her overwhelming sibling jealousy, she must have wanted him dead, but because he is not a true object of either her love or her hate, because he stands in the position where she wants to be, when he dies she becomes 'dead' like him, instead of knowing he is not her. She cannot mourn his loss.

As with Dora, behind Mildred's adult breakdown is a childhood collapse – though earlier than Dora's. Mildred was the elder of two siblings. She had had a series of breakdowns which had started when her younger brother was born when she was nineteen months old. At the time of his birth Mildred lost the ability to speak and had to learn all over again how to grow from infancy into childhood, including how to walk. She became a changed character, losing all spark and brilliance. Jack was loved and very bright; Mildred spent her childhood trying to be like him. Ever since she was a toddler, Mildred had

wanted to be Jack; when he dies, she becomes 'dead' like him –
depersonalized.

Hysteria imitates both illnesses and their cures and, particularly at
its psychotic end, is a serious condition in itself. There are indeed real
problems which Mildred brings to the adult therapy with Rosenfeld,
but once these are identified, I suggest, she mimics and magnifies them
– just as a hysteric would. Mildred's sessions with Rosenfeld are
characterized by chronic amnesia: nothing from one session can be
recollected in the next. Her mechanism of splitting everything up into
actions which do not touch each other, and parts of her self which
do not become integrated, could arise from a sense of chaos and
fragmentation which is as characteristic of hysteria as it is of schizophrenia. But also her therapist constantly draws attention to the way
she splits things, so she produces a pantomime of splitting behaviour:
this could be a hysterical imitation of the therapist's characteristic
manner of talking about different parts of the patient each having
different feelings. (Such an interpretative technique does not produce
an inaccurate picture in itself but it would encourage a hysterical
patient to present as a split or multiple personality.)

The sexual drive, no longer at the forefront of analytic theory when
Mildred sees Rosenfeld, and forbidden in therapy, is enacted by her
outside the session, with lots of women and with one man after
another. Then, knowing that she will get none of the sexual attention
which she wants from her therapist, who of course will not even
satisfy all the wants in her questionings, she turns this into a dread
of his persecutory penetration and gets married instead. Beneath the
dead depersonalization, her insistent wanting is labile; she wants
whatever she cannot have (she knows analysts do not answer questions), which makes whatever she does have become valueless. She is
able to perceive what the therapist wants and to offer this to him in
a hide and seek of symptoms and interpretations. However, it is not
enough, so the rampant seductions take place outside the treatment.

That Mildred is depersonalized, schizoid or possibly even 'schizophrenic' is not in question. However, the conditions of the treatment
rightly exclude the practice of any gratification of sexuality; but the
theory, with hysteria missing from it, wrongly does so also. With the
loss of the category of hysteria went a decline in the observation of

sexuality. In all Object Relations treatments we need to look at the sexuality that takes place outside the sessions and integrate it with behaviour such as imitation within the sessions.

In Kleinian theory the aim of the death drive is to destroy the object, but here, with Mildred, we have instead the 'death' of the *subject*. This death of the subject can be seen in the 'death by proxy' (by means of his serious breakdown) of Mildred's lover Denis, as well as in her own deathly depression. The first is comparable to the accident suffered by Herr K in the Dora case. Mildred the adult identifies with the dead brother whose death, on his birth, she had clearly wished for. Her death wishes are realized when Jack is killed but then she is punished by becoming 'dead'. But these wishes are not analysed and they persist. She finds a lover, Denis, who is clearly in many respects like her – promiscuously searching for himself in another person and hysterically avoiding the birth of someone who might displace him (in Denis's case, his own child). Denis may have identified with Mildred (we cannot know as he is not in treatment) and Mildred may have used him as a vehicle for her own death wishes. Although Denis does not die, he does break down completely. This *folie à deux* and transmission of death and sexuality is characteristic of hysteria. It is as though, in communicating her hysteria, Mildred hands on the danger, so that it is Denis who has the breakdown. Without a perception of the significance of the enactment of sexuality and the enactment of death that take place outside the treatment, hysteria becomes invisible.

It is not, then, that all psychotic patients are hysterics in disguise, but that there is often a strongly hysterical aspect to their condition which goes unrecognized if sexuality and death (often manifest as hatred) and the close relationship between the two are absent from the theory as well as from the treatment. Hysteria has a clear psychotic dimension, but hysteria also assumes a psychotic disguise if psychosis is what is required. This is not to argue against the gains made by ever finer differentiation: clinical material is bound to be confused, whereas a theoretical grasp depends on producing demarcation lines. Nor am I advocating a return to an all-inclusive label of 'hysteria' for every psychotic condition, but rather I am drawing attention to the consequences of its utter elimination. Without the category of hysteria always in mind, for the analyst, the seduction of the mimetic process in which the treatment is imitated is hard to perceive; the driven insistent wanting goes elsewhere in acted-out sex and death. This can be dangerous.

Although Libbrecht spots Mildred and others as cases of hysteria behind the psychoses of Object Relations treatment, she does not describe why they are hysterical. This absence of an account of wherein lies the hysteria is somewhat worrying, particularly when we realize that she singles out only cases of women. Is there an assumed equation on Libbrecht's part? To illustrate her contention that hysterical psychosis exists and that the hysteric has been missed out from the diagnoses, Libbrecht rewrites a number of cases. They are all female. They are taken from Object Relations theory, where the focus is all on the mother and baby. Is this 'gendering' because, although, as I would argue, it was male hysteria that led to the focus on the mother–infant relationship, the mother–infant relationship is considered typically female? Both Klein and Winnicott regard the first mother–baby relationship as feminine for both boys and girls. Winnicott, for instance, states that what is female is the primary state of 'being'; what is male comes only with some separation in 'doing'. When Libbrecht discovers the hysteria in these case histories, she is following the trend of seeing the mother-and-infant situation as 'feminine' and then making this coincide with a woman. In this way, hysteria stays feminized even in the radical rewriting of the diagnosis.

It so happens, however, that the next study of a patient in Rosenfeld's groundbreaking *Psychotic States* (1965) is a man who came to see me (though not for full analysis) for a number of years following Rosenfeld's death. My patient, Rosenfeld's 'Case A', presented himself to me as the paranoid homosexual Rosenfeld describes. It was in many ways an appropriate diagnosis – he had had many homosexual relations and certainly in most of them he had ended up feeling his lover was attacking him. But it was also a fact that the hysterical aspects of his personality were, and from his descriptions always had been, dramatically enacted outside the treatment in rages, lying and flamboyant sexual exhibitionism. The positive transference to me (whom even in the transference he experienced as a woman) and a re-construction of his actual history, which included a marriage, showed not homosexuality but the bisexuality typical of hysteria – as of

Mildred and Dora. 'Case A' was almost desperately fond of his female cat, to whom he could also be immensely cruel and whom he named after his ex-wife. The cat and, I believe, the wife were heirs to a deeply ambivalent relationship to a younger brother who does not feature at all in Rosenfeld's case history. I could have added to 'Case A' a history of male hysteria that uses a manipulation of a lateral relationship into a traumatic experience which is then protested against.

In Kleinian theory, the splitting, the delusionary aspects and the high degree of ambivalence which characterize hysteria are treated instead as developmental positions of the human infant. They are related to different aspects of anxiety but not to sexuality. Because hysteria is missing from the account, other aspects get marginalized and denigrated. Libbrecht's work shows how hysteria looked both ways – towards neurosis and, at its more serious end, towards psychosis. Without the notion of hysteria some other condition must substitute – today, where once hysteria stood, homosexuality still stands condemned as the non-normative. Because the bisexuality of hysteria is missed, anything heterosexual, such as Mildred's marriage, becomes too easily equated with psychic health.

If we look at the symptoms the patient presents in the key texts which demonstrate psychoanalytic treatment of psychotic patients (whether by Independents or Kleinians) they can be seen to be at least partially hysterical. The hysteria is either in psychotic disguise (as it was with Anne Sexton) or displays a psychotic dimension. If, as seems to be the case (and as Jung proposed), a serious hysterical condition can be resolved by the person becoming acceptably schizoid, then it follows that, at the other end of the hysterical scale, the person can also become unacceptably schizophrenic. There was a trend in Object Relations to relabel the more seriously ill nineteenth-century hysteric as really psychotic. Libbrecht's work on hysterical psychosis reverses this trend by demonstrating that a number of today's 'psychotics' are in fact yesterday's 'hysterics' and were correctly designated as such before. The difficulty is really with the theory, not the patient.

In the nineteenth century there was *folie* (madness) *hystérique*. However, with the psychiatric division of mental instability into neurosis and psychosis, the general category of 'madness' came to be considered unscientific. Much of the previous 'madness' of hysterics was siphoned off into discrete syndromes such as those that Micale describes – schizophrenia, florid MPD and suicidal anorexia, for instance. However, what would seem to have happened as well is that the 'mad' dimension of hysteria was labelled 'psychotic' so that this psychosis could then become treatable by Object Relations clinicians via an understanding of the psychotic transference. In fact, this 'transference relationship' is hysteria under its new psychotic name. The hysteric, unlike the psychotic, *appears* to be capable of a relationship; however, this apparent object relationship is simply the hysterical part of the psychosis deployed in the transference. In other words, it is not that the hysteric Anna O was really psychotic, nor that the psychotic patient Mildred was really a hysteric – but that the elements of their personalities which could become attached to the analyst in the transference were the neurotic ends of their hysteria which had not repudiated all relationships but which instead could mimic them in the clinical setting. It is possible that this object relationship, which is 'false', may be channelled into a transference and analysed so that it can be successfully dealt with – but it may just as easily remain a perfect mimicry and be missed.

Classifications are useful for declaring boundaries, but not for seeing the whole picture. Both Mildred the schizophrenic and Anna O the hysterical patient would seem, at their most ill, to have been 'mad'. However, they are also, at times, able to have social or sexual relationships, even if these are centred on themselves.

I want to move now to an illustration of an Independent Object Relations patient where again there is no suggestion in the account of hysteria, but hysteria nevertheless fits the history and many of the symptoms. In her examination of hidden hysteria, Libbrecht looks at 'Susan', a young girl described by the British analyst Marian Milner. However, Milner's account of Susan is very long and so, instead, I have selected a case from the work of Enid Balint, that of 'Sarah'. At the time of the analysis Enid Balint was herself in a second analysis with Winnicott and was married to Michael Balint, with whom she co-authored many works.

In her 1963 paper on Sarah, 'On Being Empty of Oneself', Enid Balint considers that experiences of emptiness are characteristic more of women than of men and that this state of emptiness may be one aspect of the very construction of femininity. (The well-known child analyst Erik Erikson has observed that one of the differences in girls' and boys' play is that girls are preoccupied with full and empty places and spaces[3] – Balint refers to this to support her view.) Emptiness, I believe, characterizes the hysteric – male or female. Masud Khan, a colleague of Balint, in one of the few late twentieth-century papers about hysteria, 'Grudge and the Hysteric' (1974), describes 'grudging' hysterical or histrionic behaviour (his cases are all women). It is true that both men and women hysterics are always complaining or have a grudge against someone. Khan interestingly sees this grudging behaviour as a defence against a sense of emptiness. Balint, however, does not consider the possibility of hysteria with Sarah.

Balint coins the phrase 'empty of herself' as an inversion of being 'full of oneself'. Sarah experiences herself and appears to her analyst as 'empty of herself' – there is, she feels, nothing inside her. A young woman in her early twenties, she appears to her analyst and others as a 'stranger in the world'. She cannot work and, though she can use public transport to come to her analytic sessions, she is unable to have any social life and has to be cared for by unconventional, tolerant and accommodating relatives. Balint describes Sarah as very ill indeed. Yet, when she is hospitalized following the suicide of a close friend of her own age, the psychiatric assessment, while it notes depression and a suicide risk, nevertheless declares that she is not psychotic. Presumably this is because she does not show thought disorder – and indeed the report of analytic sessions does not reveal any. If Sarah is not psychotic, is she neurotic or borderline (according to contemporary diagnoses)? Balint leaves the question unanswered. Instead she describes Sarah's experiences, symptoms and history of emptiness.

Shortly before his death in January 1970, Winnicott wrote, in 'Fear of Breakdown', of the fear that some patients have of breaking down. His argument ran that the breakdown that is dreaded has already occurred, but at a point which is, in Winnicott's words, 'prior to anything which can usefully be called the self'. According to Winnicott, patients who manifest this dread collude with the psychoanalyst in constructing an analysis of a psychoneurosis whereas their condition is in fact psychotic. This is evidence of psychotic 'splitting'. Neurotic compliance and psychotic potential both well describe severe hysteria, in which the patient seems to be getting on very well in the treatment but this conceals a madness that is enacted elsewhere. This situation, although never named as hysteria, emerges in both Winnicott's theory and Balint's analysis. That there was no diagnosis of hysteria available may also account for why neither Balint nor the psychiatric profession were able to 'diagnose' Sarah. They needed the category of severe hysteria. Sarah, according to Balint's analysis, was empty of herself because her mother had never recognized her. It would be incorrect to say that Sarah's mother had not recognized her for who she was, for she wasn't yet someone with an ego. The title of Balint's collection of essays in which this case history is reprinted, *Before I Was I*, is taken from a poem by John Donne. Sarah's formative experience of non-recognition took place 'before she was she'.

From constructions of her history it seems to both Balint and Sarah that Sarah's mother did not recognize, or love, her daughter's particular qualities. There was no match of mother's feelings and daughter's qualities – for instance, if Sarah was sad, her mother experienced her as contented. Sarah as Sarah seems to have had no significance. As a result, Sarah does not mind being alone – what she finds intolerable is being with her analyst when her analyst misunderstands something that Sarah is trying to tell her. Misunderstanding in the analytic setting is the equivalent of misrecognition in the familial. It was misrecognition, rather than the actual absence of the mother, that produced the void within Sarah as a baby. We could say that for Sarah, the void was produced by a bodily presence which was not psychically there. Enid Balint actually met Sarah's mother. She describes her as a mother who was not able to respond to the messages her baby sent out for recognition; the daughter had to conform to her mother's image of her, not to her own reality. In the therapy sessions Balint was able to reconstruct this scenario through the transference and then directly observe the actual relations of mother and young adult daughter.

Sarah's father plays no part in Balint's report of the etiology of Sarah's condition. His role, when we stop to consider it, is, however, startling. Apparently, he was a violent man without any self-control. Although he already had two sons when Sarah was born, he wanted another son and was very disappointed at having a daughter. Sarah became a tomboy. Sarah's breakdown in her early twenties occurred when her father was being particularly violent – something which would have undoubtedly disturbed Sarah. The father would not pay for the last year of Sarah's analysis; it was only during this year, apparently, that the focus of the work shifted somewhat to Sarah's relationships with her father and her brothers. For my purposes, at least as notable as the fact that no significance for the history of the illness is attached to the father, is that nothing is made of the account that Sarah gives of how, when she was about six or seven, the younger of her two brothers had sexual intercourse with her, a practice which continued until she was about twelve. This is described; the difficulties it would have occasioned are not dismissed. However, with hysteria not on the map, it is not seen to play a part in the formation of Sarah's illness.

Again, as with Mildred, no significance is attached to Sarah's many florid heterosexual and homosexual relationships. Eventually, however, after the treatment is over and Sarah would seem to feel less 'empty', she forms a satisfactory relationship with a woman with whom she lives. In the fourth year of her analysis, Sarah has a dream, which she reports both at the time and again a year later: a dog comes out of the sea, bites her and then disappears. She is reminded of a previous dream in which a bird swoops down, gashes her on the head, and then also disappears. She says that what hurts her most is that the bird never turns back, that it seems utterly unconcerned and indifferent. As a small child Sarah had lain awake at nights terrified of death, too scared to call out, imagining that something was going to crash on her head. Sometimes this 'something' was a rolling pin, sometimes a rock, or a cloud. The second time she recounts the dog dream, she comments that the dog had taken away her uterus – but that by this stage in the analytical treatment, she says that she has got it back.

Enid Balint's work, like that of Winnicott, is crucial to our general understanding of hysteria because of the importance it accords to recognition, or lack of, by the other. However, both Balint and Winnicott locate this other exclusively with the mother. Let us instead look at the pictures of both Mildred and Sarah using the concept of recognition in the context of regression, not, as do both analysts, of regression within the sessions, but of regression within the theory of illness. Hysteria, I argue, is a process of regression set up by a shock or catastrophe which is experienced as a traumatic implosion which leaves the person feeling chaotic, fragmented – or empty.

Let us look at the history of Sarah from the point of view of a possiblity of severe hysteria. Sarah is hospitalized after a friend (a young woman of the same age) commits suicide. I suggest this casts her back to an earlier catastrophic experience – we cannot be sure what. We do know, however, that when she was six or seven years old, Sarah's brother seduced her. Balint mentions that, for most of the analysis, she is unsure whether this seduction is fact or fiction – a familiar problem with hysteria. Though, of course, whether it is one or the other matters critically for Sarah, it is less important for an account of the illness. The seduction was probably actually true, and it was certainly psychically true. An incident which triggers a childhood breakdown can be a real event or a 'screen' memory, in which case it encapsulates as an image all the important experiences of childhood before that moment (see chapter 9). After the first occasion of the incestuous intercourse, Sarah went to her parents' bedroom where they did not recognize her bewilderment or distress. These feelings became manifest as Sarah feeling her heartbeat was stopping and her having night terrors of being attacked or annihilated. She was quite seriously ill. However, soon, in the daytime at least, she became the lovely, easy girl her mother thought was her true character. Eventually she left home and country for England, and this 'false' self broke down. This breakdown was characterized by an experience and appearance of 'emptiness'.

We learn very little about Sarah's rampant bisexual life, which takes place outside the analysis (and would suggest that the absence of a social life did not continue). Were these sexual encounters perhaps desperate efforts to find someone with whom she could identify – someone she could be? Sarah's father wanted a son; Sarah, until the incest with her brother, had been (like Dora) a tomboy, a younger son. The unrecognized experience of the sibling incest could well have 'emptied' her. In her nightmare, the dog or bird gash her head or steal or rip out her womb: penetrated by her brother, she could no longer be the same as him, a boy like him; instead she became a 'good girl' with an empty or missing womb. Dora continued to seek some masculine identification (such as that with her father or her suitor) after she lost her identification with her brother Otto; Sarah probably did so too. What Sarah's case can give us is the idea that when she has penetrative intercourse she experiences her insides as empty, so she has a womb that cannot be reproductive, and she has a brittle, false femininity. (Balint thinks that there may be here a possible basis for a general understanding of anorexia.) Balint tells us that Sarah's penis envy is very strong – which could well result from the overthrow of her identifications with her brothers, for we should note that it came after the emptiness. The penis envy would be subsequent because, until she discovered she could not be a tomboy, there was no need to envy her *brothers*, as she was like them, even the same as them.

The other side of emptiness is a body full of dead people. Sarah's hands are lifeless and she believes they are made of steel. She dreams (like Dora) of a fire; in Sarah's dream, however, her brother saves her. During therapy there has been a serious danger that she would kill herself. One wants the objects of one's envy and jealousy dead, but one loves them too, one has been the same as them – and so must stay so in death.

Rosenfeld, unlike Balint, puts considerable emphasis on his patient Mildred's sibling and affinal jealousies. However, he sees himself in the transference as the hated father or the mother who gave birth to brother Jack. Mildred's idealized friendships with women turn out to have been based on crippling jealousy and her male friendships on envy. Although at times Mildred cannot get to the therapy sessions and then is silent when there, and although Rosenfeld links this latter to the birth of her brother when Mildred became mute and unable to walk, it is Mildred's fiancé, not her analyst, upon whom she transfers the hysterical love and jealousy of the sibling catastrophe. When her fiancé has to go away, Mildred is overcome by grief – he might be killed like her brother – but then, once he has gone, she can hardly remember him: 'she could only feel a thrill about the prospect of getting married, but *he* did not seem to exist'. Mildred lacks feelings, but says at one point that she feels as if she has been blown up like a balloon to twelve times her size, full of 'expectancy', but that she is something tiny inside this balloon. Rosenfeld interprets this sense of 'expectancy' not (as seems obvious if one thinks of hysteria) as an empty pregnancy, but as her emptying out her fiancé because she has got inside him and made him empty through her aggressive, greedy wishes. However, Mildred's attitude to her fiancé is typical of a hysteric: he is an object she will marry, but not a subject, and this is why she cannot remember him when he is no longer present to give her attention.

We could read Sarah's and Mildred's analyses as two sides of the same hysterical coin. Although there are differences between the patients, their phenomenologies and histories are remarkably similar: the catastrophe of a death of a peer or sibling (Sarah, when hospitalized, poses a suicide risk – her friend had killed herself). This precipitates jealous rivalry, love and hate of someone with whom each closely identifies. Then there is the instant regression to an early childhood experience of just such a situation. After their childhood catastrophes both patients had apparently recovered through latency until adolescence; Sarah became ultrafeminine (like Dora); Mildred 'became' her brother and, by identifying with him, was able to relearn the skills she had lost. With the thrust of sexuality in adolescence, both girls broke down. Their analysts describe in both Sarah and Mildred all of the following: the mechanisms of splitting and depersonalization; an experiential emptiness and bodily presentation of it; an underlying sense of fragmentation or chaos; an enacted rampant bisexuality; envy and/or jealousy; a predominant orality; the possibility of fictitiousness or fabrication. We can add plagiarism to the imitation of other people. Did Sarah fear her hands might 'steal', so she stopped them? They became lifeless like 'steel'. This demonstrates a perfect hysterical symptom, showing both the desire and the prevention of that desire. In his analysis, Rosenfeld focuses on the destructiveness towards the object; in hers, Balint emphasizes the failure of recognition from the mother. Both are crucial. However, both could come together to mutual enrichment if the excluded possibility of hysteria is read back into the case histories.

Without any of the accompanying questions that would have been raised by an enquiry into hysteria, psychoanalytic Object Relations theory has developed on the basis of the psychic consequences of the first relationship to the mother. In the transference relationship, the

Object Relations psychoanalyst essentially establishes her or himself as mother, interpreting the dynamics in which the patient still deploys an infantile constellation of positions, fantasies and feelings, as ones that are related to a mother. Until the phallic stage, an infant's anxiety is without doubt at least as marked as its sexuality. This anxiety becomes evident in Object Relations treatment. If we see the hysteric as regressing back to these anxieties from the moment he is displaced by a sibling, we can also account for the sexuality – the slightly older child is a sexual child with playmates or siblings (in fantasy or sometimes in actuality, as with Sarah and possibly the Wolf Man).

With the decline in the observation of hysteria, then, there has been a decline in a focus on sexuality and on 'death' as a deadly stasis which can lead to suicide. A further problem that arose with the move to Object Relations in the context of the elimination of hysteria was the collapse of the hysterical quality of mimesis into a normative process of identification. The mimetic qualities of hysteria are testimony to the significance of identification in human life. It is as though, where animals have instincts that lead them straight to an object, humans, whose premature birth has weakened this ability, compensate with mimesis in order to ensure that the danger of separation does not arise.

Mimetic behaviour is, of course, normal, but in excess it demonstrates the regressive behaviour of hysteria. The trajectory may work something like this: a non-separation with the mother → the shock of a sibling which blasts this → a seeking out of the mother then the father to love one → an identification with the sibling (dead or alive) → a shock that disrupts this. This is the point where the hysteria comes in and traverses this path backwards. Throughout life there may be catastrophes that break an aspect of the potential hysteric's identification with peers and affines (as with Mildred and Sarah), the deaths of contemporaries, partners, friends or enemies, which can then send him or her back to that earlier catastrophe when suddenly they did not know where they stood. Hysterical confusion, mimesis, rivalry, plagiarism, and the sexualizing of the trauma, annihilation or 'death' then take place. However, if hysteria and regression from the present, which indicate the significance of lateral relationships, are not taken into account, they will be otherwise enacted outside the therapeutic sessions.

The hysterical soldiers of the First World War were shocked back into a position of helplessness where the protecting 'Motherland' was utterly absent. It was the recreation of the murders of the brother/enemy that sent them there. Their nightmares and symptoms may have been so many efforts at retaining an identification with the deaths they witnessed that were too horrific to accept but which induced guilt in them both for having survived and for having killed. The deaths thus had to be recreated in various ways in the symptoms so the dead people or parts of people were still present: a paralysed, 'dead' leg for the blasted leg of one's shell-shattered comrade; mutism for the silence of his death. In part, this amalgamation with the other would appear 'feminine' because the 'first' other who disappeared, and upon whose presence the hysteric was ultimately dependent, was a mother who necessarily, but perhaps excessively or prematurely, went missing from his babyhood. It would also appear feminine in another respect: regression to the helplessness of infancy, and helplessness in general, is ideologically perceived as a female characteristic. Object Relations theory's drift into equating infantile helplessness with femininity must be seen as the historical construct and ideological slippage it is.

Although both the cases I have considered in detail here concern women, it was, ironically, the male hysteric, undoubtedly evident, undoubtedly suppressed or denied in both the First and Second World Wars, whose condition can be seen as leading to the growth of Object Relations theory and to the increasing importance given by psychoanalysis to the pre-Oedipal state. The baby and mother became all-important. Except for an occasional interesting blip on the screen, hysteria vanished from the theory and from the treatment – but perhaps not always from the observation, for, as the British analyst Eric Brenman noted in his paper simply entitled 'Hysteria', every analyst he asked thought they saw hysteria but nobody deployed the category.

II. THE HYSTERICAL WOMAN OR
HYSTERIA FEMINIZED

The particular progress of psychoanalysis has provided an exemplary instance of a wider issue. The human potential for hysteria has been feminized. Because now in the West hysteria is said to have disappeared, and because the treatment theories that have emanated from the problem of male hysteria developed within this framework that more or less excluded the possibility of hysteria, the twentieth-century experience offers a remarkable opportunity for charting how hysteria has been turned into femininity. When, at the end of his life, Freud claimed that the bedrock beneath which psychoanalysis could not penetrate was the more or less biological one of a universal tendency by both sexes to repudiate femininity, he was making the mistake that has been widely reiterated: it is hysteria that cannot be tolerated, the conditions of hysteria that everyone wishes to repudiate. We see this time and again in psychoanalysis. Freud himself was regularly described as 'hysterophobic'; his commentators are equally so, repeatedly diagnosing Freud's clearly hysterical symptoms not as hysteria but as 'actual' neurosis, neurasthenia and so on. It is the same in other fields: anthropologists fall over backwards to eschew the term hysteria. The solution to this profound repudiation of the condition is to make sure someone else has it – structurally, through the position they have to occupy in society, girls and women are well-placed to become, not by any means its exclusive, but its chief recipients.

Within psychoanalysis from the mid 1920s onwards we hear less and less of hysteria and more and more of its replacement – femininity. This is true of orthodox Freudianism as well as of Object Relations theory, which effectively precludes the theorization of hysteria. As I have looked at the male hysteric turning into the baby-with-mother of Object Relations, in charting the transformation of hysteria into femininity I will focus on the work of Freudians as exemplified by Hélène Deutsch's 1947 two-volume study of the psychology of women, *Girlhood* and *Motherhood*, supplemented by her concept of the 'as if' personality.

Before she turned into 'the feminine', the picture of the hysteric in classical Freudian theory is one in which she will not abandon her wishes for both her father and her mother; she thinks that if anything gets in the way of those wishes, it is merely 'unfair', and she will find a way round it. She does not acknowledge that she has to accept the arbitrary prohibition on incest. The girl obviously does not have the penis with which to relate to the mother or to the mother's subsequent replacements – and so Freudians say that she is 'already castrated'. The hysterical girl does not accept this and instead she identifies with her father to possess her mother, and with her mother to possess her father. Because women cannot fear castration, it supposedly having already happened, and because (again having been already castrated) they have less investment than men in acknowledging the prohibition of material incest, there is an inbuilt proclivity in women to hysteria, particularly as there seems little reason why they should not both identify with the mother and at the same time love her as an object. This is still the accepted Freudian and Lacanian account of female hysteria, when it takes notice of it.

What, in fact, happened was a division of the woman into, firstly, a 'true' woman who accepts her 'castration' and the replacement of her missing penis by a baby, and, secondly, a false or phoney woman who only pretends to. This phoney woman is the new name given to the hysteric. Joan Rivière, a British analyst analysed by Freud who became a Kleinian but ended her life on bad terms with Klein, wrote of 'femininity as a masquerade', indicating a particular type of woman whose femininity was an act, or, I would claim, hysterical.[4] Lacan turned this notion of Rivière into 'femininity *is* a masquerade'[5] (thereby echoing Freud's mistake of a universal repudiation of femininity instead of a repudiation of the hysterical situation). In this argument one cannot be a 'true' woman or 'the' woman, as the woman is defined as being nothing to be – no penis.

Thus, in the interwar years, the problem of hysteria became resolved within the theory of femininity. Femininity was now divided into true and false. On the one hand, 'true' femininity acknowledges the prohibition on incest and accepts the feminine as the already-castrated; on the other hand, pseudofemininity grants no significance to the castration complex in establishing the division of the sexes; pseudofemininity *looks* feminine simply because it desires a man. It is interesting that in the various accounts of this pseudo-femininity, the femininity is not conceived as reproductive – there may be babies in actuality, but they have no meaning. This, I argue, is one of the defining marks of hysteria.

A heterosexual femininity which none the less avoids maternal 'womanhood' is the idea expressed in Rivière's word 'masquerade', as it is in Hélène Deutsch's notion of an 'as if' personality, which I will come to later. Pseudofemininity replaces what was once Oedipal hysteria in women. However, an important slippage also occurs: the fundamental mechanisms of hysteria are now put in place for femininity *tout court*, not simply for its excess in 'falseness'. A specific example will suffice: the *hysteric* always wants; Freud famously came to say that he could not find out what it was a *woman* wants. He wrote to his close friend the French psychoanalyst Marie Bonaparte that, in all the years of investigation, it was this question that had stumped him. The question 'What does a woman want?' has become a central question of psychoanalytic feminism. In the course of the development of psychoanalysis, not giving the patient what he or she wants has also become a central injunction. This is the so-called practice of 'abstinence', which extends from an obvious prohibition on sexual and social relationships to not answering questions. By means of this 'abstinence' the patient should come to realize that it is manageable not to have what he or she wants and instead to have an internalized image of what is missing, a representation which acts as a meaningful substitute. This technique echoes a process of mourning in which the bereaved acknowledges that the dead one is missing but can be retained as an inner image. It would have been particularly applicable to hysteria, which can never accept not getting what it wants or losing something, but by the time it was formulated, in the interwar years, it came to be applied to women in general, who always seemed to be 'wanting'. In psychoanalytic theory and practice it is *women*, not hysterics specifically (either men or women), who are considered the problem, as they can never give up yearning for what they want – which, being always of course what they have not got, is in the last analysis the penis. This is 'penis envy'.

Psychoanalysis can propose what constitutes the *mark* of the difference between the sexes, but it cannot describe what then constitutes that difference. There are of course gender differences in the experiences of every subject which will inform manifestations of the unconscious through what are known as 'the day's residues' (that is to say, what actually happens to the subject, which may be gender-related, is what will trigger the dream or symptom). However, women and men do not produce sexually differentiated symptoms, either dreams, or slips of the tongue or pen. There is no gender difference in the way in which the unconscious works, its 'language'. For social structural reasons, women may be 'more' prone to jealousy than men, but there is no such thing as *female* jealousy. One may talk of feminine masochism, but it is found in both men and women.

A conjunction of changing social patterns with an emphasis on neonatal helplessness and primal anxiety opened the door to a complete reorientation of psychoanalytic theory away from hysteria and towards its substitute, 'femininity'. The 'moral motherhood' of the nineteenth century was strengthened after the Second World War as a result of the kind of tension which often begets or strengthens new ideologies. In the earlier part of the century the European and North American women's movement had largely ensured the opening of hitherto male professions to women and had fought for greater legal and political equity (most obviously the vote). Women in all social classes had also been very actively engaged in war work, in running organizations and, most notably, in performing much of the heavy work of the kind previously associated with men in relatively developed industrial societies. Sexual practices had also become more openly liberal for women, particularly among the intelligentsia. The post-war reaction to all this when the men came home was to re-establish gender divisions, although with an extension of equal rights into so-called 'women's spheres' – legislation on women's right to child custody, marital property, divorce; issues around motherhood and the home. The tension that haunts feminism even now between wanting to be equal to men and different from men was socially put in place. An assertion of women's psychological significance rather than their secondary, inferior status was a logical result of social change.

Psychoanalysis's emphasis on infantile helplessness arose from observations of the states of dread and anxiety into which male combatants were reduced by the trauma of war; obviously it was bound to feed into the primacy of the mother in child development. After the war, Hélène Deutsch, acutely aware of the ambivalences of motherhood and the many negative consequences of a girl becoming like her mother, wrote the first and fullest account of the development of femininity, not as a response of the girl to the father (which had hitherto shouldered the burden of the analytic account of the path to femininity), but as a result of her identification, negative and positive, with the mother. The primary identification of daughter and mother, once regarded in psychoanalytic theory as a regressive characteristic of hysteria, became the model for femininity. Identification with the mother bears the weight of the creation of true femininity. The common sense notion of 'like mother, like daughter' becomes the basis of the theory. It is assumed that object choice is heterosexual unless there is what was regarded as the 'pathology' of homosexuality. In Freud's theory, homosexuality is an *in*version of object choice, not a *per*version (as later psychoanalysts tended to regard it). *Per*version is the acting out of non-genital sex and it is linked to hysteria – hysteria enacts in fantasy what perversion enacts in practice.

In Deutsch's massive study of women, there is no mention of hysteria in the index, although in the text it is noted *en passant*. Instead of hysteria, Deutsch's patients, both male and female, display the problems of 'femininity', such as: eating disorders, ceaseless longing or 'wanting', seduction as a main mode of interaction, a painful consuming envy, a sense of emptiness, and compulsive and utterly convincing lying in which fantasies are realities (pseudologia). Deutsch ties some of these together:

In our effort to find the sources of specific feminine qualities we seem always to return to our starting point. The sequence constituted by (1) greater proneness to identification, (2) stronger fantasy, (3) subjectivity, (4) inner perception, and (5) intuition, leads us back to the common origin of all these traits, feminine passivity.[6]

Deutsch has translated the real neonatal helplessness to which the hysteric regresses into 'feminine passivity' – and it is this which Freud came to believe was repudiated by everyone.

The analysis has thus become inverted. Where one could previously perceive hysteria and discover that one of its features was a regression to an identikit identification with the mother to prevent being over-whelmed by a sense of annihilation, it is now, rather, that *all* women and, because of a disturbed relationship with mother or father, some men, make a maternal identification and thus *suffer from femininity*.

One such sufferer from femininity was a male patient of Deutsch who had strong pregnancy fantasies: he wanted to be a hen in the hope that someone would find his eggs in the way in which his mother had done by putting her finger into the hen's anus. It is obvious from this illustration how homosexuality (which should be seen only as particular object choice, not a drive) came to become pathologized along with femininity. In hundreds of similar clinical descriptions, which have come to feature extensively in accounts from psycho-therapy, psychoanalysis, psychiatry and clinical psychology, the man who displays hysterical characteristics is suffering from 'feminine narcissism', 'feminine passivity' or homosexuality. In the eternal struggle to repress male hysteria, these are the new pathologies.

Deutsch's thesis about women, although purportedly following Freud, did not share his emphasis on the acceptance of being 'already castrated' as the condition of femininity – rather, she saw the conflict as lying between narcissistic self-concern and motherly altruism. Her work is an instructive tangle of trying to fit the sibling rivalries that are revealed in one after another of her case histories into the Freudian pattern of vertical relationships between parents and child. But Deutsch is doing this always in the interest of describing femininity and thus inevitably marginalizing or, more often, completely deposing hysteria. This sets a pattern that has never been properly noticed: Freud's psychoanalysis describes psychic conditions which always present as regressions to childhood or infancy. For Deutsch the psy-chology of motherhood is presented as originary; it is there in the beginning – the true mother's motherhood does not display any infantile complexes and there are no regressions to infantile states. Once motherhood, femininity and homosexuality become objects of psychoanalytical investigation they become in themselves either 'normal' or 'pathological' – they come to replace symptoms and other manifestations of unconscious processes and are made to act as though they were them.

Deutsch came to be pilloried by many second-wave feminists (who opposed Freud's view) for her Freudianism. However, this is not the main problem with her work. What Hélène Deutsch gives us is a rich panoply of theories and examples of the making of a woman from birth to grave as a progress of pathology. First she shifts femininity from a relationship to the father to a troubled identification with the mother: for Deutsch, it is not Freud's theory of castration that marks the difference between the sexes, but something inherent that enables a woman to become a 'true woman' or not. Essentially, this has to do with the struggle between narcissistic self-concern and the concern for others which is the mark of motherhood. According to Deutsch, even though girls may be socially and intellectually well-adjusted, their inherent femininity keeps them infantile: there is no need for regression – women are just children anyway. If they make the move away from their childlike femininity to motherhood, childbirth is the acme of masochistic pleasure, while breastfeeding is the reunion of self and other which was interrupted by parturition. Post-menopausal women, however, revert to an even more entrenched infantile, pre-Oedipal position. I suggest that Deutsch's argument that femininity is produced in identification with the mother necessitates this *huis clos* from the infantile to the infantile: the female begins and ends as a baby.

Deutsch's is only the fullest, and in some ways the richest, example of the tendency towards the feminization of hysteria which became general practice across the psychoanalytic board. If, however, we translate her work back into the hysteria it has replaced, we can find in it some remarkable descriptions of hysterical conditions – labelled, of course, as *feminine* conditions! I shall focus on just two of her themes: pseudologia and the 'as if' personality. The former is no longer a fashionable term, the latter has become a classic concept – and both are important manifestations of hysteria and *not*, as Deutsch and subsequent writers would have them, of femininity.

Describing teenage pregnancy, Deutsch notes that it is common for intercourse to have taken place because the girl in question was in a 'twilight state'; she frequently has complete amnesia of the event and then makes a totally pseudologic reconstruction of it. In this, someone who has nothing to do with the reality of her situation is selected by the girl as the father of the baby she nevertheless denies she is carrying.

The fantasy father feels completely and utterly right to the girl precisely because he corresponds to her fantasy; he thus fills the gap in her memory. This fantasy father of the baby will resemble the pregnant girl's own father. The fact that the girl will then completely deny pregnancy until almost the moment of birth (and sometimes even beyond this) is an unconscious statement in which the girl is asserting that there cannot have been incest: this man (who I think is my father) has fathered my baby but there is no baby. The fantasy of achieved incest is indicated in the entrenched pseudologia. The simultaneous fantasy and denial of incest are maintained by the assertion there has been no intercourse, nor any baby as a result of it. The process, then, is as follows: a state of dissociation (twilight state, trance); intercourse and pregnancy; amnesia; and a fantasy construction which reveals two contradictory ideas: I am pregnant by my father but I am not pregnant. Herein lies a perfect example of a classic hysterical conflict.

In one case history, Deutsch records how an adolescent girl is sexually completely abstinent but in fantasy she has selected a highly improbable, unattractive boy as her partner in a richly imagined range of sexual exploits. The girl keeps a diary of these supposed exploits and writes unposted letters to which she replies herself. When she does eventually tell people about her secret fantasy relationship, the pseudologia is so convincing that she is completely believed. It turns out that by having moved, over a period of years, from this boy to one after another unlikely fantasy sexual object, she has stayed loyal to her brother (in unconscious fantasy) with whom she had enjoyed some sexual exploration as a child. The conflict of florid sexual fantasy and completely asexual appearance, and the pseudologia, are classic features of hysteria. Despite the fact that Deutsch's entire work on the psychology of women depends on the exiting of the concept of hysteria to such an extent that it is not listed in the index, it keeps returning from Deutsch's suppression of it and has to be shut out over and over again.

In completing her study of a girl's path to motherhood, Deutsch notes various different destinations for femininity. In among them, the so-called 'as if' personality is discovered time and again (not surprisingly, since it is hysteria by another name). We can also see how it is 'rediscovered' in major new theorizations mentioned earlier, such as Winnicott's notion of a 'false self', in more occasional pieces such as Joan Rivière's descriptions of femininity as a masquerade, and in Enid Balint's work on 'being empty of oneself'. More recently, the 'as if' personality has been likened to a syndrome described by the British Kleinian analyst Irma Brenman-Pick as 'false concern'.[7] Perhaps whenever we note the word 'false' or its equivalent, we should make a habit of wondering whether some aspect of hysteria is being described.

Deutsch found her patients did not divide neatly into the categories of neurotic or psychotic; instead, they were often deemed 'normal' except for emotional and moral shallowness (an attribute referred to in the later *DSM* definitions of the histrionic personality). Using an instance of motherhood, Deutsch decides to explore the 'as if' personality. She explicitly claims that the 'as if' type is distinct from hysteria, yet even in her own description they merge into each other. So she writes:

[W]omen with deranged emotional lives try to find mother figures in their entourage in order to cover their own lack of motherliness by identifying themselves with these. Even then they do not have much feeling for the child, but they imitate the attitude of a loving mother so well that they themselves and the persons around them think that their motherliness is genuine. I have called such women the 'as if' type ... In women with *hysterical multiple personality or of the 'as if' type*, this process is very clear. Their motherliness goes through the same vicissitudes as their personalities as a whole: as mothers they are now one, now another person.[8] [My italics]

As Deutsch herself makes quite clear, then, there is no distinction between labile hysterical identification and the 'as if' personality. The highly successful concept of 'as if' is thus completely dependent on the exclusion of hysteria.

But to continue with the phenomenology of the 'as if' personality: if the identification or series of identifications fail, a terrible emptiness or madness results – which again has been a hallmark of hysteria through the ages. All Deutsch's 'as if' patients move from one identification to another identification. In one case, when treatment was terminating, there seemed to be an end to the possible people with whom the patient could identify. Then the patient bought a dog. Deutsch comments: 'she told me that now everything would be all right; she would imitate the dog and then she would know how she should act'.[9] Identifications with dogs, or possession by dogs who themselves are good imitators, have featured in descriptions of hysteria since the ancient Greeks. The ancient Greek hysteric experienced her body as being filled with an uncontrollable rampaging, like an animal gnawing her from within (which is quite a good description of uncontrollable desire). Her body was experienced or described as occupied by a wild dog.

Hélène Deutsch, in her own account, remained a Freudian all her life. But even in the 1920s and 1930s, when she started her work on the psychology of women, her theoretical stance and methodology were not Freud's. No less than the Object Relations theorists, Deutsch's perspective was on the 'normal' and what can go wrong with that, while Freud's was on the pathological which, he said, would show us what he called the 'ideal fiction of normality' but only as the absent figure in the carpet. Deutsch, then, instead of studying the regression of the neurotic, looked at the development (or not) of the healthy. Ostensibly there is no reason why human behaviour should not be studied in this way. However, this shift of perspective brings with it a problem: doctors, paediatricians, psychotherapists, psychoanalysts do not see normal, healthy people. So how do they, or anyone, know what 'normal' is? Normality is an imaginary, fabricated line, like the equator, to which we have to refer to make our categories.

After second-wave feminism's initial rejection of Freud and Freudianism, a positive attitude set in and psychoanalysis was used to understand the psychic construction of femininity. More recently still, some male voices asked for masculinity to be brought in from the cold and its psychic construction understood. This has more or less come to a dead end. The impossibility of charting masculinity with developmental normality as a focal point reveals the larger problem. From psychoanalysis between the wars to second-wave feminism, femininity and its discontents could only take centre stage, because femininity was seen as equal to pathology. Hysteria, then, disappeared into femininity. Under another name, hysteria does become manifest in therapies that derive from the 'talking cure': the Recovered Memory movement, or equally the 'False Memory' movement, exemplify this possibility.

Joseph Breuer, scorched by his encounter with Anna O, wrote some years afterwards to Freud: 'I at that time learned a great deal – much that was of scientific value, but also the important practical lesson that it is impossible for a "general practitioner" to treat such a case without his activity and the conduct of his life thereby being completely ruined. I vowed at the time *never* again to subject myself to such an ordeal.'[10] Breuer's reaction is often treated with easy condescension as though today we know better. In fact, Breuer's integrity stands as an early landmark. In one way or another, therapists may often get embroiled. Freud was constantly warning colleagues not only against the possibilities of sexual involvement but also those of ambition: one becomes overinvolved if one places a vainglorious value on one's therapeutic powers. Wilfred Bion much later formulated this as the need for the analyst to have neither memory nor desire – not to be a memory-haunter or to want too much. Failure to 'cure' does not necessarily constitute a refutation of the theory; it may simply indicate the limitations to which every practitioner and every patient is subject. A further reason why 'hysteria' may have disappeared from the list of diagnoses is that in its serious forms it presents almost unmanageable difficulties for anyone who has to deal with it – from spouse, sibling, child or friend to doctor, analyst, therapist. One of the reasons for this is the urgent need – and ability – of the hysteric to involve the other, as Anna O involved Breuer.

It is, however, problematic that, in nearly all versions of individual treatment, therapeutic practice and psychoanalytic theory insist on the almost exclusive importance of the parent. An emphasis on the castration complex (Freud, ego psychology, Lacan) privileges the father. An emphasis on the Oedipus complex and the pre-Oedipal (Object Relations and Self and Interactional theories) privileges the mother. Increasingly through the century other relationships have diminished in importance. Hysteria, understood as the result of problems with parents, was used to create the emphasis but was itself the fall-out of such a focus. The male hysteric led inexorably to the need for the infant to have a mother who was good enough for his burgeoning boyhood; feminizing hysteria with equal certainty meant that girls must identify with mothers for the lineage of femininity to be passed on.

After the First World War, after Otto Rank's work on the birth trauma and Freud's own highly creative confusions in *Inhibitions, Symptoms and Anxiety* (1926), Freud emerged from the doubts sown by the symptomatologies of war neurosis, the psychoses and traumatic anxiety dreams, to assert that human helplessness at and after birth was doubtless an immensely important background but one that could not of itself account for the conflicts of psychic life. Having thought first that hysterical women had been abused by their fathers, then that as infants they had desired their fathers and fantasized a consummation, by the 1920s Freud had become convinced that a father's desire for his daughter was so common as to count as normal but that one must not judge what is desired, only what is enacted.

However, the shift from a dominant stance of the prohibiting father and the castration complex to the importance of the mother in the context of the absence of hysteria has had a number of specific as well as general effects. Because of the stress, above all by Object Relations therapists, on the earliest relationships of the pre-Oedipal infant, once in the transference the therapist has become predominantly the mother, then the security against the therapist's sexual overinvolvement is stronger. The taboo on the enactment of maternal incest from the mother-therapist's side has to be all the greater because there can be no taboo for such a young infant. The pre-Oedipal infant must love and hate with impunity and the mother must only respond by containing its wilder desires. However, even so, the non-sexual involvement of the mother (and therapist) can be intense. These wishes are problematic if they are deeply unconscious or unperceived because of the therapeutic stance. The mother's desires and the therapist's problem have been recorded, for instance, in Winnicott's categorical assertion that the mother hates the baby before the baby hates her. It is possible that the mother-therapist's hatred may be more problematic than her incestuous wishes. For the Independent Object Relations analyst, the task is to hold the unstructured feelings, desperate anxieties and terrors of the infant – but the dividing line between containing on the one hand and gratifying or getting fed up on the other can be difficult.

Kleinian theory and practice is highly protective of the therapist: according to Klein, it is the baby relived by the patient who envies and wishes to destroy all the mother-analyst possesses, which seems to be everything. There is no better protection against the horrors of envy than being the one who is envied – as the hysteric knows very well, which is why he so often tries to make the other jealous. But all too frequently the hysteria gets enacted elsewhere: in the case of Anne Sexton, once her affair with her therapist was over, it was replaced by sexual violence with her husband, compulsive sexual affairs and at the same time erotic bodily involvement and violence with her small daughter. In the case of mother-transference, the hysterical element in the patient may well defend against envy by splitting: idealizing the therapist as mother, and denigrating partner, wife, husband or child. One has to be always alert to what goes on outside treatment.

Once it took me two years to realize that I could not abide a patient's wife (whom I had never met and knew nothing of save what my patient portrayed). I had not been seduced by the patient's 'love' (idealization) of me (it can easily be experienced as hollow), but I had been taken in by the conviction (the pseudologia) with which he presented a most awful portrait of a woman no one could possibly have liked. In that sense I had been seduced into his way of seeing things. A colleague once told me that the mother of a patient, whom I happened to know as a nice enough old lady, must be the worst mother in history – he too had been seduced by the pseudologia. In addition, he had also become embroiled in it, be-having improperly by talking to me and thus breaking the rule of confidentiality.

Hysterical patients used to come to therapy hoping to talk about sexuality. Now they have learnt that that is no longer the order of the day and instead they take from the ideology of whatever psychotherapeutic orientation they have chosen and imitate what is required. Knowing that reparation and concern are the current preoccupations, they will demonstrate their wish to make better what they have destroyed and show remorse for what they have done. It is often hard to distinguish between the imitation and the real thing. Once we have moved away from seeing or demonstrating the sexuality and violence of hysteria, then seduction of the therapist comes in forms other than incest. The diminution of emphasis on sexuality and violence is mainly a result of the banishment of the diagnosis of hysteria, but it is also a consequence of a move for the therapist in the transference from punitive father to caring mother. But what of the patient's and therapist's sibling rivalry, love and hate? Here the therapist and patient are in a parallel, lateral relationship. How often, when things go wrong, is it because this lateral relation has not been taken into account in the therapist's countertransference as well as in the patient's transference?

Without doubt, sexual and murderous desire for the parents and its prohibition are crucial, but their presumed exclusive supremacy would seem to be historically specific or possibly simply mistaken: first, there was the all-powerful patriarch of Victorian practice and imagination, then the all-containing 'moral mother' and 'psychological mother' of late nineteenth- and mid twentieth-century treatments. Yet a child's first fully *social* relationship, which is to say, that which breaks up the mother–child unit, is not with the prohibiting father; it is with the rival child who claims the mother's love. It is here we need to locate what is missing in the theoretical insight and clinical practice.

There is also no doubt that motherhood can be a completely (or partially) hysterical phenomenon in which childbirth, for instance, may be anaesthetized to such a degree that the mother does not know psychically that she has had a child. Both hysterical mothers and hysterical fathers are psychologically non-reproductive; in their view, the child has come from their body as a replica of themselves, not as another subject created with another subject – what I have called 'the parthenogenetic complex'. The hysterical father often identifies with a mother by hoping to give birth to himself – through an imitation pregnancy, for instance. There is, however, the possibility that motherhood can break the hysterical pattern. The idea that motherhood can end hysteria lies beyond the scope of this book; however, some points can be made. In relation to hysteria there is some validity to the old adage that the process of motherhood is analogous to creativity. The catastrophe of possible replacement of the mother by the baby (a life for a life) empties out the subject, but as always it also offers the opportunity for a 'new beginning'. To give birth can be to create something from a position in which one does survive and is recognized. But the self is not as important as it was before: now one is someone's mother and that is what counts. This is the opposite result to the overassertion of one's own importance. Until now, in nearly all cultures, motherhood has been perceived as a place of recognition for women. It may thus provide a sufficient sense of a place in the world to allow the woman not to have to overassert her identity. *Who* she is is assured by her recognized 'maternal' place: *where* she is. Once recognized, quite simply there does not have to be too much 'self'; there is the chance of not being traumatized by one's absence from the world. In giving birth, the possibilities of death and survival, rather than castration, also come into play. Even if the baby or embryo dies, the woman cannot escape the inevitability of the situation; as with death, she is subjected to a process larger than anything that can be controlled by her own will.

Motherhood can involve the absence of the ego of the subject (it is a position not an identity), as is death or castration in the castration complex: hysteria protests violently and anxiously against such a possibility. If there is a context of recognition sufficient that the prospect of such ego absence can be faced, then the desperate protests are no longer necessary. In the male hysteric's imitations of pregnancy, and in female phantom pregnancies, (as in the trial suicides), it is the protest against the annihilation of the subject that we witness. Should something enable a hysteric to face this annihilation and survive it, then the hysteria is over.

It is precisely because both death and giving birth involve the 'death' of the subject (or the subject's previous ego) that hysteria uses imitations of both as the means through which the terrors of disappearance may be enacted. Through the ages, and in all contemporary practices, hysterics, men and women, enact fantasy births to more or less the same extent as they simulate death. The enactment of the fantasy is the terror; once a place in the world is recognized which is both absolutely the same as and also different from another person's place, then the enactment of the fantasy can cease, and giving birth and dying can take place.

Because it is women who give birth, this is mistakenly taken to be another reason for the gendering of hysteria. The psychic processes of birth and death, however, can take place without their enactments. (The process, of course, does not have to be literalized; actual motherhood is also a metaphor.) In hysteria, men and women 'try on' both birth and death in order to protect themselves against these inevitabilities. Giving birth is no more *psychically* gendered than is dying. It is, however, *actually* gendered – as is having a penis, which, because it can be cut off, can also represent the annihilation of the subject.

What is there that stands as the representation of birth, as castration stands as the representation of death? Is this, in fact, creativity? Accepting the possibility of castration amounts to accepting the inevitability of the eventual death of the subject; accepting the possibility of creation amounts to accepting the death of the ego of the author. (As we shall see in chapter 9, it is analogous with telling the truth.) However, there is too much of the subject in hysterical creation, as there is in hysterical suicide. The acceptance that one's creation can live without one, and that the world will continue after one dies, are also psychologically analogous. If the subject has received sufficient recognition, then he can tolerate his insufficiency in order to experience procreation, creativity and death.

And so, the undeniable emergence of the male hysteric has led to a psychoanalytic theory of infantile helplessness and the strong emphasis being put on the importance of overwhelming anxiety. This in turn has brought the mother into prominence and made the male child come to be seen as the child in general. Hysterical wanting became feminine desire; hysteria became femininity. If, however, as I hope to have shown, we turn these last two on their heads, we can learn much from such accounts and observations.

Hysteria, once brought into existence by the subject being displaced and protesting against this displacement, does regress to an infantile situation. This regressive position is, above all, one in which the separation of the mind and body is not yet in place. When a toddler like Mildred tries to get her position back from her brother Jack, she becomes mute and unable to walk – just like a baby – and it is her body that conveys her predicament. To look at the earliest relationship is to look at the place of the mind–body or body–mind. This I shall do in the next chapter.

7

Emptiness and Possession

I. THE BODY—MIND OF HYSTERIA

Social practices change. Almsgiving, for instance, declined in Europe in the late Middle Ages. Those who had given alms felt guilty but as alms were no longer customary there was no outlet for their guilt, no accounting for it. The Church was concentrating wealth in its institution; private almsgiving was no longer encouraged. In other contexts, guilt would have been acknowledged and the reason known about; here it was just a fault of a wider social change that came about without most people being conscious of it. The guilt was an unacceptable feeling with no accompanying thought process that could have described and placed it. The feeling was best got rid of by projecting it on to another. The other was the old lady who sought alms. Made to 'contain' the anger, guilt and frustration of the would-be almsgiver who can no longer give alms, this other became the witch.

This explanation of witchcraft (with my additions about the role of the Church) emanates not from a psychoanalyst but from the historian/anthropologist Alan Macfarlane;[1] yet it perfectly describes the process of projection as understood by psychoanalysis in which unwanted feelings are expelled into the other person. Evans-Pritchard's accounts from the 1930s of witchcraft among the Azande[2] (and those of many others by anthropologists) can be similarly described. The witch may accept or repudiate the projected guilt but she does not do so by using rational thinking – rather, she returns it by cursing or enacting a curse. Cursing is so-called 'performative language'; enacting a curse entails a body performance – the two are closely linked.

Apart from walking away into another social world, which would almost certainly have been impossible, what could a witch do? The unacceptable projection is no more bearable for the person who receives it than for the person who delivers it: it must be passed on, passed back or evacuated in some physical action and discharge. But leaving aside realistic social restrictions, why not walk away? Projections do not take place *in vacuo*; there will have been some previous experience or response in the recipient that has made them a good choice. For instance, the old lady may well have scavenged for bits of food or firewood – as Wordsworth describes in his poem 'Goody Blake and Harry Gill', where the curse of poor Goody makes the relatively rich Harry as freezing cold as she had been. Harry has dispossessed Goody Blake of the 'customary' rights of the poor to 'gather'. She will be cold – so she curses him. It is not that the one-time almsgiver who projects his unconscious guilt into the previous object of his charity is necessarily hysterical, but rather that his unconscious act of projection has set hysteria in motion. This brings chaos: when social order breaks down within the body politic it may be matched by a sense of disorder within the 'body personal' – that is, within the bodies of either the almsgiver or the old woman. When the inquisitor replaces the almsgiver, the hysteria of both prosecutor and prosecuted (as with General Patton and the soldier who was not being a soldier) becomes rampant. There is a crisis in the social order and in social expectation. It is because the unbearable emotions which are released by these catastrophic shifts in the order of things are unconscious that they cannot be resolved and must be got rid of into someone else. This is the hysterical moment – when the circulation of emotions becomes compulsive and driven. And chaos has come again.

Guilt is not the only emotion that acts as a currency between people; jealousy is another. Iago cannot abide his envy of Othello's success as a lover and soldier. Even more, he cannot stand the disruption in the expected social order when Othello promotes Cassio (a brother soldier) above him. Therefore, he must make Othello experience his, Iago's, jealousy as his own – which, indeed, he ends up doing. The play *Othello* is a study in the transmission of jealousy: displaced hatred, envy, jealousy and then unconscious guilt for the fantasized murder of the rival all move from one character to another (see chapter 8).

Projection is a process of which it makes no sense to say it belongs either to the mind or to the body – it is *felt* in both and received in both. Arrested by Gill for stealing firewood, Goody Blake curses him – 'O may he never more be warm!' – and Harry Gill shivers in perpetuity. Words and the body act in unison. Similarly, Othello says of Iago, 'Demand of that demi-devil why he has thus ensnared my *soul and body*' (my italics).

The hysteric, however, starts as a displaced person. The quondam almsgiver, or alms receiver, or indeed anyone who is displaced (like, for instance, the immigrant to the city, whose situation is one in which hysteria is acknowledged to be prevalent) are displaced from the positions they once held or which held them. In these circumstances, the previous 'self' feels threatened and unbearable emotions flood in, which, when they cannot be thought about, are handed on – and may be handed back. It is because of the hysteric's need to transmit unbearable feelings on to someone else that his hysteria cannot be manifested if he is on his own. The Cartesian world is one in which mind and body are supposed to be separate. Hysteria defies this separation and, because of the explanation arrived at by Freud of the mind–body connection of the hysteric, psychoanalysis can claim to be an anti-Cartesian science. This is both true and misleading. Descartes did not completely subscribe to the division assigned to his philosophy; he argued that passions were experienced both in the mind and the body – the aim had to be to subdue them. There were, of course, also other traditions, such as the Talmudic one, to which Freud was heir. The Freud scholar and psychoanalyst Ilse Grubrich-Simitis has shown how the Philippson Bible, which Freud read as a boy, argued for complete interdependence of mind and body.[3]

If passions move equally through mind and body, and thus treat them as a single entity, is the transition from mind to body in the conversion symptom of hysteria really the 'mysterious leap' it is claimed to be? Accounts that a 'leap' has been made when a compulsive uncontrollable twitch of the facial muscles is traced to an unacceptable remark that felt like a slap in the face, assume that the mind and body are separate but that they can be bridged. The notion of conversion hysteria is that an idea or cluster of ideas which have been repressed and made unconscious, but inadequately so, 'return' from that repression, not as ideas in the mind, but as a corporeal condition such as hysterical blindness or paralysis of the leg. It is because there is a left-over quantum of feeling or affect when the representations of ideas are repressed that the body comes into play – the body expresses that surplus emotion. Freud's Lacanian commentators have been more sure than Freud was of the entire merits of this explanation.

Freud created the concept and coined the term 'conversion'. Feelings, unlike ideas, cannot be repressed and made unconscious. These feelings, of which one is not aware (as, we assume, the almsgivers were not aware of their guilty feelings) may be put into someone else – this is projection. In other cases they can get used by the body as a substitute for an idea (a painful idea becomes a painful part of the body) – this is conversion. However, because, before the repression, the affect or the feelings were connected to an *idea* through a person's associations, this idea can now be resurrected and verbalized. Then, understanding the idea behind the feelings can bring the conversion symptom to an end.

It is to this repressed idea that the 'talking cure' gains access. In this account, the thought is by definition literal. One of my patients told me how, in the morning as he was leaving for work, his wife had accused him of lying about something; having been caught telling *fibs*, he returned from work limping with an organically impossible pain in his *fib*ula. The pain and limp vanished, however, when the incident was remembered and the idea of fibbing confronted. The American literary critic Peter Brooks comments on Freud's discovery that the body was signifying something:

One cannot overestimate the radical nature of Freud's shift in interpretive paradigms here. Prior to her therapy with Freud, Frau Cacilie M has been treated by 'the electric brush, alkaline water, purges'; seven of her teeth have been extracted, on the assumption that they were causing the neuralgia; and since some of the roots were left behind, further dentistry has been performed. To move from the assumption of an organic cause for the neuralgia to the hypothesis that it symbolises the effect of a verbal insult, interpreted as a slap in the face, is to *reorient definitively our understanding of the body and how it signifies*.[4] [My italics]

What Brooks says is certainly true, but of course paradigms rarely shift as neatly as this, nor are their instigations usually so capable of such clean breaks. As I write, there is some controversy about the Italian Abbé Pio, who, it is claimed, could be in two different places at once. He also had wounds which opened and bled for no organic reason. Abbé Pio was beatified in 1999. Freud, at the same time as he was reading Frau Cacilie's body as though it were a text offering signs, was also involved in an operation by his friend Fliess on the nose of another of his patients, Emma Eckstein, in the hope that it would help cure her hysteria. Fliess had made a connection between the nose and many, particularly sexual, disturbances. The operation was a notoriously appalling failure, as Fliess left a roll of gauze in her nose which caused near-fatal haemorrhaging.

Both the mind and the body feel. Or perhaps one should say that feelings such as joy or pain, guilt or jealousy do not distinguish between mind and body – as Descartes has argued for the passions. The body can also be a repository of ideational messages because all ideas (though some more than others) are accompanied by feelings – but we may not want to feel the thought. My patient was *hurt* by his wife's realization that he had lied, and excited by the prospect that he might be caught out and punished – the fibbing became a *hurt* in the fibula. It also meant that he got attention for his pain, like a naughty child. But he probably also wanted to give or project a painful experience by lying in the first place. Macfarlane's almsgivers did not want the 'unthinkable' guilt which they felt but could not explain, so they put it into someone else's *body*. (This is almost certainly only one aspect of the explanation.)

If we talk of 'body language' and emphasize that the body *signifies*, it is in order to indicate that the mind is embodied. The body gives clues to the thoughts of this embodied mind. Always worried by the 'seductions' of the hysteria problem, Freud reflected on the connection between emotions and language in a way that has since been dismissed under the dominance of structural linguistics. Using Charles Darwin's 1872 essay on the emotions, 'The Expression of the Emotions in Man and Animals', Freud speculated that words were once used not as abstract representations of emotions and objects but rather as emotional experiences in themselves – like grunts or sighs:

[H]ysteria is right in restoring the original meaning of the words in depicting its unusually strong innervations. Indeed, it is perhaps wrong to say that hysteria creates these sensations by symbolizations. It may be that it does not take linguistic usage as its model at all, but that both hysteria and linguistic usage alike draw their material from a common source.[5]

In infancy, in autism and in hysteria, saying is doing; words are real. But, following contemporary practices of linguistic analysis, Brooks comments on this passage of Freud:

In citing Darwin, and in closing his case history with the concession that hysterical symptoms may not involve symbolism at all, but may rather reach back to a common physical source of hysteria and linguistic usage, Freud comes close to renouncing the radical nature of his discovery.[6]

It does not seem to me that we have such an either/or situation. The baby hears words he understands only later. The Wolf Man, for instance, heard his mother, referring to her bowel problems, say that she could not continue to live like this. When, in his subsequent hysteria, the Wolf Man enacts this with bowel symptoms of his own, his body is remembering the words that he did not understand but which may have communicated both fear of dying and the excitement of getting the doctor's attention. He does not want to remember the words which were frightening but nor does he want to forget them, so he enacts what they meant to him at the time – an excitement about something very frightening. The symptoms are unconsciously 'chosen' because they echo from the past the patient's present predicament. To recall the actual words would be to replace an emotional perception in the present with a memory of the past.

Brooks only likes Freud's understanding of language when it comes close to structural linguistics. In the earlier Romantic notion, the body names and language itself have a common origin in extremely strong emotions. In the later structural linguistics, the phallus has been named as the primary signifier because it does not relate to an object that it signifies, but rather to the absence of the object. It is this insight from linguistics that Lacan brought to bear on psychoanalysis. The phallus acquires its significance when it is *not* there in the mother. It then relates not to what is signified but to another signifier in a chain of signifiers – this is language. However, the child speaks before it has language and uses signs before signifiers. The hysteric regresses from his position in language to a place still only on its borders. This is to a version of 'performative' language, where words and speech are used to act, to get what is wanted, to say what is strongly felt. Anne Sexton says words are like bees in an attic, or coins in a fruit machine. These are not words in a signifying chain, but words that are things reduplicated.

As Freud was to comment in the case of the Wolf Man, all neuroses have an underlying 'earlier' hysterical layer. Linguistically, this earlier layer is not based on the referent being missing – it is always there, just as at the level of action the hysteric cannot accept that there is something he absolutely cannot have, he just thinks there is some obstacle in the way which can be removed if he tries hard enough. He is prepared to suffer from what he sees as a temporary failure, but nowhere will he acknowledge his potential but absolute loss. The lie is the best example of hysterical language because the lie institutes something that is there – by lying one can linguistically always have what one wants, nothing is missing. The hysteric is not always telling lies; nevertheless, his language is such that it is no different if he is not. This language is neither symbolic nor truly representational. Like the body, this language is a presentation, not a representation: the performative curse *does* something, it does not stand in *for* something.

If, instead of assuming that mind and body are distinct and that hysteria mysteriously overcomes this division, we postulate that initially they are one and the same thing and that hysteria *regresses* to this unitary position, we get not only a different picture but also a picture which demands a different theorization. The range that hysteria embraces would indicate that the body–mind unity is being both re-enacted and parodied in the regressions that constitute the hysterical state. There is a body which is not symbolized.

The actress Judi Dench once described how she saw the frontier of madness when she did not know the thin line of difference between herself and the part she acted; Julie Christie famously becomes completely amnesiac of who or where she might be in order to become the other she is 'playing'. Why does a 2-year-old who puts a wastebin on her head and struts up and down adamantly announcing that she is a policeman have a roomful of adults collapse in laughter, because that is just what she really seems to be? How can the act be so accurate? This presentation of another in acting treats the substitute, the fantasy, as though it were the thing itself. The great eighteenth-century thespian David Garrick could make an audience gasp with terror as he threw in the air and nearly dropped a cushion that he was pretending was a baby. Acting patrols the border between the self and the other – the hysteric *acts* because a mad loss of all boundaries is always close at hand.

The French analyst Monique David-Ménard comments in *Hysteria from Freud to Lacan* (1989) that there is 'something in the body of the hysteric that has not been symbolized'. What is this something? In extreme pleasure or pain, the body normally goes missing; similarly, one cannot feel excesses of cold or heat. If something can be acknowledged as missing, it can be represented. This has not happened in hysteria. For something to be symbolized or represented it has to have been missing or absent. Through the ages there have been records of hysterics shivering as though with cold, although they are not in fact actually cold. For the hysteric, 'cold' must be presented. The hysterical fit echoes hypothermia; there is no awareness that a numb body can be understood and represented as numb – it must be enacted. For the body to feel safe enough to vanish and return, that is to re-present itself, there needs first to be sufficient security. Children play at falling: one child stands between two others and falls first forwards and then backwards; the other children must catch the falling child before he crashes to the ground. It is a game about bodily trust. There is something radical at stake for a body to become re-presentable: its inhabitant must have sufficient trust in the other, on whom it is dependent, to be able to lose that body safely.

Throughout his work, the British analyst Wilfred Bion described the mother's role in processing the disparate, chaotic, raw elements of infantile feelings (which he called beta elements) into manageable ones (alpha elements); similarly, Winnicott showed how the mother holds and 'contains' the baby's inchoate feelings. Bion's thesis, in particular, is a part of his larger account of how postnatal feelings are capable of becoming infantile thoughts. I suggest that the hysteric regresses to an experience on this border: thought has regressed to inchoate feeling, to a sense of bodily fragmentation. It is rarely a completely authentic regression; there is often an element of simulation and acting – otherwise it would be madness not hysteria.

The hysteric (male as well as female) is commonly frigid (Lacan mistakenly thought this was a necessary aspect of the construction of femininity, in keeping with the shift from hysteria to femininity described in chapter 6); because ejaculation is mistaken for orgasm, male frigidity is usually unnoticed. The compulsive sexuality of hysteria, therefore, demonstrates a brinkmanship in which the person is driven to the edge of orgasm but never feels safe enough to allow his body to vanish. The giving up of the body in orgasm is too close, for the hysteric, to death and annihilation. The endless seductions, the repeated intercourse of hysteria can be likened to suicide attempts. Absolute loss cannot be experienced, although its possibility is always played with. The masochist tests that he has a body by having pain inflicted on it in a way that he finds pleasurable. The hysteric also tries to find out if he has a body – often, particularly in adolescence, by cutting or burning. The torturer tests out the annihilating pain on the body of the other. The hysteric cannot tolerate much pain – either physical or mental – so he emotionally tortures the other in order to hand on the pain. The torturer or rapist neither sees nor not sees the other; he simply eradicates the other's body. Loss is a condition of symbolization and representation. The hysteric cannot allow the loss (it is simply too terrifying), therefore he cannot have a symbol or representation of the body.

A non-symbolized or non-represented body is not, then, one that is 'simply there', in what Lacan calls the 'Real'. Whereas the symbolized body is a more or less accurate representation of a body with a position, a body that is 'simply there' is not. A representation of the body depends on the body being first lost and then regained as a symbol. The body can be safely lost if it is known it comes back. This entails knowing the difference between something that can return and something that cannot – as in death. For the hysteric, it is that *all* losses are deaths and that therefore he must ensure that there is no loss, so no death. In Dostoevsky's *The Brothers Karamazov*, Kolya, a 13-year-old boy, cannot face the fact that his friend Ilyshin, whom he has mistreated, is dying. He obsessively trains a dog to 'play dead' and then hysterically demonstrates this trick to the dying child; in the process of denying Ilyshin's death Kolya hastens his dying by his mad game. The baby plays at appearing and disappearing in the mirror; if it is confident that it has already been seen from somewhere else by someone else, then it can move on and perceive its own body from the perspective of the other. If there is a perspective from the mother, then this can be adopted by the subject so that the body becomes seen and recognized from elsewhere. The hysteric neither remembers nor expects to be remembered if he is not always present – so he always overinsistently presents himself.

The baby with the mirror is either there (present) or not there (absent). When it 'knows' it can reappear, it re-presents itself in the mirror. It can relinquish the game when it unconsciously knows that even though its mother or caretaker is absent, she or he has the child in mind – that it is represented. When the child feels utterly displaced by sibling or peer, it loses the knowledge that it is represented for the mother (or substitute) – that though there is another child to whom attention is given, this one too is still 'in mind'. What would a state of a non-represented body look like? The artist Francis Bacon tried to depict a non-represented state of the body in the distorted, fragmented figures of his paintings – he was trying to show what a presented rather than a represented body might look and feel like. It is as though the spoon which goes into the baby's eye, ear or cheek instead of the mouth were experienced from within as an unformed or misshapen face – because they are paintings, these are Bacon's 'representations' of the unsymbolized, unrepresented body. Regressing to this experience of his own body, the hysteric distorts and contorts his face and body; to an onlooker the body can appear either disabled or mad. Feelings make the body move: the face scrunches up or the arms clutch the stomach in emotional pain; the face creases with laughter; the torso twists with jealousy, cramps up with envy; the eyes glow with happiness or withdraw behind a veil of dishonesty.

Different times and contexts have perceived the neonate differently: as a *tabula rasa*, a small animal, a miniature adult, a being fused with its mother, an individual separate from its mother; it can be thought to have been created by its father's seed and cooked in its mother's oven, or 'immaculately' conceived by its mother with only the thought of a father, or sent by God, or brought by storks . . . However, given the already diverse perspectives of the late twentieth-century Western world, most today would agree that the infant experiences feelings from the outset. It is from such a base that the sense of the individual body and mind emerges. Although a characteristic of hysteria is amnesia, this amnesia is usually for events and ideas rather than feelings. Feelings are refelt and, in this sense, remembered in the body. Though referring to a developmental position, not to a hysterical regression, Melanie Klein called this possibility 'memories in feeling'. A hysterical patient will often recall an incident (it may not have been actual – he could equally well have imagined it) and insist on what has been said, by reference to the feeling state it produced; he will have no sense of any meaning – simply it hurt or gave him pleasure, that is what matters. The feelings will not be assignable, either to a particular mental or particular bodily experience; they will be excessive, random and free-floating – something said (or imagined to have been said) hurts and there is no 'why' or 'wherefore'.

Pain maps the body, but not always accurately at first, as with the young child who complains of a headache in his tummy: he has not yet learnt to locate feelings within the conventions of the appropriate body part. When the child says he has a headache in his tummy, he is only halfway to representing his body; his statement is somewhere between crying with pain and giving a representational description of his body. Likewise, my patient with the pain in his fibula has simply regressed to a stage when words and body parts are becoming, but have not yet become, separated out from each other. At this developmental stage a particular word *is* a particular thing; it is not part of a chain of signifiers. The Kleinian analyst Hanna Segal's phrase 'symbolic equation' is useful but not, I think, quite accurate in this context because the things being equated are not symbolized as yet. They stand for each other, are metaphors for each other, yes, but they cannot be symbols since nothing has been acknowledged as missing.

If we think of the problem from the perspective of the not-so-clearly differentiated body, we see that very many metaphors in many languages are at one and the same time body parts, abstract notions and something in between. For instance, the most prevalent hysterical symptom recorded in the London Hospital in the mid nineteenth century was paralysis of the legs. Quite apart from the sexual associations of the leg in Victorian England, when even pianos wore skirts to hide them, a vast number of objects, animate and inanimate, had legs and there were (and still are) a number of metaphors that make use of the word: 'give a leg up', 'go on, leg it', 'you haven't got a leg to stand on'. The crucial point is that sensations do not differentiate between mind and body. For instance, a child plays with snow and finds it both hot and cold; regressing to this stage, the hysteric shivers with cold whenever he is 'hot'; a patient of mine produced chattering teeth, goose pimples and shivering when she had warm feelings. When someone is 'out of their mind', we take it for granted that they are out of their body, too; they are wild-eyed and gaunt – one cannot look physically 'normal' while being completely mentally 'abnormal'. Again, as the hysteric's state is a regression, there is usually an element of acting: wracked by pain, his body presents itself as tortured.

In other words, thinking about hysteria leads us to reverse our model. It is not mysterious at all that the mind becomes the body; for hysteria directs us to the point of their non-differentiation. Sometimes this is done in parody, sometimes not. It is not a retrograde step to suggest the reinstatement of Darwinian understandings of emotion or Cartesian awareness that passions have no respect for a mind–body division. Such a move simply indicates that emotion has been inadequately theorized in most studies of human development. This biological-psychological mind-as-body zone of neonatal and early infantile life is currently the focus of considerable observational attention. Such work focuses on the mother–baby relationship. However, in returning to this postnatal and infantile state, hysteria brings that state's future back with it – the past can only be read from the present.

As André Green has pointed out, just as perception and memory cannot occur at the same time (see chapter 9), empirical observation and psychoanalytical reconstruction likewise cannot coexist, so although observation can be very interesting it cannot strictly speaking confirm or disconfirm what can be learnt from a patient's associations. From the viewpoint of the manifestations of unconscious processes, the past of the baby and mother can only ever be a hypothesis.

Instead of a radical understanding of the role of extreme pain and pleasure, psychoanalysis postulates the primacy of the pleasure–unpleasure principle, suggesting that the human being does everything in its power to produce pleasure and avoid unpleasure. Set against this is a strong emphasis on the importance for human development of accepting unpleasure, as, for instance, in cases of loss. The awful irony of hysteria is that, predicated as it is on the pleasure principle, in its compulsive pursuit of whatever it wants, it always ends up on the rock of misery. Alice James, sister of William (philosopher) and Henry (novelist) and daughter of Henry James Senior (theologian), had plenty of reasons for wanting to be like the famous males in her immediate family environment. Her father, however, was an amputee – and Alice became paralysed in one leg. Just as Dora felt considerable pain as a result of her various ailments, Recovered Memory patients truly suffer from their relived abuse and Dostoevsky had epileptic fits which resembled the death throes of his hated father's murder. Second-wave feminism has paid tribute to the radical courage of witches who mimicked power – forgetting that what they achieved was being drowned or burnt at the stake. The anorexic starves, uses enemas or colonic irrigation, vomits; teeth rot, irreversible infertility results; skinny almost to death, she looks in the mirror and sees a fat woman. Like some ghastly fairy tale, with hysteria, the more you get what you want, the worse it is. Yet there is a further twist. Although it is the body that enacts the pain, it is the mind that is truly wretched – and does not know why. The regression of the body's enactments are intended to avoid mental pain – but at the point to which the regression returns, mind and body are one and in the end both feel the pain. It is because of this that the symptom shifts so frequently. At first the body discharge enables the avoidance of pain – but not for long, so a new symptom is resorted to.

That we all want pleasure and eschew unpleasure is hardly surprising. However, few emotions, sensations or feelings are absolutely one thing or the other: masochism is the prime instance of pleasure-in-pain. For psychoanalytic theory the pleasure–unpleasure principle is the effect of the drive that needs to be discharged and that, if it is not, will give rise to feelings of unbearable tension. This takes place in the context of a social construction, a set of human relations and rules and regulations. In hysteria, the unbearable feeling is got rid of into either the body's movements or into expressions which would seem to offer some relief simply through their discharge, or by putting the emotion into someone else. In the latter instance, with bad feelings evacuated, only emptiness, not 'goodness', remains within: screaming produces exhaustion not contentment.

Wilfred Bion shows how the mother's containment of her baby's anxieties turns these into the protothoughts or feelings that will be translatable in time into ideas. This theory offers one way of conceptualizing how feelings turn into the 'mind'. Over and above biological processes, then, the mind comes out of the carer's containing of the baby's feelings. However, the theory neglects the fact that the body, too, is produced in this way beyond its biological presence, so that anxieties which have been properly contained produce a calm, coherent, contained body. Hysteria, however, regresses further back to the 'uncontained', the raw material or the beta elements, before they have separated out. The overwhelmingly unbearable feeling on the part of the hysteric that, having been dispossessed of his position in the world he feels like dying or that he is dead (translated as wanting something – 'I will *die* if I don't get what I want'), is the trigger for this regression. The regression then mimes or enacts the no-thought and the not-coherent body of the beta elements – for example in hysterical epileptic fits.

Whereas a baby's uncontained anxieties are an inevitable product of its helplessness, by the time someone has regressed through hysteria there can be no such 'pure' state. Something has made the older child or adult feel as awful as this – but because it is so bad that he feels he has been wiped off the face of the earth he does not know what it is. Minor instances repeat this major catastrophe. They are marked by unconsciousness. If the guilty almsgivers had *known* they were feeling guilty, we can assume they would have taken deliberate measures to deal with it; instead they unconsciously projected that guilt into the would-be witch ('It is not me but you who are at fault.') The witch raves and turns into an ugly hag, thereby enacting uncontained beta elements – as neither the almsgiver nor the witch's social context acknowledge her as an old woman (once a baby) in need. But in the witch as hysteric (and not in the baby) there is both a sexual and a gendered element. In the witch the helpless baby has become a woman and her corporeal and mental expression of helplessness has become sexualized. The invariable presence of sexuality and death indicates that the 'original' shock was the advent of a lateral replacement at the time when the child was both sexual and trying to understand death.

The world can be a safety net for the uncontained baby; however, it can also fail to be so. The image of Dora which Jacques Lacan uses as an emblem for her later masculine sexual identification is that of her as an 18-month-old baby, sitting on the floor sucking her thumb while clutching the ear of her 3-year-old brother. She wants for nothing, a veritable *huis clos* of satisfaction. One can imagine the dreamy, almost trancelike state of the toddler. Bion and Winnicott describe only the containing world of the mother. There is more available to the baby than this mother. Dora is 'at one' with her brother, and her own thumb is 'a good enough' provider of pleasure. As well as the mother or carer acting as a 'container' for the raw beta elements of the infant, there is also the possibility that the infant does this for itself as well. When the infant finds a thumb or another's ear, it would seem to be using the outside world as a container – in particular, a very young baby is transfixed by external movements such as the harmonious, somewhat repetitious movement of light through leaves, a mobile, or sounds (rhythms such as another's heartbeat or music) which are not monotonous but not disorganized either; soon it delights in the play and gestures of an older child. In fact, something that fits in the external world for all the senses provides (along with the mother/carer) the containment that allows the separation but also interconnection of a mind that can 'reflect' this environment and a body that can cohere to its rhythmic patterns.

Paucity or excess in the environment, however, reduces the possibility of reflection, of finding a world in which to recognize oneself, in which one is seen, heard and felt. Hysterical patients, or self-appointed hysterics such as artists and writers, complain of feeling both too full of themselves and empty, an overall existential condition exemplified in anorexia and bulimia. As one patient put it to me, she was either like a bladderfish that can inflate to fill the whole rockpool, or she was nothing. Like Sarah, she had an 'emptiness', a sense of not being there at all.

The containment of the infant's raw material of body–mind offered by the external world explains, in part, why children are 'conservative', why people nostalgically return to old haunts and experiences, even why a child will run back to an abusive parent. All these constitute moments and places from which one can see oneself recognized. One does not feel oneself to be a coherent person with a mind and a body unless one is recognized from without. I am recognized, therefore I am. When one is lost in the external world, one's body feels disorganized.

An environment which might fail to offer this 'containing' recognition might be a violent one, which is excessive and intrusive, or an inhuman institutional one, in which there is too little. But how do you ask the trees, the waves, the mobiles, the other children, whether they were 'good enough'? It is easier to fault the mother/carer and her powers of recognition – hence why she tends wrongly to become synonymous with the world. One of my hysterical patients, who had serious problems with self-perception, told me he was 'born into an empty world' and consciously talked about the prairies in which he grew up as a metaphor for this feeling. He felt he did not exist in my absence as he had felt he had not existed when his mother had shown no concern for him. He may have meant the prairies as a metaphor, but he had also in fact physically experienced the prairies, where he had been left with only impersonal care for long stretches of time, as inadequately reflective of who he was or recognizing where he might stand, and inadequately animate to contain his random (beta element) animation. For my patient, the prairies were both a metaphor for his mother's emotional non-presence and for his experience of a world insufficiently animate to reflect, mirror and contain his own aliveness. Both as subjects and as theorists, we make the mother the 'hold-all' container for all time, whereas she should really be seen as a representative but special part of the environment. The infant can find containment, mirroring, recognition that places and coordinates him in matching objects, places and above all older children – lateral relations – whose play indicates an articulation of mind and body which will hold his fragmenting, dispersed feelings so they too feel unified.

It is because hysteria is regressive, from childhood or adulthood, that it is sexual. There is a sexual-seeming frenetic discharge underlying it – which is the frantic avoidance of falling into the hole of non-recognition. Sexuality is a bodily discharge of accumulated tension. By the time of the environmental experience of 'too much', as in the case of war violence, or 'too little', as among the deprived Taita women, sexuality, along with sobbing (as opposed to a baby's crying), has become a readily available means of bodily discharge of unbearable feelings. The medieval almsgiver who finds it unbearable not to have something with which he can satisfy the old woman demanding alms discharges his feelings of unrecognized guilt or anger into her. In discharging these in her turn, the witch will probably use her body and her mind sexually – in obscene curses and perverse practices. She will regress to the shape she was as a baby before she felt 'recognized'. The monstrosity of witches is a matter of regression to the unco-ordination of infancy. When regressed to, the frenetic excitability of the infant becomes sexuality and the primitive demands of the baby become performative language.

By regressing to the unrecognized mind–body, the hysteric deploys a mind and body that are unrepresented, that do not correspond to the designations of the symbolized body. In the reconstructed, suppressed and individual history to which hysteria returns, it is experienced as though there has been insufficient reciprocity of contact between the hysteric as infant and its mother. The touch points of actual or fantasized nursing – nipple in mouth, hands cleaning anus or tending genitals – have been unable to develop into erotogenic zones, areas where the other recognizes the emerging 'self'. These erotogenic zones, had they been allowed to develop properly, would have been usable by sexuality. However, the hysteric, craving for this union, uses any bit of the body as a hysterogenic zone, that is, where complete fusion, utter identification, 'sameness' can be fantasized.

The hysteric's body is used to make him present wherever he feels he is unacceptably absent; thus, he presents it in symptoms or in acts and performances. The scene may have some actual basis or it maybe completely imaginary. One of my patients, showing me the kneeling posture he had to take up during a bronchitic attack, demon-strated both the panting of his mother in his chest spasms and the movement of his father in the sexual intercourse to which, as a child, he had listened and pictured nightly through the thin partition that separated his bedroom from that of his parents. The ultimate imagined exclusion which comes to summarize the helplessness of the human neonate is the parental intercourse that creates one: one is not present at one's own conception. If someone is traumatized by too much exclusion early on in his life, he may become the hysteric who cannot tolerate the thought of his own absence from any scene – for the hysteric does not know that in time he will fit in somewhere. A child's egocentric thought cannot imagine a scene in which he is not a participant. The exemplary scene for this absence is the so-called 'primal scene', when one fantasizes the intercourse from which one was conceived – a time before one was on earth – not the Oedipal constellation.

Klein makes much of the infant's destructive urges towards this primal scene. If, however, we look at it from the perspective of regression in hysteria, it appears somewhat differently. The child or adult who becomes hysterical has received a blow and returns to the demands for attention and to the omnipotence of infancy. In this latter, he can have babies parthogenetically. When my patient is both his mother and his father in intercourse, it could be that he is imitating the primal scene of his two parents, but it could also be that he has rolled both parents into one body – his own, which can now have sex and produce babies on its own.

The presenting body of the hysteric is also the body that is not felt to be there. A patient of mine, Matty, a woman in early middle age who was brilliant but desperately unhappy because she was virtually unable to make any personal or, in effect, social relationships of any kind, once said to me:

I'm quite nice, I want to be friendly but my body is ugly. It's the body of a little girl. I can look after it only if I remember to. My mother looked after my body but didn't know I had a soul. So my body is like something else – I must take care of it like another object. I don't really have a body.

Here she touched on a crucial truth: since the mind is part of the body, if the psyche, soul or mind is not recognized, the body cannot flourish. Even if it has been well-tended, the body, along with the 'soul', will feel non-existent. From the work of Jacques Lacan we are accustomed to the idea that in the mirror the baby gets its ego from a body *gestalt* – a whole image – a body ego. What happens to the body, however, if the mind or soul go unacknowledged? Many women record that if they are treated as stupid, they also feel physically clumsy and/or ugly.

Peter Brooks opens his book *Body Work* (1993) with the following description:

Our bodies are with us, though we have always had trouble saying exactly how. We are, in various conceptions or metaphors, in our body, or having a body, or at one with our body, or alienated from it. The body is both ourselves and other, and as such the object of emotions from love to disgust. To psychoanalysis, it is the object of primary narcissism. To religious ascetics, it is a dangerous enemy of spiritual perfection. Most of the time, the body maintains an unstable position between such extremes, at once the subject and object of pleasure, the uncontrollable agent of pain and the revolt against reason – and the vehicle of mortality.[7]

These bodies that Brooks describes in all their variety are materially and substantially existent, even if we are alienated from them. This is also true of the heterogeneous bodies described by the post-modern feminist philosopher Judith Butler in *Bodies That Matter* (1994) and it is true of the 'discursive' and 'textual' bodies portrayed in the writings of Foucault. Of course, this presence of the body is 'objectifiably' the case. Indeed, it is the body's very materiality that may account for the current academic vogue for studies of the body after decades devoted solely to 'theory'. The body is relievingly concrete.

But are bodies always there? The one thing one would seem to be able to say with confidence is that everybody has a body; but subjectively and experientially this is not always the case. Brooks' account, which concludes with a sensitive and perceptive description of the flamboyance of the hysterical body, nevertheless omits the *absent* body. The hysterical body is, quintessentially, the absent or missing body, even though, as I have maintained, it is the terror of the body going absent that drives the hysteria. The absent body is one that is unrepresentable to the subject. Therein lies a double paradox: there is no more excessively present body than that of the hysteric (in hysteria the body is always acting and thereby expressing something); however, it is exactly this bodily excess which is dependent on its subjective absence. The characteristic flamboyance is an attempt to ensure that the body which is felt not to be there, does not fall over the edge into complete non-existence. Anne Sexton talked with her therapist about dressing her body to receive a prestigious award for one of her volumes of poetry, *All My Pretty Ones* (1962). Her biographer comments:

Sexton felt she had to choose between two very different public personalities, the little girl and the vamp. The child would do very well for interviews at home: 'I was dressed like a little girl when the guy from the *Boston Globe* came – no shoes, and a shift, he couldn't tell if I had a figure.' But for New York she had chosen a costume she would have to live up to: an orchid tweed suit with a halter top, purplish, very low-cut and shocking. 'I'll have to wear a strapless bra; the top comes down low in the back. I have it all planned. I'll leave the jacket on until I'm high, then take it off.' If she had any intention of letting people get to know her, Sexton claimed, she would have to dress like a child, in flat shoes. 'When I'm that little girl I don't have any body! I can't explain that, but it's true.'[8]

We can see clearly here that one does not have a body if it has not been symbolized or represented. Sexton's doctor is reported to have echoed Sexton's self-perception by saying: '*There was almost no one there*' (my italics). In *Hysteria from Freud to Lacan*, Monique David-Ménard writes: 'The hysteric has no body, for something in the history of her body could not be formulated, except in symptoms.'[9] According to the adult Anne Sexton, if anyone was to get to know her, it would be as a young girl – and that young girl had no body. Like Sexton, my patient Matty was both a 'little girl' and someone without a body. Is there a link between the bodily symptomatology of hysteria and social attitudes towards it?

The longest standing explanation of hysteria is that the womb has gone wandering around the body. Some Hippocratic texts suggest that the womb is an animal. Helen King, however, cautions against our making too much of this:

Because it is self-evident to us that the womb not only is not a living creature, but also cannot move around the body, any suggestion that it does so move is startling, demands explanation, and may be given more weight than it deserves.[10]

However, even in the twentieth century, the womb does, subjectively, move. In a number of emotional states, such as orgasm, it is clearly felt to do so. Even if the feeling is not always as clear as this, sensations in the womb and stomach often resemble movements. The sensation of dryness and contraction of some internal organ is one with which many people are familiar. The womb, like other internal organs, moves in mysterious ways, so if the stomach 'turns', why shouldn't the womb? While not wishing to make too much of the notion that the womb moves or is conceived of as an animal, we should not dismiss other cultural descriptions of phenomena which we know about or feel ourselves – Sarah, after all, had felt her womb had been snatched away. Hysteria challenges Western scientific accounts in many fields; it is as well therefore not to rely on them too heavily.

The other standard ancient Greek notion was that the womb wishes to bear children, just as the penis was thought to be 'wilful', wishing to penetrate. As with the wilful penis of the man, the willing and desiring womb may well reflect a subjective perception of some aspects of women's sexuality. Without some explanation, such as a desirous womb, how could we even now explain the physical inflation of phantom pregnancies?

All the symptoms that accompany what has until recently been regarded as hysteria in ancient Greece would seem to indicate some loss of control or excess of need similar to the 'wanting' of the Taita sufferers. Many of the symptoms described by Greek writers feature in accounts of hysteria from the sixteenth to the twentieth centuries in the Western world: the grinding of teeth, loss of voice, cold extremities, limb pains and paralysis. As far as I know, we do not have any subjective descriptions from ancient Greece of bodies that feel absent. Experiencing her body as occupied by a wild dog, the ancient Greek hysterical woman's body is filled with a very corporeal alien presence, where the twentieth-century Western hysteric's is empty. But 'absence' is not unique; 'absences' were characteristic of nineteenth-century accounts and trances and fugue-like states, which were widely described, suggest that the body was often experienced as 'missing'. Excess and absence are once again two sides of the same coin.

When Freud came to describe the pathology of the hysteric, he talked about the unresolved nucleus of unconscious ideas whose repression, he believed, created the hysterical symptom as a 'foreign body'. The dog in the ancient Greek woman's body has become in the twentieth century a 'foreign body', an alien cluster of ideas that drives her against her conscious will. A dog is a more concrete notion than a bundle of ideas that the patient does not know she has, but otherwise are the descriptions so very different? The hysteric in both accounts has her body possessed by a foreign 'other'. What we have in both instances is a doubling self-division in which the person's empty inside is taken over or occupied.

That the emphasis should have shifted from one descriptive pole to the other – from 'too much' body to the twentieth-century Western 'too little' – may well be linked to the transition of hysteria between the seventeenth and nineteenth centuries from being seen as an illness located in the body, to be cured through medication, to being considered a condition brought about by malfunctioning 'nerves'. This indicates a shift in diagnosis from blaming the body to blaming the mind. It is, then, a short step to the nineteenth-century view that hysteria is caused by inherited neurological degeneracy. However, this is a shift only in the dominant theory, not in the experience of the patient.

There are also other partial contributory social factors: for instance, in North America and northern Europe, the current emphasis on slimming in the context of overabundant consumer cultures would tend to give support to the empty body of the anorexic and the evacuations of the bulimic. Starving and eating difficulties have been features of hysteria through the ages and in different cultures. It is impossible to do more than speculate about the causes of these. For instance, the vogue for moral motherhood in the second Industrial Revolution and into the twentieth century in Protestant countries was not really about reproduction, that is about pregnancy and parturition, rather it was about the raising and rearing of children. The image of the moral mother is not one full of maternal bounty and superabundant children, but rather that of programmed childbirth and a woman's return to an efficient body and a small family to whose education great attention must be paid. Eventually, within the worlds of work and the economy, less and less emphasis has been laid on the need to differentiate along gender lines and, even where it has, this has been less to do with women's reproductive and nurturant characteristics and more to do with the demands of child *care*. There has been little or no validation of a reproductive female body. The subjective impulses of anorexia are many and complex. It seems to rise to epidemic proportions in social contexts where the recognition of a girl or woman does not put much emphasis on the fullness of the maternal body, where ideals of physical femininity have become very close to ideals of masculinity. For instance, there was an outbreak of excess dieting among women in northern Europe and the USA after the First World War. Hélène Deutsch's understanding of this obsession with highly dangerous 'reducing' cures (which then, as now, could lead to death) was that women, particularly among the intelligentsia and bourgeoisie, having had a wartime taste of male occupations and male freedoms, were further aspiring to masculinity in their bodies.

With hysteria's mimetic propensities, hysterical presentations tend to mime their own diagnoses. A neurological diagnosis in the nineteenth century meant that hysterical women were not suffering, as their Greek and Renaissance forebears had done, from wild animals or 'suffocation of the mother', but from 'nerves'. If hysteria was thought to emanate from 'nerves' or from the mind, then accordingly the mental state rather than the physiological condition of the hysteric was more regularly described; the hysteric responded with matching symptoms – an absent body and lots to say. In 'anxiety hysteria', the illicit idea or constellation of ideas, that is the 'complex', is repressed but gives rise to such an unmanageable degree of anxiety that phobic precautions have to be taken – as with Little Hans – against the representation of the idea. In a phobia, the body flees from the idea that has caused the anxiety. It is as though, if one's body does not touch something, then one's mind does not need to think about it either: 'I'm not going to *touch* on that problem now.'

It is necessary now to get back to the apparent paradox that the hysterical body, over and above its flamboyant and rich enactments, is a 'missing' body, yet this missing body is not able to tolerate the absolute absence of the body. Absolute absence entails the fear that there may be no return, no retrieved presence. When the place the subject occupies is pulled out from under it (another child is there, for example), then the subject also vanishes. This reiterated absence/

presence next takes place not only in relation to the other person but also within the subject. An ideal passage through this catastrophe would be for the subject to feel safe enough to tolerate its own disappearance. For the subject to be able to do this, however, it is probable that his underlying experience of separation from the other person upon whom his existence depends must be that she went but also that she came back. If either the precipitating catastrophe is too great or the underlying conditions of existential reassurance too weak, then there can be no tolerance of the subject's own disappearance in conditions of extreme pleasure or pain. The hysteric's dramatizations, from fits and seizures to compulsive lying, are protests against the vanishing of his own body/mind; the drowning man's struggling cry, 'Look, I'm here!'

In the interests of illustrating these phenomena and furthering my argument without making it unnecessarily discursive, I propose to amalgamate a number of patients who, despite their different histories, have comparable hysterical responses. This amalgamation I will call Mrs Peters, because, despite a preponderance of women, there are also male patients in the material, and I would like to underscore the bisexuality of the hysterical subject. This fictional being is like a character in a 'true story' – all the elements come from direct observation, although the combination does not. The combination, however, is entirely plausible.

Mrs Peters had a recurrent dream: she went into a room and found her uncle seated there in a chair – as though sitting in state, central and enthroned. A number of her relatives were milling around, referring to her uncle though not talking to him directly. However, they behaved as though everything were normal. Only Mrs Peters knew that in fact her uncle was dead. He had been stuck together from numerous little pieces, as though he were a jigsaw. She told people this, but no one believed her. She realized that her uncle was herself.

The poet Anne Sexton once described her father as a jigsaw puzzle that would break apart at any moment. This too was a self-image. In the theoretical literature, fragmentation (the jigsaw puzzle) or the uncoordinated movements of the infant whom Lacan sees placed before the mirror in order that it will gain an alienated, cohering, posturing ego, are all evidence of a state of collapse. I would argue that this is not so. It is rather that the fantasy of fragmentation and chaos, awful as it may seem, in fact indicates the hysteric's refusal to go into the Black Hole of nothingness. It is the psychic equivalent of the frenetic body – breaking apart, or moving hectically, in order still to be there at all costs. The jigsaw puzzle, the multiple personality, the broken-up body still exist: they are the final solutions against the threat of complete absence (death). The act of torture enacts on the other the experience of mind–body fragmentation in the subject; that is, the torturer breaks to pieces the body and/or mind of the other. Threatened by a displacement that seems catastrophic, the hysteric unconsciously 'chooses' to come apart at the seams, to break into bits, rather than to disappear completely. Breaking in bits, fragmenting as a body or as a multiple personality, is a desperately insistent presence. We can therefore take the jigsaw in Mrs Peters's dream as an imago that protects against absolute loss of the subject.

In therapy Mrs Peters talked repeatedly about her older sister. It was only with hindsight that I realized that the complaints Mrs Peters made about her were really highly significant. I had got swept down the more familiar lane of the sad features she described in the relationship to her parents. These latter were certainly many and certainly relevant; but they contained neither the precipitating issue nor the catastrophic displacement to which Mrs Peters's many hysterical symptoms, both 'conversion' and phobic, were a response. I now realized that (never of course, having encountered her) I had never liked Mrs Peters's sister. Not only had she complained about her, Mrs Peters had also idealized her sister to me and set me up in competition with her in a number of ways. I found myself dealing in my mind with my rivalrous jealousy of this sister in a somewhat irritated way, by deciding I was the better of the two of us. Mrs Peters had clearly made the same decision on her own behalf. But my irritation, even my inadequate attention to the theme of sibling rivalry (though encouraged by a customary orientation to the infant–parent axis), were testimony to the fact that Mrs Peters had never found her own place in the sibling situation, that it was possible to be both the same – a child of the same kinship network and with the same parents – and different. The idealization/denigration of the sister was the mark of serious jealousy.

Mrs Peters had a 'nervous' cough, a sensation of choking, epileptic-type fits, a long history of highly disordered eating and many phobias. Her father had died of a heart attack before she was born and she had the one elder sister. When Mrs Peters was six, her mother had remarried. Mrs Peters adored her new stepfather. He played rough and tumble games with her, took her to football matches, showed her off at work and in the pub – it sounds as though she fully compensated for the very poor reception he had got from the older pubescent sister when he entered the family. To say she thought of herself as her stepfather's son and heir, and could thus find a different place from her sister, is too simple, but it conveys something of the quality of boyishness and precarious superiority with which she endowed herself as regards her elder sister. It was also how Mrs Peters at the time appeared in her body – agile and boyish.

Then, when Mrs Peters was seven, her mother gave birth to a son. The arrival of the brother was catastrophic: the stepfather was overjoyed with his natural son, and, in Mrs Peters's eyes, an over-intense, unhealthy relationship developed between father and son which seemed to exclude everyone else, in particular herself and her mother. The marriage deteriorated apace. But, unlike Herbert Rosen-feld's patient Mildred (see chapter 6), Mrs Peters did not give up: as she had become a 'boy' to outbid her sister, so she now became a 'girl' to outbid her brother, through a brightness and flirtatiousness that seems to have been comparable to the behaviour of the Wolf Man's sister. She won (as she tried in therapy likewise to win my interest over and above all my other patients). Her brother apparently became a depressed and unsuccessful child while her elder sister left home early (this leaving home meant she was also not to be at home in my mind). But Mrs Peters's victory was almost literally a 'hollow' one.

One of Mrs Peters's symptoms was shaking fits, in which she appeared to be shivering with cold. Her whole body shook and her teeth chattered uncontrollably as though she was gripped by a cold beyond endurance. When finally Mrs Peters could speak she said she knew it looked as though she was freezing (it did) but in fact she felt quite warm. Mrs Peters had sided with her mother in the hostile, disputatious marriage (to which Mrs Peters had contributed not a little) that had followed the birth of her half-brother. Mrs Peters had suffered agony on account of her mother's unhappiness, but her mother had called her 'unfeeling and cold'. There and then, Mrs Peters, acutely aware of her intense sympathy for her mother but in fact deeply ambivalent, had decided that if her mother whom she loved so much thought her emotionally cold, then that was what she was going to be. The coldness also represented the negative side of her relationship with her mother – her real coldness to the mother who had given birth to her half-brother, as well as to her elder sister. In therapy, the fits would start when I had interpreted something in such a way that made her feel warm towards me – this then was liable to reveal a more heavily concealed coldness towards me. The most profound level of hostility, however, Mrs Peters reserved for the sister whom she felt she had got rid of but somehow had not really managed to do so completely. (The hostility to me was also towards someone who had got there first – in that she felt I had been able to make my interpretations before she could. This common experience is usually traced back to rivalry with the mother or father – it was quite clearly first and foremost with the sister.) For this older sister had an unbearable advantage over Mrs Peters – she had known and been loved by their dead father for five years before Mrs Peters's birth and the father's near-coincidental death.

But Mrs Peters also had a secret: she kept imagining her natural father as a homunculus, a little man, inside her. She felt her mother blamed her for his death (as she indeed blamed her mother). Playing unconsciously on the verb 'to bear', Mrs Peters could not bear this, as later for a long time she was unable to bear (in both senses of the word) live children; instead, she bore her father inside her. The unconscious fantasy had, in this case, a nodal moment in death: a dead baby for a dead father. Most of Mrs Peters's phobic and conversion symptoms either warded off or identified with death. Mrs Peters compared herself to H. G. Wells's 'Invisible Man', a space bound in bandages, and to Italo Calvino's portrait of a knight who is not there beneath his suit of armour. She had a recurring bad dream in which she was driving a dormobile (driving in her sleep), except that she wasn't; instead she was looking in through a window and no one was driving, even though it was full of small children.

Hysterics often enact their sense of their own presence/absence by 'coming and going' with their therapists (like Mildred). Mrs Peters, however, in one session, rather than missing the appointment without warning or coming so late that she knew I would be worried (she was both accident-prone and had suicidal fantasies), instead perhaps of having a seizure, she 'disappeared' in my company. This is hard to describe but I could see her physically vanishing. First her voice faded, then I found myself wanting to stretch out to stop her falling. She went down a psychic Black Hole, such as is indicated by the concept of 'blank psychosis', which may happen in moments of trauma. André Green, in his work on 'the negative', theorizes that this state of complete absence, the 'blank' of psychosis, is an expression of the death drive. He argues that, in neuroses, states of feeling empty result from suppressing fantasies, but that in psychoses the absence comes first and must be subsequently filled with fantasies. I would argue that in hysteria (which can be both neurotic and psychotic), the abundant fantasies, the wild acting-out, the florid symptoms and the awareness of emptiness indicate both a suppression of 'unthinkable' ideas (Green's neurotic absence) and a defence against utter and complete absence (the psychotic absence). Balint's patient Sarah preferred the wild wolves in her head to a void within. The shock of sibling substitutability for the subject leads to fragmentation and even to multiple personalities as avoidance of the absence beneath. In Mrs Peters's case, 'disappearing' herself – though it frightened me to watch – was her first recognition (when she came back) that her father could *not* come back, could not be present in her body, that she was there, but that he was not. From here she was eventually able to be sad *for him* that he had died without seeing his daughter. This was a shift out of the hysterical perspective in which there was only room for her to count. The hysteric is like an empty vessel, free to be flooded with the other: there is too much of the 'other' in the empty body of hysteria. The excess, the ostentation of the symptom, depends on the vacancy. It is as though the walls can shake and tremble because the object within (like the Greeks' dog) does not fill the space. If there is to be 'recovery', then the subject has to disappear completely and then come back. It is the terror of this disappearance, the lack of any sense that one will indeed come back, and at the same time no knowledge that one does not come back from death, that underlies the hysterical reaction in all of us.

There are, then, two levels to a sense of emptiness. One, which I will call 'secondary', is the most prevalent symptom of hysteria and this can be filled. This secondary sense of emptiness both reflects and guards against the Black Hole. In order to bear a dead father (and thus not acknowledge his death), Mrs Peters needed to be secondarily empty. In this state the body is empty, the mind thought-free, and others as objects or the projections of others may flow in. But regression to this state involves an evacuation of what have become, or what might become, one's own feelings: anger, guilt, jealousy, envy. Because the feeling is unbearable, the witch who receives the projections of unconscious guilt from the almsgiver repeats the same process that the almsgiver had hoped to accomplish – she re-evacuates any feeling of guilt, jealousy or envy. The other, the 'primary' level, is really a psychic Black Hole – such as Mrs Peters eventually fell into. Until then she had felt empty and her symptoms had been dependent on that emptiness. The primary emptiness that underlies this play of secondary emptiness and possession is, as it were, psychic death. Very often a crucial death – Mrs Peters's father, for instance – has not or could not be mourned. This primary emptiness, the Black Hole, is the necessity to know and experience an absolute absence. Knowledge that the other person is dead allows the knowledge of one's own death.

All this involves Green's 'neurotic' blankness, which I am calling secondary emptiness in order to indicate how a hysteric becomes secondarily empty so as to be filled with wild dogs, wolves or homunculi, or the guilt of others. The Black Hole beneath (the primary or primal void) is defended against by this secondary emptiness and the many objects and alien states of mind that rampage within it. Whenever hysteria has truly disappeared, that is because it has been 'cured' by the social equivalent of the knowledge that Mrs Peters was able to acquire after going down her Black Hole, the taking on board, as a deep internal knowledge, of the fact that the world exists without one. Such knowledge involves a process of mourning for one's own self and also for the dead other person. If there is no mourning-equivalent process, then the labile hysteria is merely in hiding.

II. THE GENDERING OF POSSESSION

Current Western pathological symptoms which play on the relationship between fullness and emptiness are anorexia and bulimia. In looking at what was once regarded as hysteria and its manifold expressions, our psychoanalytic theory follows these Western symptoms in emphasizing eating, greed and orality – but overall in relation to the mother. I think these features of hysteria are important, yet the prevalence of 'possession', both historically and cross-culturally, may provide a different and useful model for the experiences of voids and foreign bodies, of the emptiness that must precede both the inhabitation by wild dogs as well as by envy and creativity.

The twentieth-century decomposition of hysteria in the Western world into its many constituent parts and an analysis of the diverse phenomena that once went under its umbrella appellation has an analogue with the ethnography of 'possession'. Here there are now seen to be a number of discrete phenomena which for a long time had been analytically merged. Following the anthropologist Evans-Pritchard's breakthrough in understanding witchcraft among the Azande of central Africa in the 1930s, there was a move to demarcate and differentiate its various phenomena – sorcery, witchcraft, possession – into discrete instances. As with the breakdown of hysteria into different elements, much was usefully learnt about these, but, perforce, at a cost of not seeing the larger wood because of the many trees; what the conditions had in common disappeared before the increasingly subtle distinctions that were made between them. Here I shall retain the categories but, while referring from time to time to witchcraft, I will give pride of place to 'possession'. However, to maintain the connections between those various manifestations is essential, since they are all connected in hysteria.

It is sometimes observed by anthropologists that witchcraft disappears almost overnight once an attempt has been made to stamp it out or another ritual or religious order – such as Christianity – has been imposed. This disappearance almost certainly parallels the so-called disappearance of hysteria in the twentieth century: with witchcraft, there are probably some hidden and occasional instances that persist, but then, like hysteria, it simply expresses itself in another form.

In 1923, offering an analysis of a case history of a Renaissance painter, Christoff Heizzman, Freud commented that whereas in medieval and early modern times hysteria took the form of possession, in the twentieth century it manifested itself in seemingly organic illnesses. Given my emphasis on the importance of the role of the physician in the case of Dora, this is a doubly interesting observation. It may be that there is more at stake in this aspect of hysteria than the imitation of whatever are the prevalent social diseases, dilemmas and treatments at the time. Our modern conception of biology is a case in point – it offers a way of thinking that is particularly appropriate to hysteria. Our medical knowledge of anatomy, since at least the days of Leonardo da Vinci, has extended the emphasis on the interiority of bodies as containers in which things take place, even grow and change shape, when illnesses occur within. Organic illness offers the hysteric a model of the inner body that can be filled; he does not need to invent, only copy it. During my own pregnancy, which I did not hide, one patient could not see it for what it was until finally, in my eighth month, I confronted him with it as an absolute and unavoidable fact. Until that point, despite my repeatedly telling him that the growth was in my belly not his, he developed first a stomach ulcer and then, with full medical support, supposed cancer of the stomach. There is little difference between the imaginary growth in this patient and the homunculus in Mrs Peters. The latter was only deploying a somewhat 'medieval' mode of fantasy in keeping her father inside her; the former was using contemporary medical knowledge and, as Freud comments, became ill instead of being possessed.

We do not commonly come across instances of overt 'possession' in the contemporary Western world. But the hysteric's description of his experience is often that of emptiness and possession. The *saka*, and numerous ecstatic dances or raves described historically and cross-culturally, take up and 'bind' the frenetic movements whereby the hysteric discharges through the body the unbearable feeling– thoughts of his impotency, jealousy, rage and so on. Likewise, our modernist medical model has the concepts of inner and outer, invasion and infection, some of which reflect culture-specific ways of experiencing. Medieval 'humours' – hot, cold, dry and moist – do not distinguish between the inner and the outer body; modern notions of a tumour that both invades and grows demand a sense of separate interiority. It is not that the medieval world had no conception of interiority, it is just that this interiority belonged to religion rather than medicine. Our medical conceptualization and psychiatric, and even more particularly psychoanalytic, theory, then, has taken over what in other times and places belonged to non-medical discourses, not to illnesses but to spiritual experiences. Even within the so-called objectivity of medical observation, there is a relationship between an illness and its treatment. This is true of medicine, of psychiatry, but even more so of the utterly dialogic practice of psychoanalysis. Hysteria and psychoanalysis were born together, 'speaking' to each other, however much hysteria became neglected, even forgotten, later. Because witchcraft and possession are no longer privileged expressions of hysteria in the Western world they have been absorbed into the culture in the form of political witch hunts, such as the McCarthyite ones of the 1950s, or into the practices that try to understand and cure them. The psychoanalyst is often referred to as the 'witch doctor' or 'shrink' (head-shrinker) or compared, more seriously, to a shaman – such incorporation of these figures into popular metaphors within the general culture points to the link with religious understandings of hysteria.

This is true not only of colloquialisms but also of theoretical conceptualizations. As previously mentioned, the notion of possession is very close to the German *besetzung*, which features centrally in psychoanalytic theory. '*Besetzen*' means to 'occupy', in the sense in which an invading army may *take possession* of a castle or contemporary equivalent. James Strachey, Freud's English translator, controversially interpreted *besetzung* as 'cathexis' – one 'cathects' a person or object when one wants it so passionately that one takes it over. 'Cathexis' is insistent; like 'possession' it stretches along a continuum from the normal to the excessive or pathological. Similarly, in our Western cultures, the child 'possesses' a teddy bear or a secret, but one can also become 'possessed' with rage. The Kleinian notion of 'projective identification' is a rewriting and sophistication of the *process* of possession, seen from the viewpoint, not of the possessed, but of the possessing infant, who projects a whole or part of himself into the other person in order to harm, control or *possess* it.

The relationship between demonological accounts of hysteria and modern medical practices is well illustrated in a Central American example described by the British-Belizean anthropologist Byron Foster: among the Garafuna of the coastal regions of Honduras, Guatamala and Belize, spirit possession is common. For this impoverished refugee Carib population, possession seems a means of maintaining a community and its traditions when under threat. It is as though the Garafuna deliberately negotiate their situation by deploying a ritual of possession in a context where modern Western medicine has hegemony. First a woman is taken ill with what amounts to a severe hysteria with death-like symptoms. Then, very intentionally, the dominant Western medicine is tried, but to no avail; the ill woman becomes increasingly 'absent' and comatose. It is only when she is at death's door, and beyond the help of all Western-style doctors, that it is decided she is possessed by a dead mother who has been offended by the group's neglect and disloyalty in turning to Western practices (which have anyway proved useless). Ecstatic dances and gifts honour and restore the importance of the mother to the community and, with this, traditional values.[12]

Within anthropology, as within psychiatry and psychoanalysis, the practice of making ever greater distinctions between various hysterical or cult forms has seemed to give not only a richer picture but also scientific credence to the investigatory method. Again, however, although a lot can be learnt from such distinctions, something is also lost from the larger human picture.

It was in order to countermand this trend for increasing differentiation that, in the 1980s, I. M. Lewis argued in *Religion in Context* that it was incorrect to regard witchcraft, spirit possession, cannibalism and shamanism as four discrete phenomena found in different social contexts in different places and times. Instead, Lewis contended, they are just so many diverse aspects of mystical power or charisma – the various faces of one phenomenon. Looking at the ethnographic data, Lewis showed their common features. Although he eschews the term hysteria, the hysterical element that unites them runs like a thread throughout Lewis's analysis. But, as we saw in chapter 1, it was not by considering their common hysterical features that Lewis arrived at the unity of his subject matter; it was by asking who were the chief actors. Occasionally they were disadvantaged men, but nearly always they were women. Deprivation and social disadvantage unites the actors in cults which both express the problem and make an attempt at solving it through the gaining of magical power. However, jealousy also seems at issue. For instance, in the *sar* of the nomads of northern Somalia, the possessing spirits, often djinns, are greedy, covetous and envious. *Sar* possession is regarded as an illness but in every instance the possessed woman has some grudge against her spouse, such as that he is often away for long periods. Frequently, in this polygynous society, the onset of *sar* coincides with the husband's search for another wife.

Lewis observed four clearly defined contexts for spirit possession. In all, it is easy to see the evidence of what we would call hysteria, and, indeed, despite himself, that is how Lewis describes the behaviour. The first is a version of love-sickness when the rejected girl (or sometimes boy) becomes possessed by the loved one who gets inside her. (Lewis compares his observation of this state to the famous account of the possession of the seventeenth-century prioress 'the hysterical Sister Jeanne des Anges', whose infatuation with Canon Urbain Grandier was diagnosed as a possession by malevolent spirits. Grandier was judged the active agent who 'occupied' the prioress; he was convicted and burnt as a witch and Sister Jeanne recovered.)

In Lewis's three other categories of spirit possession, the possessing spirit is not another human being but a nature sprite. In these instances the symptoms of the possessed person range 'from mild hysteria or depression to actual organic injury'. Lewis gives an instance of possession among the deprived youths who tend the camels in virtually complete isolation from the social life of the tribe: these young camel herdsmen, he says, are prone to 'bouts of hysteria' and, on their return to camp life, sometimes develop 'symptoms of hysteria'. This is attributed to possession by *sar* sprites and regarded as a mild and usually temporary form of madness.

Overworked married women with grudges against their husbands, who may be about to take another wife, form the next category. Here, the inhabiting sprites are said to be consumed with envy and greed so that they desire to be appeased with gifts of luxurious clothing, finery, perfume and dainty goods. The husbands accuse the wives of 'malingering' and consider the possession yet another instance of the deceitful tricks women play on men. Such practices – grudges, deceit – and such attitudes towards them – accusations of 'malingering' – are common in modern Western expressions of, and responses to, hysterical behaviour. The husbands' attitudes are similar to those found among the Taita described by Harris.

The final category in Lewis's panoply are 'psychologically disturbed (men) who experience particular difficulties in bearing the pressures and burdens of their society'. These are particularly serious cases. It is notable that in the psychoanalytic literature of the Western world the extreme seriousness of hysteria, when it is found in men, is nearly always emphasized.

Lewis's actors are Muslim, nomadic pastoralists of northern Somalia. He gives numerous other locations for possession cults, in describing which the term 'hysteria' keeps slipping in despite his intentions. In the Tanzanian 'Devil's disease' the possessing spirit 'manifests its presence by hysterical and other symptoms', and in an interchange of possession between Thonga and Zulu women 'in both cases there is the familiar pattern of hysterical and other manifes-tations', as well as requests for gifts and for the mounting of a cathartic dance paid for by the husband. Among the Zulu today, this affliction – known locally as 'Bantu disease' – is widely seen as a form of conversion hysteria; it most commonly involves possession by Indian spirits and by the *tokoloshe*, which are imagined as obscene little sprites with thick-set bodies and huge penises.

Moving on from Africa, which he knows best, Lewis writes:

Finally, a diligent search of the literature will, I think, yield examples outside Africa of the particular type of mystical sanction we have been discussing. Certainly ... women and persons of other subject categories figure promi-nently in many spirit cults elsewhere in the world, and not least in our own shamanistic tradition, where the sexual element is certainly by no means absent. One well-established non-African phenomenon that seems to support this argument is found among the polar Eskimos and other Siberian peoples and is usually known as 'Arctic hysteria'. This is a hysterical affliction mainly affecting women and particularly prevalent during the harsh winter months in northern Greenland. Gussow (1960), who interprets this condition in Freudian terms, considers the hysterical flights to which those affected are prone as unconscious seductive manoeuvres and invitation to male pursuit. They are, he argues, the refuge of those women who in hardship and crisis seek loving reassurance. Stripped of its Freudian cadences, this interpretation suggests my own line of analysis. It is, moreover, particularly significant in this connection that this hysterical condition, which is generally attributed to spirit-possession, plays a vital part in the selection, training, and ritual performances of Siberian shamans – who are frequently women.[13]

These, then, are some cross-cultural examples of possession cults, which are using one expression of hysteria. In the West, possession as a feature of hysteria also has a long history. It is clearly perceivable in the ancient Greek notion that the woman ill with hysteria had a hungry raging dog in her womb.

Lewis considers that the nature of its practitioners – women and disadvantaged groups of men – indicate that 'possession' as a means to power and control results from an attempt to remedy deprivation. However, deprivation is more than just a social phenomenon. The richest people can feel forever poor, being unable to give anything to anyone since that would indicate they have something to give – one patient told me he needed to own very little, otherwise he would be envious of himself. A sense of 'emptiness' may relate to a real situation of disadvantage, but it may also simply be triggered by a psychic state. It is by no means necessarily the wretched of the earth who feel empty 'of themselves' and possessed by alien 'bad feelings'. Deprivation should be read not simply in the context of the wealth or good that is missing, but as the absence of a sufficiently recognized social place, for instance, in not feeling adequately recognized as a wife or mother.

We can both widen the sense in which possession is used and treat it more strictly. A wider use suggests one can be possessed by supervalent thoughts, ideas one cannot get rid of; or by recovered memories of apparently actual abuse (whether today or in Freud's pre-psychoanalytic work in the late nineteenth century) and Oedipal fantasies of paternal seduction. These are variations of the *sar* notion of a sexual incubus. We are 'possessed' by envy, jealousy and the rest. Badly behaved 'alters' in instances of hysterical multiple personality could also be seen as forms of sprite. More narrowly, phantom pregnancies and Mrs Peters's belief that she carried her father inside her, as with Allon White described below, are latterday cases of possession.

It is important to emphasize that hysteria and possession experiences are not the privilege of 'backward' societies or 'neurotic' people; they are attendant on certain conditions. When Allon White, a young university lecturer, knew he was dying of leukaemia, his sister, who had drowned tragically in his childhood, took up residence within him. He wrote:

it is impossible to say whether my illness is connected with the death of my sister all those years ago ... In the early days of my leukaemia two years ago I was convinced that this death wish, this identification with my drowned sister, was responsible for my illness. Three things, tangled up together but separate, seemed involved. The first was identification: inside me somewhere Carol actually constituted a part of my being, she was me. Not as a part of my personality, but as something much more physical, an hysterical body, a violence which terrifies me even when expressed as mere words on the page. I can hardly begin to approach this level of my being: Here Be Monsters.[14]

With hysteria and, in particular, hysterical possession, there is more in heaven and earth than is dreamt of in our philosophy. In White's case, this is inhabitation by a dead sister, as Mrs Peters was by a dead father. In Freud's case one can see him struggling *not* to reach a knowledge of his own dead brother in his analysis of male possession hysteria after brother had killed brother in horrific profusion on the battlefields of Europe. Freud made everything come back to the Oedipal or pre-Oedipal parents, in order to avoid the dead brother. This unacknowledged dead brother can be said to have 'possessed' the theory of psychoanalysis, ever present in the accounts but completely unintegrated into the theory or practice.

In 1923, Freud was shown manuscripts recounting the possession of a sixteenth-century painter, Christoph Heizzman. Heizzman suffered from visions, fits and seizures; he had sold his soul to the Devil following his melancholic depression and inability to work after his father's death. The Devil, according to Freud, inherited the ambivalence with which Heizzman regarded his father. However, all but one of Heizzman's paintings of the Devil portray him with breasts. One level of Freud's analysis shows this to be what he regarded as a typical male hysteria in which the painter has projected his own feminine desires on to the other, expressing his repressed wish to produce a baby with his father. Another level indicates that, after the repression of this illicit wish, Heizzman's ego approved the choice of selling his soul to this breasted Devil as it would mean he could be looked after by a mother figure. And indeed, having been offered the sexual temptation of beautiful women in magnificent buildings, the painter has his 'possession hysteria' cured by entering a monastery and being looked after for the rest of his life.

In Freud's post-First World War analysis of 'possession', Heizzman's shock at his father's death made him regress to a sense of the helplessness of infancy, in which the world is dominated by the mother in her provision of essential nourishment. We cannot know whether Heizzman felt 'empty' without this but, as his paintings showed multiple pendant breasts and as he feared not being able to earn his daily bread, it is possible that he felt deprived of food and potentially disadvantaged; his melancholic depression would certainly indicate this. The temptations the Devil offers, then, are his desires and these are expressed as desires for wealth and sex. Money and sexuality commonly fill the 'emptiness' in the adult as they act as later versions of the infant's need for food.

As we have noted, Freud acknowledges the historical specificity of hysterical manifestations as at one time 'possession' and at another as quasi-organic illness. However, more importantly, he adds to his earlier picture of hysteria. The well-established conflict in the conversion symptom between desire and its prohibition in the interest of self-preservation is given an added dimension by the part played by the ego in protecting itself against helplessness. As I have shown in charting the rise of Object Relations theory in chapter 6, this addition arose from the wartime awareness of the mass phenomenon of male hysteria. The postwar analysis is that some shock makes the recipient feel helpless. This instigates a neediness in which the temptation is to fill oneself up with other objects of which one has been deprived; it is most likely that these would be illicit satisfactions, such as the luxuries that the sufferers of *saka* or *sar* crave. These 'wantings' are assigned to some other being by which one is 'inhabited' or 'possessed'.

At the end of the essay on Heizzman's possession, Freud pulls himself back from seeing a catastrophe as the precipitant of hysteria. He notes that a failure in business or some equivalent occurrence can trigger a neurosis, but then he re-emphasizes that the hysteria itself reflects the conflict of libidinal desires and their prohibition. Freud, although he makes this crucial comparison between 'possession' and contemporary hysterical illness, eschews the term 'hysteria' even for Heizzman's possession. I suggest that, like displacement by a sibling, the collapse of a businessman's enterprise is a catastrophe which may make him lose his social position, just as the woman in the polygynous tribe temporarily loses her position when her husband looks for another wife. Whatever the present catastrophe, in one way or another it is a repeat of the catastrophe in which is echoed the earlier childhood catastrophe of sibling or sibling-equivalent displacement. The serious-ness of its effect may vary according to circumstance, but it is structur-ally the psychological occurrence that renders one helpless and infantile: the discovery that one is not unique. We know nothing of Heizzman's history in this respect, but his later collapse on his father's death and his wish to become the only infant who has the breast of the Devil Mummy suggests an earlier experience of catastrophic displacement.

In hysteria, then, the group or individual is disadvantaged in some way, whether this is as an early modern gleaner-turned-witch, an Allon White with leukaemia, a poor painter whose supportive father has died or as a Garifuna Carib in a shanty town. The Garifuna show clearly how 'possession' restores the power of the mother. Lewis's accounts, which eschew any explanation in terms of hysteria, neverthe-less reveal the condition as the underlying motif. Freud's analysis of Heizzman shows Freud moving away from the all-importance of the father to that of the mother. Psychoanalysts always look from the perspective of a subject who has regressed to infancy; hysteria is regression to the grandiosity of narcissistic omnipotence in the toddler, but in it there is also the infant's possession of the mother. The wish to possess becomes inverted as the wish to be possessed. The infant or hysteric takes on the power of the mother. The psychology of motherhood is not of course identical to that of the infant who identifies with (or is possessed by) her. But why has motherhood so often been seen as the cure for hysteria? Are hysterical manifestations such as witchcraft and certain instances of possession the power expressions of the dispossessed in terms of motherhood?

To emphasize the helplessness or disadvantaged position and not to analyse the powerfulness of possession would be to examine only half the story. When the shocked person regresses to infancy and identifies with the mother whom he wants to have as his alone, it may be that the helplessness of the infant is uppermost – greedily demanding food, love, attention; however, it may equally well be that it is the powerful 'inhabiting' mother who predominates.

Among the Garifuna Caribs it is almost exclusively women who are possessed, and the chief possessing spirits are the women's deceased mothers. 'Sisters', a term the Garifuna use to mean far more than direct blood kinship, are crucial participants in the rituals that appease the possessing spirits. In this practice we can see clearly spelt out the role of hysteria in establishing a link between daughters, sisters and mothers. Possession is a way of presenting, not representing, what has been made absent; the mother has not been lost. It is not a process of uterine transmission through mourning, but a continuation of the past as the present. The other comes back; she is not lost or dead in spirit – hysteria and its performances enable the presentation of absence rather than the representation of loss. The emptiness is the absence, the possession the restoration of a presence. The Garifuna are a dispossessed people, existing between a past in which the group, at least in their popular imagination, is unified and cared for by traditions, and a deracinated present, in which they are only very precariously recognized as a social group at all. They can presumably overcome, to a degree, the helplessness of their past by enacting the protecting presence of the mother. But this re-establishment of the 'primal' mother tends to gender 'possession' no less than Oedipal or pre-Oedipal accounts of the girl's identification with the mother genders hysteria – except that it is seen from the point of view of the importance of the mother rather than the helplessness of the infant. The Garifuna possession confirms the gendering, but upsets the power play: through placing the mother in the centre of the group, it is not the baby but the all-powerful matriarch who comes back. The women are constructing a tradition by, in Virginia Woolf's words, 'thinking back through their mothers'.

Anna O, the first patient of psychoanalysis, effected a self-cure after the end of her treatment with Breuer. First she gave herself a social position by writing fairy tales of young girls caring for the sick (as she did) and then by identifying with a seventeenth-century ancestress (described by the historian Natalie Zemon Davis),[15] Glikl of Hameln, a wife, widow and matriarch and successful businesswoman. In many times and places 'motherhood' has been recommended as the cure for hysteria and it has often been observed to be successful.

Our culture assigns an asymmetrical position to the woman over and over again; her hysterical protest then expresses an unacknowledged envy, jealousy and guilt for the imaginary murder of the rival, be it sibling or the husband's new wife. Either by statute or by custom, until very recently indeed, nearly all cultures have been polygynous, making women by definition the displaced and hence, even if the co-wife is consciously welcomed, potentially the repositories for the unbearable feelings that arise from this dethronement of their subjecthood.

Writing up her 1960s field work among the Gonja of west Africa, the anthropologist Esther Goody noted that male witches were regarded positively: their power was seen as a force for good. Women witches, on the contrary, were seen as bad, a force for evil. When she questioned the women, they explained that women as such were 'evil'.[16] Goody suggests that because this is a polygynous society in which there is a considerable amount of jealousy, envy, bitterness and rivalry among wives, it may be that both men and women perceive those who express such unbearable feelings as 'evil'. This example shows how witchcraft and possession are only secondarily gendered negatively as female: they are not gendered either way when they express power, and only negatively when this power is expressed by jealous women. If this is so, once more we see that it is neither witchcraft nor hysteria that is feminine; and excess jealousy is socially (not biologically) prescribed.

As I. M. Lewis found, the actors of all the rites that operate as alternatives to dominant religions are predominantly women and some disadvantaged men. However, we cannot leave the matter there. This particular type of disadvantage – for instance, to be made the bearer of guilt or jealousy – is already gendered; for disadvantage is first and foremost assigned to females, and then considered as an aspect of individual sexual difference ('feminine', whether male or female).

The male hysteric can have his condition ritualized in the couvade, in which it is socially recognized that the father enacts childbirth, 'dies', and then recovers from being displaced by a newcomer. The recovery and, with it, the realization that he, like the mother, still has a position after the birth, ends, at least for the time being, the hysterical element. Men's fantasies of childbirth in cultures which do not practise couvade have tended to seem as strange to outside observers as the hungry dogs in the bellies of ancient Greek women. But every child is a 'Little Hans' who merrily gives birth to babies parthenogenetically and assures his father he can do likewise. 'Possession' is the same process, the same reaction to threatened or actual displacement. Within a limited range, what possesses will vary. When the Garifuna women are possessed by the dead mother, it is testimony that the culture has *survived* its transplantation and uprooting and that they have 'undone' their guilt at 'murdering' the mother through their assimilation of Western practices.

But not all possessions are by the powerful mother or father. When the medieval almsgivers lost this aspect of their position in a new social and religious order that did not recognize such almsgiving, the wish to kill whoever seemed responsible for that loss of a particular position produced unconscious guilt: they evacuated this into the old woman whose witch status indicated she was possessed by evil thoughts in the shape of the Devil. Her death was therefore ensured.

When Allon White realizes that all his life he has borne within him the younger sister whose tragic death when he was five years old was an accident, he understands that this possession is a consequence of guilt:

How a child takes on the guilt of death and separation I don't know, but before the body had been found something inside me had already decided that I was responsible for the crime, that I had a dreadful guilty secret that

I would henceforth carry with me unknown to myself for thirty years. And like the sense of seduction in Freud, the truth or falsehood of the matter was utterly irrelevant.[17]

However much he adored his little sister, he also wanted her dead and out of the way. The guilt is for this unholy wish that everyone has. Accidents can lead to the appalling realization of one's worst wishes.

On the whole, cultural practices have favoured men in the process of handing on to women the awful feelings, craving, wanting, murders and jealousy that the threat of annihilation through displacement entails. The process is one of projection, so the other is possessed by the awful feelings. These projected feelings, however, always have some point of coincidence in the receiver – because everyone has been threatened with displacement at some point or another and responded accordingly. The 'possessed' thus bears the weight of cultural displacement and expresses the overwhelming wanting to be reinstated at whatever cost.

8

The Hysterical Lie

I. DON JUAN AND THE NORMALIZATION OF MALE HYSTERIA

Today in the Western world the conditions once associated with hysteria – eating disorders, multiple personality disorder, amnesia, false memory and recovered memory syndromes, histrionic personalities, manipulativeness, mendacity and so-called 'borderline conditions' – are all associated in the popular imagination and according to the statistics with girls and women. This continues hysteria's previous trajectory: in the nineteenth century hysteria and femininity were equated, then male hysteria was 'discovered', hysteria 'disappeared' and women reassumed hysteria's characteristics as the feminine. In the context of this history there is bound to be an absence of male hysteria, not only from the theory but also from the observation. Male hysteria is seen as a brief response to trauma or as a psychotic pathologizing of such a response. In this chapter my interest is not in such obviously extreme instances but in showing how aspects of male hysteria are regarded as so normal as to be invisible.

In using Don Juan and Iago as my main examples I intend to indicate, in the first instance, the normalizing of male hysteria and, with the second, how even an extreme example can be missed by the community which cannot detect the lie. Men are rarely visible within the component illnesses and conditions into which hysteria has been decomposed, but they can be seen instead in the psychopathologies of everyday life.

Firstly, though, I would like to introduce 'Mr Smith'. Like Mrs Peters, he is a 'fiction', a true story created from several patients of mine who were predominantly hysterical. Whereas we learn almost by default of the compulsive sexual behaviour of Mildred or Sarah outside their therapy sessions, Mr Smith brings me tales of his sexual exploits as though for congratulation. Each one is presented as a new heroic tale which conceals the fact that each one is also a compulsive repetition, to all intents and purposes identical to the last – thus marking the violence of the death drive that is being sexualized. He is also highly, but urgently, creative as a would-be musical composer, but if the creative activity cannot be sustained he becomes worryingly depressed. As well as forming a composite from several of my patients, I will transpose on to Mr Smith's family history the Hungarian psychoanalyst Michael Eisler's case history of the tram man, 'A Man's Unconscious Phantasy of Pregnancy in the Guise of Traumatic Hysteria' (see chapter 5), both because it is appropriate and because Eisler and then Lacan, who rewrote the case, make nothing of the sibling relationships that, to me, form an essential part of it. In none of my patients' histories which comprise Mr Smith was the family quite so large, but each had one or other feature of the tram man's sibling problems. Mr Smith's nearest sibling is a girl, which probably accounts for the predominantly heterosexual nature of his relationships; but each woman is someone with whom he hopes to identify and each is idealized in turn and then condemned. He is married, but although his wife has children from a much earlier marriage and Mr Smith hopes for a son who will be 'just like him', with Mr Smith there are no children. In the transference I am idealized, although always made to realize that I have several predecessors (I do; he has had a number of therapists). This idealization of me is at the expense of a splitting: his wife has inherited the endless criticism he had of his sister; she can do nothing right. He is also violent, physically and verbally, to her daughter, his stepdaughter.

Mr Smith is a teacher, with not only clear aspirations but the clear possibility of becoming a professional composer. He has had a number of his works performed. His creativity is significant but we both feel there is an obstacle to its full realization. Nothing hinders him in actually conceiving and writing down his compositions; however, as with his sexual encounters, the compositions are repetitions of a theme. He describes the works to me with no sense of awareness that I might not understand the special nature of his work, and I realize that each composition, like each woman, is a presentation of his own triumphant survival brought to me for my congratulation. The limitation on his creativity is that in each work he himself is more important than the work – he assumes my knowledge because for me not to understand the intricacies of musical composition is tantamount to not understanding or recognizing him. Inevitable failure (mine and the world's) entails the endless oscillation of near-manic hopes and complete, deflated, depressed collapses into states of emptiness. In fact, if he feels I appreciate his endeavours, in time it has the same effect; like the *saka* dance, it only assuages what he wants for the time being. The creative objects, the compositions, are not subjects in their own right, but rather objects that can be identified with. They are parthenogenetic births in whom no one else has a share. As I have failed to give him sufficient recognition through praise of his composition (which is himself), he builds up a fantasy world of his successes in which I find it difficult to tell where the truth ends and the fiction begins.

One session, in which Mr Smith's anxiety was palpable, led to him telling me two dreams in quick succession. He often answered anything I might say about one dream by telling me another – for dream situations had to be repeated, like the women and the musical compositions.

In the first dream, Mr Smith had lost his hand and arm from the elbow downwards. Instead he had an artificial arm that ended in three black claws. The next dream referred to his house, which, he said, was even worse than in reality; the whole structure was dark and crumbling. I started to say something about the first dream but he interrupted and said the second was really very much worse and that he realized he himself *was* the house and that, although we had done lots of work in the therapy, the house was who he was, that was it. I realized that he could not tolerate an intervention from me and in normal circumstances I would probably have kept quiet until the time felt right later in the session, or in a future session, for me to say something. However, as I was shortly to take a holiday, I conventionally linked his anxieties to my impending departure. He was vehement: he did *not* mind my departure but was overcome by fury that I seemed confident that I had told him of this on an earlier occasion when he was positive I had never mentioned it. He brought so much evidence to bear that I became confused and doubtful of my own memory. He then recollected another dream. It was about a ventriloquist and his dummy. The description of the dummy was graphic; it resembled a swaddled baby but, through his associations to the memory of a real ventriloquist employed at the birthday parties of his childhood, this baby-dummy changed into an unpleasant, snotty toddler. At first, as he was talking of the baby-dummy, Mr Smith cradled its imaginary presence in his arms like a baby. But as he did so, its head became that of a grotesque adult – which reminded both Mr Smith and myself of his descriptions of his mother. Mr Smith commented that he had absolutely never been able to tell the difference between the ventriloquist and his dummy. Mr Smith then returned to the first dream and told me of a successful younger colleague of his who had an artificial forearm. This colleague had displaced Mr Smith in reality and in Mr Smith's mind.

When something is terrifying, the body/mind feels in chaos. The hysteric's solution is to create this chaos for everyone else in the world around and to insist on firm footholds for himself. The confusion also serves to prevent other people from seeing what is true and what is false. If for a moment he does not feel firm, then the danger is of falling into the chaos which has only been projected out in the first place. Mr Smith felt sure and I felt confused, but to sustain this reversal there had to be a slide into fantasy passed off as 'truth'. First I had been told a dream about an artificial arm – this may truly have been a dream or it may have been an identification with something which formed the basis for a fantasy: Mr Smith had become his successful colleague, but he knew there was something artificial/untrue/false about this. Previously we had discussed his creativity and he feared this fantasy was an aspect of his own creativity. He was also wildly jealous of the colleague, whom we had previously linked to one of his 'unimportant' brothers, and would have willingly 'clawed' him. But Mr Smith did not want to discuss any of these possibilities with me; so instead he told me the dream of his crumbling house and how he knew that that was what he really was – in other words, a derelict building, not a jealous colleague. It is easier to feel 'disadvantaged' than to acknowledge jealousy. However, the important message here was that there was nothing to be done about it: he was not going to change and I was therefore useless. So, when I linked Mr Smith's anxiety to my going away, he was furious because, having established a state of stasis in which I was unnecessary, why would he mind my departure? His confused, conflictual feelings – he did not need me but was frightened by thoughts of my absence – led to his making sure I was confused. He then tried to build up a picture in which he could look after his own baby-self (cradle the 'dummy') while I was the idiot baby who looked like the grotesque mother. These associations were probably fictive, but he now realized that if he made me confused, he was not a lot better off than when he himself was confused: there was nothing to choose between us and I then could not help. We were both unpleasant babies; furthermore, there was no difference between the ventriloquist and the dummy. The rapid move from dream to dream was a considerable creative effort, partly consisting of authentic dreams, partly of forced associations that nevertheless revealed real fears and wants.

There was, of course, much else at stake, but we can note a trajectory in which Mr Smith regrets having told me about his colleague who might overtake him, whom he wants to get rid of and whom he fears he is like (for he is worried that he too is artificial), but whom he also wants to be. This is the unacknowledged sibling. Then Mr Smith takes over the analysis, making the sort of interpretation that, from all his experience as a dab hand at analysis, he expects me to make – that he is a ruined house. Confused about whether or not he needs me, he tries to manipulate the situation. This does not help and the excited series ends in a state of sad depression. The fictive parts of Mr Smith's dreams are both the house and the dummy who is first a baby and then a grotesque mummy. They have *a* truth but they are also parodies of psychoanalysis: a house is often seen to be a symbol of the body–self, likewise a typical psychoanalytic interpretation would be to note the confusion between mothers and babies.

Mr Smith is trying to create an alternative, safer world. He is psychoanalytically informed and thinks that if he acknowledges his crumbling psychic condition, this will be evidence of therapeutic progress; in fact, it is the resource of the hysteric, through a hysterical, mimetic identification in which he becomes part of the psychoanalytic wallpaper. He managed my impending departure by identifying with what he saw to be an aspect of the analytic process. But, like each woman in his compulsive sexual encounters, and each musical composition in his creative endeavours, and each dream in the series of dreams, each identification is only a waystation on the relentless path down which some catastrophic moment of non-recognition has driven him, overwhelmed with jealousy – even as he presents himself as a perfectly charming, apparently creative, Don Juan.

Mozart's *Don Giovanni*, based on the Don Juan story, was Freud's favourite opera. In the opera, Don Giovanni has deserted his betrothed, Donna Elvira. He is about to seduce Donna Anna when her father the Commendatore discovers him; he kills the Commendatore then tries to seduce a virgin bride, but is prevented from doing so by her peasant groom, Masetto. Don Giovanni is then threatened with death by the ghost of the Commendatore, whom he invites to a feast. The stone statue of the Commendatore appears at the feast and drags the still-unrepentant Don Giovanni to Hell.

There are one or two interesting asides on the character of Don Juan in Freud's letters and notes, but no proper exploration of it anywhere else – and nothing of note in his published works. In chapter 2 I wondered whether Freud was a fantasy Don Juan. In the 1880s he was working with the male hysteric with whom he closely identified, the patient whom he called 'E' in his letters to Fliess. The five-year treatment was crucial to the foundation of some of the main tenets of psychoanalysis but it was never written up. As I also discussed in chapter 2, one of 'E''s disabling symptoms was a compulsive fantasy Don Juanism that he struggled to suppress. He suffered from agoraphobia and in particular could not go to the theatre or opera for fear that he would blush compulsively. He blushed because whenever he spoke to a woman he imagined seducing or raping her. At the same time as he was analysing 'E', Freud told his friend and colleague Karl Abraham that the omitted associations to his own famous dream of Irma's injection, the specimen dream of *The Interpretation of Dreams*, were that he, Freud, 'had all the women'.

Psychoanalysis uses myth and literature as explanatory devices – most obviously, the story of Oedipus. In this context, the absence of Don Juan from Freud's writing is striking. The general absence of Don Juan from the Freudian corpus indicates the repression of male hysteria from the theory and practice of psychoanalysis: where Don Juan had been, there Oedipus came to be. Sexuality and murder are completely intertwined in the Don Juan story: Don Juan, the son, kills and defies the father substitute who has done nothing to him, where Oedipus defies and then kills the father who has twice threatened his life. On killing father substitutes, Freud remarks of Hamlet's murder of Ophelia's father Polonius that this displacement from the actual father to the father of the woman in whom he is interested is a typical hysterical substitution. Don Juan kills the Commendatore, Donna Anna's father, and is as indifferent to his deed as is Hamlet, who, though he claims to repent his murder of Polonius, shows little sense of its significance: 'I'll lug the guts into the neighbour room.' Where Oedipus weds his mother Jocasta and together they have four children, Don Juan seduces and deserts his women; neither consummation nor marriage is likely, and procreation is unimaginable. Oedipus in the psychoanalytic complex is the man who is punished for his filial transgressions (killing his father and marrying his mother), blinded (castrated), rendered helpless but ultimately, because of his acceptance of his punishment, redeemed and honoured in death. Don Juan, who does not repent of his sins and so rots in Hell, cannot be collapsed into Oedipus; no more can the story of the male hysteric turn into an Oedipal one.

It is almost extraordinary that Don Juan does not feature in Freudian theory, which is so crucially about sexuality and death in human life. However, there has been one major study. Otto Rank, who subsequently left the psychoanalytic movement, but at the time of his initial study was a follower of Freud, wrote *The Don Juan Legend*. The first of many versions of this complex, indeed overcomplicated, work was published in 1922. Interested in the story since his youth, Rank had been catalysed into his original publication by his attendance at an outstanding performance of Mozart's *Don Giovanni* at the Vienna opera house in November 1921. He explains that Mozart has split his hero in two. One half is, of course, the philandering Don Giovanni; the other half, or 'double', is his servant Leporello, who represents the voice of ordinary conscience, of anxiety and criticism. Leporello is also, Rank argues, the precursor of the Stone Guest, the ghost of Donna Anna's father whom Don Giovanni has killed. In mythology and in the psychoanalytic interpretation of dreams, doubles always presage death; conscience is a kind of doubling of the subject, a precursor of a sense of guilt. In psychoanalytic terms Leporello is the ego ideal whose formation precedes the superego. An ego ideal is formed by identification with another, whereas a superego is formed by internalizing the meaning of the other after there is an awareness that the other can be lost. The superego is thus linked to the ability to symbolize. Classically, the superego is an internalization of the father after the castration complex has been negotiated. Rank sees the ghost of the Commendatore as threatening paternal chastisement (castration) from the grave. But the women are also implicated. According to Rank's interpretation, these are 'bad' women who all represent a mother figure who uses her youngest son (Don Juan) to get rid of the primal father (more usually represented by a husband). But this mother is treacherous – in the end she looks only to her own freedom and becomes awesome, as do both Donna Anna and Donna Elvira. This is Rank's first analysis of the story. One could hardly read an account that performed more contortions to confine a story to an Oedipal explanation.

When Don Juan is thus introduced into psychoanalytic theory, his transformation is likewise most extraordinary. In exactly the way that was to be taken up later by Melanie Klein, Otto Rank argues that Don Juan's endless women are all versions of the unattainable mother. The men he abuses, and indeed kills, are versions of the father whose right to the mother Don Juan cannot tolerate. In Rank's account, Don Juan does not appear as a sexual profligate who is without a conscience, but as someone in need of a mother. Later, when Don Juan does get mentioned by Klein, sexuality is no longer a centre point of the theory. Rank's later versions also demote sexuality.

Because at this stage of his thinking Rank was trying to stay loyal to Freudian theory, he rewrites the myth that he believed to lie behind the Don Juan story in terms of Freud's reconstruction of an imaginary history in *Totem and Taboo* (1913). In *Totem and Taboo* Freud hypothesizes that in mankind's prehistory a gang of brothers have conspired to kill the primal father, who has been keeping all the women for himself. Rather straining the point, Rank suggests that the Don Juan story substitutes women for the brothers. This introduces a homosexual element into the reconstruction of human prehistory: Don Juan has conspired with the women against the father, and thus has a feminine identification. This is in staggering conformity with the shift I have traced from hysteria to femininity. Rank's account falls over backwards not to see hysteria and instead to pinpoint homosexuality as the problem – Don Juan desires the father (as well as the mother). However, in his adjustment of *Totem and Taboo* Rank foreshadows his break with classical psychoanalytic theory: the women are both the 'bad' mother who murders the father and the siblings (here sisters for brothers) who also do so. Instead of perceiving a problem in this conflation of mother and sisters, at this stage Rank uses it to emphasize that the 'feminine' identifications of Don Juan are thus doubly strong.

This rewriting of the myth of *Totem and Taboo* may go a small way to explaining the absence of the Don Juan story in psychoanalytic theory in general, the absence of which is commensurate with the absence of the male hysteric. In *Totem and Taboo*, women feature only as sexual objects, whereas in Rank's version the mother is all-powerful, sisters and brothers (who are seen to be the same as sisters) unite to overthrow the father. This, though masquerading as loyalty to Father Freud, is a different story altogether. It is one much more true to the male hysteric than it is to the Oedipal constraints it contorts itself to maintain. Otto Rank's first analysis, then, of the legend presents at best a paradox; more accurately a distressing confusion. He interprets the story in such a way as to privilege the mother. He nevertheless struggles to keep it within an Oedipal framework with a castrating father, in the person of the Commendatore who is murdered – not only by Don Giovanni but by the women who are the Don's 'brothers'!

In this post-Great War account, then, Rank, like his fellow psychoanalysts working with war hysteria, was struggling to keep all psychic development within the terms of the Oedipus complex. He does not describe Don Juan as a hysteric. Instead, his account offers the structure for male hysteria in terms that provide a transition from earlier psychoanalytic accounts of hysteria to postwar accounts of femininity – the feminizing of hysteria as described in chapter 6. Rank's later versions of the story make this shift explicit. However, even in this first account, there are observations useful for an understanding of hysteria and for perceiving its suppression from the account.

According to Rank, Don Giovanni is split into himself and Leporello. If we were talking about an actual person being portrayed as split, he would be a schizoid character; however, as it is a fiction, this dual personality is portrayed as two separate people. Anna O and Anne Sexton both described their good and bad selves in this way; the good and the bad are not polar opposites, but, on the contrary, almost contiguous states. Leporello has a conscience, but it is not a very effective one – otherwise he would have progressed to superegoic internalizing of moral values rather than merely identifying with them. He is anxious, but unable to truly experience the pain of not doing whatever it is that the force which 'masters' him (as represented by Don Giovanni) wants. Leporello is weak – he has as much of a conscience as a Don Juan character could ever muster.

To achieve this reading of Don Juan, Rank himself had to split the story; in doing so he finally relegated the hysteria, even the sexuality of the story, to popular understanding. He points out that literary and artistic versions differ importantly from popular conceptions. The former focus on Don Juan's failures, the latter on his sexual successes. Rank argues that it is the portrait of the failures that mark the greatness of the myth, that the popular image of the arch-seducer is trivial. Thus it is sin, guilt and damnation that are the human universals and the compulsive sexuality only a means to the depiction of this end. To Rank, Don Juan is Faust rather than Don Juan:

one notes ... that the action portrays anything but a successful sexual adventurer; on the contrary, it presents a poor sinner pursued by misfortunes, who finally arrives at the destiny of the Christian hell that is appropriate to his era and background. Imagining the happy, gratifying time if the real Don Juan is left to the fantasy of the audience – who appear only too happy to make use of this privilege – while the stage is given over to presentation of the tragic features of the moral law.[1]

Rank's tragic version is not correct. Before the story became part of our cultural heritage and so was simply referred to by its hero's name, it was best known as the play *El Burlador de Sevilla*, written by Tirso da Molina in 1630. A *burlador* is a trickster and hence the original play draws attention to the characteristic that was to become fully incorporated in the popular version of the Don Juan story. Don Juan is not simply a desperate sinner, he is also a trickster. It does not make sense to separate the literary from the popular version – both are present, as both are present in our imaginations when we hear or view the play or opera. The image conjured up for us most readily, however, is undoubtedly the popular one.

Obviously bothered by how this story did not fit his theory, Rank amended his interpretation of Don Juan a number of times over a ten-year period. The alterations also mark his break with psychoanalysis. The first of the alterations shows how the story was forcing him away from the Oedipal interpretation and towards something more useful to us in understanding hysteria. For Don Juan just will not fit the model.

That Don Juan had been read ignoring the importance of sexuality is an all too accurate indication of the fate of psychoanalysis itself. When psychoanalysis turned towards the centrality of the mother after the Great War, it was as though the ultimate taboo on mother–child incest came to operate at the level of the theory: what the child really wants (and the mother, too) is not sex but care and nurturing. The Greek womb desiring to produce a child is one thing, but the notion that the mother has sexual feelings for her offspring is quite another. Henceforward, once the mother is the centrepiece, the disruptive nature of sexuality disappears from the account. Subsequent psychoanalytic theory explains pathological and characterological problems largely either through the excessive violence or envy of the infant or through the inadequacies of the mother. Sexuality is conspicuously missing and so, too, is hysteria.

When the soldiers who fell psychologically ill during and after the First World War were initially diagnosed as hysterics or malingerers, the focus for this ascription was on their bodily malfunctioning. The repeated one-night stands, the compulsive sexuality so well described by Pat Barker in *The Ghost Road* (1991) that often accompanied the falling ill was not seen as part of the pathology. In the same way today, the prevalence of rape in wartime is linked not to serious illness but to masculinity. As we have seen, we would have a better explanation of wartime rape, I think, if we saw how it was connected to hysteria. Rape is not sexuality that is violent but violence that has become sexualized. We can instructively use Don Juan for the purpose of understanding this.

Following the First World War, Rank also proposed and published a thesis that shook the psychoanalytic world, *The Trauma of Birth* (1923). In it he argued that it was the trauma of birth, not sexuality, that was the cause of mental illness. In this theory, infantile anxiety is the prototype of all anxiety and it originates with the first separation from the mother. Because of the mother's expulsion of the infant at birth, the mother (and therefore all women) is ever afterwards regarded with a great deal of ambivalence. In so far as it features, sexuality in this account is an attempt to get back to the mother.

In 1925, nearly two years after the publication of *The Trauma of Birth*, Rank reneged on his interpretation and returned to the psychoanalytic fold, emphasizing once again the centrality of the Oedipus complex. Prompted by Rank's work and the increasing emphasis among his colleagues on the importance of the pre-Oedipal phase of development, in 1926 Freud published *Inhibitions, Symptoms and Anxiety*. This amended his own earlier contention that anxiety was the effect of repressed sexuality and suggested that there was, in addition, a primary anxiety, though this was prepsychic. Among other things, the book is remarkable for the way in which hysteria keeps raising its problematic head and also for the way in which Freud throws in the sponge in relation to it: 'Why the formation of symptoms in conversion hysteria should be such a peculiarly obscure thing I cannot tell; but the fact affords us a good reason for quitting such an unproductive field of enquiry without a delay.'[2]

Rank and Ferenczi (who was always interested in hysteria) began to experiment with different analytic techniques, their focus being on the caring or uncaring mother and the intrusion of adult sexuality into a non-sexual infantile world. Rank became increasingly antagonistic to psychoanalysis and started to revise *The Don Juan Legend* yet again, this time in accordance with the very ideas he had abandoned when he reneged on his thesis in *The Trauma of Birth*. Two themes emerge from Rank's revision of his study of Don Juan. First, he places yet greater emphasis on Don Juan's wish to merge with the mother. Second, he takes the several versions of the story which portray the betrayed women as coming back to haunt Don Juan as evidence that the Stone Guest represents not the power of the castrating father but that of the primal mother come to reclaim her son in death. The all-powerful mother, bearer of birth and of death, comes to hold centre stage in an even more absolute way. If we look at the terms of Rank's analysis there are important ways in which, without ever using the category, he can be seen to be describing hysteria.

The legend of Don Juan indicates the fate of hysteria in the Western world since the Renaissance. It is useful as a way of indicating hysteria's presence as an alternative response to the conditions of human existence in which seduction is a keypoint.

The first theory from which psychoanalysis developed was that hysteria was the result of a father's seduction of a child in infancy. The French psychoanalysts Laplanche and Pontalis have subsequently demonstrated how the very notion of psychosexuality has still preserved its origins in this initial idea – even though it seems to go so strenuously against them, by asserting that it is the child's fantasy of a phallic relationship to the mother, that is, the Oedipus complex, which is the starting point of all psychic health or all neurotic difficulties. Later Freud suggested that the infant's fantasies had a *real* basis in the necessary seductions which the mother uses in the care of her baby.

Seduction has featured prominently in Western literature since late antiquity. For a time the theme was suppressed by Christianity, but when it re-emerged in the twelfth century with chivalry and courtly love, it did so in connection with heresy. Seduction celebrated love outside marriage. Threatened by the success of heresy, the Church had to take notice of this seduction. It did so by integrating it into a version of the Fall: the Devil seduced Eve. Seduction and sin were therefore linked. Marriage assumed a new religious and legal status. In Catholic countries the Council of Trent of 1545–63 established marriage as an indissoluble sacrament for which a priest, two witnesses and a church ceremony were essential.

The Don Juan legend arose in Spain in the immediate aftermath of the Council of Trent. In its first versions it is a moral tale promoting the importance of paternal authority and sacramental marriage. Don Juan is the opposite of the earlier chivalric seducer, the courtly lover, for he has neither code nor ideal. He is portrayed as an iconoclast out to destroy all values. In fact, the values Don Juan is protesting against were only just in the process of being established. The irony is that his opposition is as potent a force for their construction as were the edicts of the Council of Trent. For he is, despite his amorality, a propagator of new values. Parodying marriage by offering it to all and entering into it with none, Don Juan shows an alternative to the new stress on marital fidelity and obedience to fathers for the sake of the transmission of property: he is the rebellious son, the anti-Christ, the flipside of the coin. But at the same time as he foreshadows the decline of the Church, Don Juan asserts, in his very rejection of it, the rising importance of secular patriarchy. The story seems to have lost its religious emphasis fairly soon. By the time of Molière's version and then of Mozart's *Don Giovanni*, the story had become more or less completely secularized.

Though more popular in Catholic countries than in Protestant ones, Don Juan is surely the most dominant representation of male sexuality in the modern period. For 400 years he has been its prototype. Exuberant, promiscuous, amoral, he has stood for a youthful sexuality that knows no boundaries and will dare the abyss. Men are supposed to hanker nostalgically after his image, women to adore him.

By the middle of the twentieth century there had been literally thousands of renditions of the story from Japan and Russia through all of Europe to North and Latin America and although its importance seems to have declined somewhat in recent decades, a Don Juan day is still celebrated in Peru. The most immediately striking feature about the Don Juan story since its origin in seventeenth-century Spain is its infinite variety. Don Juan may be the hero of tragedy, comedy or farce: his antics may be acted out in churches to point a moral, he may be the spokesman of a political revolutionary creed, a pretext for a day's holiday, a Faust, or the silly, polymorphously perverse plaything of numberless women. Yet his is always fundamentally the same story: that of the noble, attractive, amoral seducer of countless women.

Don Juan's absence from psychoanalytic theory is testimony to the absence of the male hysteric and to the feminizing of hysteria. To read him back into the theory is to shift its centre of gravity, or at least to give it two focal dimensions: an intergenerational one and a lateral one; parents as representatives of the vertical axis *and* siblings as representatives of a lateral axis. Don Juan's story likewise gives a phenomenology of male hysteria which is otherwise missing from most psychoanalytic observation. The thrust of his story is the hysterical transmission of lateral jealousy.

Let us start with the hysteria. If we use the text of Da Ponte's libretto for Mozart's *Don Giovanni*, we can see how close he comes to giving us a portrait of a triumphant hysterical universe in which 'wanting', getting or willing what one wants reigns as the paramount value: 'Do what you will is our only law/All that you may desire/May here be done!/Do as thou wilt, is here the law.' 'No man shall call me coward/I feel no fear/I will.' God is parodied: 'Thy will be done, thy will be done.' The opera is full of frenzied dancing which serves to confuse anyone who might subscribe to other values. As with the hysteric, nothing is ever Don Giovanni's fault. We hear constantly of 'his shameless love of lying', 'his words are all a lie'. 'Whom are we to believe/Which one should we believe/Whose word believe?/When ought we to believe?/he lies.' The frenetic laughter within the opera recalls hysterical giggling – 'your laughter will not last, even till morning'. A sexual compulsiveness is conveyed in oral terms: 'All his appetites are vicious/I can hardly bear to watch him/Watch him guzzling in that way.'

Don Giovanni creates a lying universe and, as with the pseudological world of the hysteric, any penetration of this by truth or reality would drive him mad. In typical hysterical manner he closes his ears as a way of keeping his mendacious world intact ('Talk if you must but talk to yourself, then listen I won't'; 'Heed you I don't'). Finally, harsh reality does nevertheless impinge: 'He's mad and getting madder', and Leporello, his split-off saner part, realizes that he must break away or 'I shall soon go crazy too'.

The key theme in *Don Giovanni* is jealousy. Don Giovanni is driven by the need to make others jealous so as not to be tormented by jealousy himself. Compulsively, desperately, he makes Masetto the bridegroom jealous by seducing his bride-to-be, and he makes every woman jealous of the other. The hysteric whose passion of wanting is fuelled by remorseless envy and jealousy always fears he will fall into madness. Instead, the hysteric drives the other mad by making the other jealous, as Iago does Othello, as Don Giovanni does Donna Elvira: 'She's crazy.'

Finally, however, this great seducer is only a storyteller whose conquests are listed in Leporello's copy book. The aim of storytelling, as exemplified in the repetitions of *One Thousand and One Nights*, is to deny the inevitability of death. This refusal to recognize the meaning of death is depicted explicitly in Don Giovanni's challenging of the Stone Guest, the father figure whom he has murdered, to a feast. The repetition–compulsion of the list of conquests is a sign that death as a conqueror is both making his presence felt and being desperately resisted. Descriptively, then, Don Giovanni presents a good image of the hysterical personality; how well does this match an analytical investigation?

The British Independent Object Relations psychoanalyst Adam Limentani concludes his 1984 essay entitled 'To the Limits of Male Heterosexuality: the Vagina Man' with these words:

I . . . hope that the acceptance of this concept [of the Vagina Man] could lead us to review some of our stereotyped ideas about homosexuality, or of many cases of promiscuity. Its acceptance also means that we do not need to take a romantic view of Don Juan as someone who was hoping to find the ideal woman (the primal object), to the last; neither do we need to accuse him of being a latent homosexual. Perhaps Don Juan is nothing more than a man who has found a way of avoiding the outbreak of some primitive anxiety which threatens to destroy him, by turning to the pursuit of a chimera.[3]

Limentani's 'Vagina Man', who is narcissistic, intelligent, charming, obscurely 'feminine' and bisexual, has escaped some overwhelming primitive anxiety by identifying with an undifferentiated protector. The 'Vagina Man', a Don Juan, is, I would claim, a clear case of male hysteria. In the face of an untenable situation there is for the 'Vagina Man' an instant retreat into an identification with the otherwise lost object he needs – the woman as mother. This ensures that the object is not lost – except, of course, that it cannot exist in its own right. If the infant in its helplessness feels that whatever ensures its survival is missing, it experiences this absence as a total death or what Wilfred Bion calls 'nameless dread'. If this happens too early, as it does to all of us to some degree, then the absence must be denied in a primal identification – one becomes what one needs. If we do not call this hysteria, we miss the sexualization of the process: what Limentani describes as the fundament of a 'Vagina Man' is the ground plan for everyone's hysteria, the position to which all hysteria regresses. As a total way of life, it denies that the object is also a subject. With his endless women, Don Juan never loses anything; but he never has anything either, which is why the hysteric goes on wanting . . .

The story of Don Juan is a possible tragedy, but certainly not as Mozart understood it. Hysteria can be horribly sad, but not tragic. Mozart's *Don Giovanni* is the story of the permanent hysteric. We can try to see Don Juan, as Rank does, as a neurotic Oedipus, in what seems a heroic resistance to death and castration, but this is not the thrust of the opera. Don Juan is empty: here hysteria finds its meeting point with schizoid conditions and with paranoia: the object and the ego are decomposed. However, Don Giovanni's emptiness, which is shallow, makes Mozart's opera a troubling rather than a tragic opera.

An Oedipal interpretation of Don Giovanni is the stuff of which tragedy is made. But for Mozart's version, there is something wrong with such an account; for whilst the Don may have Faustian courage to dare the abyss and lose all, there is something missing both in the role he is accorded and in the quality of his arias. In *Don Giovanni*, as indeed in all the versions, there is an emptiness at the centre. The philosopher Bernard Williams writes:

The opera is of great and unsettling power . . . a seducer is at the centre of it . . . *the seducer is virtually characterless* . . . he expresses more than he is. He seems to have no depth adequate to the work in which he plays the central role. He has, in a sense, a character . . . to a considerable extent, a bad one. But we are not given any deep insight into what he really is, or what drives him on. We could not have been: *it is not that there is something hidden in his soul*. It is notable that he has no self-reflective aria – he never sings about himself, as Mozart's other central characters do.[4] [My italics]

This is a good description of the hysteric. Because he is made to sing we can also consider the question of Don Giovanni's creativity in general, which is lacking in self-reflection. Don Giovanni's arias, like his women, have no existence independent of himself in his mind, so they cannot constitute positions from which he himself can be recognized. His arias cannot be self-reflective because they are not separate from him. They are performative utterances, words as actions rather than as thoughts.

In 1941 Melanie Klein moved to Pitlochry, Scotland, in order to avoid the Blitz in London. While there she undertook the analysis of an evacuee child, 'Richard'. Writing up the case later, she noted of Richard, 'His behaviour with women was very precocious, in some ways like that of a grown-up Don Juan.'[5] Klein used six sessions that took place after she had made a brief return visit to war-torn London – the city that symbolized for Richard all death (while she was away Richard was terrified that Klein would be killed). Klein's understanding of Richard was that he had split women into the tender, idealized mother and serial women, who were sexualized and towards whom he felt both flirtatious and contemptuous, that is, the classic Madonna and the whore. In the actual narrative of Richard's case history, written directly from her notes, Klein does not refer to Don Juan. She does, however, mention both infidelity and the boy's feminine identification – perceiving homosexuality beneath the infidelity. Klein proposes that the boy is relentlessly seeking the father's penis in the woman's body; the feminine identification is an early Oedipal envy and hence there is possessive and cannibalistic identification with the breast and womb of the mother. Klein does not link these features with the Don Juanism she is later to accord Richard. Yet, if we read the accounts in reverse, we can connect this supposed femininity and homosexuality to the Don Juan he is to become in Klein's subsequent understanding. According to Klein, Richard has only a weakly developed, positive Oedipus complex, for he still has his mother in identification rather than in (genital) object love and he seeks (as object rather than as source of identification) his father's penis. The problem with this account is that Klein's thought is too relentlessly object orientated: if the mother cannot be observed to be a proper object, then the father or his penis steps in. But the hysteric does not have a proper object relationship.

The difficulty with Klein's account of Don Juan becomes self-evident when we consider that both homosexuality and femininity lie a long way from our received notions of Don Juan. Surely if anyone is the representative of extravagant male heterosexuality in the Christian (particularly Catholic) world since the seventeenth century it is Don

Juan? Something very odd is going on when Don Juan is turned into a homosexual by the theory. Limentani's version of Don Juan suffering from primal dread resists this homosexual version but at the expense of losing sexuality altogether. The Kleinian analyst Eric Brenman notes his hysterical patient's Don Juanism, linking it, however, to a complete identification with a woman, just like Limentani's 'Vagina Man'.[6]

Some years before she met Richard, in her 1937 essay 'Love, Guilt and Reparation', Klein muses about infidelity: 'I have found that the typical Don Juan in the depths of his mind is haunted by the dread of the death of loved people.'[7] In her subsequent work with Richard, Klein ascribes his Don Juanism to a split that he makes in women as his love objects, even though to Klein herself he is both tender (as with his mother) and debasing (as with the women towards whom he is unfaithful). However, there is no actual split; only ambivalence. In Klein's account Richard is using sex with mother substitutes to heal the mother he has damaged in his greed and envy. Yet Klein, his analyst on whom he is dependent, has returned from the Blitz in London. Surely, Richard's primitive dread of her death has some bearing on his fantasies?

When a person is threatened by the prospect of pain, annihilation, displacement or dethronement, he retreats to a splitting device; this splitting, which leaves him with a sense of emptiness – an absence of himself – is his hysterical destiny. Although the regression is deep, there is, as Bernard Williams commented of Don Giovanni, no depth to his personality. The hysteric goes down Alice's tunnel; but his fall lands him in a place where his problem is not vertical but horizontal. It is a problem of his siblings or, in the present of his adult life, his friends and affines; or, for Don Juan, the problem of his female peer group.

Don Juan does not want the pain of jealousy, so he makes others jealous instead of feeling the emotion himself. Richard is appallingly and agonizingly jealous of Klein's other patients. These other patients and Don Juan's women are sisters rivalrous for the father's love. Donna Anna is the 'sister' whose position with the father, the Commendatore, Don Juan does not have. Don Juan is the one who is unrecognized and who must therefore endlessly make everything revolve around only him.

Klein's Don Juan, Richard, is proving to himself that the loved mother, whom he fears might die because of his own destructiveness towards her, is not indispensable, since she can always be refound in other women towards whom he has passionate but shallow feelings. At the same time, he preserves her by making her a timeless ideal Madonna. This may be so, but it is redundant to postulate innate envy and destructiveness, except as secondary experiences, when jealousy can be provoked by a social occurrence such as the birth of a sibling and the consequent displacement of the subject. Envy follows suit.

Faced by lateral rivals, Don Juan regresses to the pain of losing the mother and the father, neither of whom are there for him alone. Death is only one more thing to be opposed and conquered. The point about death is, of course, that it cannot be conquered; it does have dominion. 'The worst' is ultimately the situation in which we are completely helpless, and, as Shakespeare realized, the worst does not exist while one can talk about it. To talk about it is to have survived, but there are also the phenomena of repetitive lists and compulsive storytelling. Such lists and such storytelling fend off death without allowing the subject to 'die' in the act of creation. Repetition of an object defends against a fear of the absence of that object.

The absence of any significant place for Don Juan in the corpus of psychoanalytic theory perfectly expresses the comparable absence of the male hysteric. The repression of the story of Don Juan has allowed all psychoanalytic theory to establish male sexuality as the norm and in doing so to avoid its analysis. Don Juan, the male hysteric, was absorbed into Freud's own character; repressed and at the same time identified with. The early Freud, in his self-image, was the scientific *conquistador* (see chapter 2). The acknowledged need to keep the male as normative ensured first the suppression of Don Juan and male hysteria, then the transformation of hysteria into femininity. But the elevation of the mother in Object Relations theory effected further suppression. The mother represents both presence and absence, and her absence elicits anxiety. Made anxious by displacement, both boys and girls mimetically fix on the mother at a moment when she is simultaneously the object and the source of identification. The theory again echoes or mimes this: the Object Relations therapist believes that the mother is everything. When the boy grows into a man and chooses a woman apparently as a love object, he may in fact be making a hysterical identification *with her* – this is Don Juanism.

Much anthropological observation notes the presence of male hysteria in a limited way; most link it with jealousy, envy and 'wanting' in the context of deprivation. For men and women, deprivation may be temporary and the hysteria occasional, as among the Taita women, or it may be 'permanent'. It is, I believe, always triggered by displacement by lateral relations, whether siblings or peers in childhood or affines and peers in adulthood. Laterality must be added to vertical descent. Overall in the modern period there has been a weakening of the importance and power of descent in the West. Patriarchal lineage systems call a boy into his heritage; in the relative absence of such systems, the *where* one stands gives way to the *who* one is. However, identity, as opposed to position, is predicated on the mother–child relationship. The anthropologist Meyer Fortes has argued that in patrilineages, individuality depends on the ties to the mother, not to the father. In relation to the father, descendants stand in identical positions – everyone is of the same descent line – but who the mother is is what differentiates them. Transposed to the individual, this would suggest that females and males within a family are all in the same position *vis-à-vis* their father – they all take his name – but to differentiate themselves from each other they must rely on their mothers – she must see each one in his or her uniqueness. Whenever a sibling is born, it is this differential position that is threatened once more – the child must rely on the mother to let it know that it has not just been 'repeated'. As the mother becomes more important with the decline of the importance of patrilineage, so the situation becomes more precarious for both boys and girls – and therein lies the essential threat to the subject's uniqueness. Hysteria is a response to that threat.

There is only one Don Juan. But he is also a modern phenomenon and – male or female – with the growth of individualism, his may be a particularly common fate for the modern hysteric. The progress of Don Juan leads us thus towards some of the specific qualities and conditions of hysteria in contemporary industrial societies. Threads come together: the mother of Object Relations theory is a late stage in the growing importance of ties to the mother for the creation and preservation of individuality. Where the emphasis is on oneself as an individual, the erosion of one's position and the retreat to the mother is likely to be all the more intense.

II. 'HONEST IAGO' AND DIABOLICAL SPEECH

In the Western world, then, the last 400 years have witnessed an uneven but nevertheless noticeable shift of emphasis from one's position within the patrilineage to a sense of individuality and identity dependent on the mother. The individual, less sure of his position than before, is more likely to feel threatened in his identity. This has coincided with the roles of men and women becoming more similar in their work, home and social lives. Though girls and boys have different positions in the kinship system, they are most similarly placed in their infantile relationship to the mother. A sister may be almost as much a rival to a boy as a brother. The intensity of rivalry – murderous and hating – is also a condition of the intensity of love that can replace it. However, just as there has always been a hysterical response to a threat to the subject in his individuality, although it may now be more exaggerated, so there has also always been hysterical language. The prevalence of 'talking cures', and the wider movement of the information revolution, have helped the expression of hysteria to migrate from the body to the story. Language has always had great power: in the witch's curses, in seduction, in compulsive lying, in the words used in sexual arousal. However, because these sorts of words are not ritualized in the West, as they are, say, in Trinidadian 'cussing sessions', their power can be easily missed, privatized or met with embarrassment and ignored.

The language of hysteria has been described in a number of different ways: 'pseudosymbolic', 'performative', 'excitable speech'. I would choose to call it 'literal', in order to distinguish it from the so-called 'concrete' thought processes of psychosis. Hysterical language is a language of equations rather than of representations, as it is with young children. I once came home to find my 2-year-old daughter jumping incessantly over a row of toy bricks she had constructed; she told me that she was 'fencing' – a sport her childminder had just left to pursue. For her, one sort of fence equalled a completely different sort of fence. Only if 'fencing' had stood for something that she knew she did not know about would it have been a representation. However, rather than search for a theorization of what is undoubtedly a complex field in its own right, I will produce a description.

The key features of Don Giovanni's linguistic performance are the following: he rages, he lies, his story is 'empty', he giggles and makes others giggle, he refuses to hear when it does not suit him, there is no self-reflection. Through his servant Leporello, Don Giovanni makes lists – words without a relationship to each other within a signifying chain. An analysis shows him following the trajectory described by Lacan: the patient starts by talking about himself but not to the therapist; then he talks to the therapist but not about himself. However, the treatment only ends when the patient can talk to the therapist about himself – self-reflection. Don Juan does not reach that point of cure. This is a linguistic enterprise that parallels that of the hysterical body – from only body to no body and back again.

Shocked by something, the hysteric has no position from which he can see himself. His antics are a performance to get the other's attention but he has no idea how they look to others; transposed to speech, he talks to get what he wants, but has no idea of how what he says is perceived by others – he cannot see himself from another's perspective. Though intent on an effect, he has no concern with that effect – sometimes his moods are a discharge of an emotion that he finds impossible to contain; sometimes his moods aim to kill – to get the other, who has impinged, out of the way. Alternatively, feeling insufficiently existent, the words of the hysteric can be acts of verbal seduction, reflecting his need to take over the other in order to fill his own inner void. The shock, the breach in his defences, that has precipitated his hysteria has been experienced as violent. This is repeated every time his ego feels too threatened; that received violence is then verbalized and sent out into the world in order to annihilate the other as the hysteric himself has felt annihilated. Don Giovanni rages and lies.

Ferenczi accused Freud of abandoning hysterics: he could not forgive them because he had believed their lies. What were their lies? In part they were wanting what the other wanted; grasping Freud's nascent theory of infantile seduction as the cause of their illness, they identified with it and told him stories about it – 'E', for instance, apparently recollected an incident when he was seduced as a baby. But that does not by any means exhaust the problem. Hysterical lying is not occasional, but compulsive. That does not mean that the hysteric lies all the time but that he uses it as a persistent mode of defence whenever it feels necessary.

As the British analyst Wilfred Bion has demonstrated, the nature of the psychoanalytic process is such that it would be rather unlikely for an analyst to knowingly accept a compulsive liar as a patient. In theory, this would exclude from treatment a serious case of hysteria, except that if the analyst cannot detect the lying, then it is very likely that the prospective patient is equally unaware of it. To a certain extent, its very compulsiveness is a sign that the lying is unconscious. But a liar, conscious or unconscious, needs an audience, and this makes him vulnerable. The liar accumulates evidence to bolster his position and becomes driven further and further into fabrication, as Macbeth is driven further into murder: 'returning were as tedious as to go o'er'. The audience that accepts the lies is, in Bion's terms, the host to a parasite – and the lie then destroys both. This is the communal destruction we see in *Don Giovanni*. Don Giovanni lies and tells each woman that he loves her; she then becomes host to that lie and all is destruction. But if someone refuses to be a host, then the liar experiences them as a persecutor – someone attacking not only his distorted world view, but the liar himself. The 'true' liar is his lie. To expose the lie is to call the liar's being into question – just as it was his sense of his existence being apparently called into question that made him create the lie in the first place. For a lie is not only words, it is a state of being. Indeed, the lie depends on this state of being, for:

The lie requires a thinker to think. The truth, or true thought, does not require a thinker – he is not logically necessary . . . we may consider that the difference between a true thought and a lie consists in the fact that a thinker is logically necessary for the lie but not for the true thought.

Nobody need think the true thought: it awaits the advent of the thinker who achieves significance through the true thought. The lie and its thinker are inseparable. The thinker is of no consequence to the truth, but the truth is logically necessary to the thinker. His significance depends on whether or not he will entertain the thought, but the thought remains unaltered.

In contrast the lie gains existence by virtue of the epistemologically prior existence of the liar. The only thoughts to which a thinker is absolutely essential are lies. Descartes' tacit assumption that thoughts presuppose a thinker is valid only for the lie.[8]

The hysteric regresses to the fantasized omnipotence and need-to-control characteristic of the young child. The child turns round the 'lies' it has been told in its upbringing ('If you don't eat all your dinner up you won't grow big and strong') to achieve his importance in a world where he is becoming aware of his insignificance. The hysteric's lies are the child's fictions, with all the accretions of his subsequent history. The hysteric lies so that he can fill the world. To tell the truth (just as to truly create or procreate) means to acknowledge his own unimportance. The truth, the work of art, the child, are logically necessary to the thinker, the artist and the parent. Their significance depends on whether they will entertain the thought, the work or the child, but the thought, the work and the child remain unaltered.

We all, at times, lie. Why do we believe lies? And why are we sometimes unable to detect them? The lie is usually eloquent, and it uses a closed system (which is why it must be replete with so-called 'evidence'). We also shrink from breaking into the lying structure as to do so turns us into persecutors. Dr Rosenfeld became a persecuting Daddy Devil for Mildred (see chapter 6) perhaps in part because he was not seduced by her 'lying' tales of female Don Juanism. If one is not a persecutor, then one can only collude, become a host to the lie. To facilitate this collusion, the lie the hysteric tells creates confusion. The cited evidence for the lie may be real evidence but it is utterly irrelevant; the speech used is the opposite of symbolic – it is 'diabolic', that is it jumbles things up deliberately. This diabolical speech is defined by the philosopher Gemma Corradi Fiumara:

A pseudosymbolic process which has the appearance of symbolism but is not conducive to dialogic interactions is 'diabolic' in the etymological sense of the word – the Greek term 'diaballo' being a compound word of the word *dia* ('across') and *ballo* ('I throw'). Hence a 'diabol' could be something that flings things across, and as a consequence jumbles them up.[9]

Don Giovanni jumbles things up so everyone within the opera is confused. However, as spectators, we watch but do not fully participate in the confusion – we do not collude. The lie is central to hysteria and thus is an indication once again that hysteria (like its manifestation, the lie) is a possible general response to the human condition. I want to illustrate how the lie infects the group and the group becomes hysterical by using what should become a *locus classicus* for understanding how a social group acts as host to the lie: the case of 'honest Iago' in Shakespeare's *Othello*. Here we can see the overlapping of language and emotion that underlies hysteria. Iago would appear to be less 'hysterical' than either Don Giovanni or Hamlet because he does not have any feminine features (he is no 'Vagina Man'), nor does he display any bodily symptoms or violent mood swings. Iago is, however, verbally perverse and the symptom he displays is, above all, the hysterical lie.

The play *Othello* opens with Iago's sense of displacement at his brother soldier Cassio having been promoted to lieutenant, the position Iago expected. Iago plans revenge on his general, Othello, for thus having given Cassio what he considers his place. His first act is to rudely awaken Brabantio, the father of Othello's bride Desdemona, telling him that his daughter has eloped with Othello, that 'an old black ram/Is tupping your white ewe'. In an effort to produce civil unrest, he also urges Brabantio to disrupt the Duke's council. His tactic is to incite a fear of 'illegitimacy', in the form of black–white miscegenation. This effort at creating chaos and confusion fails in a way that is all too familiar: the society he is trying to disrupt unites by going to war. Left with his jealousy, excluded from the society that has banded together, Iago turns to projecting his unbearable jealousy: he will make Othello mad with it. And so he hints that Desdemona is having an affair with Cassio. It is only when Othello resists this ensnarement and demands proof of Iago's allegations of Desdemona's infidelity that Iago becomes frightened. At this point he turns to elaborate deceits and constant lying, and the manufacturing of 'evidence' in the absurd form of a lost handkerchief. He thus builds up a pseudological world in which the innocent are guilty and Othello becomes possessed with Iago's emotion – murderous jealousy. Pushkin rightly described Othello as trustful rather than jealous. Othello is inhabited by Iago's jealousy. This sequence demonstrates the mechanisms and emotions that underlie hysteria: jealousy, confusion, revenge, deceit and the production of the violent unbearable emotion in the person one holds responsible for one's situation.

From the sublime of Shakespeare's extraordinary play, we can descend to the ridiculous of everybody's ordinary experience: the child, Iago, has been replaced by a new brother, Cassio, who seems preferred; he feels overpowering jealousy and wants to destroy the parent, Othello, who has shown preference for this new baby. He feels utterly confused at having lost what he thought was his rightful place and so wants to evacuate or project that awful feeling of confusion by bringing chaos and confusion to the world. He wants to kill the new sibling and to make the offending parent feel all the jealousy and hatred which he himself feels. At a moment in this wild rage, he is terrified by the greater power of the parent: this is the moment of trauma. There could be a route out, which would be to acknowledge that one has created mayhem and is overwhelmingly jealous. However, Iago chooses to deny this and to make the other feel the unbearable feelings. He uses his fantasies to create a pseudologic universe which takes everyone in. In this reductive scenario we can say that, where Don Juan takes a first step along the path, Iago goes the whole way. We can see him build the hysteric's story. He decides to believe that it is he who has been betrayed: Iago plays with the thought that Othello has committed adultery with his own wife, Emilia. This is the 'mad' theory with which Iago can explain his need to project the jealousy and exact the revenge on which his pseudologic system is built; he is, like any child, jealous of any sibling the parent seems to prefer – and the young Desdemona here is more Iago's and Cassio's Venetian sister than she is a mother figure.

The first stage of jealousy and hatred deploys fantasy – how to get one's own back. Caught out and asked to prove the truth of one's fantasies, the fantasies become an entire lying world. But why is everyone taken in? Why do lies work? It is not simply because they fall on the fertile ground of emotions we all share, though this plays a key part. In *The Brothers Karamazov*, Mitya does not murder his father – but he wanted to. The apparent evidence against him sticks because he feels guilty – guilty because he wanted to kill his father and guilty because he mistakenly thinks he has killed an old servant. *In the Name of the Father*, the film of the story of the Guildford Four, who were innocent of the bombings for which they were imprisoned, reveals the same thing. The accusing lies of the prosecuting police are effective because their victim feels guilty about something completely different: he has kept some money dropped by a prostitute. His protestations of complete ignorance of the bombing are less effective than they should be because he gets confused, as all the time he is thinking of how he is guilty of something else. The lie falls on the ground of the accused's irrelevant guilt.

In Othello's case, Iago's *coup de grâce* is when he converts Othello's total bewilderment into a real possibility by suggesting that there is no reason why Desdemona should not be false to her husband, since she was false to her father in marrying him. It is usually argued that Othello cannot resist the hurt of this assertion; in fact, is it not rather that Othello himself feels partly guilty for having encouraged his wife to offend her father? In Christa Wolf's novel *Medea* (1998) (an allegory for the West German attack on Wolf for her role under communism in the former East Germany) Medea stands accused of murdering her children in revenge against her husband Jason for his infidelity. In Wolf's version she is innocent of the murder. Initially, though, she is accused by the Corinthians of having sacrificed her younger child-brother: she has not done so in any literal sense, but she is guilty of a political plot that would have used him as a pawn in a larger conspiracy to replace her father. Medea is not guilty of the main crime of which she is accused, but she is partly guilty of another one. However, the Corinthians' own power is built on their hiding their king Creon's secret sacrifice of *his* daughter. Guilt is the currency that moves between people. A sense of guilt makes someone desperate to escape its consequences by projecting it into others – so that it becomes a currency of exchange. Everyone feels guilty for the death of the sibling, or its substitute, for everyone has some version of a sibling who is a rival that could have replaced them.

The point about this emotional scenario is that a particular type of language emanates from it. Iago turns the beauty and the truth of creation into a lie, and in time everyone joins in the process, because everyone's ego has become so threatened that the only resource appears to be an overassertion of their selves. This entails destruction of the other: lying or murder.

Iago is the perfect foil to Othello. He is a bluff man of action, endlessly insistent on his own white soldierly presence. 'What do you think of me?' he keeps asking – to which, as a refrain throughout the play, comes back the answer, 'You are "honest Iago".' No one can listen properly to the story Iago tells because all the time they are having to confirm his identity for him.

Othello, however, is a true hero and a true poet, presenting the truth and the miracle of creation without an awareness of himself except as the bearer of the story of 'the wonders' he has seen. When Iago tries to create havoc by getting the Senate to see the 'truth' of black Othello's marriage to white Desdemona, Othello explains to the assembled council that he simply told Desdemona about the amazing deeds and sights in which he had partaken. He had seen 'the Anthropophagi, and men whose heads do grow beneath their shoulders . . .' The company listen, and, like Desdemona, they do not see Othello, they see the world he opens up. This is, as the Duke concludes, a tale that would win his daughter, too. The creation, not the creator, counts.

Creativity and the truth occupy the same position: they are, as Bion describes truth, there *before* the teller. The teller gains his existence by being their bearer. Desdemona loves Othello as the bearer of a world he has seen and experienced and he loves her because she can see it. Iago is able to turn this world from poetry into a lie at the very point where he can force Othello to assert his ego rather than see the world. This comes about when he makes Othello fear he played host to a deceit. He shows Othello that Desdemona was a deceiver of her father and that Othello was host to that deceit. This is both true – and completely false. Even technically, by eloping Desdemona deceived no one: according to the statutes and kinship regulations of the time, it would not have necessarily been the case that Desdemona and Othello needed her father's consent – the Church could have wed them like some mature Romeo and Juliet. Shakespeare's plays make profound use of his time's kinship confusions and changing legisla-tions, hence they give us rich insights into the intertwining of kinship and language, as in Hamlet's 'more than kin and less than kind'.

However, what Iago's intentional paralleling of Desdemona's apparent betrayal of her father and of her husband achieves is an instance of the apparently correct being put to the service of the utterly untrue. By confusing correctness with the truth, Iago can then pose his lie as truth. Because, at least momentarily, he is confused and thinks he is guilty of helping to deceive Brabantio, Othello is undermined. He crashes down into a desperate assertion of his drowning self. Othello enters Iago's world, a world that manipulates a technicality (Look what she did to her father) to construct a diabolical lie (Look what she is doing to you). Othello hosts Iago's lie, seeing Desdemona through his eyes, and is doomed.

The language of the lie in this play is sometimes empty eloquence, but more often it is the sexual vulgarity of the 'honest', plain-spoken soldier: crude sexuality stands against erotic beauty – and wins. But the empty eloquence which Iago occasionally uses in a parody of Othello's true eloquence also collapses into the same posturing obscenities. These two dimensions of the hysterical world – the perverse and the dishonest – are manifest linguistically as the complete absence of the subject alongside a bombastic self-assertion. This is conveyed through Iago's pointless rhetoric. The thrusting, assertive body with which he must fill the world is present in his language of insults and assaults. In today's idiom this language is 'in your face' and obscures all else from view. 'It is as sure as you are Roderigo,/Were I the Moor, I would not be Iago./In following him, I follow but myself': beneath the apparent awareness of difference (If I were Othello, I could not be Iago), there is no awareness – there is no meaning to this difference; beneath the seemingly significant thought, there is only banality.

What the play of *Othello* demonstrates so powerfully is how easily the ordered social world can degenerate to the level of Iago's uncontrollable hatred and jealousy, into, that is, a hysterical universe. This is shown to be not only a world of hysterical action but also of hysterical language: the two are inseparable. In a play that has some of the most beautiful blank verse ever (Othello's 'Keep up your bright swords, for the dew will rust them'), Iago speaks in prose or crude rhyming couplets ('There's none so foul, and foolish thereunto,/But does foul pranks which fair and wise ones do'). Trying to explain something incomprehensible in what Iago says, a Shakespeare scholar, M. R.

Ridley, finally suggests that it may be utter banality, for when Iago seems eloquent he is saying nothing. Iago's empty speech is used for 'diabolic' purposes. However, when the chaste Desdemona is able to backchat with Iago's bawdy talk, Ridley argues that this is a lapse on Shakespeare's part.[10] He is surely wrong. This is no lapse on Shakespeare's part. Desdemona has, even if only momentarily, agreed to enter Iago's linguistic world of perverse bodies. Lying begets lying; perverse talk begets perverse responses. It is not only guilt but hatred and jealousy that circulates through language. This is language as violence and sexuality, and violence and sexuality as language. It circulates between people because the audience of the posturing liar can make only one of two choices: either act as host, thereby echoing the performance, or break into it and cause the breakdown of the liar. (It is the same with perversion.) Hosting the lie as she does, Desdemona's verbal innocence is also endangered. Othello's knowledge that they loved each other because they shared the wonders of the world (she loved him for his telling her, and he loved her for seeing it) is likewise endangered. Reasonably and tragically, Othello can no longer believe her or believe in her; it is no longer possible to 'tell' the truth or to 'tell' what is true from what is false. Othello can no longer believe in the poetry of his mother's handkerchief woven by a sybil with which he endowed Desdemona in honour of all women. Through Iago's theft and lie, the handkerchief becomes just a piece of cloth Desdemona dropped, as she could have become in this lying world just a body for Cassio. Through accepting the transformation and debasement of the handkerchief from a symbol of honour to a token of dishonour, Othello too has played host to the lie.

Othello is 'undone' the moment Iago finds the weak spot where he can turn Othello, the bearer of truth and poetry, into a man implicated in lying deceit. That moment comes when Iago implants the notion that Othello's wondrous story was a 'lie' which seduced Desdemona into betraying her father (so she may likewise betray him). What turns the creativity of stories of Anthropophagi into the dross of lying? The difference between the lie and the creation comes entirely as the result of the position of the teller. It is not true that there are people with heads below their shoulders, but it is true that the world is an amazing place. It ceases to be an amazing place, however, the moment the teller becomes more important than what is being told.

The lie, then, is not a matter of telling it like it isn't, it is rather the position it occupies in asserting the very being of the liar. The lie is the liar's overimportance. The lie demands of the other that he plays host – confirming the liar's existence, thereby being at one with the liar. Here we can go back to the linguistically simpler story of Don Giovanni. Don Giovanni does not have a relationship with any of his many women; he seduces, makes the women mad with jealousy of each other and then records *his* conquests on a list kept by Leporello. A list is a piece of writing (or singing) in which there are only small differences within the pattern of repetition – the narcissism of small differences. One of my hysterical patients could not understand that his kin were also each other's relations; as far as he was concerned, everybody in his large kinship network related only to him – an aunt was *his* aunt (not his uncle's wife or his cousin's mother), his grandfather only *his* grandfather; nobody was related to anyone else except him. A list such as Don Giovanni's expresses this absence of any relationship between the parts; there is no relationship except to the list's author. If the list's author is not known – if one finds a shopping list on the street by chance, for instance – it is very boring, for the author is all.

According to the anthropologist Jack Goody, what we find at the emergence of writing are lists, not the many wonderful myths and tales we hope for. I suggest that when a culture becomes more complex, the previous group ego is under threat. Writing provides a means of asserting some control over the new and threatening complexity in which others take one's former place. Lists offer some form of control. However, the language of listing does not serve as a communication between people, but rather as an account of what one has got, an enhancement of the body or body of the group at a time when it may have been threatened. This language has no relational parts of speech, the words do not relate to each other, only to their author – just as my patient's family members bore no relationship in his mind to each other, only to him. The language of lists is not symbolic; it is an enumeration given meaning only if one recognizes it as the accoutrements of the subject. Anne Sexton gave a good description of this hysterical, non-relational language: 'words are like labels, or coins, or better, like swarming bees' – in other words, serial repeats of each other, not parts of a signifying chain.

All these hysterical expressions and symptoms and use of words destroy or deny relationships between others – allowing a 'relationship' only of an audience to the subject. Corradi Fiumara describes this process well, but misses the dangers:

[E]ven an attack on symbolic links – namely an attempt to induce confusion and disruption (as is reported in the more serious forms of mental pathology) – may turn out to be, paradoxically, an active effort for organization, preferable to being passively absorbed by incomprehensible situations. For in this case it is a subjective nucleus of the self which is producing disorder, as opposed to being overwhelmed by what is perceived as a chaotic milieu.[11]

The subjective nucleus of the subject may resort to diabolical speech, to lies, to projection, to violence as an active act just as (according to Winnicott) psychopathy is a sign of health – they contain the necessary aggression of life rather than the passivity of death. However, if we look only at the subject's survival, we are in danger of missing the real evil created. Diabolical speech, lying and violent sexuality are intimately connected, and while they may be an act of survival for the subject, their social effects, or effects on the other, may be disastrous. These symptoms are not just healthy aggression; they are also marked by the violence of a death drive. Iago cannot tolerate his jealousy of Cassio, nor his hatred of Othello who has seen the world. Because of Iago's unbearable jealousy and hatred, Othello murders Desdemona and kills himself.

Like Don Giovanni, Iago has the emptiness of the displaced person. This he projects into Othello – 'Othello's occupation's gone!' The self-assertion with which he compensates is also transmitted; at Iago's insistent suggestion, Cassio can be concerned with little else than getting back his 'position' which he lost when Iago made him drunk. Desdemona gets caught in the same web – she too wants her own way, pestering Othello to reinstate Cassio as proof of his love for her. Both join Iago in the 'look at me' posturing. Jealousy makes for turbulent emotions; these Iago projects to create the chaos of the world around him.

Othello and Desdemona won each other by their respect for the wonders of the world. Stirred up by Iago, Desdemona's father Brabantio had accused Othello of using witchcraft in his wooing. By the end of the play, the wonders of creation indeed have turned to witchcraft. Othello's language has changed: his mother's handkerchief with which he had endowed Desdemona, allowing her 'to think back through her mothers' (Woolf), has become 'witchy', steeped in the juice of mummies, woven by sibyls with magic. Othello's 'performative' description is designed to terrorize. Desdemona is frightened even before she fears he will murder her. The language of poetry has toppled over into the language of action – sexually perverse and murderously violent.

Throughout the play Iago is portrayed as a man of action. Cassio explains Iago's lewd banalities to Desdemona by saying he is a soldier, not a scholar. Hysteria and the enactments of perversion are two sides of the same coin. The states of mind are the same. Thus Iago's diabolical speech uses symbolic equations or literality and this is also enacted. For instance, he decides that it suits the lies he is to set in motion if he believes that Othello has slept with his wife, Emilia. That suggests the equivalent – that he would like to sleep with Desdemona. Then he stirs Othello to jealousy by describing how when he, Iago, was sleeping beside Cassio the dreaming Cassio mistook him for Desdemona and not only spoke sexually to the imagined Desdemona but also put his leg over Iago as in the act of sex. The fantasized perverse act is also perverse language. Iago's position of perversion in word and deed is the position of the hysteric – the hysteric fantasizes; the perverse man enacts. Both Don Giovanni and Iago enact the polymorphously perverse behaviour and fantasies of the displaced child – perverse sexuality is also perverse violence. Both are driven by jealousy. Both are men; action and perversion as alternatives to hysteria are favoured by authors depicting men – as indeed they are by men themselves. Hysteria and perversion alternate – their literal language and their compulsive lying reveal their fundamental unity.

9

Trauma

I. HYSTERIA, MEMORY AND TRAUMA

Trauma has always played a part in hysteria. It features prominently in *Studies on Hysteria*. The trauma that is implicated may be actual, imagined or induced. Or the trauma may be 'displaced'. The *saka* illness of the Taita women that was triggered by the unusual sight of a car parked in a road, or by the sudden noise of the striking of a match, may be the result of displaced shock. Something has occasioned the illness and that something is experienced as a shock or trauma, but the shock that triggers is not the 'original' shock. Any shock or trauma will do.

A more open question is the possibility of the hysterical reaction to trauma. Hysteria may need its trauma, but does trauma produce hysteria? It would seem that between the trauma and the hysterical reaction there is always a delay, so that if there is a hysterical response it is not immediate. The shock the soldiers of both World Wars received only later appeared as hysterical mutism, for instance. Sometimes the delay is far greater. It has been observed that the children of survivors of the Holocaust, rather than the survivors themselves, tend towards hysteria. This suggests that an actual trauma in one generation may not be induced until the next, when it may be lived as hysteria. The delay may thus not only be within any individual's experience, but within a social context too. Trauma's effects may be transmitted *as* hysteria.

Trauma and hysteria are both also closely connected to questions of memory. Hysterics characteristically suffer from great gaps in memory but they also suffer from what are described as 'reminiscences'. There can be a compulsion to go down 'memory lane'. Trauma victims, rather than remembering the events that traumatized them, experience a compulsive repetition of the traumatic moment. Trauma sufferers have been described, for this reason, by the American cultural historian Cathy Caruth as victims of history, since the 'Real' (Lacan) has invaded them.[1] I do not think this is quite correct. To examine the link between trauma and hysteria will help to redefine the problem. I suggest that in the case of the trauma victim and the hysteric, *memory has regressed to perception*. Perception and memory are incompatible. We need not 'remember' what we see, hear, touch, smell at the time. We cannot see something and simultaneously remember it. Even when it is recollected in the body, as what Melanie Klein calls 'memories in feeling', something is only remembered when it must be reperceived in its absence. At the very moment of trauma there is neither perception nor memory. Something experienced as traumatic shock eradicates the victim's capacity for memory as re-presentation. In its place comes the perception, the presentation of the experience. Blasted limbs, a hole in the stomach, come into the mind's image with a vividness that is near-hallucinatory. This presentation of sensory aspects of what happened is not the same as the experience itself coming back in its actuality. It is not 'the Real' nor a representation of it as memory. It is an iconic presentation. Perception necessarily distorts and is individual. It is this perception that returns as the iconic images, or 'frozen' movements such as running without moving across some railway tracks as the train approaches, of the traumatic nightmare – the inescapable, repeated perceived presentations of an aspect of the experience, not the experience itself. The trauma victim and the hysteric are akin (or are sometimes one and the same person) because they cannot remember, they can only perceive. It is not that the 'Real' invades them, it is that they have too much perception. This formulation means that we need to examine further the differences between perception and memory.

Memory

At the end of the last century the first questions in the enquiry that was to lead to psychoanalysis addressed the drastic gaps in memory, the 'absences', noted in the hysterical patients of Vienna of the 1880s and 1890s.

Hysterics seemed to be 'suffering from reminiscences' as well as having gaps in memory – as though they had both too much and too little memory. The reminiscences were found to be of cut-off bits of story somewhere between daydreams and memories. The huge memory gaps came as a result of internalizing the prohibition on thinking those thoughts and feeling those feelings. These feelings and thoughts were seen within the context of an event, in which memories of that event had been 'repressed'. What was repressed was the memory, not the event – hence the 'event' could return in another form, as it does after trauma. Freud argues: 'All repressions are of *memories*, not of experiences; at most the latter are repressed in retrospect.'[2]

Although his emphasis changed, Freud continued to maintain the notion that the hysterical symptom is the expression of a repressed memory. The symptom contains within it both the representation of the agency that brought about the repression – the prevention of the wish being realized – and the wish and impulse that has had to be banished from consciousness but which has its own force and can reassert itself in this pathological, symptomatic form. Although the emphasis on repression and consequent amnesia became over-shadowed by the post-Great War emphasis on earlier infantile experiences, it continued an 'underground' life and re-emerged in Freud's later thought on hysteria. In 1928 he argued that in a hysterical epileptic fit (Freud used here the example of Dostoevsky), the symptom – the fit – can be translated as follows: You want to be your father (the desire); you cannot be your father (the repressing agency); you want to be your father anyway; he is dead; you can be a dead father (the symptom, i.e. the fit). The epileptic fit mimes this death. The wish is no longer a memory, it is an enactment in the present.

Memory is an essential part of the process of humanization; psychoanalysis is concerned with the workings of, and the formation of, unconscious memory. When, in the late nineteenth century, it was still officially thought that sexual awareness only arose with puberty, Freud argued that an infantile experience, even if overtly sexual (such as sexual abuse in early childhood), could only be experienced as sexual after puberty. The first, for the infant, non-sexual experience (an experience empty of the sexuality that becomes its hallmark) is experienced as sexual later, in the present. It is not that the present reinterprets the past, but that there is what we could call a retardation of meaning altogether. This is crucial for all Freud's work. It is also crucial for an understanding of trauma. As regards memory, this perspective argues that the past means nothing until it comes into being in the present. 'What emerges from the unconscious is to be understood in the light not of what goes before but of what comes after.'[3] There are no memories *from* childhood, only *of* childhood.

There are currently roughly three strands of psychoanalytical understanding of memory: American ego psychology; French structuralist, post-structuralist and deconstructionist thinking; and British Object Relations theory. In American ego psychology, even where groups and individuals have broken away, the dominant paradigm, so far as memory is concerned, is the notion that experiences which have already been constituted as potential memories have been repressed. The patient must therefore be helped to find his 'narrative'; his conflict-free ego must make conscious, in order to control, the conflictual disturbances caused by these repressed memories. It is not by chance that psychohistory, the contemporary cult of narrative and narratology, and the Recovered Memory movement all originate from the psychodynamically informed culture of North America. Is this orientation of identity as history the product of a country that still feels itself a new nation, a nation in need of a past?

For the French, memory is never constituted. It may seem odd to put such figures as Lacan, Derrida, Laplanche and André Green into the same camp: even on the issue of memory, their creative work is often produced in disagreement with one another. Yet these diverse arguments and developments of ideas of memory all have a common base, and one that is very different from that of American ego psychology. The key concept for the French is Freud's original notion of

a 'deferral', '*nachträglich, Nachträglichkeit*'. This has been emphasized in different ways by Lacan and Green, expanded on and deployed
by Derrida in order to develop his key concept of '*différence*', and
retranslated by Laplanche into English as 'afterwardness'. Memory
comes after the trace. There is nothing, no event, experience, feeling,
to remember, there is only a past whose meaning is realized in the
present.

American ego psychology and Lacanian and post-Lacanian psychoanalysis are usually virulently opposed to each other, but they have
two things in common which are relevant to the concepts of memory:
they are both orientated to language and to the father. In this respect
British Object Relations theory is very different from either. Again,
within British Object Relations theory the controversies are perhaps
more important than its unity as an orientation, but that unity can
represent a particular position with regard to memory. Whether they
are Independent Object Relations therapists or Kleinians or neo-
Kleinians, British psychoanalysts focus on the 'two-person relationship', that is, the interaction between patient and analyst. Object
Relations theory (see chapter 5), with its emphasis on the pre-Oedipal
child, is concerned with the conditions in which 'memory' can come
into being, rather than with the instances when it fails. Within Object
Relations psychoanalysis the task of the analyst is to provide the
context – the 'container', the focus of reverie – in which the baby/
patient can come to have thoughts and memories of its own.

Wilfred Bion theorized about the role of the mother's 'thinking
ability', what he called her 'alpha elements', to contain and process
the undirected anxieties and sensations of the infant, the so-called
'beta elements', and hand them back transformed into manageable
feelings to the baby who will thereafter, hopefully, be able to use them
for the formation of its own thinking and remembering. If there is
'enough' of a mother, the infant will be able increasingly to 'hold her
in mind', in other words to begin to remember her, in her absences –
always provided that these are not too long. 'Memory', in this theory,
is a matter of human development taking place within the social
context of mother and child. A failure of memory will thus be a failure
of the original context, which hypothetically will not have been
matched to the infant's developmental stage.

For example, one of my patients, Mrs A, found it very difficult to remember anything from one session to the next. Shortly after we met and started working together, she told me that she needed me to remember why she had gone into a shoe shop. It was not like going into the grocer's and forgetting the sugar – anyone can do that – but she did not even know why she had gone into the shoe shop at all. She added, somewhat embarrassedly, that she did not need me to know too well why she had gone into a shoe shop, that would be absolutely awful. In asking me to remember for her, Mrs A was asking me to hold her overwhelming anxieties in my mind.

Although only words are used in Object Relations practice (as in all psychoanalytic treatments), its interpretations are of a relationship that tends to be preverbal, in which affects (feelings and emotional states) and the body are also used as sources of information about the psyche. Whether the emphasis is on Winnicott's reverie or facilitating environment or Bion's alpha function of the analyst to contain and transform the anxieties and beta elements of the patient, the model is the mother and the nature of her memory is seen as crucial to the development of memory in the infant. Instead of reconstructing a past like the Americans, or deconstructing the past like the French, the British emphasize the so-called 'here and now' of the session. Although not all Object Relations therapists would subscribe to the pre-eminence of this practice, yet even when the notion is opposed, the 'here and now' dominates over any reconstruction of the patient's history through the patient's memory. The present, in which the past assumes meaning, is everything. Winnicott claimed that the catastrophe that the patient fears as impending is one that has already taken place in the infantile past at a stage before the subject could process it. In one way this suggests deferred meaning (like the French and the Freud they use), in another it argues, to the contrary, that there was a relevant, real experience in the past.

We have, then, first the notion that memories exist, are expressed and can be retrieved, and that a history (either of real experiences or of feelings and impulses) can be reconstructed. Secondly, beside this or against this, we have the thesis that memory is laid down upon a series of inscriptions or traces which have no origin and no content in themselves. And then there is the third perspective, in which the mother's/analyst's holding of the baby in mind will facilitate the development of the preverbal baby's/patient's memory; here, however, it is the relationship, not the memory, that counts. These are not three different psychoanalyses, rather they are three aspects of theories of memory which have received different degrees of emphasis. What links these diverse strands is, in fact, the *absence* of memory. Whether that absence is due to repression (the Americans), deferral of meaning (the French), or the immature developmental state of the patient as a preverbal infant (the British), the starting point is absence. All three schools of thought have their roots in clinical experience and Freud's theories.

A hundred years ago, psychoanalysis started not with memory but with forgetting. Observing the pathological gaps in memory displayed by hysterical patients led Freud in time to formulate a 'normal' universal amnesia of the first years of life: however hard we try, we do not remember, at least in any continuous way, our infancy. Freud saw that those hysterical characteristics were particular manifestations of a general human characteristic. Between these two instances of forgetting (the hysterical-pathological and the normal) – and really, one could say, because of them – came the great discoveries that are the objects of psychoanalytic theory and, to a greater or lesser degree depending on the psychoanalyst's orientation, the focal points of therapy: an unconscious which is structured and which functions in a way that is completely different from consciousness; repression and other modes of psychic defence; the Oedipus complex and infantile sexuality. At the turn of the last century this was the field that was laid out between the hedgerows of the observation of hysterical forgetting and the theory of human infantile amnesia.

Although there may be biological explanations, for psychoanalysts no physiological, neurological or anatomical explanation fully accounts for this observation. It can, however, be explained by the particular nature of human interaction. The extreme dependence of the human infant induces a situation in which the objects on whom it is dependent become overcathected, that is, they matter too much. There is too much emotion, both love and hate, towards he who protects and she who nourishes, and in the interests of human society this excess must be forgotten, repressed. This act of repression makes the representations of these wishes and impulses unconscious and, because it is so major and momentous an act of obliteration, it drags with it all potential memories of this earliest period.

Although memory is individually and culturally quite variable, no psychoanalyst believes anyone can fully recover those earliest years of splendour in the grass or glory in the flower or of terror and anxiety as actual specific *memories*. The most that can happen is that they will be relived and given meaning in the present of the therapeutic session and that something may be reconstructed from them.

One of the reasons why biology does not satisfactorily account for infantile amnesia is that there are some memories that seem to stand out from the general background of infantile amnesia with extraordinary clarity. One of my patients could clearly remember the first time she stood up. She had been placed on top of the fridge by her father, who had been holding her under the arms, but then stood back to steady her just by her outstretched hands and fingertips. He let go so she stood for a moment alone, ecstatic and shocked, before she sat down with a bump on top of the fridge. The memory was incredibly vivid and various details made it possible to date it to somewhere around her ninth to eleventh month. This type of iconic memory is called a 'screen memory' and in fact, on analysis, would seem to be a mixture of childhood experience and unconscious fantasy. Its structure is like that of a symptom – something that has been repressed returns in a new, displaced image; if that image can be traced to the fantasy and the experience, then we have a clue to the infancy otherwise lost in amnesia. Freud writes of screen memories: 'Not only *some*, but *all* of what is essential from childhood, has been retained in these memories. It is simply a question of knowing how to extract them out of analysis. They represent the forgotten years of childhood as adequately as the manifest content of a dream represents the dream-thoughts.'[4] The notion of the screen memory gives a clear structure within which to explore the underlying unconscious memory. These screen memories are like positive versions of the iconic images that can come back after trauma or in nightmares. Though in appearance like neither a symptom nor a dream (except in its clarity), the screen memory is none the less an implication of unconscious processes.

Even when he credited his own and his patients' memories of

incest as truthful, Freud's notion of 'memory' was not one of literal reproduction. In the following letter to his friend Fliess, Freud was writing of memory in general, not just unconscious memories formed by the repression of sexual events or fantasies:

I am working on the assumption that our psychologic mechanism has come into being by a process of stratification: the material present in the form of memory traces being subjected from time to time to a *rearrangement* in accordance with fresh circumstances – to a *retranscription*. Thus what is essentially new about my theory is the thesis that memory is present not once but several times over, that it is laid down in various kinds of indications.[5]

It is to this theory of the formation of memory that both the French and the British look. Memories, then, are 'ideas' that flow over and over again along the same trace marks. Consciousness is the state that is without such traces; memory and consciousness are thus alternatives (they cannot happen at the same time). This notion of consciousness became defined as a system known as 'perception-consciousness'. It is to this perception-consciousness and not to 'history' that I believe trauma returns its victim when her memory is shattered.

In his *Project for a Scientific Psychology*, posthumously published but written in the late 1880s, in the heyday of the so-called sciences of memory, Freud tries to ground his psychological observations in neurology and the use of nerve pathways. Later, although essentially he builds on this earlier description of memory filling the breaches in the psychic apparatus, he uses instead the image of a 'printator' or mystic writing pad to indicate how memory works. This 'mystic pad' is made of a block of wax with a piece of wax paper and a protective sheet of cellophane placed over it. Both the wax paper and the cellophane are attached to the block only at one end so that they may be lifted away from it, although not removed entirely. If you write on the cellophane with a pointed instrument the marks go through the wax paper on to the pad beneath, but these marks on the cellophane may be wiped off by lifting the cellophane and wax paper away from the pad beneath. The cellophane would not be liftable were it not for the wax paper, but the cellophane is essential to protect the wax paper, which would tear if you wrote straight on to it. The analogy with our mental apparatus is that we must have something like the cellophane to protect us from too much stimulus. In this way we may go on receiving impressions and recording them, while remaining open to new ones. Memory is a process of marking, forgetting, and being reimpressed over and over again.

Memories flow along already scored traces; the cellophane and wax paper representing the system of perception-consciousness. They can be repeatedly cleared and made available for reinscription. However, if one examines the wax pad underneath, even when the paper is cleared, it is found to be scored over and over with a network of fine traces.

In *The Interpretation of Dreams*, Freud describes the unconscious latent thoughts that he hypothesizes must lie beneath the manifest thoughts that appear in the dream. These, he said, resemble the mycelium of the mushroom – there is no navel to the dream, no root, no origin or centre point, only a tangle of threads beneath the surface. We may transpose this image to memory: memory has no direct origin or root in a past object or experience. Before memory there is simply a mass of traces.

The French, and, in a very different way, the British, are interested, not in the recovery of secondarily repressed memories, but in the formation of memory itself. This formation of memory falls within a process known as 'primal repression'. Primal repression is a necessary hypothesis: for something to be repressed at all it needs to be both pushed into the unconscious from one direction and pulled into the unconscious by something that attracts it that is already there. The question is, how can there be a something there already when it would have to have got there by the same process? A hypothetical explanation of the necessary existence of something which does not have an origin in the unconscious but is already there is given by Freud as follows:

It is highly probable that the immediate precipitating causes of primal repressions are quantitative factors such as an excessive degree of excitation and the breaking through of the protective shield against stimuli.[6]

This is, in fact, a picture of trauma. The shift away from searching for the patient's memories necessitated also a shift in therapeutic techniques from using the analyst's conscious memories of the patient's sessions towards focusing on the process of unconscious communication between patient and analyst: 'It is a very remarkable thing that the unconscious of one human being can react upon that of another without passing through the Cs [conscious] . . . descriptively speaking, the fact is incontestable.'[7] Through the deployment of the fundamental technique of 'free association', the patient is meant to say whatever comes into his head and the censorship, which would otherwise operate to prohibit unconscious material from coming to the surface, is bypassed. Commensurate with this is the fact that the analyst should offer 'evenly suspended attention', listening with a part of herself that is not the logical conscious mind.

If the analyst must come to each session without either 'memory or desire', this does not mean that she does not have the patient in mind. However, if she consciously either recalls the last week's session or the patient's childhood, or prompts him to have memories, this will interfere with the unconscious communication between his freefloating association and her suspension of conscious attention. Of unconscious communication Freud wrote:

Experience soon showed that the attitude which the analytic physician could most advantageously adopt was to surrender himself to his own unconscious mental activity, in a state of evenly-suspended attention, to avoid as far as possible reflection and the construction of conscious expectations, not to try to fix anything that he heard particularly in his memory, and by these means to catch the drift of the patient's unconscious with his own unconscious.[8]

Therefore, if it is claimed that there is a real memory of a real event, this will set an obstacle in the way of the creative process of remembering, that is, one in which something is allowed to find a place within the capacity for memory. With this shift of understanding, traumatic events may be understood very differently. It is not, of course, that trauma is collective but that the traumatic breach in each and everyone taps into a shared human situation. Unconscious communication can thus bypass consciousness.

When psychoanalysis came into being at the turn of the century, a prevalent explanation of pathological, and above all hysterical, symptoms was of an earlier actual trauma. This was almost always given as the background to male hysteria. When women were studied, the traumatic accident turned instead into the suggestion of sexual trauma. But then twice over – during the 1880s and 1890s and again after the First World War – Freud argued that, although of course people have a psychic response to trauma, trauma itself is not the explanation for the formation of neurosis. But in psychoanalysis, as in the formation of memory itself, ideas that are entertained rarely disappear altogether. If we look back at the theories of memory, or the hypothesis of primal repression which establishes the fundament of unconscious memories, what are these theories, if not modelled on trauma?

Psychic trauma, like physical trauma, breaks through the subject's protective shield so that there is an influx of excitation which cannot be mastered or tolerated. The trauma happens *to* one and one responds with an unconscious act of 'primal repression' to deal with the 'excessive degree of excitation and the breaking through of the protective shield against stimuli'. The mystic pad, as a model for memory, describes the breaching of the protective cellophane and wax paper to form the ineradicable, permanent marks below; always the language is of quantities of excitation and of breaching. Derrida glosses Freud's ideas on the formation of memory thus: 'Life already threatened by the origin of memory which constitutes it, and by the breaching which it resists, the effraction which it can contain only by repeating it.'[9]

The hypothesis of primal repression implicates the particular conditions of human existence. The prematurity of human birth necessitates a degree of dependence that entails the risk of death if the conditions of survival are under threat. Prototypically, one might almost say mythologically, the absence of the all-providing/caring mother is equivalent to death. In the absence of protection and nurturance, too much of the world invades the neonate, puncturing whatever protective psychic shield it may have. The Taita woman whose *saka* is triggered off by the noise of a striking match is reminiscent of the baby who bursts into tears at a sudden unexpected sound; the woman whose *saka* is started by the sight of a strangely placed car has parallels with the infant of around eight to ten months whose 'stranger anxiety' makes it frightened of an unfamiliar face. In *saka*, as in hysteria in the Western world, we are dealing with the regression to a very early response. This regression repeats or parodies the response when an 'excessive degree of excitation' breaks through. Some mark from this incursion is retained by the subject as a track or groove along which repeated perceptions travel – this is the 'memory' with which human life is initiated: next time (or even twenty years later) the unexpected sound will be a repetition of this perception rather than of the trauma itself. The hysteric responds to this shock not with memory or thinking but, as it were, with a repeat of the original perception. Remembering the infant's shock, the hysteric repeats it as a perception: a perception of an actual noise or sight that breached its protective shield. This perception enables the hysteric to enact or tell it as a fantasy which seems completely real.

There is too much consciousness in the traumatized child. There is likewise too much consciousness in the hysteric. Without the capacity for memory, which acts as a safeguard, a protection against the potential trauma of being helpless in the face of the superabundance of the world, there could be no human society; memory and its absence structure and differentiate the conditions that surround us. Human beings are born with their eyes wide open; after the first week or so the eyes become less focused. It is common for traumatized babies to stare longer and harder than normal ones and then to retreat quickly into infantile autism. Hysteria may be a relatively brief response to traumatic impingement, as in shellshock, or it may be a more established regression to earlier responses to trauma. The general traumatic basis of the human condition entails the possibility that instances such as being passed over by one's partner, deprived of what one wants, can be experienced as unmanageable, 'traumatic'. In themselves they are in fact only 'catastrophic'. The regression is not a 'pure' return to infantile experience, since the person has moved on. The subsequent history is pulled into the regression. The older child or adult is a sexual being – and hence trauma revisited becomes trauma sexualized. But if there has been too much actual trauma, such as in physical or sexual abuse, the breach itself will become sexualized: the 'death' entailed in the violation will fuse with sexual energies to produce a tragically perverse child. This is the perversion which is the other side of the coin to hysteria. It is not the same as hysteria, for there is no repression – instead there is 'acting out'.

Recovered Memories

Hysterical patients often claim to have 'repressed memories' of sexual events, most particularly of intercourse with the father. When therapists of the Recovered Memory movement, which hit the US in recent years like an epidemic, sought to release the dissociated or 'multiple personalities' of their clients from the defences they had erected, they searched back to actual abusive events. In November 1993, in a review article entitled 'The Unknown Freud' in the *New York Review of Books*, Frederick Crews launched this decade's attack on Freud and psychoanalysis. Crews' arguments were that Freud was a fraud as a thinker and a malpractitioner as a clinician. Just over a year later, Crews also undertook a virulent critique of the abuse-hunters of the Recovered Memory movement, in which he argued that these abuse-hunters are Freud's true heirs. According to Crews, the spurious popularity of psychoanalysis has led to the supposed recovered memories of childhood abuse being seen as the causes of adult malaise or pathology. As Crews rather inadequately acknowledges, this is a peculiar claim. Indeed it is a very peculiar one, since it was precisely by *rejecting* the notion that his patients had recovered memories of real events, in favour of the realization that they were in the grip of fundamental human fantasies, that Freud established the basis of psychoanalysis. Yet, according to Crews, 'the ties between Freud's methods (and theirs) are intricate and enveloping – and immeasurably more compromising to both parties – than they imagine'.[10]

The Freud in question is the Freud who believed the stories that his first hysterical patients told him when they were able to fill in the amnesiac gaps in their consciousness. It is not a question of asking whether or not the stories were true or false. The result of coming to see them not as actual but as fantasies was, quite simply, psychoanalysis. For, there would have been no Oedipus complex, no theories of the unconscious, of defences, of infantile sexuality if what Freud had been dealing with were instances of actual abuse. This shift from seeing hysterics as victims of specific acts of abuse to believing that all children, by virtue of their common humanity, both desire and repress the desire for their parents – the Oedipus complex – changed the nature of the enquiry from one that was concerned with a discrete pathology, to one that had to do with the formation of the human psyche. By saying that patients with pathologies such as dissociation or Multiple Personality Syndrome (MPS) *have* suffered actual childhood abuse, Recovered Memory therapists are saying that these people are *not* like the rest of us – they are a special population. When Freud came to the conclusion that he himself, like his hysterical patients, was fantasizing his father's abuse of him in childhood, he turned a marginalized, discrete pathology (hysteria) into a central aspect of the human condition. Psychoanalytic practice, in training for which the future analyst must undergo a long analysis herself, incorporates this shift: the analyst must first, and in a sense always, be a patient. For neurosis and normalcy are on a continuum. Concepts of memory played a central part in this crucial change.

In *Rewriting the Soul: Multiple Personality and the Sciences of Memory* (1995) the philosopher Ian Hacking argues that in the twelve years from 1874 to 1886 in France, 'memory' replaced the notion of 'the soul' as the source and explanation of personal identity. This period saw the advent and efflorescence of the multiple personality and then, in ways that were both similar to and different from today's epidemic, recovered memory produced the unified person who had split and dissociated himself only in order to cope with trauma. Initially multiple personality was not a syndrome on its own, it was considered a manifestation of hysteria. Hacking, a highly sophisticated, original and interesting thinker, writes:

The recovered memory people and the false memory people may seem completely at loggerheads, but they share a common assumption: either certain events occurred and were experienced, or they did not and were not. The past itself is determinate, true memory recalls these events as experienced, while a false one involves things that never happened. The objects to be remembered are definite and determinate, a reality prior to memory. *Even traditional psychoanalysis tends not to question the underlying definiteness of the past.* The analyst will be indifferent as to whether a recollected event really occurred. The present emotional meaning of the recollection is what counts. Nevertheless, the past itself, and how it was experienced at the time is usually regarded as definite enough.[11] [My italics]

While this observation is interesting, it is completely wrong about psychoanalytic theory. Yet, as a Canadian, Hacking is likely, of course, to be thinking of American ego psychology, with its emphasis on repression – which gives his misunderstanding some plausibility. However, for psychoanalysts the 'past' is never definite. It is the patient who initially thinks it is definite. Any psychoanalyst aims only at a constant deconstruction of the past and a replacement with a new version. In the end, one settles for a 'history' that will have to suffice – not that is 'correct'.

In advocating the notion of the indeterminacy of the past, Hacking invokes the philosopher Elizabeth Anscombe's idea of an 'action under description' – so that a handshake can be saying hello or goodbye, clinching a business deal, or it can be offered in congratulation. In fact, the notion of 'indeterminacy', or anyway Anscombe's 'action under description', may well have been derived *via* Wittgenstein from psychoanalysis.

Clearly, psychoanalysis can be seen, as Hacking sees it, as both emanating from within, and then becoming exemplary of 'the sciences of memory'. Discussions and theories of memory at the time Freud was formulating his ideas were highly complex. Yet, even when Freud was going like a sleuth after hysterics' apparent memories of incest, it was never with the notion of memory as a reproduction of a fixed event, true or untrue. The amalgamation of Recovered Memory therapy and psychoanalysis, as in Crews' account, presupposes just such a notion to have been at work. There must be some explanation for this misunderstanding.

In what follows I have divided the subject of memory in two. Firstly, there are perceptions of experiences, whether internal or external, which follow old mnemic traces – the marks over the marks over the marks on the wax pad. Then, within this general category are the specific memories that are perceptions of experiences which are illicit sexual memories. Sexual memories become repressed by a process of secondary, not primary, repression and so form part of what Melanie Klein called 'the repressed Unconscious'. In one sense, because they follow old traces, these memories may seem to be already constituted as memories and as such may be considered retrievable. However, they only *appear* to originate from an actual starting point in childhood. In fact it is the trace, not the memory, that is there. It is to this trace that I believe many ego psychologists address themselves. Given such an emphasis it becomes understandable (just) that non-psychoanalytic writers like Crews and Hacking should place such memories in the same camp as those sought by the Recovered Memory therapists. To do so, however, is to misunderstand the psychoanalytic explanation of memory.

Freud's abandonment of the so-called 'seduction theory' and his replacing of sexual trauma with infantile sexual fantasy as the key factor in his hypothesis on neurosis came not as the result of a revelation on a scientific road to Damascus; it was very much a part of contemporary debates about trauma, degeneration and *specific* causes of mental disturbance.[12] Despite the now infamous claims of Jeffrey Masson that Freud was simply cowardly and did not dare indict fathers of abuse, there has never been any question but that actual abuse exists, indeed is alarmingly prevalent. However, in the first place, does sexual trauma produce neurosis? And, in the second, have people suffering from psychoneurotic or psychotic symptoms always been traumatized? Coming out of these questions is the issue, too, of whether or not sufferers' stories of such abuse, initially repressed and then revealed, are necessarily true. The two questions on the relationship of trauma and mental illness are clearly important. Whether or not the stories are true has serious practical implications. However, their theoretical significance lies not with any factual accuracy but with the place and nature of fantasy in the human psyche.

Crews claims that the new Recovered Memory therapists and Freud are identical fantasists. Using Freud as a fall guy he argues that Freud palmed off his own propensity for making up stories on to his first hysterical patients – the women he treated in the 1880s and 1890s. He also thinks Freud was so confused with his later obsessional patient, the 'Wolf Man', whom he treated in 1918, that his reconstruction of the 'primal scene' in which the Wolf Man witnessed the copulation of his parents was probably Freud's fantasy about the sexuality of his own mother and father. Similarly, Crews speculates that Freud may also have projected his own fascination with sexual initiation by serving girls on to the Wolf Man. Put like this, Crews can make Freud sound very like the contemporary therapists whom he likewise accuses of inducing false memories in their clients.

Crews charges Freud not only with being a bad and inhumane therapist, but also with being a cheat as a scientist, with showing 'grave flaws of reasoning or even outright fraudulence'. Crews' amalgamation of Recovered Memory therapy, in which the therapist helps the patient discover and express a story of abuse, and Freud's entirely contrary argument, in which he abandons this very position in favour of a notion of infantile desire that must be repressed (the Oedipus complex), rests on a particular assumption about hysteria. Ironically, the theory of recovering memories itself depends on the same assumption as Crews': that there is no hysteria, only trauma. The American psychiatrist Judith Herman, in her highly successful book *Trauma and Recovery* (1992), lists three phases in the recent methodologies of trauma: firstly, at the end of the nineteenth century, there was *hysteria* which she claims was really trauma; then, following the First World War, came war neurosis; the final 'real trauma', she says, is the 'sex wars of the 1990s'. The effects of trauma are labelled as 'complex post-traumatic stress disorder'. Herman's work has led the way to a veritable 'trauma industry' in American academia. Herman writes: '[This] formulation reunites the descriptive fragments of the condition that was once called hysteria and reaffirms their common source in a history of psychological trauma.'[13] However, the more super-subtle the analysis of trauma becomes, the less subtle is its place in the human soul. Not all is trauma, though all humans may have become human through an initiating trauma – the impingement of the world into their prematurity.

Crews, meanwhile, says of Freud's relationship to Dora in 'A Fragment of an Analysis of a Case of Hysteria': 'Freud's treatment . . . constituted psychiatric malpractice . . . [forcing] prurient suggestions upon his virginal teenage patient.' His opinion of hysteria is no better: 'so-called hysteria – itself a faddish malady whose distribution was suspiciously well correlated with possession of the means to pay for treatment'; 'hysteria, of course, has vanished along with the doctors who battened on it'.[14] Crews' primary aim here is to attack psychoanalysis, but underlying that attack is an assertion of the non-existence of hysteria. He is also, of course, attacking the Recovered Memory therapists, whom he sees as feminists. But they, by labelling everything as 'trauma', are likewise asserting the non-existence of hysteria. Ironically, then, Crews and the Recovered Memory therapists whom he vilifies have become intellectual bedfellows.

In fact, what Freud, the Recovered Memory therapists, Crews, or anyone else for that matter, could have as a common thesis is of the human propensity for a hysterical response to trauma, either real or imagined. The hysteria may replace the memory. To argue this last point is not the same as to suggest that regaining an actual memory would replace the hysteria. Psychoanalytic experience suggests that where there is memory there can be no hysteria, but what is meant by 'memory' here is a *capacity* for memory, not the remembrance of a particular event. The two different problems have been disastrously confused. A simple illustration may be taken from the prevalence of hysteria among children of Holocaust survivors mentioned earlier: they have no *memory* of their parents' trauma, but they can have an imaginary *perception* of it. Their hysteria is thus perception, as though they could experience it. If instead of a perception they can develop the capacity for memory, they will remember that this is their parents' unspeakable experience – not theirs.

II. WHERE AM I? TRAUMA AND THE
QUESTION OF RECOGNITION

In an everyday context we tend to look at a range of difficult or tragic occurrences from an observer's point of view and label them 'traumatic'. Instead, I want to define trauma from the perspective of the person who experiences it. This means, firstly, that the same event will not necessarily be traumatic for all who experience it and, secondly, that if different events are experienced as traumata at all, they have some lowest common denominator. The exception to this is what I would describe as the originary 'trauma' of an effraction that institutes life by setting up an unconscious nucleus through primal repression. In common, too, is the capacity for memory, sexuality

and a death drive. That is, there is the trauma of the world's impingement on our premature birth which we all share as part of the human
condition. The traumata I wish to consider here, however, all happen
later when what may from the outside appear to be the trauma is in
fact only the catalyst that brings to the surface an experience which,
were it not for this later event, might not even in itself have been
traumatic. Even so extreme an experience as the Holocaust may not
breach the defences of particular individuals. Thus, although the
Holocaust is one of the most grotesque events known to mankind,
this does not automatically qualify it as traumatic in itself. The
catalytic event in the present (here the Holocaust) triggers an earlier
occurrence which only becomes traumatic by virtue of the meaning
it attains in the present. This has nothing to do with the horror or
cruelty of the experience. Too often cruelty and trauma are made to
be synonymous. Trauma, I think, should be specified not as the content
but as the action of breaching. So that, for instance, if the crisis in
the present, however appalling, does not breach the defences and
evoke an earlier, potentially traumatic experience it will not constitute
a trauma.

My stepfather endured several years' incarceration in the Nazi
concentration camps; although his account of what man can do to
man confirms, even extends, all that Primo Levi and others have
described, this experience does not appear to have constituted a trauma
for him. He had been born very prematurely, the only survivor of
many miscarriages, a so-called *krepeirl* – an infant who can neither
live nor die. This early survival, which was neither life nor death,
coupled with his profound belief in reincarnation, are probably the
means by which he endured his experience. Afterwards, what he did
need to do for a time was to become frequently physically ill – so that
he could be looked after (and look after himself) and legitimately
nurse his ego – a necessary narcissism. He did not deny or foreclose
on the experience – his suffering was no less than anyone else's. My
argument here is that I do not think it was *traumatic*. What it 'repeated'
was not earlier infantile trauma, but infantile survival. It did not
breach a protective shield.

We can see the role of illness and the contrast between its necessary
narcissism and hysterical excess of ego very clearly in *King Lear*. In

Shakespeare's play King Lear decides to hand over his kingdom to his daughters on condition that they each swear they love him most in the world. Cordelia, his youngest daughter, states that she loves him as his daughter but will love her future husband as a wife. Lear insists that he must have all her love. Five times she says 'No.' Lear becomes increasingly hysterical, crazily overasserting his position as king and father in need of all the love and attention. His elder daughters then deprive him of any shred of recognition of these positions. 'Who is it who can tell me who I am?' he demands and, as no one but the Fool answers, he plunges into a cauldron of violent sexualized madness. His sanity is restored only after a doctor recognizes this breakdown as an illness needing care and facilitates a long, curative sleep. When Lear wakes, his younger daughter Cordelia is there to recognize him both as her father and as the ageing king. This transformation of hysteria into illness is the condition on which the survivor loses his hysterical excess of ego in situations of care such as can be produced by therapy. Without this 'going over the edge' into nothingness (as Mrs Peters also did), I doubt if there can be any real recovery from the hysteria.

Among my patients, Mrs A made me expect for a long time that we would come across some unbearably dreadful experience in the past. We didn't. Yet a certain event – a period when she went away with her mother but left her father – which, on the face of it, would not have seemed as difficult as some others she recounted, had evidently been traumatic for her. Mrs C, by contrast, nearly convinced me that the death of her father when she was a child was insignificant. Although she had sought treatment, Mrs C assured me it was only for reasons of intellectual curiosity; there was nothing amiss. The 'nothing amiss' was linked to the fact that her father's death had no significance.

Mr B was an aspiring writer who could compose brief, fluent, inessential journalistic pieces but never the sustained work to which he urgently aspired. We were to see in time how this was linked to language for him. Interested in the theory and history of language, he claimed that what was extraordinary about humankind was not the ability to speak, but metaphor. A successful man in early middle age, he told me that when he was much younger he had had a fleeting thought that his mother, who had died when he was a little boy, might really be alive somewhere but that if she was and he were to meet her he would not recognize her. He then told me about a real event in his life which exactly paralleled this. As an adolescent he had had a very serious relationship with a girl for over three years. He had been devastated when she broke this off and he had entered a depression. Some years later, she telephoned him out of the blue. Although he knew who she was, wasn't even particularly surprised to hear from her, had full recall of their relationship, throughout the phone call and even after it he said that he did not *recognize* her. We puzzled together about the nature of this lack of recognition.

We talked about the quality of recognition, agreeing that a split between cognitive and affective recognition, knowledge and feeling, did not adequately serve to explain or even describe his experience. Probably all animate matter can be traumatized. In humans the breach occurs in the particular context of our premature birth. However, this general breaching opens up the possibilities of either recognition or rejection, upon which our response to trauma is predicated. We can postulate that my stepfather was *recognized*, not rejected, as a *krepeirl*, and succoured into life.

Mr B's mother had died after a prolonged illness when he was six years old. He had no recall of her at all. Indeed, if he saw a photograph of himself with his mother, as far as he was concerned it was evidence of the fact that the woman was not his mother. In his company, she was signed with a negative. He knew who she was, and if he saw her in a photograph with someone else, such as one of his siblings, then she was his mother; but if she was with him, then she couldn't be.

After his girlfriend abandoned him, Mr B dreamt the only dream about his mother that he could recollect ever having had. As he told me this, he started to wonder whether, before the break-up with his girlfriend, he had in fact had just ordinary, continuous memories of his mother. As we talked about these things we both found we had odd memory sensations, recollecting some things neither of us would expect to remember and forgetting others, so that the exchange was a crisscross of repetitions, revelations, certainties and uncertainties taken to an unusual degree. At one point I said, musingly, 'I wonder if, when you were going to visit your mother in hospital towards the end, someone warned you in advance that your mother wouldn't recognize you?' Mr B answered, 'Yes, they certainly did; I can remember that clearly.' As he said this, I both sensed the revelation of a new bit of understanding and realized that I had, in fact, merely repeated something Mr B had told me long before.

We can treat this question of his mother not recognizing him as an iconic instance. My question is: What would a young child experience/ imagine if he was told his mother wouldn't recognize him – and then, of course, she didn't? Somehow the latter seems less problematic than the former. A child of six is sufficiently mature to be able to ascribe the actual experience of non-recognition to the mother's serious illness. However, the abstract idea that one is in the world, but that the person who 'put' one there cannot recognize one, is profoundly disturbing. In the context of being told this without the presence of the sick person in whom the idea can be rooted – he was in the back of a car, not at her bedside – what would a child make of it? I imagined the 6-year-old Mr B, a highly gifted child, trying to grasp this notion intellectually and imaginatively.

I suggested to Mr B that he had reversed this impossible idea so that, instead of being unrecognized himself, he had imagined that he would not recognize his mother and, in fact, subsequently did not recognize his ex-girlfriend. Sitting in the back of the car, a small boy visiting his dying mother, he may have, so to speak, 'tried on' the idea of her not recognizing him by his not recognizing her. What would 'recognition' or non-recognition entail in this context? Could it be that he would know who she was, but would not know she was his mother when he was with her? He knew she was his mother when he saw a photograph of her with one of his siblings – nobody had suggested anything to the contrary. This was knowledge of a status or standing of someone named 'mother', just as he knew who his ex-girlfriend was when she telephoned, but this would not entail recognition of a relationship that gave him a particular position. And if he did not recognize her, then, by definition, she could not be *his* mother – as in the original hypothetical situation, how could he, unrecognized by her, be her son?

André Green has suggested that absence is the precondition for fantasy: in the originary absence of oneself from one's own conception, one dreams up the primal scene.[15] My own emphasis would be on the dilemma of one's own absence from the world at large: that simple but extraordinary bewilderment of childhood that the world is there without us. Someone or something gives us a place in that world. They see me, therefore I exist. Equally, in the peek-a-boo game of the very small child, if I close my eyes you cannot see me; you cannot see me because I cannot see the world. Do we feel secure in familiar places and insecure in strange ones not only because we are attached to known objects, but because we feel the known environment sees us where the unknown one does not?

'Recognition' is an extremely important concept in the work of Winnicott, who describes how essential it is for psychic growth. However, what I want to do is look at the notion and process from the perspective of its catastrophic failure. I think that if we do this we will get a fuller picture and some more elements to add to both the theory of trauma response and the nature of trauma – real or constructed – in hysteria.

Unlike Freudian or Lacanian theory, Object Relations theory such as Winnicott's has normal, healthy growth as its methodological centre point. However, we can apply Freud's methodology of interrogating the 'abnormal' or pathological instead of the fictional 'normal' to object relationships?

The relevant extreme 'abnormality' for questions of recognition is autism. Autism would seem to be based on appalling primary non-recognition; the autist is experienced as, and therefore experiences himself as, an alien. It is puzzling that so brilliant a psychological researcher as Frances Tustin, who transformed the understanding of autism, nevertheless should, at the eleventh hour of her life, give in to the notion that there must be some biological underpinning to autism. There may be. It has not been proved either way. However, for a number of reasons some of which have a bearing on our consideration of trauma and hysteria, a biological explanation of autism seems redundant. This does not mean, though, that the experience of autism, and therefore the observation of it, is not based in a problem so fundamental that it appears to be biological. Indeed that, I posit, is exactly what occurs.

Theories of trauma also often revert to neurophysiological models or scientific formulations based on biology. There can be nothing biologically causative about the Holocaust or a mother's death, or about their possible effects. So why do theories of trauma fall back, often despite our best intentions, on to biological models? I do not believe that this is because we cannot conceptualize the psychic at such a level of experience. It is, I suggest, rather that the level of the experience *is* a biological level. For here we are talking about the originary breaching event, through which subsequent trauma is experienced, that instantiates human life in the neonate and so appears 'biological'. We then use natural science explanations because they echo our existential experience.

Many theorists of trauma write of the hole (*trou*-ma), breach, or failure of the holding environment that has been broken into as the condition or expression of trauma. But it could be the other way around: these breaches or holes may only come about in the context of a primal non-recognition which is, to a greater or lesser extent, everybody's human lot, but which could in some instances, as in the situations that produce autism, be abnormally severe.

An experience or event can only fracture the protective shield if it resonates with an internal state. As with the formation of memory and primal repression, there must be something already there to draw the event/experience in, thereby enabling it to breach the protective shield and so constitute the trauma. Or what one has been recognized as being might turn out to be not what one is. This is more than just the notion of a 'false self'. My stepfather did not experience the outrageous horror of the concentration camps as traumatic because he managed to get himself recognized once more as what he had originally been recognized as in infancy, a *krepeirl*. But Mr B's dying mother's probable non-recognition of him as a boy might have been traumatic because, having been brought up by nannies because of his mother's long illness, he was already unsure about being his mother's son. The Wolf Man was told that his sister was his mother's child but that he was his father's baby – which is exactly how he saw himself, as someone to whom his father had given birth. The question, then, is: Who am I for this person/world I see? Mr B could believe his brothers were recognized by his mother; he had no doubt that his father was too; but was he? This 'Who am I?' is not a question of a self-sufficient identity, but rather one of positioning, of 'Where do I stand?'

There was clearly a link between Mr B's sense that he would not recognize his mother with his inability to write in a sustained way. He and I both wondered whether his inability to write had something to do with the inhibition of an Oedipal desire for his mother. It may have; however, more immediate was his identification with his mother's death than any inhibition that related to her life. When she died, after brain surgery, the 6-year-old Mr B raced around with a hood over his head like the bandages that she had worn; he would not be parted from his 'crash helmet' – a physical metaphor that condensed his experience of his mother's death as a crash into an identification with her and her brain surgery. If I am you or he is she, then you, she, 'the other', cannot be recalled as there is insufficient distance between the two terms – in this case between the terms of mother and son; he was his mother as the moon is blue cheese. A metaphorical equation does not allow for a position which necessitates, not equivalent, but *different* terms, such as 'mother' and 'son'. It was as though, in his mind, Mr B and his mother had become metaphors for each other. Hence his high regard for metaphor rather than language, which requires distance and difference.

The good enough mothering which Winnicott describes as essential for psychic health facilitates the development of the 'true self', but it does not ensure categorical knowledge; it fails to give a place, to establish kinship or say where one belongs in the world. Mr B did not develop a false self probably because he had a wonderful nanny who was 'good enough', but he did not know *where* he was positioned in the world. As far as he was concerned, the nanny loved him as *her* baby, not as his mother's son. Not knowing his position *vis-à-vis* his mother, Mr B could only make a hysterical identification with her – being the same as her, he could not see her in his mind's eye.

In autism, the recognition that is missing would seem to be at the most basic level. The baby's body is repudiated, found disgusting and utterly alien at a time when the body – the cries, the smiles, the manifold body products – is what the baby *is*. It is because the lack of recognition takes place at such a physical and primary level that it is experienced as biological. Explanations, then, tend to follow suit and offer biological accounts. I believe that the condition that underlies the hysterical reaction has a lot in common with autism – both crucially involve non-recognition. Likewise, after a trauma, the position that the subject is in is the autistic one of non-recognition.

One of the best descriptions of autism from the perspective of the person who experiences it is Donna Williams's *Nobody, Nowhere* (1993). Autism is often regarded as a state of self-enclosure, except that, as Donna Williams's account makes starkly clear, there is no 'self' to enclose. Life is lived in sensations and, perhaps, fantasies which have no apparent reference to external reality and no 'I' to think them. If there is language at all it would seem to be used to control the environment (animate and inanimate), certainly not to communicate with another person.

Nobody, Nowhere recounts the life of its author growing up to young adulthood in an Australian suburb. Labelled retarded, imbecilic, spastic, mad, schizophrenic, Donna is nearly institutionalized and for a time is sent to a special school. Yet, through sporadic, surprise academic successes, she gets to university where she also has some psychotherapy treatment which provokes a suicide attempt, a break-down (what I have seen as the necessary illness) and then the beginning of a recovery in which she sets out on the trail of her own history and, I imagine, eventually, this remarkable book.

All too completely, in her autistic state Donna Williams becomes like whatever she looks upon: at first she consciously copies a girl in the park – Carol – and then one day she looks at 'herself' in the mirror and instead sees Carol. Fully becoming Carol costs her some effort but, as Carol, she can have a social and later a sexual life – a charming, brittle, seductive and tragic hysterical imitation of life. However, for a different sort of protection, she also needs to be Willie, the raging, violent-eyed boy from her own surname. Willie, she claims, is a mimic of her mother's anger and taunts. In my experience these 'violent eyes' develop when the baby looks into the 'mirror' of its mother's or father's face and finds, instead of recognition, the inquisitorial stare of a parent who, for some reason or other, finds the baby alien. These staring eyes show the presence of excessive perception which itself indicates trauma. There is a passing question (made nothing of) in the book as to who are Donna's biological parents which made me wonder somewhat fancifully whether perhaps her father had stared at her wondering whose child she was.

The autist, Donna, is not really there as a self to be named, except very occasionally. However, even when she is, appropriately enough she addresses herself as 'you'. This Donna is the body which makes messes on the floor, screams, paints her face wildly, swings in total ecstasy from the trees, cuts and batters herself. In between the autistic non-existence and the hysterical mimesis, however, Donna has instances of total identification – neither goings-out (projection) nor takings-in (introjection) – but what I can only describe as transubstantiations. By inviting absolutely anyone into her bed in the same way that a friend of hers, Trish, had once invited her, Donna 'had become Trish'. When dressing herself, the pretty objects put on are not objects, but instead they become her actual body. It is her body, then, not words, that expresses her autistic state of being:

Around this time I was again tested for partial deafness, for although I could speak I often didn't use language in the same way as others and often got no meaning out of what was said to me. Although words are symbols, it would be misleading to say that I did not understand symbols. I had a whole system of relating which I considered 'my language'. It was other people who did not understand the symbolism I used, and there was no way I could or was going to tell them what I meant. I developed a language of my own. Everything I did, from holding two fingers together to scrunching my toes, had a meaning, usually to do with reassuring myself that I was in control and no-one could reach me, wherever the hell I was.[16]

As Donna Williams herself says, a great deal about the manifest behaviour of autism is at some unimaginably extreme edge of everyday experiences. Autistic children communicate (often just to themselves) with body signs. Yet in the dentist's chair or at the truly extreme edge, under torture, anyone's body may be used self-referentially in order to control pain. In autism the body would seem to be used to control the emotional pain which is experienced as a physical sensation and to create the encapsulated frantic excited pleasure which is the same as pain. This is the way of handling the break-up of the protective shield. In autism it is as though there is more breach than there is protection. The moments of the effractions are simultaneously sexual and violent.

In autism, instead of recognition, there has been primary repugnance and repudiation. Interesting questions, then, are raised about the thought and language processes. It would seem that the autist has the capacity for inner thinking and speaking without the ability to communicate, as though that capacity had persisted outside of the social context needed for its realization. The language that emerges is very impoverished, often only a series of giggling and babbling. Another psychotherapist with extensive experience of autism, Ann Alvarez, writes of a child patient: 'Robbie was excited and tickled, not by the content of the stories, but by particular words . . . sounds were felt, quite literally, to touch him, caress him, tickle him, or strangely, to provide visual thrills.'[17]

Of course every baby is caressed, tickled and made happy by words she hears and sees – what else is the impact of lullabies? What would seem to have happened in autism is that from this state we have a frozen stasis. Something impinged traumatically and was trapped and eternalized. Henceforth it bears the mark of the breach – sexual and violent. In autism, the ability to express oneself through body movements and protowriting is there. Donna Williams writes:

[The picture] had been drawn by a young autistic girl and was featured in a book by a psychoanalyst who worked with such children. The adult analysis of the picture was that it expressed this girl's longing for the breast. When, after becoming close to her counsellor, she drew two white squares in the darkness, this was interpreted as two breasts. When she then reversed the picture, with a black square now in the middle of the white paper, this was taken to be her version of the 'bad breast' as opposed to the 'good breast'. I laughed myself stupid when I read this. I had drawn the same picture over and over, writing beside it: 'Get me the hell out of here'. This was the symbolic representation of my trap which was due to the infantile nature of my unreached emotions. The blackness I had to get to was the jump between 'my world' and 'the world', though I had never been able to make it in one piece. I had learned to fear the complete loss of all attachment to my emotional self, which happened when I made the jump, and to do this was the only way which made communication possible. Giving up the secret of this was simply too deadly. Too many well-meaning people would have tried mercilessly to drag me through the darkness unprepared, and killed my emotional self in the process. I may never have died physically, but psychically

I had died many times in the effort. I had multiple fractures of the soul as a result.[18]

Through the body, through making marks and noises, the presence of the subject is asserted. But despite Williams referring to this as 'symbolic representation' it is not really either symbolic or representational. Writing, words, even thought are there, yet this is *presentation* not representation – it cannot be. For re-presentation to occur the object must have been acknowledged as lost and then regained as a symbol. The mocked pschoanalyst was trying to make the autistic patient use a picture as a symbol of a breast. Williams shows that it is not a symbol – it is a presentation of the state of no communication between her world and the world. In the case of autism, there has been no loss of the caretaker to be managed because the caretaker is the 'well-meaning' person who is in fact murderous, repudiating the child. The communication is not what we ordinarily mean by social communication. Presentation, according to Freud, is one of the features of the id, and so it is as though the subject has survived for itself as an 'it' – not an 'I' that has been recognized.

There are, then, a number of aspects to recognition. I am positing that it is some basic aspect of recognition that has never been there in autism and which is catastrophically eroded in trauma. We could put it like this: human life starts for everyone as the traumatic impingement of the world into our prematurity. The social context can confirm this trauma by repudiation/non-recognition, which may induce autism. Alternatively, it may recognize the infant but a later trauma, such as happened to Mr B, will cut through the recognition and give meaning to the primal trauma. In this case the later incident 'finds' the non-recognition within the subject and is drawn through the protective shield to join it. In other words, the later breaching instance (what is normally called the trauma) is only the instance which pierces to this human level of the need for recognition, and the failure of it.

The British analyst Enid Balint told me that, when questioned about the devastating effects of the Blitz in the Second World War, a bombed-out Londoner refused to mention the bomb but instead complained incessantly that her neighbour had failed to return the pound of tea she had lent her – that is, there had been a failure of recognition of who she was as a generous neighbour. Shocked by the bomb, what she asked for was recognition of where she stood and so she expressed her need for this by compulsively recalling an instance in which her need for recognition had not been met. The point is that it is recognition of where one stands, not of what one has suffered, that is important.

A primary rejection of the neonate's body by the person on whom it utterly depends prevents it from developing the sensation and primitive conceptualization of what Freud called the body–ego. This comes before the possibility of structured language. It is the rock bottom of a person's psychic existence. Trauma can reactivate aspects of these states in anyone because some minor degree of rejection of the body/I, some small sense of the body/I as alien, is probably the human lot. In *The Power of Abjection* (1986) Julia Kristeva writes of 'abjection' to describe the state from the viewpoint of the one who rejects. Autism is the result for the one who has been repudiated.

Mrs A asked me to name her body parts for her – she could not do so herself. She also did not expect me (or anyone else for that matter) to recognize her except by external insignia, such as the time at which we had made an appointment. If she came at another time, she was sure I would not know who she was. There was both truth and a degree of contrivance in Mrs A's somewhat melodramatic behaviour, which marked it as a hysterical regression rather than as an autistic state of alienation – yet that alienation is what is imitated. Mrs A lived permanently in a state of extreme anxiety; she feared her own or another's death at every moment. I became anxious that her reckless behaviour might end in suicide; however, her actions made me think, more than anything, of an accident-prone or drastically risk-taking child who is trying to alert one to something traumatic in its environment which it cannot formulate. When she was already a young adult, Mrs A's father had died, probably in a violent quarrel. Like much else in her life, his death left her predominantly with feelings of confusion and uncertainty rather than the emotions that should conventionally have accompanied the event. Her confusion was partly hysterical, so that she did not have to feel or think about where her father's death left her: did she love him or hate him? was she happy or sad that he was dead? However, it was also a 'genuine' expression of her uncertainty about whether he really was her father.

What, however, seemed to constitute the trauma was not the horror of the violent, disintegrating home which had been hers but rather that when Mrs A was two years old, her mother had taken her children and left her husband for a period of about three years. Apparently, before this, as a baby, Mrs A had adored her father. She didn't see him for a period that was too long for a young child to retain a memory and when she returned it would have been to a stranger. If her father was a stranger, then she could not be positioned as his daughter. She did not know where she was, or where she 'stood'. This was both experienced and also in hysterical fashion it was literalized when she herself had daughters: she could not stand up to walk.

To be placed in a position demands a perceiver of that position. It is not only a question of mirroring the baby to itself. On the death of his mother, Mr B put his anorak hood over his head and raced round with his 'crash helmet' on. When her father died in her childhood Mrs C, on the contrary, was already well armoured through some earlier instance or situation which she had experienced as traumatic and recovered from. However, when her father was finally taken off to hospital she recollected collapsing over his bed. She felt herself merging into the bed; she became both the bed and the father. At the same time she was told she would never see her father again. Language was also literal for Mrs C. Like Mr B, Mrs C never did 'see' her father again in any sense at all, for she could never thereafter either remember him or see him in her mind's eye. There was a conflict between the Oedipal excitement of having got rid of the father as a rival for her mother and of his becoming a missing 'father' who could not be seen. As a result of this conflict one of Mrs C's symptoms was fainting fits, in which she became temporarily the dead father. For all three of my patients, the physical literalness of their symptoms was what marked their condition as hysteria, for it showed a regression away from the possibility of representation to that of presentation.

Mrs A, Mr B and Mrs C all had difficulty finding their position in the world – for the parent who would have offered the key kinship position from which they could take their bearings was dead and so the experience of absence for Mrs A, of the dead persons themselves for Mr B and Mrs C, was mimetically identified with instead of being experienced as an event or person who was a separate object of concern. They simply could not imagine the parent. Not one of these three could see how hard it would have been for the parent to have lost the child: their own preceding traumatogenic states of not being recognized had been too severe. Without this concept of the loss of oneself to another there can only be unsymbolizable absence/emptiness or possession-as-presence in cults or nightmare. It is the loss of the self to the other in all its terror that the hysteric has to experience if he is to overcome his hysteria. Mrs A, Mr B and Mrs C all suffered from either being 'too much' there, filling all the available space, or alternatively from being non-existent, merging into the background; commensurately, not being able to understand another's loss, they could not perceive what it would mean for someone else to be without them. Hence, they did not have access to the play of presence and absence, existence and non-existence – the knowledge that, although they remained in the world, they were lost to their dead or abandoned (or abandoning) parent. But none of these three patients was only or entirely hysterical. Mr B, in particular, although he used hysterical mechanisms of identification, did not have many hysterical symptoms. He had been able to use his *identity* as his nanny's beloved baby, but he still could not find his *position* as his mother's son.

When the nuclear family disintegrates, the problem of the child is how to be a child without a parent. If a parent dies or disappears, where does the left-behind baby or child fit in? The question is one of positioning, rather than of identity. In terms of a position, the child who cannot understand what the dead person has lost cannot see himself alive from the tragic perspective of the dying parent. As a result of this missing position, he can only take up a stance of being the victim of the death; this orphanhood is not to be a positioned child but to be a person marked by death. The hysteric always presents as victim.

It may be that if one parent dies or disappears, for the child to ask for a history from the other parent is too intimate, incestuous; for it is to enquire only about the parents' relationship between themselves, as there is not a child position to ask about. The child then fantasizes about and is haunted by this exclusive parental relationship – its version of the primal scene. The parent does not even have to totally disappear; he or she may simply withdraw from the family through infidelity: thus, Dora thought about her parents to the exclusion of all else. This preoccupation in turn may lead to widespread sexualization of the surroundings. The death, or disappearance or betrayal of or by a parent captures the sexuality of the parents as a timeless icon. As I said before, this is the static icon of the dyadic primal scene rather than the moving possibility of the Oedipal triangle in which any two can always exclude a different third. Mr B had a horror that he wouldn't recognize his mother were she (secretly) to be still alive. He complained that his father never talked to his children about their dead mother – as indeed he may not have done, from the same sense of excess intimacy of the two-person primal scene that Mr B may have had. The potency of the idea that his mother might still be around somewhere suggests that, in this area of his mind, Mr B did not know death – as indeed young children do not. When he was shattered by his mother's death, he identified with her (the crash helmet) but could not be concerned about her because such concern would have necessitated being able to see from *her* perspective – a state which appears close but which is in fact a million miles away from the mimetic identification to which he had resorted.

Commentators on trauma often see it as a death-like experience. It seems rather, in fact, to be an experience of a violent gap which stands in for a conception of death, as a presentation rather than a representation of death. The patient who had a screen memory of the first time she stood up on the fridge illustrates some of the issues involved. Her screen memory *did* – as screen memories do – encapsulate the experiences of her infancy. When she was six months old, her mother had died of a septic abortion and her father had cared for her until she was about three years old. He then moved away to form a new family and left my patient in foster care. Excited and terrified at standing on her own two feet with her father's support (under the arms and then just by the fingertips), she collapsed psychically just after he left her for good. Of course she could not remember her mother's death, although she did have some recall of her father before he left. The screen memory, like the dream image, is a condensation of different losses and abandonments into an incident which, though probably unrelated, nevertheless serves to express the experience. All the elements in the condensation are probably accurate, but it is the congregation of them that produces a metaphor. It may have been her foster mother (not her father) who held her, on a table not a fridge (which would have represented her shivering cold with fear as well as inverting her 'hot' excitement), she may have sat down suddenly in the park – the factors that can be displaced and reunited in the image are endless.

The prolonged absence of the mother or key caretaker is thought to be experienced by the infant as a 'death'. This may be so – but it is in fact, of course, not a death. In time, through play and repetition the child realizes that absence and presence alternate. Death is something else: it is a loss that cannot be made good in actuality, only through memory. Memories are ways of thinking, not literal transpositions of actual experiences. The first time the patient who collapsed on the fridge 'remembered' her mother was in a dream during therapy: she dreamt she received a brief phone call from her. She was wittily ironic in recounting this long-awaited experience which was, however, an enormous relief. The form of the 'memory' was probably induced by the therapeutic transference – I sat out of sight behind her and offered some brief verbal comments or interpretations. However, this may well have 'joined up' with early experiences of her mother. Presaging recent work on infant responses, Freud commented in the last century on how hysterics construct fantasies from things that are heard but not understood in the earliest months of life. Through her dream, my patient could recognize for the first time that her mother had been alive and then that her mother *was* her mother. In time this recognition was enough to give my patient her own position. Through the transference to me, she realized that her mother had known she had a daughter.

It has been shown that, as small infants stare at objects, their motor activity begins to escalate about a second before they look away. At the height of that motor activity, the infant's visual attention disengages and the activity begins to subside.[19] This would seem to be the process that sets up Melanie Klein's notion of 'memories in feelings': the body retains what has been seen. The traumatized infant, however, continues to stare and its movements stay at excess peak levels: it cannot safely give up its object, nor therefore remember that object in its body. When the object has been given up and retained it will no longer be the object itself pure and simple, but the object in the context of the baby's feelings and, even more crucially, within a setting. By contrast, when the object has not been given up safely, then it features too much – and a replica of this excessive object will 'return' if some later occurrence breaks through the protective shield. This replica may seem to be the object or event itself, but it is not: it is a presentation of it.

To remember is always to discover, never to recover. An officer in the Great War, the psychoanalyst Wilfred Bion later wrote up his memoirs. In these he describes an incident in which a young messenger was about to reach him in the trench when he was hit in the chest and his throbbing heart and pulsating lungs were left hanging out. Before dropping dead, the soldier gasped, 'Will you write to my mother, sir?' to which Bion replied, 'Yes, damn you, I will.'[20] The violent, shocking image of the blasted chest is made particularly poignant by its being set in the context of social class – the 'sir' on the one hand, the 'damn you' on the other. This is memory.

Trauma, the incident that breaches the protective shield and opens up the traumatic response, makes the subject respond directly to neither the object nor the event itself, nor even to a memory-in-the-mind of it, but to the perception of that object or event. This may be a mental perception, or it may be enacted bodily. The fits, such as hysterical epileptic fits, that shocked people are subject to may be repetitions of the infant's bodily movements which become excessive when it is not safe enough to give up staring at an object. To discover a memory is to put that object in a particular context. If the infant is not traumatized, gradually its frantic movements will lessen and it will look away from the object and remember it in the body/I in the context of other objects, feelings and histories. As it ceases to be the focus of overattention, the object may be given up; the infant does not need to check it out to see that it is still there. The trauma victim oscillates between the poles of absolute absence and absolute presence, perception and non-perception. For the trauma victim to recover, however, absence and presence must become first loss and presentation in memories-in-the-body-ego, then representation and memory-in-the-mind.

The excess stimulation of the world which causes the breaching of the protective shield establishes the crisscross of traces along which this process of remembering will go – the marks on the wax of the magic writing pad. In a young baby, the 'too much' object becomes 'not too much', so that the baby can turn away from it. The breaching marks become marks through its protective shield along which memories may travel. If stressed too much the marks are not open but blocked with the excessive perception of the object or event. In hysteria, an object or event which has been experienced as 'too much' blocks the pathway for memory; all is perception. In hysteria if something is not there, then it is completely absent (not temporarily lost) and its presence is craved. An actual incident of abuse or specific trauma need not take place for there to be hysteria. Rather, hysteria models itself on trauma.

10

Hysteria: From Catastrophe
to Trauma

There is no way in which hysteria cannot exist: it is a particular response to particular aspects of the human condition of life and death. Cross-culturally and transhistorically, its modalities will vary, but these will all be variations on the theme of a particular way of surviving. There is the ego which is overinsistent because it is not felt to exist. Then there is the emptiness or absence in the hysterical subject which allows for possession by another; however, this is not the absence of some primordial self but of the necessary 'other' whose presence gives life its possibility and meaning. If one does not allow hysteria to disappear, there is another theory of psychoanalysis to be written – one which takes on the full import of the conflictual death and life drives constructed in the context of the condition of the prematurity of the human birth. But it is also one which must give full import to laterality – that horizontal relations can replace one and drive one back to those earlier states of depending on one's parents, first for survival at and after birth, and then for love and care within the Oedipal and preOedipal phases. But all theories need to take on board the full significance of the repeated feminization of hysteria.

For this feminization we also need to write in the parthenogenetic complex. The normal infantile fantasies of parthenogenesis need the differentiating prohibition from the mother: you cannot be a mother now, but you, a girl, can grow up to be one, and you, a boy, cannot. The hysteric refuses this law – continuing to insist that he can produce a baby from himself.

Unless we take hysteria into full consideration, the significance of much that we observe, as well as theorize about, will be missed. This is not an idle contention. No one working with the middle-aged multiple personality or with the charming borderline Don Juan or the teenage anorexic would necessarily be alert to the possibility of domestic violence to partner or child, the transmission of accident-proneness or even death by proxy which, with its powerful emotional exchanges between people, the overarching nature of hysteria allows. If, however, we reassemble these various conditions and illnesses under the umbrella framework of hysteria, then, with all the insight gained from their having been treated as discrete entities, we can make the connections first between them, and then between hysteria and the other missed dimensions of human behaviour.

Above all, we need to read our history backwards. Dethroned and displaced by the advent or overwhelming presence of the so-alike yet so-different sibling, and later by friend, colleague, enemy or partner, we seek out, through seduction, tantrums, the grandiosity of telling lies, and the demands of ill health, the love of our parents (or their substitutes) that we think has gone to our rival. Towards this rival we stand on the razor-sharp edge of ambivalence. I can well recall the day I dashed with joy in my feet and love in my heart to nursery school to tell my adored teacher of my brother's birth, only to meet her warm, enthusiastic question as to what he looked like with the firm reply, 'a bad egg'. My brother, somewhat jaundiced at birth, grew up with my jaundiced nickname for him well beyond infancy. When I commented to a patient that he presented his relationship to his family as though he were adopted, my patient responded by mentioning that, to this day, his elderly mother seethes with rage when she recalls how her older siblings insisted she was the child, not of their mother, but of a pastry cook of 'ill repute'. Little Hans thought storks would be better employed taking babies *away*. The Wolf Man's sister tortured and tormented him with his terror of animals and seduced him so that he did not know if he was her – or him. Mrs Peters had a pet hamster that her mother loathed but that she and her stepfather loved: her starving it to death coincided with the birth of the brother she so came to love. Actual siblings both as regards to their general position and as regards to their individual and incidental histories are clearly important. However, the major consideration is the introduction into psychoanalytic theory of laterality – it is one's horizontal, not one's vertical relations, that both threaten and confirm one. Ambivalence is the name of the game; torturing and being tortured is one set of rules. In time, we more or less sort out this ambivalence into who or what we like or dislike. Hysteria, however, reverts to this unbearable ambivalence of being. When Mrs A became confused as to whether or not her father was her father, she had returned from a three-year absence – a long time for a small child. However, in addition, on their reunion her parents conceived another child. Mr B's non-recognition of his mother certainly expressed the trauma of her death in his childhood. However, he also had no doubt his mother belonged to his brothers – only he, the youngest, was in doubt. His unconscious fear was that his birth had killed his mother and that therefore his live mother had only recognized his brothers as her sons. Even with Mrs C, the trauma that she had 'survived', which meant her father's death did not signify, was the death before she was born of a half sister (by a different mother). Her jealousy of the predecessor contributed to her not recognizing the significance of her father – nor of his death.

The emotional spur to both recovery and survival, on the one hand, and, on the other, to making the rival take possession of one's ghastly feelings and occupy one's marginal place, thereby leaving one centre stage, is jealousy. When loss of place and face is translated into surviving through getting what one wants, then envy is added to the green-eyed monster. From one's marginal place one seeks to be once more the only one for the mother or, failing that, the father. One craves to be all and everything for and to her. But with the awareness of the presence of a sibling this wanting is no longer that of the baby one once was. The insistence of the wanting, its desperation, comes from the child who has also most likely explored sexual pleasures with a friend or older sibling. Once wanting becomes sexualized, it is prohibited. If the child cannot give up the desperate wanting at this point, then the retreat to being at one with the mother becomes more urgent – the child wants to be her, giving birth as she does (but without a father), as well as being her baby. If something stands in the way of this fantasy, then the subject is exposed to the dangers of re-experiencing the terrors of human birth, at which death is an ever-present danger if someone does not answer one's cries. Here, the striving for life and the reaching backwards after what feels like death are experienced together. And here too we come full circle: every time a trauma or an accumulation of small traumata in later life occurs, this is the point to which we are cast back.

Starting off from the catastrophic displacement by the sibling or its substitutes, hysteria ranges from a temporary Oedipal response to a delusionary psychosis. Moreover, the one can slip into the other. In a footnote to the case of Frau Emmy Von N in *Studies on Hysteria*, Freud describes a hysterical girl, one of whose symptoms is a compulsive moving of her feet and wriggling of her toes – she is convinced that her feet are too big. One element in the manifold meanings attached to this conviction is that in childhood her siblings had relentlessly teased her about her big feet. In 1924 Freud added a further footnote: he had learnt that her hysteria had become a *dementia praecox* – in other words, a psychosis or schizophrenia. Hysteria is on a continuum at the psychotic end of which the hysteric is overwhelmed by death. Jacques Lacan considered male hysteria was always more serious than female hysteria. This is to miss the point: hysteria ranges from the near 'normal' to the quite mad. Our associations to masculinity and femininity are superimposed on this general condition. So a man thinking he is his mother simply appears more disturbed than a woman thinking she is her mother.

There is no question but that men can be hysterics. Galen affirmed this in the history of Western thought in the first century AD; it was soon rejected. It was revived deliberately in the seventeenth century, when it was once more rejected; the late nineteenth-century conviction of its prevalence was eventually not disputed. However, the whole category of hysteria was soon set to disappear. Hysteria has been noted by anthropologists in many regions of the world – from among the disadvantaged groups of the Samburu of east Africa, in west Africa and Indonesia, to the wild man behaviour of the Bene-Bene in New Guinea to the 'Arctic hysteria' of the Inuits of northern Canada. However, in Western accounts and in anthropological observations, as in psychoanalysis, there is a tendency to treat hysteria in the male as more serious than hysteria in the female so that, if it is recorded at all, it is frequently labelled 'hysterical psychosis'. More usual is that the notion of male hysteria is rejected, and then other categories are used to encapsulate acute hysteria and its male sufferers: melancholia and hypochondria in the seventeenth century; schizophrenia at the turn of the nineteenth century; traumatic neurosis and then 'borderline' after the two World Wars of the twentieth.

However, everywhere and at every time women are made to be the main carriers of the hysterical condition. This is true not only of times and places where the diagnosis of hysteria is made, but also of the subcategories and variations that come into being when hysteria is not in fact a term readily deployed in diagnosis: in this century, eating disorders, 'as if' personalities, borderlines, multiple personalities – all predominantly 'belong' to women.

Describing, let alone analysing, hysteria is beset with difficulties. But an attempt at even a partial understanding must take into account this gendering of a human condition; it simply does not make sense for us to relegate its gendering to a secondary position in any analysis. For this reason, Greek explanations of hysteria based on the womb, or medieval ones of intercourse with the (male) Devil, have a pertinence that is missing from many twentieth-century psychogenic explanations. An account such as that of Thomas Szasz,[1] which argues that hysteria is not a disease but a mimicry of a disease for the purposes of a malign form of communication, may have some validity but cannot explain the gender bias. This is true, too, of many other accounts.

Of course, one must ask whether hysteria itself has a gendered dimension or whether such an ascription is in fact an ideological imposition, by implication a derogatory way of describing women analogous to asserting the inferiority or degeneracy of a racial or ethnic group. In other words, are men and women equally prone to hysteria, but by and large women are more likely to be labelled thus? It would appear that women and hysteria are found synonymously unattractive, so a hysterical man is 'feminine'.

The human situation of premature birth makes both genders equally vulnerable to hysteria. The fact that we are born in such a state makes dependency on another human being stand in the place of instincts in the struggle for survival. The psychoanalytic concept of a 'drive' addresses this: a drive is a force that impels the subject to release a state of untenable tension. But, in order to achieve its aim, the drive comes up against the condition of our neonatal need for an object, another human being (or even a wolf mother). Such an instinct exists irrespective of who or what the object is. A drive always heads for an object, but its destination, its object, is not fixed. A drive is not gendered, nor is premature birth, nor the resulting human dependency in which the all-important object is bound to be loved and hated. Therefore, none of these factors common to us all can account for hysteria falling into the lap of women.

However, the different placing of girls and boys, men and women, within kinship relations does expose women more than men to the possibility of a hysterical reaction to dependency. Siblings are differentiated according to gender within kinship systems. The femininity of hysteria has been structurally established by human social organization, by the different positioning given to girls and boys. Only then does custom follow this social organization with a value system. The prospect of death stands at the threshold of life for everyone because those who care can also kill, but because of socially ascribed value this human vulnerability is differently figured for girls and boys. For instance, in most cultures infanticide of girls is more common than infanticide of boys. (This is not true, however, in sub-Saharan Africa, where the exchange of bridewealth, as opposed to dowries, gives value to women.)

The classical psychoanalytic account explains both the possibility of male hysteria and the far greater prevalence of female hysteria in terms of the Oedipus complex. In this theory, both boys and girls initially desire their mother; then, in the course of events, both come to accept that this desire is taboo. The boy hopes one day to be a father in his own right with a woman of his own, so long as he accepts first and foremost his own father's claim to his mother. The girl, however, accepts that she can never possess the mother nor her substitute as her love object; instead, she must first give her mother up and then identify with her, then become a love object for the father. This normative trajectory is beset with more difficulties for the girl than for the boy because she must change both her object (mother to father) and her sexual zone (from clitoral/phallic activity to vaginal receptivity) on the model of her secondary identification with her mother. Within this theory, the greater difficulty of her task is the explanation of her greater proclivity to hysteria: she is 'more' bisexual because she first wants her mother, then she must become the object of her father. Moreover, she is not so subject to the strictures of the castration complex as the boy since she is already lacking the phallic possibilities of attaining her mother – she thus has less of a superego (the internalization of the father in the castration complex) and as a consequence less of a role in culture. As has often been said, femininity is the good end and hysteria the bad end of this Oedipal trajectory. The hysteric refuses to settle for her role as object of desire for a man (initially the father), but instead roams ceaselessly between this feminine identification as object of desire and the masculine position of subject of desire. So reads the classic account.

In the Oedipal account, all the symptoms and characteristics of hysteria are quantitative consequences of this different position between girls and boys in relation to their parents. For the girl, there is more need to pursue identifications, more shame, more anxiety, a greater likelihood of regression to bodily expressions of trance, possession, conversion symptoms, above all to complaint, grudges and longing for what one has not got. It is easy from here to see simply a way of righting the balance and suggest that, since the deprived are the hysterical, ending deprivation will end hysteria. But this is in itself a hysterical solution. Hysteria is not feminine; on the contrary, it is that girls and boys are structurally put in different places. The place of the girl or boy may be rich and famous, but it is their position relative to their 'others' that counts. Everyone experiences the displacement by lateral relations; it is the hysteric who cannot overcome this – cannot find his own position as both the same as and different from his rivals. Instead he turns this displacement into an ineradicable trauma.

Only for male hysteria is this the dominant ascription. Motherhood has often been proposed as a cure for female hysteria – this can be so because what the hysteric unconsciously cannot face is sexual reproduction as opposed to parthenogenetic procreation. Sexually reproductive parenting implies the future death of the parent in the birth of the offspring; accepting this allows psychological motherhood and fatherhood to take place.

In its account of the consequences of Oedipal difference, psychoanalytic theory joins up with other explanations, seeing a girl's deprivation as genital (she has not got the phallus the mother desires) rather than social in the wide sense of the term. The problem with this arises the moment one tries to fit male hysteria into the scheme. According to the Oedipal theory the male hysteric has adopted a feminine position for his hysteria. If he moves searchingly across the bisexual possibilities, whenever he tries to be an object for a man his stance becomes homosexual, and when he desires a woman then he happens to look like a normative heterosexual male. Of course, neither is the case: Don Juan, the male hysteric, is not taking a woman as a love object; he has utterly identified with her. He projects his rampant jealousy into a series of women making them enact what he would otherwise feel. The story is not about his conquests but about the jealousy which he stirs up in these women. In this he behaves as any good hysteric would when threatened by the unbearable feelings which well up within him when he is displaced. His list of conquests amplifies his narcissism to make him feel at the centre of the universe.

He is also identified with the women he seduces. But his jealousy having been projected into the women, he has to move on in order not to feel it by identification. Projecting it has also further emptied him. Don Juan, however, brings us back to the possibility that men and women are equally liable to hysteria, but that in our prejudice we see only the woman as hysterical. In the classical psychoanalytic account, the hysteric of either sex has not accepted the taboo on the relationship with the mother. The notion of a castration complex depends on a social law assuming its meaning from a biological condition. The law prohibits incest with the first object of love and care; both sexes are subject to it. But the physiological difference between their genitalia confirms their different social fate: girls must be like mothers and boys must aspire to possess their replacements. Social prescription refers to biological sex differences. However, the idea that there are psychical consequences to anatomical differences, while probably correct, is also unnecessary. It is redundant as an explanation. It is the kinship displacement of the girl, rather than her socially inscribed definition of anatomical 'inferiority' that renders her more subject to the more visible dimensions of hysteria – it is this which sets up a social relationship between femininity and hysteria which is then wrongly read as necessary. There is no difference between male and female hysteria. However, the girl may be more often or more seriously displaced within the patrilineage than the boy. She may overcome her displacement or she may treat it hysterically. Social displacement, not the hysterical possibility to which it can give rise, is what distinguishes girls from boys. The mistake of seeing male and female hysteria as different, or hysteria as female/feminine results from us ignoring lateral sibling or quasi-sibling relationships. The minimal difference between brothers and sisters is the difference that must be socially established. It is here that various relationships are encouraged or forbidden. It is here that sexuality is first realized and prohibited.

I am not for one moment suggesting that the infant's relationship to its mother and father are not crucial, nor am I disputing the existence and significance of Oedipal and castration fantasies. However, both from clinical material and from the exigencies of the theory, a social description that finds its explanation within a social experience seems to me to make better sense than one that rests on a different field. Biology is, of course, extraordinarily important, but it does not provide the meaning of the social. If we consider what happens when the child is displaced by a sibling or lateral substitute or must abandon its near-complete identification with a sibling, then its position, the place where it is recognized as existing, is pulled away from under it. Everyone, in different degrees, has this experience. In this crisis of annihilation, when the 'Thrones and Altars' of childhood fall, the child will seek, in Oedipal ways, to regain its foothold, its meaning, its position. Given the universality of kinship systems which variously differentiate along gender lines, the dethronement will be different for girls and boys. Sexuality – even indeed biological sexual differences – takes on its meaning within kinship. This, too, shows the strength of the understanding of the Oedipus and castration complexes. The problem of that theory, however, is that it gives attention *only* to vertical intergenerational relationships at the expense of lateral sibling and affinal ones. Additional problems about understanding hysteria are raised in many theories, in particular Object Relations theory, because they also propose a developmental perspective where the clinical material of hysteria (and the theories of Freud) indicate that we should always be aware of regression.

When his sister Hanna is born, Little Hans is no longer his mother's baby: the question is not *who* is he, but *where* does he stand now his place has gone? Hanna is like him, but not him – love and murderousness are the emotions that arise towards one who is like enough to be adored and so alike as to need to be killed. To regain his place and escape his overwhelming, self-destroying, chaotic emotions, Hans wants to be his mother's baby again – but he wants this with all the energy of his 5-year-old self; there is nothing passive here. But also, in order not to lose his mother to his sister Hanna, he becomes like his mother – able to have babies, just as she can. So he identifies with some conjuncture of mother and baby. But that conjuncture is one of life and death and his own violence repeats the violent experience of a human trauma, a neonatal vulnerability to death. The violence he feels towards his rival sibling and towards his mother for her betrayal brings with it the terror of punishment. It is now that the father, as father of his sibling, mate of his mother, comes into the picture, with the prohibition, the law of what Lacan calls the Symbolic Order, the castration complex. Hans would like to kill his father for giving his mother this baby sister – instead, he develops a phobia so as not to have to witness the death and devastation to which his wishes would give rise. Hans will not leave the house in case he sees a horse whose fall metonymically slips and slithers as an enactment of his mother in the throes of childbirth and his father falling down dead. But he fears his father will kill him. We must add: he also needs to acknowledge his mother's prohibition – he cannot make babies either now or in the future if he is to be a 'boy' and a 'man'.

If Hanna were to die, as Freud's brother Julius died, there would be less chance of reparation, of making up for the fantasized murder through future love of the sibling and its replacements – no honour, love, affection, nor troupes of friends. Or if, like Hamlet or Don Juan, no sibling were to be born, his mother's inevitable withdrawal would become a point of obsession. Then, as well as brothers to surpass, every woman, every Ophelia or Donna Anna, would be the threatening sister, the replica of the subject who is yet so different; who was so wanted, but ambivalently so – and who in this case has died before she was conceived. It is telling that both Tirso da Molina and Shakespeare imagine their hysterical fictional characters as only sons, *fils uniques*. It is not, of course, that only children are more liable to hysteria on the contrary, it is that the hysteric is fighting to be an only child – a *fils unique* – and Hamlet and Don Juan are pertinently pictured as having succeeded in this.

A youngest child is, as far as hysteria is concerned, a variation on this theme. Like the only child, he unconsciously expects a repetition of himself which is not forthcoming, but he will also have formed a crucial aspect of his sense of his position in an identification with an older sibling. Freud's case presentation of an infantile neurosis, popularly known as the history of the 'Wolf Man', named after a traumatic dream (actually a nightmare) the small boy had of wolves, shows a version of the hysterical response to an older sibling. The Wolf Man suffered in early childhood from anxiety hysteria manifest at first by spectacular animal phobias. He had been a very quiet baby; his elder sister had been the tomboy, mischievous, very tormenting of her younger brother, sexually provocative and very clever. Between his second and third year, his sister had seduced him into sexual games. He had refused these seductions but started to behave sexually with his 'Nanya' (who was a complete mother substitute). His sister's seductions and tortures transformed the quiet boy into a wildly misbehaving, almost 'lunatic' child. Without doubt, his sister (displaced on to a servant girl with the same name), in his fantasies and in his behaviour, could be said to have taken precedence over his Oedipal Nanya/mother.

Freud's reason for not integrating the sister into the etiology of the Wolf Man's psychopathology is that this would make the power games of rivalrous siblings rather than the prohibition exemplified in the castration complex (and failure of the prohibition) determinate of psychic life. Freud had got near to this idea of the importance of superiority and inferiority in his early writings on hysteria. Subsequently a bowdlerized version of it had been advocated by Alfred Adler in his theory of the 'masculine protest' against the femininity of dependency.[2] Adler replaced sexuality with a drive to power – no one wants to be powerless, as is the feminine position. Such an argument still underlies many non-psychoanalytic accounts of hysteria and needs to be examined. However, bringing in laterality and the sibling does not, in my opinion, necessitate a shift of emphasis from the disturbances of psychosexuality to the more anodyne problem of power play. Power and rivalry are obviously present – but it is not these that are determinative.

If we see the transformation of the Wolf Man's infantile character as an identification with the 'wicked sister' (becoming as 'impossible' as she was), then power play may be an expression of the ensuing conflict. However, the conflict itself does not arise from a power struggle but from a catastrophic confusion as to where the Wolf Man stands in the family. Before this he seems to have taken literally (as hysterics do) his Nanya's metaphorical statement that he is 'his father's baby': a strand in his unconscious psychic thinking is that he was born from his father and that he can be his good baby. However, when he is about two years old, his parents take his older sister away with them on a trip, leaving him behind; subsequently, his father clearly prefers his sister to the little boy (as his mother has always done). By becoming awful like his sister, he gets not only attention but also the prospect of a favoured place like hers. This place is intricately bound up with sexuality; to be like a boy, paradoxically, he must become his tomboy sister; but, if he is a boy, he must also want his sister as a sex object (and then his Nanya/mother). From this perspective the mistake in the case history comes when Freud interprets the Wolf Man's gloss on his sister's seduction. The little boy has been passive and resistant but his later fantasy is that it is he, and not his sister, who has been the active, aggressive initiator of the sexual play between them. Freud explains this as the boy's masculinity asserting itself. It may be that the older Wolf Man thus edits his earlier history in favour of masculinity, but it is a mistake for an analyst or theorist to follow suit. The Wolf Man becomes wild and aggressive – like the sister – after the seduction. The seduction of a small child with not as yet fully formed boundaries would indeed induce such a bodily identification with the wild, aggressive, seducing sister – it is for this reason that sexually abused children become sexually precocious. For the Wolf Man it is not power play but the permutations of sexual positions and identifications within his extensive family and household of servants that are at stake.

Dora, another younger sibling, is exiled from her identification with her older brother at the age of six or seven, when, in my interpretation, the doctor fails to recognize that, though a girl, she too can masturbate and be like her brother. Experiencing this catastrophe as traumatic, she becomes hysterical and tries to avoid the strictures of the Oedipal and castration complexes into which such an exile casts her. The younger Wolf Man, aged two or three, is not exiled from a place but rather made to become utterly identified with his bad sister through sexual games and socially through this being the only place recognized by both parents. Once he has lost the position of being his father's baby there is no distinct place for him. He is not trying to find a place as one of three within an Oedipal triangle; he is having a nightmare in which his discrete existence is threatened. The nightmare of annihilation is followed by the 'bad dream' of a dyadic primal scene which utterly excludes him. He then has an Oedipal relationship with his Nanya/mother and his father. The fact is that he cannot entirely become his sister because, firstly, she is the preferred older child and he is not, and, secondly, because he must also want her as an object just as his father seems to do. The emotions of hate, love and the lust for preference and power may give form to these strivings for a position where he is recognized. The content of the striving is a conflictual sexual struggle in which he is baby, sister, mother . . . Power struggles *succeed* the loss of recognition and position, at the core of which is sexual rivalry with the one whom he must love as himself.

The struggle is not, Who am I? but, Where am I?; not one of identity (though it is often confused with this) but of, What is my position in this kinship scenario? Mrs Peters had been the beloved heir of her stepfather, accompanying him to work and to football matches until a younger half-brother was unexpectedly born: she was lost, and enacted her lost self by losing objects that stood for her former relationship with her father. Rosenfeld's patient Mildred felt nothing when her popular younger brother was killed in the war, but subsequently she broke down completely. His birth had triggered an infantile crisis: 'From the time she first saw Jack [her brother] she became completely silent and withdrawn . . . Not only did she give up speaking for a considerable time, but her ability to walk suffered as well', and later, 'She had quite consciously tried to adopt his personality and his interests, but had failed.'³ Not speaking and not walking are states to which later hysteria commonly reverts.

A younger sibling is a repetition of the older child, occupying the place it previously had; an older sibling monopolizes the place the subject thought it shared. The response is like the territoriality of many animals transposed into the context of human kinship – if one's space is invaded, this is experienced as what indeed in a sense it actually *is*: a catastrophe. More often than not, this displacement is a more serious and more long-lasting catastrophe for girls than for boys. Everyone has to try to overcome the catastrophe – find another place, or room within the same space, get on with the other occupant. Agnatic kinship systems (relationships through the male which are everywhere the most common) are slanted to favour boys in this endeavour: at the simple level boys are sons and heirs irrespective of sibling rivals; they are thus preferred.

At a deeper level, once flung on to the Oedipal constellation, the inevitable catastrophe of the annihilation of the subject by the advent of the sibling is displaced on to the trauma of the castration complex. According to classic psychoanalytic theory, castration is only recognized as a possibility when it is discovered that the penis is absent in the woman; femininity is construed as the 'already castrated'. That castration then symbolizes death or annihilation of the subject is thus socially determined. For, beneath this is the ungendered, unsymbolized danger of death in the fact of birth. The castration complex with its gender implications symbolizes this death. The male hysteric, however, who does not take on board the castration complex (the 'Vagina Man') is testimony to the fact that an unsymbolized death which can be sought and dreaded without being understood is not intrinsically gendered. It may be equally traumatic to discover that one cannot produce babies parthenogenetically and that reproductive sexuality implies the death of the parent. Everyone has actual or possible siblings, everyone is therefore cast back thereby to the life/death struggle, to a state of psychically being or not being. If the child accepts the taboo on what I have called the parthenogenetic complex, then the way is open for the acknowledgement of the other in sexual reproduction. It is here that kinship systems and social mores come in to differentiate between the sexes – a mother is always known, not so a father. Polyandry is very rare so customs such as polygymy have been largely non-reciprical between women and men.

A resolution of the Oedipus complex is the dominant theory and practice of psychoanalysis. Overcoming this is the desired path of both masculinity and femininity. The failure to achieve this, however, is not, as is commonly contended, the same as hysteria. The normative path of femininity and masculinity actually resolves the parental relationship; castration becomes the trauma that replaces the catastrophe of where one cannot be, which is with the mother. The hysteric, however, stays stuck with the catastrophe of displacement by a sibling which throws him or her into the Oedipus complex, the primal scene and helplessness of premature birth, all of which he protests against by fantasies of parthenogenetic omnipotence and by overasserting a self that has also gone absent.

Without a lateral axis to the theory, there is no place in it for the male hysteric to take up residence, except in the place of the woman: in the dominant psychoanalytic theory and practice he is therefore feminine or homosexual. This means that it is not recognized that homosexuality, heterosexuality, femininity and masculinity, are only variations on a fictive normality; in themselves, in fact, they cannot be either actually normal or actually pathological. Indeed they are not the proper objects of psychoanalytic research into the unconscious and sexuality at all. Because of a bisexuality in everyone, hysteria is far more likely to be heterosexual than homosexual in both men and women. However, even if a mass of children result from this heterosexuality, the hysterical position is a non-reproductive one. The basic fantasy here is a parthenogenetic one in which the baby is a reproduction of the subject.

A catastrophe is an event which produces a change in the order of things – it may be disastrous for a time, but it can be overcome. The word 'trauma' comes from the Greek word for a 'wound' – the psychoanalytic use of it carries over its physical implications into the psychical: a wound, experienced as a violent shock, affects the whole organization. Hysteria makes an individual or collective trauma out of a catastrophe. When the Taita woman had a shock on seeing a car in an unusual place, followed by an attack of *saka*, she was converting a change in the order of things into a personal violent shock which affected her whole being: a catastrophe became a trauma. At one end, hysteria is harmless, even funny and inventive, an emptying-out of the subject that can be a prelude to creativity; at the other is the major trauma into which a catastrophe, minor or major, can be converted and a lifetime spent protesting it.

In itself the sibling situation is catastrophic, not traumatic. Entering the Oedipus complex seems the solution to the catastrophe of the displacement by the sibling, but this incestuous hope of being the mother's only love is vanquished by the trauma of possible castration. Woman, constructed as the one who is 'already castrated', is the site of that trauma for men, but can she be so for women as well? There is no doubt that women featuring in dreams and nightmares do sometimes symbolize a trauma as an experience of castration. It is here in having turned the catastrophe into trauma and that trauma then being symbolized as castration that hysteria comes to seem more typically feminine – the fate of women. This can take its rightful place in the theory when we see that men must also submit to a prohibition on their parthenogenetic fantasies – they have to become 'those who cannot give birth'. Castration introduces only *one* mode of symbolization. Biologically there is, of course, in infancy and childhood no other part of the external body that can be generically missing according to gender in the same way as the penis. The penis seems so highly cathected and crucial because it is a means of linking people. The penis also seems to have a life of its own. But hysteria indicates that the fullness and emptiness of the erotic breast and fullness and emptiness of the womb as a reproductive organ are also both highly cathected. The womb, in particular, is also a representation of something that can be missing and which seems to have a life of its own (not only for the Greeks). The small child plays with the fullness and emptiness of the tummy/womb. The fat belly of having eaten well or of pregnancy is also an external sign of absence and presence. Freud dreams of his mother as miraculously thin after the birth of his brother: the hysteric asks about the absence and presence of the full/empty womb and, like the small child who puts a cushion up its jumper, sometimes tries it out for himself in phantom pregnancies or persistent fantasies of parthenogenesis. The future, as with the future of the phallus, is different for girls and boys: one can, the other cannot grow up to conceive. Just as a little girl may want a penis, so Little Hans is determined not to be left out of pregnancy or giving birth.

Trauma is reached in the regressions of hysteria. What follows is an enactment of the trauma that has apparently broken and effracted the boundaries which protect the subject, leaving him or her with no 'I', just a conflict of forces or fragmentation by terror. The 'original' trauma manifests as a death drive. Pontalis writes of the death drive (which he calls 'pulsion' and which has been unfortunately translated as 'instinct'):

The introduction of the death instinct as referent or as primal myth confronts us with another problematic which 'narcissistic personalities' and 'borderline cases' are making us increasingly aware of. In this instance, the psyche becomes a body. 'What does that mean?' becomes 'what does that want?' Death is no longer localized in the consciousness or in the unconscious, it is at the very roots of the unconscious. It is no longer the property of one psychical instance, but the principle of 'discord' in each one of them. It is a-topia. It is no longer speech but silence, cries or fury . . .[4]

We can read 'hysteric' here for both narcissistic and borderline cases. The trauma at the origin of life introduces discord which can only be enacted as something compulsive, driven, a violence that cannot be remembered but only activated when a subsequent trauma throws the subject back into its vortex. At this point, the mind becomes the body and wants and wants – there is no meaning – as a bid for survival. In turning the catastrophe into a trauma, the hysteric becomes driven, expressing reiterative wanting through his body.

It would seem that Freud could not think through the death of his younger brother in early childhood. Like a symptom, this fact both usefully preserved the notion of trauma as crucial to the whole edifice of his psychoanalytical theory and at the same time prevented its importance from ever being realized fully in that theory. Defensively, Freud always tried to throw the emphasis on castration in relation to the father rather than on the death wishes towards siblings that confirmed the terror of being murdered and murdering in infancy. The formulation of the Oedipus and castration complexes hid the death of Julius Freud, sibling rivalries and deaths that could have been Freud's own, from the practice and. theory of psychoanalysis.

Hysteria, which opened the door, was pushed out of the room or made to conform to the Oedipal–mother problematic; the trauma is represented by castration alone.

Shortly before the fantasies of the origins of hysteria that Freud devised with Ferenczi and never published, he wrote to his younger colleague of a fainting fit he had had in Jung's presence: 'the attacks point to the significance of cases of death experienced early in life (in my own case it was a brother who died very young, when I was a little more than a year old). The war dominates our daily life.'[5] With Ferenczi Freud worked out an idea of the origin of hysteria in human history. This fantasy of the phylogenetic location of hysteria was that in the first Ice Age, when there was insufficient food for survival, all reproduction had to be curtailed. Though Freud did not chart how he had arrived at this notion, one can see that, from the individual case, one can construct the myth of a world historic trauma (the Ice Age), sexuality without procreation, starvation to death (anorexia). Even icy coldness fits in; the hysteric is frequently cited as experiencing 'cold' – he reverses the heat of passion into the cold of death and vice versa. (The hysterical fits I have witnessed or heard described resemble the juddering of hypothermia rather than epilepsy.) Individual hysteria combines these key features and provides the material for the phylogenetic fantasy.

It is psychical processes, whether in dreams or in the symptoms and formations of neuroses, whether as defences, resistances, or as the psychotic mechanisms (such as splitting and dissociation) and neurotic ones (such as repression), which are the proper object of psychoanalysis. The hysteric forms symptoms through processes of conversion, his anxiety produces phobias, fits, breathing difficulties, and so on. A symptom contains conflict. It is here, in the question of the symptom and its conflict, that the problem with accounts of hysteria as the result of a power struggle or of powerlessness need to be located.

Elaine Showalter's study *Hystories* privileges powerlessness. However, there are problems with such an account. I have not had first-hand access to Weir Mitchell's case report of Robert Conolly, the watchmaker who suffered from hysterical movements described as pendulum spasms. Showalter discusses him, so I am using Conolly simply to make a point. Had Conolly only felt inarticulate frustration at his job, as Showalter suggests, it is highly unlikely he would have compulsively swung his arms like a pendulum. The driven quality, the very real inability to stop, suggests something else at play as well – something which made its presence felt insistently. This is the compulsion of the death drive; he could not stop. Conolly had a thought which he could not fully repress: he may, for instance, have been well aware of Voltaire's famous comparison of God to a watchmaker. Such hubris would have to have been repressed; when the idea returned from the failed repression, it made a compromise with the ego which had repressed it – otherwise it would not stand any more chance of expression than the original idea. This compromise becomes the symptom. With the wit of the unconscious, the watchmaker who wants to be God finds that, as Voltaire said, it is God who is the watchmaker. We can only speculate – my point is that some such conflict of a wish for omnipotence and a prevention of it would be needed to explain the compulsion of his movements. The Taita woman who wants to suck her husband's blood needs a trance state, a demanding sprite within, or a frantic, breathless body, to allow the expression of this unacceptable wish. What the ideas and wantings have in common is not power or powerlessness; it is that they insist on recognition, but are simultaneously unacceptable.

When the child is replaced by the sibling, initially this feels like annihilation; 'murder' is the reaction of the fittest. But the child also more or less simultaneously loves its replica as the child was itself loved when it was a baby. However, the child also fears that if that other baby can die, or even be affected by murderous wishes, then what distinguishes it from the child itself? Although based on this, murderous feelings towards a rival are not only directed towards the sibling. They can come up whenever it seems there is a need to save oneself from the catastrophe of someone else's demands which suggests that they, not the subject, need attention: 'I have told you,' she said, 'that I was not fond of the child. But I might add that one could not have guessed it from my behaviour. I did everything that was necessary.' This is Frau Emmy in 1895. And Anne Sexton of her eldest daughter in 1957: 'I've . . . never loved Linda . . . Something comes between me and Linda. I hate her, and slap her in the face – never for anything naughty; I just seem to be constantly harming her.'[6] Sexton wrote a poem expressing the not-unusual experience that a growing daughter steals a mother's being.

I suggest experiences of annihilation of the subject through dangers of death and trauma at the origin of human life, to which the hysteric in part regresses, give rise, not to wish-fulfilling dreams, but to nightmares. The fulfilment of a wish in a dream is supposed to ensure sleep. One wakes screaming from the nightmare because one is disappearing, being killed, or destroyed in some way. Over fifty years ago, Ernest Jones, the only psychoanalyst to study nightmares in depth, interpreted them Oedipally. Is this correct? The nightmare can be alarmingly full of bizarre happenings and objects because one imagines one's absence through this sort of monstrous plenitude. Children, still finding their place in the world, have lots of nightmares. The *Studies on Hysteria* are replete with appalling nightmares. 'She had had some fearful dreams. The legs and arms of the chair were all turned into snakes; a monster with a vulture's beak was tearing and eating her all over her body . . . she had been going to pick up a ball of wool, and it was a mouse and ran away . . .'[7] Was there an element of wish-fulfilment on Freud's part that from the material of *Studies on Hysteria* he wrote instead *The Interpretation of Dreams*, an account of dreams fulfilling what one wants?

Between the nightmare and the dream are 'bad dreams' – these are unpleasant but not so utterly terrifying as nightmares. Bad dreams are, I suggest, survival dreams in which, in a confused way, one maps oneself on to the person on whom one is utterly dependent so as not to lose the love, which would be tantamount to dying (as I have described how Don Juan or Limentani's 'Vagina Man' become the woman in order to avoid the nameless dread of bad dreams). After a bad dream of Freud's, from the height of his hysterical period, he woke in a terrible fright, having in his dream dissected his own pelvis, which left him in doubt of the strength of his legs. This is a useful example of a 'bad dream' because it shows the difference between a 'good dream' and a 'bad dream'. In a good dream, the ego is mobile, occupying different people in different stances. In a bad dream this ego mobility is excessive, frantic and bizarre. We can see how such excess is linked to survival in a bad dream such as Freud's, where, in another part of it, he is at one moment a baby being carried, but also himself carrying out his self-analysis and himself having to cross a bridge towards old age and death as his father had done; in having his pelvis dissected he is also a bleeding woman. Bad dreams offer the chance of identification in the interests of survival, but they are full of incongruous juxtapositions suggesting the iterativeness and compulsiveness of the strategy: the ego is not mobile so much as driven from pillar to post.

Dreams enable the dreamer to sleep by giving the dreamer what he wants; bad dreams offer survival strategies; nightmares enable the dreamer to wake up. The dreamer of a nightmare experiences death but he can scream himself awake. Identified with the dead, the carnage has happened, but when he awakes he is still there. After a trauma such as the experience of war, the nightmare enables the traumatized to 'die' safely. Without the useful nightmare, the vulnerability of living and waking is much greater. But by not overcoming a catastrophe and instead experiencing it as a trauma, a hysteric typically subjects himself to repeated nightmares, such as are common with children.

I have called the advent of a sibling, or the discovery that one is not the same as one's elder sibling, or that no sibling arrives and hence must have died, a catastrophe – not a trauma. A catastrophe is the event that produces the overthrow of a certain order of things: this is exactly the sibling predicament. Winnicott wrote of patients who always feared a catastrophe was about to happen and who needed to come to realize that it had already happened when they were too young to make sense of it; this was a catastrophe not a trauma. A trauma is a wound, a breaching of the body or psyche. A catastrophe can be overcome. On the contrary, although a trauma heals over, the scar of the wound is always there. The notion of castration is a notion of trauma – a psychic breach expressed as a body wound. Carnage in war may trigger hysteria, but if the hysterical combatant can realize that this is a catastrophe not ultimately a trauma, then he will recover. If, on the other hand, not getting what one wants is experienced as a traumatic wound, then instead of being able to ask: 'What does this sibling's presence mean? Where did it come from and where does it place me', the hysterical response will be to convert that question of the mind's meaning to the body's wanting: he will be forever hungry and craving. Instead of understanding what has happened, the hysteric suffers for ever his physical emptiness. If only I can get enough milk, buy enough clothes, suck his blood, watch him play football, have his bandolier . . . I will survive. Anne Sexton wrote, 'This [wanting] is like pills or drugs but much more complex . . . The aura of this thing is more strong than alcohol.'[8] Both Anne Sexton and Don Juan eventually die of their wanting, a hunger that invites death to a feast. One can perhaps only grasp this move from the displacement of the catastrophe to the wound of trauma through metaphor. A wound is gaping, it leaves the subject empty, driven to fill up the cavern that has opened up. A catastrophe demands that one shift perspectives, sees the situation differently.

The hysterical movements, actions, identifications and demands to satisfy the wants are designed to restore the order of things before the catastrophe struck. From this arise the manipulativeness, the histrionic protests, the complaints, the victim status, the pseudologia. In order not to think about a catastrophic situation, the hysteric has a traumatic reaction and this has to be repeated over and over again.

The real shock of displacement, then, is replenished by an act which treats displacement as traumatic. The triggering 'trauma' thus is often trivial (the striking of a match for the Taita woman) but the displacement that it recollects was probably particularly catastrophic. The tram man described by Eisler and redescribed by Lacan was addicted, not to his pains but to his hospital treatment with surgical instruments. A minor accident at work when he fell from his tram entailed the dread and excitement of an internal examination. This awoke his parthenogenetic fantasies and was experienced as the exciting and dreadful trauma of a mother with a dead baby being dismembered inside her which he had witnessed as a child. But also, hysterically bisexual, in his chest pains the tram man became Adam whose rib produced Eve. The hysteric has regressed in such a way to such fantasies that the triggering catastrophe is incomprehensible and so, because it is incomprehensible, it is traumatic. It is not, then, that it has necessarily really taken place at an age prior to comprehension, as Winnicott suggests, but rather that something from early experience is being used to express a catastrophe that is experienced as a trauma.

Freud commented already in the 1890s that hysterics make use of words that they have heard as early as six to eight months. These are not, of course, understood at the time, but are later unconsciously used to turn the catastrophe into the trauma on which to base the symptoms. The Wolf Man as an adult produces bowel pains and bowel dysfunction, but he does not want to change (or cannot change) the catastrophic situation in which he finds himself. His symptom is modelled on some abdominal pains suffered by his mother during his infancy. He had overheard his mother tell the doctor, 'I cannot live like this.' At the time he had not understood what she meant but when in later life he wants to both preserve the *status quo* and at the same time complain that it is intolerable, he produces this symptom to enact her words. But this symptom is also associated with his infantile fantasy that babies are born anally – which makes him, a boy, as eligible as his mother for their production.

The trauma that is used cannot be consciously remembered – indeed, it may not even have been one's own trauma that has to be enacted. The children of Holocaust survivors tend towards hysteria: their parents' real trauma is their children's catastrophe, but the children treat their catastrophe as though it were a trauma. Of course there are as many variations as there are individuals. But with their own history blasted, with no kinship, no nation, no homeland, no generally shared basis but the traumatic emptiness of their suffering, the parents would have had no place from which to 'recognize', that is to say, from which to position their own children. The children experience the catastrophe of non-recognition, but enact instead their parents' trauma. Annie, a survivor's child, was a luminously beautiful blonde ghost; ten days into her therapy with me she made a suicide attempt with consequences that prevented my seeing her again except on a visit to her in hospital. I had not had sufficient time with her to do anything more than register that this attempt felt like a message that there was not yet enough of her to talk about, and what there was of her was an identification with something she experienced as having died in her parents. She had presented herself as somehow 'absent'. Then she had to enact and make real this absence by a suicide attempt.

The pattern for a hysterical reaction is, then, one that moves from a shock in the present to a catastrophe in the past to enacting a trauma, using any real trauma or the potential trauma at the origin of life. The shock may be either a present trauma which may be very real, as in war, or it may be fabricated from nothing, such as was most likely the case with the *saka* fit that was induced by the striking of a match. The trauma shock, serious or trivial, causes a breach that 'empties' the subject. If the hysterical reaction stops there, as it often does when the present trauma is real, it will wear itself out, as Rivers noted among his patients in Craiglockhart in the First World War. In this instance of a response to overwhelming violence there is first a short circuit back to the earliest trauma of helplessness. Recovery will involve realizing that, as a survivor of the violence in which one's brother soldiers have died, one is heir to a new order, but not guilty of their death, even if it was unconsciously wished. It is a catastrophe. If, however, the hysteria is more entrenched, then the present trauma/shock will act as an overlapping event on the structural catastrophe of having been displaced in childhood, which will then be experienced and used as an earlier trauma. The traumatic element in the vulnerability of human infancy is everybody's lot, but its degree will vary individually, as will our ability to overcome it or live with it. Its expression is some version of death and brings with it the quality of the drive to death – insistent and compulsively repetitiousness. It is the danger of death that the hysteric turns into excitement.

Death by identification is crucial to hysteria. Sometimes this may be an essential way of registering the death of others. In modern warfare, with its minimal ritual, the problem is not that the shell comes too quickly for registration, but that death, or even total decimation, happens too fast. An identification with the dead, feeling paralysed like the dead, mute like the dead, deaf like the dead, is a necessary psychic stage; nightmares from which one can awake are part of the process of survival and recovery. Playing dead has featured in accounts of hysteria both throughout history and cross-culturally. What are some of hysteria's most commonly repeated features, such as breath-holding, choking 'to death', if they are not death experiences from which (hopefully) one can return? 'Often, very often, Sylvia [Plath] and I would talk at length about our first suicides [*sic*]; at length, in detail, and in depth between the free potato chips . . . We talked death with burned-up intensity, both of us drawn to it like moths to an electric light bulb sucking on it,' writes Anne Sexton.[9]

Imitation of death can be a brief early stage in the process of accepting the loss. If it becomes entrenched, then we have hysteria; the compulsion displays the dread and the excitement behind the imitation. For instance, at a girls' school in Lancashire in the mid 1960s there was an outbreak of an illness in which the girls were 'dropping, slumping over desks, feeling sick and having difficulty in breathing'. Tension and anxiety were noted. It was thought to be caused by a virus, then diagnosed as encephalitis and then as 'winter vomiting disease'; toxic fumes were seriously considered as a possible cause and demolishing potentially dangerous buildings was talked about. The disease was reported in other girls' schools without connections being made. The *British Medical Journal* discussed the incident. *The Times* of 16 October 1965, however, concluded its reports with an editorial:

Vapour or Virus?

The unfortunate schoolgirls . . . are perpetuating a mystery which has baffled the medical profession for some thirty years. Periodically throughout this period there have been similar outbreaks of fainting and collapse mainly among schoolgirls . . . So far as it is known viruses have no particular predilection for either sex . . . [It is] mooted that hysteria may play a part. To make such a suggestion in these days of scientific materialism is verging on *lèse-majesté* but it is a possibility that cannot be ruled out with absolute certainty . . .[10]

There was only one reported observation from a victim. This was a year later, when one of the girls told her doctor on a routine visit to his surgery that they had started to feign illness as a joke, but then found they could not control their subsequent actions or mental state. The summer and autumn of 1965 had witnessed major outbreaks of polio. The girls could have been playing with their anxiety and excitement about death but then their 'anxiety' started to play with them. The hysteric cannot control his symptoms, whether it is gasping for breath (hysterical asthma) or compulsive rhyming. Anne Sexton became very frightened by the fact that she could not stop rhyming. The compulsion, the repetitiveness, that takes over the hysteric is the mark of an originary trauma, a manifestation of the death drive.

It is the compulsive element that differentiates hysterical conversion symptoms, even behaviour, from psychosomatic illness. It indicates the switch from catastrophe to trauma. By experiencing a catastrophe (outbreaks of polio, syphilis, TB, cholera, the plague, all of whose symptoms have been convincingly mimed in hysteria) as a trauma, hysteria moves the catastrophe into the realm of the death drive: a drive towards the inorganic, towards annihilation that can only be repeated as a way of ensuring one has survived it. In order to ensure his survival, the hysteric turns the danger into excitement. To do this he uses the body which would have experienced the original catastrophic blow, but he uses it sexually, with all the rhythms (including the rhythms of rhyming) which mark autoeroticism. It is the autoeroticism of the child who is exploring how he might give birth.

In the turning of a catastrophe into a trauma, the serious hysteria sufferer shifts the register from a position or place in any world order into a crisis of identity. The 'Where am I?' becomes the 'Who am I?' The hysterical recovery will then come at an individual level through a reassertion of grandiosity, a regression to the stage of when one was 'His Majesty the Baby', the omnipotence alternating with helplessness before one had a position within the social system. Focusing on identity, there is either no 'I' at all, or alternatively nothing but an 'I'. On the one hand, the 'I' has been evacuated and the very emptiness it leaves draws the other in to fill it up. On the other hand is the aggressive, assertive 'I', as illustrated by the demanding aspect of the wanting or seduction. The process is also evidenced in groups: the grandiosity of political rhetoric, of nations after defeat, are obvious examples. There is likewise too much 'I' in the lie. It is an assertion suggesting that the world is 'as I say it is', yet the construction of the lie also demonstrates that there is too little of the subject. The lie occupies its utterer and takes over like an incubus; the true liar cannot stop, he is in the grip of a fantasy that possesses him and from which there is no going back. When a histrionic drama of excessive self-assertion is in full swing, it will always be found to be replete with lies – they take over without conscious volition by the subject. It is nearly impossible for another person to break into the immaculate fiction. In the first place, it is very difficult to detect, as the liar has unconsciously worked so hard, collecting evidence from wherever he can, to construct his alternative, fabricated world; his degree of absolute conviction carries conviction. If one does detect the lie and one does break in, the liar can go berserk – for to find a crack is to find the catastrophic absence of the subject beneath the carapace of the lie.

It is insufficiently appreciated that the free association of psychoanalysis interrupts the lie. The truth asserts itself as much through the body as in the words that arise against the ego's censorship. Becoming subject to the processes of the unconscious, to the slip of the tongue or pen, the associations to a dream, the play of one's fingers, the movement of one's symptoms, is to have the chance to learn something true about oneself. More importantly, this subjection of oneself to a force that comes from within, but is beyond one's control, is to accept that the world is larger than oneself. However, the serious liar does not (or cannot) free associate; the manifestations of the unconscious do not break through for him. The lie is immaculate.

Hysteria's moment is the moment when the displaced ego reasserts itself as a subject, fragile but too insistent. The Oedipal drama it plays out is on a stage; hysteria is not a malnegotiation of the Oedipus complex but an enactment of it, a masquerade of object relations in the service of narcissism. In so far as hysteria is gendered female, it is because human cultures, by and large, hand on the name and all that goes with it to the son and heir while the girl is displaced and put in *her* place. When she turns her catastrophe of displacement to trauma, the trauma that is found to dominate is castration – her place is 'to be castrated'. But the male hysteric can simply hide his hysteria by presenting it as merely a subplot. Don Juanism appears heterosexual and normative but the women are not true objects of Don Juan's love. Rather they are either an audience to his autoerotic narcissism or repositories into which he projects the wild play of the desperate travails of a jealousy no less violent than that of the *sar*-possessed Somali women whose polygynous husbands are moving on to another wife.

Most psychoanalytical theory added the importance of the pre-Oedipal mother to that of the father. It is this mother that feminism has explored in order to understand femininity. But there is no pre-Oedipal mother – or rather, she is the caregiver, for better or worse, before she is Oedipalized by the displaced child regressing to demand that it will be her only lover. This Oedipalized mother then prohibits the child's fantasy of parthenogenetic procreation: You cannot make babies. If this prohibition is accepted and the possibility abandoned and mourned, then the girl will grow up to be in the position of the mother (in whatever way – actual or symbolic – she may use it), but the boy will not. This prohibition we might call 'The Law of the Mother', on a par in principle with 'The Law of the Father' in the castration complex. In principle, because kinship practices and ideological stances obscure it; hysteria reminds us of its existence because the hysteric flouts it. No more than he has accepted the law of the castration complex, has the hysteric accepted the prohibition on parthenogenesis: he continues to make babies in his fantasies or to treat real ones as though they were his clones. Because our theory and our observations have missed this, so too have we continued to miss the male hysteric. And of course it works the other way round too: without an awareness of male hysteria we can miss the parthenogenesis prevalent in all hysteria, miss the cloning in the mind of the apparently 'normal' heterosexual wife and mother. Hysterics – and the hysterical in all of us – use partners only as audiences to their parthenogenetic creations – but somewhere these audiences are never good enough, nor do these cloned babies satisfy. Finally, hysteria leaves the hysteric craving, like the Taita, whose endless wanting, like that of the nostalgic child or reminiscing adult, can be temporarily released through the body's antic dances, but returns to plague them another day. The violent demands and disputes of heterosexual marriages and partnerships, the sororities and fraternities of adolescent hysterical illness, are testimony to the love/hate relationship of siblings or sibling substitutes, to which, for better and worse, lateral relationships of friends and enemies, peers and partners are heir.

The autotraumatism of hysteria, the wiping out of the self can, along with its identifications, be preconditions for fantasy and creativity. Hysteria is part of the human condition, the underbelly of 'normality'; it can move in the direction of serious pathology or in the direction of creativity in life and art. Yet either pathologically or creatively, it is a way of overestablishing one's uniqueness in the world where one both is and is not unique, a way of keeping control of others where one both does and does not have such control. If the work of art, which has been made possible by the induced trauma offering the possibility of a new beginning, still remains only at a hysterical level, then there will be too much of the creator in the work. The hysteric is an author in search of her characters; for it is the display of the artist herself that dominates the picture.

The hysteric's dramatic engagement with other people led to an understanding of how the individual psyche is constructed from its relationship to others in the Oedipus complex. But this apparent engagement with others is, for the hysteric, only a masquerade. The prevalence of male hysteria led immediately to its elimination in the Oedipus theory and thereby the disappearance of the category from psychiatry and psychoanalysis. It continues, however, a very active life as a popular designation indicating clearly that we cannot lose it. We need to resuscitate the category. Hysteria, if seen, offers an important challenge to how we think about ourselves as 'self' and 'others'.

Reading hysteria along a horizontal as well as a vertical plane changes our mapping of human relations. In the social world it opens up reflections on contemporary familial and sexual patterns, on questions of creativity in current performance theory and of the prevalence of evil in today's Iagos.

Why at the beginning of the twenty-first century have I partially returned to Freud's work to consider some aspects of the question of hysteria? Most obviously, Freud's theory is still immensely influential in the Western world – even if it is the focus of criticism or refutation. There are probably few places where we could have learnt more about hysteria than in psychoanalysis – and initially the gain was mutual. The importance of unconscious processes – the thrust of the psychoanalytic endeavour – was revealed largely through hysteria. What happened? The subsequent history of the relationship between the two virtually occluded hysteria: certainly, little progress was made. Psychoanalysis concentrated on other issues and hysteria was said to have 'disappeared'. Undoubtedly, something went wrong in our understanding of hysteria in psychoanalytic theory. One mis-direction, or missed direction, took place after the First World War with the failure to use the problems raised by the similarities and differences between traumatic and hysterical neurosis in men to question elements of the psychoanalytic edifice. The situation is being repeated yet more widely today when trauma is once more being used as a catch-all term.

The problem was inherent from the outset with the recognition of male hysteria, and simultaneously, but largely unconsciously, with the need to assign hysteria to women and both to marginality. To understand how hysteria is a possible universal response we need to look at lateral relationships of sameness and difference, uniqueness and replication. This involves more than just adding siblings (however different cultural groups may define them) to the Oedipal recipe and mixing. Inserting lateral relationships enables us to see the partheno-genetic complex, which reveals another axis of sexual differentiation, another prohibition and 'law'. Beyond this, hysteria insists that we notice 'siblings'; seeing 'siblings' forefronts hysteria as a persistent feature of the human condition.

Notes

1 Hysteria

1 Harris, G. (1957), p. 1046.
2 See Veith, I. (1965), p. 148.
3 Ibid., p. 169.
4 *The New Encyclopaedia Britannica* (1991), p. 6207.
5 Veith, op. cit., p. 209.
6 Slavney, P. (1990), p. 190.
7 It is easy to see how this approach has developed out of American ego psychology, but to trace this is beyond the scope of this book.
8 Personal communication from Dr Sidney Carlish, Birmingham (1986).
9 Freud, S. (1910), p. 47.
10 Freud, S. (1916–17), pp. 333–4.
11 Freud, S. (1900–1), pp. 250–51.
12 Winnicott, D. W. (1936), p. 47 and in Winnicott, D. W. (1975).
13 Showalter, E. (1997), p. 63.
14 Cited in Anderson, P. (1999), p. 24.
15 See Felman, S. (1983).
16 Eliot, T. S. (1963), p. 34.

2 Sigmund Freud: A Fragment of a Case of Hysteria in a Male

1 Masson, J. (ed.) (1985), p. 261 (14 August 1897).
2 Freud, S. (1925), p. 15.
3 Masson, op. cit., p. 412 (7 May 1900).
4 Ibid., p. 181 (14 April 1896).
5 Freud, S. (1900–1), p. xxvi.

6 Masson, op. cit., p. 202 (2 November 1896).

7 Ibid., p. 204 (22 November 1896).

8 Ibid., p. 230 (11 February 1897).

9 Ibid., p. 198 (29 September 1896).

10 Ibid., p. 147 (31 October 1895).

11 Ibid., p. 152 (29 November 1895).

12 Ibid., p. 73 (21 May 1894).

13 Ibid., p. 183 (26 April 1896).

14 Ibid., p. 243 (16 May 1897).

15 Ibid., p. 311 (18 May 1898).

16 Ibid., p. 317 (20 June 1898).

17 Otto Weininger took the credit for the idea. Fliess alleged that Weininger got it from his friend Otto Swoboda, who was Freud's patient, and hence from Freud, who told his patient of Fliess's idea. Confusion and ultimate break-up is not uncommon in creative relationships (as in marriages). It has always struck me as curious that no one mentions it in the case of the end of the close friendship of Joan Rivière and Melanie Klein. Rivière wrote a most interesting paper on primal jealousy; Klein renewed her own fame with a theory of primal envy. In Rivière's theory there is an initial jealousy of actual or potential siblings; in Klein's, an envy of all the mother possesses. Subsequently Klein, however, headed the monograph 'Envy and Gratitude', in which she worked out her theory, with a quotation from Saint Augustine about infantile *sibling jealousy* – which suits Rivière's thesis much better than her own.

18 Masson, op. cit., p. 433 (25 January 1901).

19 Ibid., p. 456 (11 March 1902). Subsequently, Freud was to postpone publication of his work frequently.

20 Ibid., p. 457. *n.* 1.

21 For reasons to do with recognition (see chapter 9), names are very important. Fliess's only daughter was called Pauline and his son Conrad. 'Conrad' was Freud's nickname for his own troublesome bowels!

22 Masson, op. cit., p. 392 (21 December 1899).

23 Ibid., p. 269 (3 December 1897).

24 Winnicott, D. W. (1956), pp. 300–305.

25 Masson, op. cit., p. 301 (10 March 1898).

26 Ibid., p. 33 (6 November 1898).

27 Ibid., p. 255 (7 July 1897).

28 Ibid., p. 261 (14 August 1897).

29 Ibid., pp. 391–2 (21 December 1899).

30 The degree of this restriction is culturally specific. In the dream books of

the ancient Greek physician Artemidorus there is the category of (a man's) dreams of intercourse with the mother. The meaning of the dream depends on the posture assumed in the intercourse.

31 Masson, op. cit., pp. 272–3 (15 October 1897).
32 Ibid., p. 328 (27 September 1898).
33 Ibid., p. 268 (3 October 1897). Julius died at the age of six months on 15 April 1858. Sigmund Freud was probably born on 6 May 1856.
34 Freud, S. (1900–1), p. 483.
35 Ibid., p. 253.
36 Ibid., p. 252.

3 Dora: A Fragment of a Case of Hysteria in a Female

1 Freud, S. (1905), p. 75.
2 Ibid., pp. 44–5.
3 Ibid., p. 116.
4 Ibid., p. 115.
5 Ibid., p. 49.
6 Ibid., p. 59.
7 Ibid., p. 69, *n.* 2.
8 ibid., p. 70.
9 Ibid., pp. 75–6.
10 Ibid., p. 18.
11 Ibid., p. 22.
12 Ibid., p. 44.
13 Ibid., p. 82, *n.*
14 Masson, J. (ed.) (1985), p. 329 (27 September 1898).
15 Freud, op. cit., p. 56.
16 Cited in Carter, K. C. (1983), pp. 186–96.
17 Freud, op. cit., p. 73.
18 Lacan, J. (17 July 1949) and in Lacan, J. (1966).
19 Winnicott, D. W. (1968).
20 Freud, op. cit., p. 60.

4 Where Has All the Hysteria Gone?

1 Micale, M. (1995).
2 Ibid., p. 29.
3 Trillat, E. (1986), p. 274.
4 Slavney, P. (1990), p. 190.
5 Forrester, J. (1997).
6 Libbrecht, K. (1995), p. 217.
7 Abraham, H. C. and Freud, E. L. (eds.) (1965).
8 Libbrecht, op. cit., p. 135.
9 Ibid., p. 221.
10 Middlebrook, D. W. (1991), p. xiv.
11 Rivers, W. H. R. (1920), p. 2.

5 Sexuality, Death and Reproduction

1 Middlebrook, D. Wood (1991), pp. 147–8.
2 Ibid., pp. 147–8.
3 See chapter 1, *n.* 12 above.
4 Dostoevsky, F. (1880), pp. 119, 130.
5 Freud, S. (1928), pp. 182–3.
6 Eisler, M. J. (1921).
7 Lacan (1956).
8 Deutsch, H. (1947).
9 Eisler, M. J., op. cit., p. 272.
10 See Conran, M. (1975).

6 From Hysteria to Motherhood

1 Cited in Showalter, E. (1997), p. 74.
2 Rosenfeld, H. (1947), p. 20.
3 Erikson, E. (1964).
4 Rivière, J. (1932).
5 Lacan, J. in J. Mitchell and J. Rose (eds.) (1984).
6 Deutsch, H. (1947), vol. 1, p. 109.
7 Brenman-Pick, I. (1995).
8 Deutsch, op. cit., vol. 2, pp. 240, 289.

9 Ibid.
10 Breuer, J. in P. Cranefield (1958), p. 319.

7 Emptiness and Possession

1 Macfarlane, A. (1970).
2 Evans-Pritchard, E. (1937).
3 Grubrich-Simitis, I. (1997). For details of this bilingual Hebrew/German Bible, published by the Philippson brothers in Leipzig in 1858, see D. Anzieu (1986), particularly pp. 301–9.
4 Brooks, P. (1993), p. 227.
5 Freud, S. (1895), p. 181.
6 Brooks, op. cit., p. 229.
7 Ibid., p. 1.
8 Middlebrook, D. W. (1991), p. 194.
9 David-Ménard, M. (1989), p. 61.
10 King, H. (1993), p. 28.
11 Green, A. (1993).
12 Foster, B. (1986).
13 Lewis, I. (1986), pp. 38–9.
14 White, A. (1993), pp. 41–2.
15 Davis, N. Zemon (1995).
16 Goody, E. N. (1970).
17 White, op. cit., p. 42.

8 The Hysterical Lie

1 Rank, O. (1975), p. 38.
2 Freud, S. (1926), p. 112.
3 Limentani, A. (1984), p. 203.
4 Williams, B. (1981), p. 117.
5 Klein, M. (1925) and in Klein, M. (1975), vol. IV.
6 Brenman, E. (1985), pp. 423–32.
7 Klein, M. (1937), p. 323.
8 Bion, W. (1970), pp. 102–3.
9 Corradi Fiumara, G. (1992), p. 82.
10 Ridley, M. R. (1965).
11 Corradi Fiumara, G., op. cit., p. 16.

9 Trauma

1 Caruth, C. (1996).
2 Freud, S. (1910, 1963), p. 31 (10 January 1910).
3 Freud, S. (1909), p. 66.
4 Freud, S. (1885), p. 233.
5 Masson, J. (ed.) (1985), p. 207 (6 December 1896).
6 Freud, S. (1926), p. 194.
7 Freud, S. (1915), p. 194.
8 Ibid., p. 194.
9 Derrida, J. (1978), p. 202.
10 Crews, F. (1994), p. 206.
11 Hacking, I. (1995), p. 246.
12 See Makari, G. J. (1998).
13 Herman, J. (1992), p. 126.
14 Crews, op. cit., p. 206.
15 Green, A. (1976).
16 Williams, D. (1993).
17 Alvarez, A. (1992), p. 52.
18 Williams, op. cit.
19 Robertson, S. Research in process reported in the *Cornell Chronicle* (10 December 1998). Robertson's interest is in the baby's foraging of the new environment; my emphasis is on the opposite – on how the object to be lost is 'retained'.
20 Bion, W. (1997).

10 Hysteria: From Catastrophe to Trauma

1 Szasz, T. (1961).
2 Adler, A. (1910).
3 Rosenfeld, H. (1947), pp. 130 and 131.
4 Pontalis, J.-B. (1981), p. 189.
5 Masson, J. (ed.) (1985), p. 440 (9 December 1912).
6 Middlebrook, D. W. (1991), p. 73.
7 Freud, S. (1895), p. 62.
8 Middlebrook, op. cit., p. 147.
9 Ibid., p. 107.
10 The incident is reconstructed and described in Wijewardene, G. (1976).

Selected Bibliography

Abraham, H. C. and Freud, E. L. (eds.) (1965) *A Psychoanalytic Dialogue. The Letters of Sigmund Freud and Karl Abraham 1907–1926*. London.

Abraham, K. (1927) 'The Psycho-sexual Differences Between Hysteria and Dementia Praecox' in *Selected Papers of Karl Abraham*. London.

Adler, A. (1910) 'Inferiority Feeling and Masculine Protest' in H. L. Ausbacher and R. R. Ausbacher (1956) *The Individual Psychology of Alfred Adler*. New York.

Alvarez, A. (1992) *Live Company: Psychoanalytic Psychotherapy with Autistic, Borderline, Deprived and Abused Children*. London.

Anderson, P. (1999) *The Origins of Post-modernity*. London.

Anzieu, D. (1986) *Freud's Self-analysis*. London.

Appignanesi, L. and Forrester, J. (2000) *Freud's Women*. London.

Balint, E. (1963) 'On Being Empty of Oneself' in J. Mitchell and M. Parsons (eds.) (1994) *Before I was I*. London.

Balint, M. (1952) *Primary Love and Psychoanalytic Technique*. London.

Barker, P. (1995) *The Ghost Road*. London.

Bart, P. B. (1968) 'Social Structure and Vocabularies of Discomfort: What Happened to Female Hysteria?', *Journal of Health and Social Behaviour* 9, pp. 188–93.

Bart, P. B. and Scully, D. H. (1979) 'The Politics of Hysteria: The Case of the Wandering Womb' in E. S. Gomberg and V. Franks (eds.) *Gender and Disordered Behaviour: Sex Differences in Psychopathology*. New York.

Bateson, G., Jackson, D. D., Haley J. and Weakland, J. (1956) 'Toward a Theory of Schizophrenia' in *Behavioural Science* 1, pp. 251–64.

Bernheimer, C. and Kahane, C. (1985) *In Dora's Case: Freud–Hysteria–Feminism*. New York.

Bion, W. (1962) 'A Theory of Thinking', *International Journal of Psycho-Analysis* 43, pp. 306–10.

(1970) 'Lies and the Thinker' in *Seven Servants: Four Works*. London.

(1970) 'Attention and Interpretation' in *Seven Servants: Four Works*. London.

(1991) *A Memoir of the Future*. London.

(1997) *War Memories 1917–19*. London.

Bowlby, J. (1952) *Maternal Care and Mental Health*. World Health Organization.

(1953) *Child Care and the Growth of Love*. London.

Brenman, E. (1985) 'Hysteria', *IJPA* 66, pp. 423–32.

Brenman-Pick, I. (1995) 'Concern – Spurious or Real?' *IJPA* 76, pp. 257–70.

Breuer, J. and Freud, S. (1895) *Studies on Hysteria*, see Freud SE2.

Bronfen, E. (1998) *The Knotted Subject*. Princeton.

Brooks, P. (1993) *Body Work: Objects of Desire in Modern Narrative*. Cambridge, MA.

Butler, J. (1994) *Bodies That Matter: On the Discursive Limits of 'Sex'*. New York.

(1998) *Excitable Speech*. New York.

Bynum, W. F., Porter, R. and Shepherd, M. (eds.) (1998) *The Anatomy of Madness: Essays in the History of Psychiatry*. 3 vols. London.

Carter, K. C. (1980) 'Germ Theory, Hysteria, Freud's Early Work in Psychopathology', *Medical History* 24, no. 3, pp. 259–74.

(1983) 'Infantile Hysteria and Infantile Sexuality in Late Nineteenth-century German-language Medical Literature', *Medical History* 27, no. 2, pp. 186–96.

Caruth, C. (1996) *Unclaimed Experience: Trauma, Narrative and History*. Baltimore.

Charcot, J.-M. (1889) 'Clinical Lectures on Diseases of the Nervous System', W. F. Bynum and R. Porter (eds.) (1991).

Cixous, H. (1981) 'Castration or Decapitation?' *Signs* 7, no. 1, pp. 36–55.

Colonna, A. and Newman, L. (1983) 'The Psychoanalytic Literature on Siblings' in *The Psychoanalytic Study of the Child*, vol. 38, pp. 285–309.

Conran, M. (1975) 'Schizophrenia as Incestuous Failing'. Paper to the International Symposium on the Psychotherapy of Schizophrenia (August 1975). Oslo.

(1984) 'Fantasies of Parthenogenesis in Schizophrenia' in *Confidential Bulletin of the Psychoanalytical Society*. London.

Corradi, Fiumara G. (1992) *The Symbolic Function: Psychoanalysis and the Philosophy of Language*. Oxford.

Cranefield, P. F. (1958) 'Josef Breuer's Evaluation of His Contribution to Psychoanalysis', *IJPA* 39, pp. 319–28.

Crews, F. (Nov. 1993 and Dec. 1994) 'The Unknown Freud', *New York Review of Books* and in Crews, F. (1995) *The Memory Wars: Freud's Legacy in Dispute*. New York.

Darwin, C. (1872) *The Expression of the Emotions in Man and Animals*. New York.

David-Ménard, M. (1989) *Hysteria from Freud to Lacan: Body and Language in Psychoanalysis*. Ithaca.

Davis, D. A. (1990) 'Freud's Unwritten Case', *Psychoanalytic Psychology 7*, pp. 185–209.

Davis, N. Zemon (1995) *Three Women*. Cambridge, MA.

Derrida, J. (1978) *Writing and Difference*. Chicago.

Deutsch, H. (1934) 'Some Forms of Emotional Disturbances and Their Relationships to Schizophrenia', *Psychanalytical Quarterly* (1942), vol. II, p. 301.

(1947) *The Psychology of Women: A Psychoanalytic Interpretation*. Vol. I, *Girlhood*. Vol. II, *Motherhood*. London.

Donnet, J. and Green, A. (1997) *L'enfant de ça. La Psychose blanche*. Paris.

Eisler, M. J., (1921) 'A Man's Unconscious Phantasy of Pregnancy in the Guise of Traumatic Hysteria', *IJPA* 2, pp. 255–86.

Eliot, T. S. (1963) *Collected Poems, 1909–62*. London.

Erikson, E. H. (1964) 'The Inner and Outer Space: Reflections on Womanhood' in *Life History and the Historical Moment* (1975). New York.

Evans, M. N. (1991) *Fits and Starts: A Genealogy of Hysteria in Modern France*. Ithaca.

Evans-Pritchard, E. E. (1937) *Witchcraft, Oracles and Magic Among the Azande*. Oxford.

Fairbairn, R. W. (1954) 'Observations on the Nature of Hysterical States', *British Journal of Medical Psychology* 27, pp. 105–25.

Felman, S. (1983) *The Literary Speech Act: Don Juan with J. L. Austin, or Seduction in Two Languages*. Ithaca.

(1993) *What Does a Woman Want? Reading and Sexual Difference*. London.

Ferenczi, S. (1909/1952) *First Contributions to Psychoanalysis*, M. Balint (ed.). London.

(1950) *Further Contributions to the Theory and Technique of Psychoanalysis*, M. Balint (ed.). London.

(1955) *Final Contributions to the Problems and Methods of Psychoanalysis*, M. Balint (ed.). London.

(1968) *Thalassa*. New York.

(1988) *Clinical Diary*, J. Dupont (ed.). Cambridge, MA.

(1993–6) *The Correspondence of Sigmund Freud and Sándor Ferenczi*, E. Brabant, E. Falzeder, P. Gampieri-Deutsch and A. Haynal (eds.). Cambridge, MA.

Figlio, K. (1978) 'Chlorosis and Chronic Disease in Nineteenth-century Britain: The Social Constitution of Somatic Illness in a Capitalist Society', *Int. J. Health Services* 8, pp. 589–617.

Finney, G. (1989) *Women in Modern Drama: Freud, Feminism, and European Theater at the Turn of the Century*. Ithaca.

Flaubert, G. (1857) *Madame Bovary*. Paris.

Forrester, J. (1997) *Truth Games: Lies, Money and Psychoanalysis*. Cambridge, MA.

Fortes, M. (1949) *The Web of Kinship among the Tallensi*. London.

Foster, B. (1986) *Heart Drum: Spirit Possession in Garifuna Communities of Belize*. Belize.

Foucault, M. (1976) *Madness and Civilization*. London.
(1978) *The History of Sexuality: An Introduction*. Vol. I. London.
(1980) *Herculine Barbin: Being the Recently Discovered Memoirs of a French Hermaphrodite*. New York.

Freud, A. (1937) *The Ego and Mechanisms of Defence*. London.
(1968) *Indications for Child Analysis and Other Papers*. London.

Freud, S. (1953–74) J. Strachey (ed.) *The Standard Edition of the Complete Psychological Works of Sigmund Freud*. 24 vols. London.
(1885) 'Report on Paris'. SE1.
(1895) *Studies on Hysteria*. SE2.
(1900–01) *The Interpretation of Dreams*. SE4 and 5.
(1905) 'A Fragment of an Analysis of a Case of Hysteria'. SE7.
(1909) 'Analysis of a Phobia in a Five-Year-Old Boy'. SE10.
(1910) 'Five Lectures on Psycho-analysis'. SE11.
(1913) 'The Theme of the Three Caskets'. SE12.
(1913) *Totem and Taboo*. SE12.
(1915) 'The Unconscious'. SE14.
(1916–17) *Introductory Lectures on Psycho-analysis*. SE16.
(1918) 'From the History of an Infantile Neurosis'. SE17.
(1919) '"A Child is being Beaten": A Contribution to the Study of the Origin of Sexual Perversions'. SE17.
(1920) *Beyond the Pleasure Principle*. SE18.
(1923) 'A Seventeenth-century Demonological Neurosis'. SE19.
(1923) *The Ego and the Id*. SE19.
(1925) 'An Autobiographical Study'. SE20.
(1926) *Inhibitions, Symptoms and Anxiety*. SE20.

(1928) 'Dostoevsky and Parricide'. SE21.

(1963) *Psycho-analysis and Faith: The Letters of Sigmund Freud to Oskar Pfister*. H. Meng and E. L. Freud (eds.). London.

(1965) *A Psycho-analytic Dialogue: The Letters of Sigmund Freud and Karl Abraham 1907–26*, H. C. Abraham and E. L. Freud (eds.). London.

(1987) *A Phylogenetic Fantasy. Overview of the Transference Neurosis*, I. Grubrich-Simitis (ed.) London.

(1993) *The Correspondence of Sigmund Freud and Sándor Ferenczi*, E. Brabant *et al.* (eds.). Vol. I 1908–14. Cambridge, MA.

Gay, P. (1988) *Freud: A Life for Our Time*. New York.

Gilman, S., King, H., Porter, R., Rousseau, G. and Showalter, E. (eds.) (1993) *Hysteria Beyond Freud*. Berkeley.

Goldstein, J. (1991) 'The Uses of Male Hysteria: Medical and Literary Discourse in Nineteenth Century France', *Representations* 34, pp. 134–65.

Goody, E. N. (1970) 'Witchcraft among the Gonja' in M. Douglas (ed.) *Witchcraft, Confessions and Accusations*. London.

Goody, J. (1962) *Death, Property and the Ancestors*. Stanford.

(1987) *The Interface Between the Written and the Oral*. Cambridge.

Green, A. (1976) 'The Dead Mother' in *On Private Madness* (1986). London.

Green, A. (1993) *Le Travail du negatif*. Paris.

Grubrich-Simitis, I. (1997) *Early Freud and Late Freud*. London.

Hacking, I. (1995) *Rewriting the Soul: Multiple Personality and the Sciences of Memory*. Princeton.

Hare, E. (1991) 'The History of "Nervous Disorders" from 1600 to 1840, and a Comparison with Modern Views', *British Journal of Psychiatry* 159, pp. 37–45.

Harrington, A. (1988) 'Hysteria, Hypnosis, and the Lure of the Invisible: The Rise of Neo-mesmerism in Fin-de-siècle French Psychiatry' in vol. 3 of W. F. Bynum, R. Porter and M. Shepherd (eds.) *The Anatomy of Madness* (1998). London.

Harris, G. (1957) 'Possession "Hysteria" in a Kenya tribe', *American Anthropologist* 59, pp. 1046–66.

(1978) *Casting Out Anger: Religion among the Taita of Kenya*. Cambridge.

Harris, R. (1991) *Introduction to Clinical Lectures on Diseases of the Nervous System, by J.-M. Charcot*. London.

(1988) 'Melodrama, Hysteria and Feminine Crimes of Passion in the Fin-de-siècle', *History Workshop* 25, pp. 31–63.

Herman, J. L. (1992) *Trauma and Recovery: From Domestic Abuse to Political Terror*. New York.

Hunter, D. (1983) 'Hysteria, Psychoanalysis, and Feminism: The Case of Anna O', *Feminist Studies* 9, no. 3, pp. 464–88.

Hurst, L. C. (1982) 'What was Wrong with Anna O?' *Journal of the Royal Society of Medicine* 75, no. 2, pp. 129–31.

Hutschemaekers, G. (1988) 'Hystérie, cent ans après – résumés'. Abstracts of papers delivered at the seventh annual conference of the Association française de psychiatrie, Paris, January 22–4, *Psychiatrie française* 19, special number.

Israël, L. (1979) *L'Hystérique, le sexe et le médecin*. Paris.

Jennings, J. L. (1986) 'The Revival of "Dora": Advances in Psychoanalytic Theory and Technique', *Journal of the American Psychoanalytical Association* 34, pp. 607–35.

Jones, E. (1931) *On The Nightmare*. London.

Jorden, E. (1971, 1603) *Brief Discourse of a Disease called the Suffocation of the Mother*. New York.

Khan, M. R. (1974) 'Grudge and the Hysteric' in *Hidden Selves: Between Theory and Practice in Psychoanalysis* (1983). London.

King, H. (1993) 'Once Upon a Text: Hysteria from Hippocrates' in S. L. Gilman, H. King, R. Porter, G. S. Rousseau and E. Showalter (eds.) *Hysteria Beyond Freud*. Berkeley.

Klein, M. (1975) *The Writings of Melanie Klein, Vols. I–IV*. London.

(1925) 'The Psycho-Analysis of Children'. Vol. III. London.

(1937) 'Love, Guilt and Reparation'. Vol. I. London.

(1957) 'Envy and Gratitude'. Vol. III. London.

(1945) 'The Oedipus Complex in the Light of Early Anxieties'. Vol. I. London.

(1961) Narrative of a Child Analysis. Vol. IV. London.

Kristeva, J. (1986) *The Power of Abjection*. New York.

(1989) *Black Sun: Depression and Melancholia*. New York.

(1995) 'Hysteria – A Counter-transference Phenomenon' in *New Maladies of the Soul*. New York.

Krohn, A. (1978) *Hysteria: The Elusive Neurosis*. Monograph 45/46 of Psychological Issues 12, nos. 1/2. New York.

Lacan, J. (1956) 'The Hysteric's Question' in *The Seminars of Jacques Lacan. Book III The Psychoses 1955–1956* (1993). New York.

(1968) J. Roussel (trans.) 'The Mirror-phase as Formative of the Function of the I', *New Left Review* 51. Paper read to International Congress of Psycho-analysis at Marienbad (1949), reprinted in *Écrits* (1966).

(1984) 'Intervention on Transference' in J. Mitchell and J. Rose (eds.) *Feminine Sexuality in the School of Jacques Lacan*. London.

Laplanche, J.-P. (1970/1976) *Life and Death in Psychoanalysis*. London.

(1965/1992) *La Révolution copernicienne inachevée*. Paris.

(1989) *New Foundation for Psychoanalysis*. Oxford.

(1992) *Seduction, Translation, Drives*. London.

Laplanche, J.-P. and Pontalis, J.-B. (1964) *Fantasme originaire, fantasmes des origines, origine des fantasmes*. Paris.

(1973) *The Language of Psychoanalysis*. London.

Leed, E. J. (1979) *No Man's Land: Combat and Identity in World War I*. Cambridge.

Lefkowitz, M. R. (1981) *Heroines and Hysterics*. London.

Lewis, I. M. (1971) *Ecstatic Religions*. London.

(1986) *Religion in Context: Cults and Charisma*. Cambridge.

Leys, R. (2000) *A Genealogy of Trauma*. Chicago.

Libbrecht, K. (1995) *Hysterical Psychosis*. London.

Limentani, A. (1984) 'To the Limits of Male Heterosexuality: The Vagina Man' in (1989) *Between Freud and Klein: The Psychoanalytic Quest for Knowledge and Truth*. London.

Lloyd, G. G. (1986) 'Hysteria: A Case for Conservation?' *British Medical Journal* 293, pp. 1255–6.

Lowenberg, P. (1983) 'Otto Bauer, Freud's "Dora" Case, and the Crises of the First Austrian Republic' in *Decoding the Past*. New York.

MacDonald, M. (ed.) (1991) *Introduction to Witchcraft and Hysteria in Elizabethan London: Edward Jorden and the Mary Glover Case*. W. F. Bynum and R. Porter (eds.) Tavistock Classics in the History of Psychiatry. London.

Mace, C. J. (1992) 'Hysterical Conversion 1: A History', *British Journal of Psychiatry* 161, pp. 369–77.

Macfarlane, A. (1970) *Witchcraft in Tudor and Stuart England*. London.

Macmillan, M. B. (1979) 'Delboeuf and Janet as Influences on Freud's Treatment of Emmy von N', *Journal of the History of the Behavioural Sciences* 15, no. 4, pp. 299–309.

(1988) 'Freud and Janet on Organic and Hysterical Paralyses: A Mystery Solved?' in O. Zentner (ed.) *Papers of the Freudian School of Melbourne: Australian Psychoanalytic Writings*. Melbourne. Reprinted in *International Review of Psycho-Analysis* 17, part 2, pp. 189–203.

Makari, G. J. (1998) 'The Seductions of History: Sexual Trauma in Freud's Theory and Historiography', *IJPA* 5, pp. 867–72.

Masson, J. F. (1985) (ed. and trans.) *The Complete Letters of Sigmund Freud to Wilhelm Fliess 1887–1904*. Cambridge.

(1985) *The Assault on Truth: Freud's Suppression of the Seduction Theory*. London.

McGrath, W. J. (1986) *Freud's Discovery of Psychoanalysis: The Politics of Hysteria*. Ithaca.

Merskey, H. and Merskey, S. (1993) 'Hysteria, or "Suffocation of the Mother"', *Canadian Medical Association Journal* 148, no. 3, pp. 399–405.

Merskey, H. and Potter, P. (1989) 'The Womb Lay Still in Ancient Egypt', *British Journal of Psychiatry* 154, pp. 751–3.

(1991) 'Shell Shock' in G. E. Berrios and H. L. Freeman (eds.) *British Psychiatry's Strange Past: 150 years of British Psychiatry, 1841–1991*. London.

Micale, M. S. (1985) 'The Salpêtrière in the Age of Charcot: An Institutional Perspective on Medical History in the Late Nineteenth Century', *Journal of Contemporary History* 20, no. 4, pp. 703–31.

(1989) 'Hysteria and Its Historiography – A Review of Past and Present Writings' (2 parts), *History of Science* 27, no. 77, pp. 223–61 and no. 78, pp. 317–51.

(1990) 'Charcot and the Idea of Hysteria in the Male: Gender, Mental Science, Medical Diagnosis in Late Nineteenth-Century France', *Medical History* 34, no. 4, pp. 363–411.

(1991) 'Hysteria Male/Hysteria Female: Reflections on Comparative Gender Construction in Nineteenth-Century France and Britain' in M. Benjamin (ed.) *Science and Sensibility: Essays on Gender and Scientific Enquiry, 1780–1945*. London.

(1995) *Approaching Hysteria: Disease and its Interpretations*. Princeton.

Middlebrook, D. W. (1991) *Anne Sexton: A Biography*. New York.

Miller, E. (1988) 'Behaviour Modification Mid-Nineteenth-Century Style: Robert Brudenell Carter and the Treatment of Hysteria', *British Journal of Clinical Psychology* 27, no. 4, pp. 297–30.

Milner, M. (1969) *The Hands of the Living God*. London.

Mitchell, J. (1974) *Psychoanalysis and Feminism*. London.

(1984) *Women: The Longest Revolution*. London.

(1986) (ed.) *The Selected Melanie Klein*. London.

(1986) 'From King Lear to Anna O', *Yale Journal of French Studies*.

Mitchell, J. and Oakley, A. (1986) *What Is Feminism?* Oxford.

(1997) *Who's Afraid of Feminism: Seeing Through the Backlash*. London.

Mitchell, J. and Rose, J. (eds.) (1984) *Feminine Sexuality in the School of Jacques Lacan: Lacan and the école frendienne*. London.

Mitchell, W. S. (1904) 'A Case of Uncomplicated Hysteria in the Male'. Unpublished manuscript in Philadelphia College of Medicine. Cited in E. Showalter (1997).

Molina, T. da (1630) *El Burlador de Sevilla.*

Mullan, J. (1984) 'Hypochondria and Hysteria: Sensibility and the Physicians', *The Eighteenth-century: Theory and Interpretation* 25, no. 2, pp. 141–74.

Oughourlian, J.-M. (1982) *The Puppet of Desire.* Stanford.

Owen, W. (1918) 'Strange Meeting' in *Collected Poems* (1963). London.

Pierce, J. L. (1989) 'The Relation Between Emotion, Work and Hysteria: A Feminist Reinterpretation of Freud's "Studies on Hysteria"', *Women's Studies* 16, nos. 3–4, pp. 255–71.

Pontalis, J.-B. (1981) 'On Death Work' in *Frontiers in Psychoanalysis: Between the Dream and Psychic Pain.* London.

Poovey, M. (1988) *Uneven Developments: The Ideological Work of Gender in Mid-Victorian England.* Chicago.

Ramas, M. (1980) 'Freud's Dora, Dora's Hysteria: The Negation of a Woman's Rebellion', *Feminist Studies* 6, no. 3, pp. 472–510.

Rank, O. (1929) *The Trauma of Birth.* New York.

(1975) *The Don Juan Legend.* Princeton.

Reichard, S. (1956) 'A Re-examination of "Studies on Hysteria"', *Psychoanalytic Quarterly* 25, no. 2, pp. 155–77.

Ridley, M. R. (ed.) (1965) *Othello*, Arden edition. London.

Rivers, W. H. R. (1920) *Instinct and the Unconscious.* Cambridge.

Rivière, J. (1932) 'On Jealousy as a Mechanism of Defence' in A. Hughes (ed.) *The Inner World of Joan Rivière* (1991). London.

Rosenbaum, M. and Muroff, M. (eds.) (1984) *Anna O: Fourteen Contemporary Reinterpretations.* New York.

Rosenblum, E. (1973) 'Le premier parcours psychoanalytique d'un homme relaté par Freud', *Études psychothérapeutiques* June–Sept., pp. 51–8.

Rosenfeld, H. (1947) 'Analysis of a Schizophrenic State with Depersonalisation' in *Psychotic States* (1965). London.

(1987) *Impasse and Interpretation.* London.

Roustang, F. (1986) *Psychoanalysis Never Lets Go.* Baltimore.

Rubinstein, B. B. (1983) 'Freud's Early Theories of Hysteria' in R. S. Cohen and L. Laudan (eds.) *Physics, Philosophy and Psychoanalysis: Essays in Honor of Adolf Grünbaum.* Dordrecht.

Safouan, M. (1980) 'In Praise of Hysteria' in S. Schneiderman (ed.) *Returning to Freud: Clinical Psychoanalysis in the School of Lacan.* New Haven.

Satow, R. (1979) 'Where Has All the Hysteria Gone?' *Psychoanalytic Review* 66, no. 4, pp. 463–77.

Seccombe, W. (1993) *Weathering the Storm: Working-class Families from the Industrial Revolution to the Fertility Decline.* London.

Segal, H. (1957) 'Notes on Symbol Formation', *IJPA* 38, pp. 39–45.

Sexton, A. (1962) 'All My Pretty Ones' in D. W. Middlebrook and D. H. George (eds.) (1991) *The Selected Poems of Anne Sexton*. London.

Shorter, E. (1986) 'Paralysis: The Rise and Fall of a "Hysterical" Symptom', *Journal of Social History* 19, pp. 549–82.

— (1989) 'Women and Jews in a Private Nervous Clinic in Vienna at the Turn of the Century', *Medical History* 33, no. 2, pp. 149–83.

— (1990) 'Mania, Hysteria and Gender in Lower Austria, 1891–1905', *Psychiatry* 1, no. 1, pp. 3–31.

— (1992) *From Paralysis to Fatigue: A History of Psychosomatic Illness in the Modern Era*. New York.

Showalter, E. (1987) 'Rivers and Sassoon: The Inscription of Male Gender Anxieties' in M. R. Higonnet *et al.* (eds.) *Behind the Lines: Gender and the Two World Wars*. New Haven.

— (1987) *The Female Malady: Women, Madness and English Culture*. London.

— (1990) *Sexual Anarchy: Gender and Culture at the Fin de Siècle*. New York.

— (1994) 'On Hysterical Narrative', *Narrative* 1, pp. 24–35.

— (1997) *Hystories: Hysterical Epidemics and Modern Culture*. London.

Simon, B. (1978) *Mind and Madness in Ancient Greece: The Classical Roots of Modern Psychiatry*. Ithaca.

— (1979) 'Hysteria – The Greek Disease', *Psychoanalytic Study of Society* 8, pp. 175–215.

Slavney, P. (1990) *Perspectives on 'Hysteria'*. Baltimore.

Spanos, N. P. and Gottlieb, J. (1979) 'Demonic Possession, Mesmerism, and Hysteria: A Social Psychological Perspective on their Historical Interrelations', *Journal of Abnormal Psychology* 88, no. 5, pp. 527–46.

Stallybrass, P. and White, A. (1986) *The Politics and Poetics of Transgression*. London.

Szasz, T. (1961) *The Myth of Mental Illness*. New York.

Thomas, L. (1979) *The Medusa and the Snail: More Notes of a Biology Watcher*. New York.

Trillat, E. (1986) *L'Histoire de l'hystérie*. Paris.

— (1987) 'Hystérie et hypnose (une approche historique)', *Psychiatrie française* 19, special number, pp. 9–19.

Veith, I. (1956) 'On Hysterical and Hypochondriacal Afflictions', *Bulletin of the History of Medicine* 30, no. 3, pp. 233–40.

— (1960) 'Hysteria', *Modern Medicine* 28, no. 4, pp. 178–83.

— (1965) *Hysteria: The History of a Disease*, Chicago.

(1977) 'Four Thousand Years of Hysteria' in M. J. Horowitz (ed.) *Hysterical Personality*. New York.

Vittorini, P. (1998) 'Self and Attachment in Autism'. Unpublished MPhil Essay. Cambridge.

Weissman, H. P. (1982) 'Margery Kempe in Jerusalem: Hysteria Compassio in the Late Middle Ages' in M. J. Carruthers and E. D. Kirk (eds.) *Acts of Interpretation: The Text in Its Context, 700–1600: Essays on Medieval and Renaissance Literature in Honor of E. Talbot Donaldson*. Norman, Okla.

White, A. (1993) *Carnival, Hysteria and Writing: Collected Essays and Autobiography*. Oxford.

Wijewardene, G. (1976) 'Hysteria and Religious Behaviour'. Cyclostyled pamphlet, Dept. of Anthropology, ANU, Canberra.

Williams, B. (1981) 'Don Giovanni' in J. Miller (ed.) (1990) *Don Giovanni*. London.

Williams, D. (1993) *Nobody, Nowhere*. London.

Williams, K. E. (1990) 'Hysteria in Seventeenth-century Case Records and Unpublished Manuscripts', *History of Psychiatry* 1, no. 4, pp. 383–401.

Winnicott, D. W.

(1936) 'Appetite and Emotional Disorder'. Paper read before the Medical Section of the British Psychological Society. London.

(1949) 'Hate in the Counter-transference', *IJPA* 30, pp. 69–74.

(1956) 'Primary Maternal Preoccupation' in *Collected Papers* (1958). London.

(1968) 'The Mother as Mirror' in P. Lomas (ed.) *The Predicament of the Family*. London.

(1969) 'Mother's Madness Appearing in the Clinical Material as an Ego-Alien Factor' in *Psycho-Analytic Explorations* (1989). London.

(1974) 'Fear of Breakdown', *IJPA* 55, pp. 103–7.

(1975) *Through Paediatrics to Psycho-Analysis*. London.

Wolf, C. (1998) *Medea*. London.

Young-Bruehl, E. (1998) *Subject to Biography: Psychoanalysis, Feminism and Writing Women's Lives*. Cambridge, MA.

Index